Applying Social Statistics

Applying Social Statistics

An Introduction to Quantitative Reasoning in Sociology

Jay Alan Weinstein

ROWMAN & LITTLEFIELD PUBLISHERS, INC.
Lanham • Boulder • New York • Toronto • Plymouth, UK

Published by Rowman & Littlefield Publishers, Inc.
A wholly owned subsidary of The Rowman & Littlefield Publishing Group, Inc.
4501 Forbes Boulevard, Suite 200, Lanham, Maryland 20706
http://www.rowmanlittlefield.com

Estover Road, Plymouth PL6 7PY, United Kingdom

British Library Cataloguing in Publication Information Available

Library of Congress Cataloging-in-Publication Data

Weinstein, Jay A., 1942-
   Applying social statistics : an introduction to quantitative reasoning in
sociology / Jay Alan Weinstein.
      p. cm.
   Includes bibliographical references and index.
   ISBN 978-0-7425-6373-5 (cloth : alk. paper) – ISBN 978-0-7425-6374-2 (pbk. :
alk. paper) – ISBN 978-1-4422-0313-6 (electronic)
   1. Sociology–Statistics methods. 2. Sociology--Methodology. I. Title.
   HM535.W45 2010
   301.072'7—dc22
                              2009038558

∞™ The paper used in this publication meets the minimum requirements of
American National Standard for Information Sciences—Permanence of Paper
for Printed Library Materials, ANSI/NISO Z39.48-1992.

Printed in the United States of America

Contents

14 Regression Description and Induction in the Sociological Study of Globalization   325

15 Supplemental Material Online at http://www.rowmanlittlefield.com/RL/Books/WeinsteinStats/

The Role of Additional Variables in Frequency Distributions

Confidence Intervals with Nominal- and Ordinal-Level Data

Margin of Error and CIs Using the Sampling Distribution of Proportions

An Example from Political Polling

Difference of Proportions

The Procedure

An Illustration

Chi-Square with Three or More Variables

Multivariate Correlation

Partial Correlation

Multiple Correlation

Multiple Regression

An Illustration

Boxes, Tables, and Figures

Boxes

Tables

Figures

Symbols Used in This Book

n	The number of units, or cases, in a sample.
f	Frequency; the number of times a specific attribute occurs in a frequency distribution. $f_1, f_2, \ldots, f_i, \ldots, f_n$: the frequency for the first, second, $\ldots$, general (ith), $\ldots$, and last (nth) attribute (see Appendix B).
Σ	Summation; take the sum of $\ldots$. $\sum_{i=1}^{n} f_i$: the sum of each of the quantities designated as f, from the first to the last (nth). In a frequency distribution, where f_i is a given frequency, $\sum_{i=1}^{n} f_i = n$ (see Appendix B).
p	Proportion or probability. $p_1, p_1, \ldots, p_i, \ldots, p_n$: the proportion or probability for the first, second, $\ldots$, general (ith), $\ldots$, and last (nth) attribute.
m	The midpoint of an interval in a grouped frequency distribution. $m_1, m_2, \ldots, m_i, \ldots, m_n$: the midpoint of the first, second, $\ldots$, general, $\ldots$, and last interval.
ll	The lower limit of an interval in a grouped frequency distribution. $ll_1, ll_2, \ldots, ll_i, \ldots, ll_n$: the lower limit of the first, second, $\ldots$, general, $\ldots$, and last interval.
ul	The upper limit of an interval in a grouped frequency distribution. $ul_1, ul_2, \ldots, ul_i, \ldots, ul_n$: the upper limit of the first, second, $\ldots$, general, $\ldots$, and last interval.
pct (or %)	Percentage. $pct_1, pct_2, \ldots, pct_i, \ldots, pct_n$: the percentage for the first, second, $\ldots$, general, $\ldots$, and last attribute.
cf	Cumulative frequency; the observed frequency for a given attribute plus all of the frequencies for the attributes beneath it in a frequency distribution table. $cf_1, cf_2, \ldots, cf_i, \ldots, cf_n$: the cumulative frequency for the first, second, $\ldots$, general, $\ldots$, and last attribute.
$col\%$	Column percentage
$row\%$	Row percentage
$total\%$	Total percentage

$c\%$	Cumulative percentage
	$c\%_1, c\%_2, \ldots, c\%_i, \ldots, c\%_n$: the cumulative percentage for the first, second, $\ldots$, general, $\ldots$, and last attribute.
x	An individual attribute (value, score, etc.) on a numerical variable.
	$x_1, x_2, \ldots, x_i, \ldots, x_n$: the value of the attribute for the first, second, $\ldots$, general, $\ldots$, and last unit in a sample. Also, $x_1, x_2, \ldots, x_i, \ldots, x_k$: the first, second, $\ldots$, general, $\ldots$, and last independent variable in a multiple correlation or regression.
$mode$	The attribute with the highest frequency.
mdn	Median; the middle case in a frequency distribution.
$\bar{x}$	The sample mean.
$(x - \bar{x})$	A deviation (from the mean).
	$(x_1 - \bar{x}), (x_2 - \bar{x}), \ldots, (x_i - \bar{x}), \ldots, (x_n - \bar{x})$: -the value of the first, second, $\ldots$, general, $\ldots$, and last deviation.
R	The range.
s^2	The sample variance.
s	The sample standard deviation.
z	A standard score
	$z_1, z_2, \ldots, z_i, \ldots, z_n$: the value of the first, second, $\ldots$, general, $\ldots$, and last standard score.
q	The probability that a given event will *not* occur (where p is the probability that the event will occur).
	$q_1, q_2, \ldots, q_i, \ldots, q_n$: the probability that the first, second, $\ldots$, general, $\ldots$, and last event will not occur.
μ	The population mean.
σ^2	The population variance.
σ	The population standard deviation.
σ_p	The standard deviation of a probability distribution.
$\sigma_{\bar{x}}$	The standard error of the mean.
CI	Confidence interval.
ME	Margin of error.
t	t-score (Student's t).
$t_{calculated}$	Calculated t value.
t_{table}	t value from table of t distribution (table A.2 in Appendix A).
$d.f.$	Degrees of freedom.
	$df_{between}$: degrees of freedom between groups.
	df_{within}: degrees of freedom within groups.
	df_{total}: degrees of freedom total.
H_r	Research hypothesis.

H_0	Null hypothesis.
$\sigma_{\bar{x}_1-\bar{x}_2}$	Estimated standard error of the difference between means.
F ratio	The statistic used in analysis of variance. $F_{calculated}$: calculated F value. F_{table}: F value from table of the F distribution (table A.3 in Appendix A).
MS	Mean square. $MS_{between}$: mean square between groups. MS_{within}: mean square within groups.
SS	Sum of squares. $SS_{between}$: sum of squares between groups. SS_{within}: sum of squares within groups. SS_{total}: sum of squares total.
s_p	Standard error of proportions.
π	Population proportion.
$s_{p_1-p_2}$	Estimated standard error of the difference of proportions.
p^*	Combined sample proportion.
χ^2	Chi-square. $\chi^2_{calculated}$: calculated chi-square. χ^2_{table}: table value of chi-square (table A.4 in Appendix A).
f_o	Observed frequency.
f_e	Expected frequency.
r_s	Spearman's rank-order correlation coefficient. r_{scalc}: calculated rank-order correlation coefficient. r_{stable}: table value of the rank-order correlation coefficient (table A.5 in Appendix A).
r	Pearsonian (bivariate, linear) correlation coefficient.
ρ	Population correlation coefficient. ρ_s: population rank-order correlation coefficient.
$\bar{y}$	Mean of the dependent variable in correlation and regression.
s_y	Standard deviation of the dependent variable in correlation and regression.
SP	Sum of the products in correlation and regression.
SS_x	Sum of the squares (squared deviations) in x.
SS_y	Sum of the squares (squared deviations) in y.
r^2	Coefficient of determination. $r^2_{calculated}$: calculated value of the coefficient of determination. r^2_{table}: table value of the coefficient of determination (table A.6 in Appendix A). $1 - r^2$ coefficient of alienation (non-determination).
$r_{x_1y \cdot x_2}$	Partial correlation coefficient: correlation between x_1 and y controlling for x_2.
$R_{x_1x_2 \cdot y}$	Multiple correlation coefficient: correlation between x_1 and x_2, together, and y.

$R^2_{x_1 x_2 \cdot y}$	Coefficient of multiple determination.
b	The slope of the regression line $b_1, b_2, \ldots, b_i, \ldots, b_n$: the value of the first, second, ..., general, ..., and last slope in multiple regression.
a	The y-intercept of the regression line.
$\hat{y}$	Predicted value of the dependent variable in a regression equation.
e	Residual (regression error).
SS_{error}	Sum of squares error (in regression).
$s_{y \cdot x}$	Standard error of the estimate.
B (uppercase beta)	The slope of the bivariate regression equation in the population.
s_b	The estimated standard error of b.
$MS_{regression}$	Mean square regression.
MS_{error}	Mean square error.
$SS_{regression}$	Sum of squares regression.
SS_{error}	Sum of squares error.

Preface

Students and instructors today who are looking for a good, useful textbook on elementary social statistics have a wide range of possible titles from which to choose. Some are brief and others are long. Some are very serious and others are quite funny. Some are entirely oriented to personal computer applications and software, such as IBM SPSS, whereas others make little or no mention of computers at all. Yet none, to my knowledge, is explicitly designed to assist in the *application* of sociological and related social scientific concepts and principles. As an applied sociologist, and one who has for several years been involved in promoting the cause of sociological practice, I have endeavored here to satisfy this unmet need. This text, like most others in its field, is "about" social statistics. However, as the brief discussion that follows emphasizes, it is first and foremost a book about how sociologists *apply* statistics.

The book is intended primarily for courses in introductory social statistics, offered in departments of sociology, criminology/criminal justice, political science, social work, and occasionally in geography and planning programs. These courses, which are typically listed at the sophomore level and above, have for the past few years been counted as satisfying a university's basic studies/general education requirement in mathematical reasoning. This is the case at Eastern Michigan University, where I teach.

The range of disciplinary interests and the levels of preparation of students have changed substantially over the past several years. Instructors can no longer assume that they are addressing sociology majors exclusively, who need to be prepared for more advanced (perhaps graduate-level) courses in research methods or statistical analysis and who are likely to be using the material later in research projects. Rather, one must seek to emphasize the basic and transdisciplinary aspects of statistical reasoning, and to show how these principles can be applied to numerous problems in a wide variety of contexts—to answer effectively the question "What's it for?" In brief, the goal of instilling expertise or virtuosity has been replaced by the aim of addressing practicality.

Thus, although this presentation is strongly committed to teaching sociology along with the statistics, it does not neglect the need to make clear the importance of the two main branches of statistical analysis. These are: (1) understanding and communicating to others the meaning of our observations expressed quantitatively; and (2) generalizing properly from our observations to related but unobserved phenomena, that is, inductive reasoning.

This change represents one of the two major discernible trends affecting the way social statistics courses with an applied orientation are now being taught. The other is the dramatic increase in computer literacy among students of all backgrounds. In fact, I have learned that the students generally do not require instruction in the use of the PC. Rather, they only need to be shown where to "point-and-click" to use SPSS or other statistically related packages effectively. In addition, it is now possible to incorporate into the course the use of actual online data sets from the U.S. Bureau of the Census and other authoritative sources. Finally, there is now a considerable amount of material about statistics, including several complete courses, on the Internet. Thus, an important part of the instructor's responsibilities today is to teach the student how to make the transition, as effortlessly and as meaningfully as possible, from the textbook (and lectures) to the vast world of related information on the web.

A Note from Instructor to Instructor

Without question, the most pressing challenge for me in achieving my course objectives in introductory social statistics—and I know this is shared with most other statistics instructors today—is what I refer to as "anxiety management." A large proportion of my students, ranging from 50% to nearly 100% in any given semester, feel very insecure about their math abilities. For some, I have learned, it is because they never studied math in high school, or did very poorly in it, and have taken no college-level math course prior to statistics. Others, who may actually have a fair grasp of algebra and geometry, have nevertheless been frightened by teachers who themselves may have had a poor grasp of or a dislike for the subject. In any case, I feel obliged to assure them all that they *can* succeed in basic social statistics because, in effect, they know it all already but have either forgotten or suppressed the skills and facts they need to do well.

As noted, there are many textbooks in elementary social statistics currently available, some of them very good. Nevertheless, none of the approaches employed in these books effectively addresses the needs and opportunities I have come to view as top priorities in over three decades of teaching the course at several universities, to all sorts of students. This is to say that in seeking a special orientation or a unique "take" on the subject, other texts fail to address the importance of application and the intellectual diversity of the intended audience. At the same time, in making the translation from the spoken to the written word, they lose sight of the techniques that actually work in the classroom.

Moreover, many existing texts appear to stress the need to give a "complete" presentation of the topics at hand. The result is that a considerable amount of space is given over to esoteric issues that most students will never need to address, whereas the main task—helping improve the student's skills at quantitative description and induction—is often underemphasized. In fact, no text of this type can be complete, nor should it attempt to be. Some things that are considered important to authors or their peers will always be left out. The challenge is to decide what to cut and what to include. And in this regard, I reiterate that nothing should take precedence over the primary goal of teaching mathematical reasoning or over the pedagogical methods that have proved to be effective in the classroom. All of the material ordinarily included in an introductory social statistics course is presented here in only 14 chapters. This economy of presentation has been accomplished by reorganizing the discussion in several minor ways. In three instances, this is accomplished by covering topics usually treated as distinct variations on a common theme.

- Chapters 10 and 11 are presented as two closely related approaches to the difference of means, for two and for three or more groups, respectively. This allows us to treat one-way ANOVA as an extension of the difference-of-means *t*-test.
- Chapter 12 deals with two nonparametric measures of association (and related inductive applications): chi-square and rank-order correlation.
- Chapters 13 and 14 consider bivariate correlation and regression as a single topic.

This strategy is possible, in part, because the topic of testing hypotheses, which applies to *all* of the subsequent chapters, is treated separately in Chapter 9.

- An additional chapter, Chapter 15, is available online. It contains supplemental material on (1) multivariate applications and (2) confidence intervals around proportions and differences of proportions.

Because most academic semesters are 14 or 15 weeks long, this chapter organization allows the instructor to vary the amount of time dedicated to various topics. For example, one might proceed more deliberately at the very beginning and more quickly at the very end of the course. In my experience, this seems to be more realistic than attempting to cover one chapter per week regardless of the subject matter.

Nevertheless, *Applying Social Statistics* is hardly "watered down." Rather, it challenges the student to "reach up" to the material—essentially the same as is covered in other texts. They are encouraged to do so via the anxiety management approach just mentioned. All along the way, the students are reminded that they have done this before, that they know this concept, and that, based on what they know, this is evident, and so on. It would be inaccurate to refer to this as a Socratic method, because that term really applies to oral communication. However, the proposed text endeavors to come as close as possible to such an approach, and it can easily be adapted to all styles of teaching, from the purely Socratic to the one-way lecture-monologue.

Special Features

As indicated in the title, this book is not meant to turn students into master statisticians. Nor is it especially intended to expand one's general mathematical horizons (although it can do that). Rather, its purpose is to help the student learn how to apply social statistics in any of several contexts. Each chapter of *Applying Social Statistics* ends with special sections that address these needs. First is a set of new words introduced in the chapter. In the text these terms are usually presented in italics, and in the "Key Terms" section they are briefly defined. Of course, these terms are also indexed. The second special section is "Web Sites to Bookmark." Here the students are introduced to web sites, data sources, and the like that relate to the subject of the chapter. One of these sections, in Chapter 3, includes an annotated presentation of Internet sites (such as http://www.census.gov) that provide free data to be used for the SPSS applications and exercises that follow.

Each chapter includes a set of exercises (some using the Internet) on the major principles, concepts, and techniques introduced in the text. These are referred to as "Solution-Centered Applications," a type of learning tool introduced in the late 1990s by the leading applied sociologists Stephen Steele, AnneMarie Scarisbrick-Hauser, and William Hauser. Many of these applications are based on the work of these and other colleagues in the applied and clinical social science community. The exercises can be used in a variety of ways, including by the instructor for quizzes and by the student for self-study.

Each chapter also includes one or more brief essays that connect statistical concepts and principles with a contemporary sociological theme or issue. Most of these "Statistics for Sociologists" applications are featured in boxes, which are listed by chapter, along with the tables and figures following the Table of Contents.

Finally, in the accompanying *Study Guide* an SPSS application for the major techniques and principles in the text is included for most chapters of this book. Here students learn how social statisticians actually manage the data and perform the calculations they are learning, and it will give them hands-on experience with this leading statistical software package. The illustration for Chapter 2 involves creating a data set, and many of the applications and illustrations in subsequent chapters employ this data set. Unlike some texts that acknowledge the importance of SPSS, ours can be readily used with other packages, such as the increasingly popular SAS, or without any computer applications. This matter is essentially left to the instructor.

A main learning objective of this text is to help students understand how and why social statistics is used. Yet its style and substance are based on the recognition that it is of equal, or even greater, importance that students begin to learn how to apply these principles and techniques themselves.

The Data Sets

The SPSS applications and some of the other exercises in this book use three data sets that can be downloaded from http://www.rowmanlittlefield.com/RL/Books/ WeinsteinStats. The first, "colleges.sav," has been made available by the Institutional Data Archive (IDA) on American Higher Education. It was created by Steven Brint and his colleagues at the University of California, Riverside, with support from the National Science Foundation, the Spencer Foundation, and Atlantic Philanthropies. Portions of the IDA are used by permission. It consists of data on over 380 colleges and universities in the United States. The second is the World Population Data Sheet, distributed by the Population Reference Bureau, Inc., Washington, DC, and used with their permission. It contains demographic information for over 200 countries. The third consists of U.S. Census Bureau data on the 56 counties of California. All of these data sets are in SPSS ".sav" format, and the variable view defines the variables. Depending on the needs of the students and instructor, these data sets can also be used for homework assignments, practice quizzes, and other applications.

Statistics and Sociology

Computation and Application

This book is designed to provide you with a set of tools that can and should be readily *applied* to solve certain kinds of problems. Although there are several ways in which the subject of social statistics might be introduced, we have selected the approach that is the most *practical*. Obviously, this is not because it is the only way or even because it is somehow the "best" way. Rather, it is because this approach will help you to see clearly and immediately why and how you can benefit from learning the concepts, principles, and techniques that are presented.

Even while you are taking your first course in statistics, you will be able to use what you are learning here in other classes in which you are enrolled this semester. These classes might be in sociology, in another one of the social science disciplines, or in other fields. Knowledge of basic statistics will serve you well in more advanced courses in social science and in graduate studies if you choose to go on after your bachelor's degree. Your research reports and term papers will reflect a more mature grasp of the strengths and the limitations of the scientific method, and of what one can (or cannot) "prove" with factual observations. On a more general level, your reasoning powers will become more orderly and more disciplined than they might otherwise have been. Ultimately, the lessons learned from a practical introduction to statistics such as this will serve you well in getting a job in any of several professions and in doing good, effective work after you are hired.

The "applying" part of the title of this book is reflected in several small ways and in two major themes that run throughout the chapters that follow. One of these focuses on how we *use* social statistics with the personal computer (PC). The second focuses on how applied sociologists and other practicing social scientists *apply* statistics in their assessment research, evaluation studies, community organizing, and various types of consulting for governments, nonprofit organizations, and businesses. The next few pages introduce these two themes and discuss how they are integrated with the basic principles and techniques of social statistics.

Statistics for Sociologists[1]

The Origins of Sociology and Modern Statistics

One could argue almost endlessly about who the founder of sociology was. A major reason why this question is difficult to resolve is that sociology did not have one inventor. Rather, several scholars in various parts of the world developed the elements of the discipline over the course of centuries. However, if we had to select the person most often identified as the first "true" sociologist, it would be Auguste Comte (born in Montpellier, France, 1798, and died in Paris, 1857).

Comte is accorded this place in intellectual history partly because he invented the term (*sociologie* in French). But his fame is also the result of the set of principles he summarized, which have endured as the foundation of the field to this day. These are:

1. The scientific study of human relationships and the application of the results of this study to improve the human condition are necessary components of contemporary society. As in any other scientific field, the truths of sociology must ultimately be based on careful observation of relevant phenomena. What we observe (see, hear, etc.), not what we deduce or wish was the case, forms the raw material of sociological thinking. Following his teacher, Henri Saint-Simon, Comte referred to this doctrine of "seeing is believing" as *positivism*—another of his concepts still in use.

2. In contrast to psychology and biographical research, the focus of sociology is not on individuals as such but on aggregates: relationships (e.g., friendships, buyers and sellers), families and other groups, organizations, institutions, and societies. This is not to deny the importance of individuals, for they obviously are the participants in relationships, members of families, etc. However, specific friendships come and go, family members die and new ones are born, organizations experience turnover, yet the aggregate forms endure. In an important sense, there are no lone individuals in this world: all of us are defined by and act within the framework of aggregates. Thus, to understand humanity in an authentic scientific manner, we must understand the aggregate level of behavior.

3. Human behavior and experience at the aggregate level are exceedingly complex compared to the objects of study of other scientific fields. Numerous, sometimes enormously many, variables affect how we relate to one another, from two-person interactions (*dyads*) to international relations. Also, unlike the phenomena studied by other sciences, humans in the aggregate set goals, act with intentions, and make and execute plans—granted, often without much success and with frequent unintended outcomes. This means that the social world is shaped by a combination of physical, biological, psychological, and environmental forces,

but also by behavior motivated by the goal of affecting the shape of the social world. This fact underlies Herbert Spencer's invention of the term *superorganic*. This concept indicates that the principles that govern sociocultural phenomena include but also extend beyond the principles that govern other biological phenomena.

4. As in other sciences, those who study superorganic matters need a common language. This language must be universal in scope, it must avoid ambiguity, it must be precise, and it must facilitate inductive as well as deductive thinking. In brief, this common language must be mathematical.

If we ask what mathematical language deals most effectively (1) with truths based on observation, (2) at the aggregate level, and (3) with highly complex phenomena, the answer clearly is *statistics*. As Comte was living during an era of significant breakthroughs in mathematics, especially in probability theory and statistics, he viewed these fields as the most appropriate tools for sociological discourse. In recognition of this, he first called his new "positive science" *social physics*. However, he settled on *sociology* because "social physics" had been popularized by the Belgian statistician and sociologist Adolphe Quetelet (1796–1874; figure 1.1). As the *Collier Encyclopedia* notes, Quetelet

> developed many of the rules governing modern census taking and stimulated statistical activity in other countries. Applying statistics to social phenomena, he developed the concept of the 'average man' and established the theoretical foundations for the use of statistics in social physics or, as it is now known, sociology. Thus, he is considered by many to be the founder of modern quantitative social science.

Comte and Quetelet are two of the best-known founders to appreciate the fact that scientific sociology and statistics are closely related. However, in their age as in ours, this observation has been made and demonstrated by many researchers (in both fields). This book presents another illustration of the strong ties between statistics and sociology. We are not merely applying statistics to sociological examples, although there is much of this as well. Rather, we demonstrate that many of the key sociological issues of today—public sociology, civil society, sexualities, social inequality—are also, at root, statistical issues. That is, they are capable of formulation in statistical terms and they can be better understood through the use of statistical techniques.

FIGURE 1.1   Adolphe Quetelet (1796–1874), founder of statistical sociology. Photo by Milton Micallef, used with permission.

Using Social Statistics with the Personal Computer

When the digital computer began to be used for business and educational applications in the years following World War II, it became clear to statisticians that a new era had dawned on their field. As you will soon see, many of the formulas employed to calculate statistical measures are quite simple in appearance, and they are also easy to understand once they are explained. However, when the number of units[2] to which these formulas are applied is large (in some cases even 10 or more is large), computation even with a good desktop calculator could be long, tedious, and prone to error. The mainframe computer introduced in the postwar era was ideal for such number crunching. The increased capacity to perform many repetitive calculations relatively quickly allowed social statisticians to work with larger and larger samples. In addition, it allowed them to test established theories and principles that had been developed prior to the computer era in experiments that used only a small and (what was then) a manageable number of cases.

The Origins of Statistical Computing

The development of computer-oriented techniques of data analysis occurred in conjunction with the evolution of computer hardware. In the late 1950s, still during the mainframe-only era, a few programming languages were created that were in some respects the precursors of the codes used today. One of special interest to statisticians is FORTRAN (for "FORmula TRANslator"). This language, invented in 1959, is well suited to handling large databases and calculating all of the statistical measures discussed in this book: sums, averages, correlations, frequency distributions, crosstabs, and the like.[3] Several of FORTRAN's features led programmers to experiment with what we now term "packages." These are program-like languages that are compiled on a FORTRAN base (or a similar language) but that allow the user to write commands and to input data directly. By far the most widely used of these packages among sociologists and other social scientists is IBM–SPSS, which was known until 2009 as SPSS® (originally Statistical Package for the Social Sciences), produced by SPSS, Inc., based in Chicago and having a web site at http://www.spss.com. PASW began as mainframe software that quickly caught on among computer-oriented social researchers because of its ease and its repertoire of commands that fit well with the ongoing interests of users. Since the 1960s, it has served to teach uncounted hundreds of thousands of students (and many of their teachers) how to employ the computer in quantitative research. (As of October 2009, SPSS, Inc., was acquired by IBM, motivating the name change to PASW and a new advertising emphasis on the use of the software to support business decision making.) By the late 1980s, statistical computer applications, and SPSS in particular, had made the transition to the PC. SPSS-PC, now known as IBM–SPSS and available for Microsoft Windows, Macintosh, and Linux, is a powerful, easy-to-use package that has turned a task that once required a thick manual and some ingenuity to decipher it into a point-and-click operation. The computer applications presented in this book are all geared to recent SPSS versions.

The Fundamentals of Statistical Computing

Most of the chapters of *Applying Social Statistics* include an IBM–SPSS application in the *Study Guide* that accompanies this book, for a total of 11 in all. Each application uses SPSS-PC, version 14.0 or later, and one or more of the data files included with the software. Topics and the corresponding chapters are:

Chapter 2: Opening a Data File, Sampling, and Comparing Two Data Files

Chapter 3: Creating Your Own Data File

Chapter 4: FREQUENCY and CROSSTABS Commands

Chapter 6: Central Tendency and Variability

Chapter 7: Sampling and Sampling Distributions

Chapter 8: Finding and Using Confidence Intervals

Chapter 10: Two-Sample *t*-Tests

Chapter 11: ONE WAY Analysis of Variance

Chapter 12: Chi-square, Confidence Intervals and Differences of Proportions, and Spearman's Rank-Order Correlation

Chapter 13: Correlation

Chapter 14: Regression

Social Statistics in Application

Until the early 1980s, few people thought of majoring in sociology or related social science disciplines as preparation for a nonacademic occupation. Rather, students and instructors alike viewed a B.A. in sociology, political science, anthropology, etc., as essentially a basic studies degree with no particular career focus. It was expected that a small minority of B.A. holders in these fields would continue with graduate studies and eventually earn a Ph.D. This, in turn, would lead to a career of conducting research and teaching at the college or university level. Most undergraduate majors would, however, end up doing something that had no direct ties to sociology; the rest would find themselves teaching college-level sociology and perpetuating the pattern.

Since that time, much has changed. Increasingly many opportunities now exist for graduates with a bachelor's or master's degree in sociology and related disciplines to apply outside of academe the skills they have acquired. Professional organizations dedicated to promoting application have been created and are actively involved in changing the teaching philosophies and the public images of social science. Their goal is to make it clear that one can "do something" with a degree in one of these fields other than teach it. Two of the most important of these organizations are the Association for Applied and Clinical Sociology (AACS) and the Sociological Practice Section of the American Sociological Association (SP-ASA).[4] To emphasize how social statistics is used in solving real-world problems, this book discusses the work of these and similar organizations and their members at several points. In particular, each chapter includes one or two case studies based on the publications of AACS that illustrate the chapter's main concepts or techniques *in practice*.

These studies and other aspects of this book that are application-focused will make it clear that one of the most valuable skills that an undergraduate degree in sociology or a related social science offers is the ability to understand statistical reports and to perform basic statistical operations, especially with SPSS. Unlike many of the other social science courses required for a degree, in fact unlike most other courses regardless of the discipline, basic social statistics provides skills that can immediately be added to one's résumé and pay off on the job market. Although it remains difficult for a graduate to find a job as a "sociologist," or a "political scientist," employers are very interested in someone who can fit the requirements of a "statistical analyst," a "statistical report writer," or an "SPSS statistical programmer." Of course, neither this book nor any introductory statistics course can make one an expert in such fields. But they can give you a considerable head start in becoming an expert on the job and/or with continuing technical training.

By way of illustrating how social statistics can be used in practical contexts, each chapter includes "Solution-Centered Applications" that accompany each of the main principles and techniques introduced in the text. These are drawn from actual projects on which applied sociologists have worked during the past few years. They were provided by some of the leading practitioners in the field: Robert A. Dentler, William J. Hauser, AnnMarie Scarisbrick Hauser, Stephen F. Steele, Roger Straus, William DuBois, R. Dean Wright, and Richard E. Stephens. The authors and titles of these books are listed at the end of this chapter, and full citations are included in the reference section following Chapter 15.[5] You are expected to give some careful thought to each of these projects, to carry each out with the statistical tools that are provided in the text, and to write a brief report on each. As you work toward achieving these goals, it will become obvious that social statistics is meant to be *applied*, and you will better appreciate how it can provide a very *useful* set of skills for solving real-world problems.

The Limits of Statistical Sociology

Statistics clearly plays a central role in sociology, especially in applied sociology. Yet it cannot substitute for well-developed theory, careful data collection, and old-fashioned hard work. A debate has been going on since the middle of the twentieth century between sociologists who are strongly committed to quantitative methods and computer application, on one side, and others who believe that such a commitment has led the field astray. The latter faction has argued that statistics is in danger of becoming a *substitute* for good sociology.

As with most other debates of this type, a middle ground does exist. It is not always appropriate to conduct research with quantitative variables that are susceptible to statistical analysis using SPSS or similar software. Whether such techniques are applicable depends on the problem at hand, the specific groups and individuals who are the subjects of the research, the availability of previously collected data, and numerous other factors. At the same time, quantitative research in sociology does have many advantages, including precision of findings and economy of presentation. Thus, statistical applications have a place, and an important place. In some respects they are a necessary part of the enterprise. But statistics is only *one part* of the enterprise. It may often be necessary, but it is not a sufficient basis for doing good sociology.

In Box 1.1 is an excerpt from an essay by William Foote Whyte about the limits of statistical, computer-assisted sociology. Whyte was a pioneer in participant observation research, made famous by his study of a Boston neighborhood, *Street Corner Society* (Whyte, 1955).

Looking Ahead

Now that we have outlined the main ways in which this is a first course in applied statistics, the next step is to get down to the business of examining the kinds of things you can expect to encounter as you learn. In this spirit, Chapter 2 turns to an overview of the field that includes basic definitions, a discussion of the relationship between statistics and the scientific method, and a close look at the processes of observation

BOX 1.1	**Statistics for Sociologists**

Participant Observation and Statistical Sociology

WILLIAM FOOTE WHYTE

Until recently, it appeared to me that [participant-observer] research had gone out of style, overwhelmed by questionnaires processed with all the sophisticated methods made possible by modern technology. If I were to write a history of sociology from World War II into the 1970s, I would be inclined to give it the title of "Captured by Computers." It seems to me that the computerization of sociology began during World War II with the large-scale and impressive surveys leading to *The American Soldier*. Since that time, computer technology has advanced with such extraordinary rapidity as to make possible statistical and mathematical analysis hardly dreamed of in earlier periods.

Many sociologists have become so impressed with the powers of the computer as to lead them into planning research in terms of what the computer can do rather than in terms of what needs to be learned to advance knowledge regarding human society and social change. Let me hasten to add that I am not advocating abandonment of the computer. In collaboration with others more competent in surveys and statistical analysis, I have benefited greatly from the use of the computer. I am simply arguing that surveys—the most commonly used method of data gathering for computer processing—are not the only research method to be practiced by sociologists and learned by students.

I see encouraging signs that increasing numbers of sociologists now share this view. On the other hand, we should recognize that this is still distinctly a minority view. I was depressed recently to hear that in the graduate program of one of our leading departments of sociology, the standard way for a student to do a doctoral thesis did not require any field work at all. The student just got hold of a tape from the Institute of Social Research, the National Opinion Research Center, or some other research center, figured out a set of hypotheses different from those involved in the original survey, re-ran the tape through the local computer, reported the figures that came out, and then went on to try to find some plausible explanations for the apparent support or non-support of the hypotheses. To be sure, at this university students are not told that it is against the rules to go out and get their own data, but those who insist upon "doing it the hard way" are looked upon as rather peculiar types by their fellow students.

Apparently this is not a unique case. The chairman of a department at a major university described to me his recent experience in recruiting a new assistant professor. The department invited nine candidates from a number of departments to visit the campus and give a talk on their doctoral theses. The professor reported that eight of the nine presented theses that conformed to the pattern I have described. When, in the discussion following the presentation, professors asked questions about what was going on in the field from which the numbers were produced, the candidates were unable to answer. Furthermore, their reactions suggested that they considered such questions illegitimate. They seemed to be saying, "If we have command of the numbers, what else can you ask of us?"

If this is to become the only way that sociological research is done, in the future we can visualize a complete division of labor between those who gather the data and those who design the research instrument, analyze the data, and publish the results. In this research style, the professional skills of research design and analysis are concentrated among people who have little if any contact with the field they study, and the field work is done generally by people without advanced training in sociology or any other social science. In fact, as is well known, in sociology or any other social science. In fact, as is well known, large survey organizations prefer to hire as data gatherers housewives, school teachers, and others without advanced social science training.

This style of research also deprives the sociologist of the experience necessary for effective performance in applied sociology or action research. It is a rare case indeed in which a sociologist simply reports how the numbers came out and then finds practitioners able to make practical use of the findings. Those who learn to interview and observe in the field are also acquiring skills of social interaction that are transferable in the action side of action research. The sociologist who can only interact with the computer and with his academic colleagues will not be able to work effectively with people in that "real world" beyond the Ivory Tower.

I expect increasing numbers of students to be attracted to field work, including participant observation, but many will still be troubled by the question of the legitimacy of such field methods. They will ask: "Are these methods scientific or artistic?" In my view, both science and art are involved. The student must not only grasp intellectually the nature of the skills required; he or she must also learn to perform those skills—which is where art comes in, for we must assume that some people will become more skillful than others.

At the same time, we are selling participant observation and related field methods short if we view them simply as art. These methods rest upon a scientific foundation, . . .

Those who fail to recognize this scientific foundation may be misled by a common error in describing the interviewing we do, along with participant observation, as nondirective or unstructured. If we are rigidly nondirective in the sense that we simply encourage the respondent to talk and let the respondent completely determine the content of the talk, it is impossible to gather comparable data from a number of informants.

It seems to me that "flexibly structured" is a more accurate characterization of what we do with interviewing in the field. We do not pin the respondent down with a rigidly pre-structured series of questions, but neither do we simply invite the respondent to talk about whatever topic comes to mind in whatever way seems most comfortable to the respondent.

With [this] research style . . . the structure emerges in the mind of the field worker as he or she gains increasing familiarity with the people and problems in the field of study. We begin in a highly unstructured fashion, recognizing that we won't know really what are the important questions to ask until we have learned the lay of the land socially. As we see patterns emerging out of our data and out of our personal experience, we gradually build more structure into our field work. Increasingly, we focus questions designed [to] support or deny the pattern we think we see emerging. Even as we close in on this structure, we try to keep our minds open to the possibility that there is some important element that we have overlooked, and therefore we encourage the respondent to go beyond simple answers to our questions in ways that may point out to us relationships among topics that we had not previously perceived.

_____

Reprinted from *The Journal of Applied Social Science*: 1, 2: 1–3, with permission from The Association for Applied and Clinical Sociology.

Professor Whyte was a pioneer in the method of participant observation, living four years in an Italian community in Boston researching street gangs. He wrote over one hundred articles and 20 books, including the classic *Street Corner Society*, 1943; *Money and Motivation: An Analysis of Incentives in Industry*, 1977; *Worker Participation and Ownership: Cooperative Strategies for Strengthening Local Economies*, 1983; *Making Mondragon: The Growth and Dynamics of the Worker Cooperative Complex* (with K. Whyte), 1988. He served as the president of the Society for Applied Anthropology in 1964 and also of the American Sociological Association in 1981.

and measurement. At times, we may find ourselves deeply involved in technical details, which is to be expected in a course such as this. If this does occur and you find yourself asking, "What is this all for?" it will help to remember the preceding overviews of IBM–SPSS and applied social science. This might also be a good time to explore the IBM–SPSS exercises and the solution-centered projects provided at the end of most of the chapters. Although these aspects of the book may not always help to make every detail perfectly clear, they will allow you to see the larger picture and to make better sense of the place of the smaller details in it.

An Overview of
Applied Social Statistics

This section discusses the contexts in which the tools and techniques of social statistics are applied. The several topics covered here are meant to answer in advance many of the questions that are likely to arise as the details of descriptive and inductive statistics are introduced: What is statistics? Why is the field increasingly viewed as a necessary part of an undergraduate education? What is its relationship to the scientific method? What are the basic concepts in the field?

In addressing these concerns, the material is divided into two parts. The first, to which Chapter 2 is devoted, is the more philosophically and methodologically oriented. For many readers, this will be more of a review of principles presented in other courses, including courses on the philosophy of science and social research methods, than the presentation of entirely new ideas. Yet, even for those of you who are familiar with concepts such as *theory*, *sample*, *hypothesis*, and *variable*, this is likely to be your first encounter with the specific roles that these play in statistical applications.

Chapter 3 focuses on the fundamentals of scientific observation. Beginning with a closer look at variables (the topic with which Chapter 2 ends), the discussion is guided by three main sets of learning objectives: (1) to become familiar with the notion of data and the related concept of information, (2) to understand how measurement is applied to observations and data, and (3) to learn how data are collected. With these goals achieved, the connections among the other concepts and techniques presented throughout this book—up to and including those in the last chapter—should be clear and easy to grasp.

A course in statistics, like a course in language or music, is highly cumulative. Every idea builds on every other. It is true that if one falls behind in such a course, it is difficult to catch up. Yet it is also true that if one does attain a good grasp of earlier material, there are few "surprises" later on. Every new concept or principle is related to something else learned earlier. It is with this in mind that the chapters in this section are meant to be truly a foundation for what is to follow.

Statistics

What It Is and Why Sociologists Use It

You are about to embark on your first course in social statistics, and most likely your first course in any kind of statistics. Based on that assumption, this chapter is designed to provide you with an overview of the portion of the field covered in this book. As mentioned in the introductory chapter, our primary interest is in application: how and why the principles and techniques we discuss are used in research, in planning, in program evaluation, and in many other contexts. This means that we will not be especially concerned about methods for deriving the equations and formulas we use or with certain refinements of the techniques we introduce. Such an emphasis should not suggest that these more technical matters are unimportant, for they are very important in the larger scheme of things. But because a one-semester course cannot do everything, we have decided to stress those aspects that will be immediately relevant to your future studies in sociology, political science, and related fields and, most important, to everyday life.

The applied spirit is reflected in this chapter, which consists of three main sections, beginning with the more general topics and ending with the more specific ones. The first section discusses the term *statistics* itself. Here we see that the term (and the field itself) extends surprisingly far back into history. We also note that, even today, it has not just one meaning but several.

The next section focuses on the role played by statistics in the scientific method, with an emphasis on understanding the method as a type of inductive thinking. Induction, the orderly process of going beyond what is immediately observed, is one of the two major functions of statistics in science. It is sometimes referred to as "inferential" or "decision-making" statistics.

We then conclude with a look at the other main function of statistics: description —communicating to others what we observe. In this context, the key elements of descriptive statistics are introduced and defined: units, samples, and variables. These elements determine the specific fields and subject areas of statistical application, such as engineering statistics, biostatistics, and—as in our case—social statistics. Although every field employs the same basic procedures and rules, some use them to understand physical forces, some are more concerned with life processes, and others with human relationships. The examination of variables that begins in this latter section continues in greater detail in Chapter 3.

What Is/Are Statistics?

Perhaps you have read or heard the word *statistics,* been reminded of the word *status* or *state,* and wondered whether there is a connection. The answer is, yes; all three words have the same Latin root, *status,* meaning "how affairs stand." The name of the field that today is known as *statistics* (which has the Greek endings *-ist-* and *-ic*) still refers to that meaning as the science that informs us about the status of situations, phenomena, or events of interest. According to Webster's *International Dictionary,* 2nd ed., statistics is "(1) a science dealing with the collection, analysis, presentation, and interpretation of masses of numerical data." That, I think, is a fair catalog of the things you will be learning about this semester: collection, analysis, presentation, and interpretation.

Of course, understanding the word *state* in its political sense, the connection might also suggest that statisticians are especially concerned with government data.[1] This is certainly true to an extent, because the kinds of data collected by governments, such as census findings, are especially appropriate for statistical treatment. In fact, we will collect and analyze data from the United States and other national censuses at several points in the following chapters. However, this connection is after the fact, so to speak; it is not part of the original meaning of statistics, which is far broader and could apply to any kind of data.

You may also have wondered why the word *statistics* is always in plural form, like the names of other sciences such as economics, physics, and mechanics. In all of these cases, the plural is a carryover from Greek, in which physics (*ta physika*) originally meant "those things that pertain to material nature" (*physis*). Then, you might have wondered, is there such a thing as *a* statistic? Here, too, the answer is, yes. The word *statistic* in the singular (formed from the plural in what linguists call a "back formation") refers to a single piece of information, one that represents an observed characteristic. As we discuss below, we call the data that we observe collectively a *sample.* Thus, a statistic is a measure of a characteristic of a sample. In contrast, we also speak of a *parameter,* which is a characteristic of a larger whole (which we generally do not observe) from which a sample is drawn: a population or universe. Our dictionary makes this point as follows: A statistic is "(3b) a quantity that describes a sample and is thus an estimate of a parameter of a population."

One last point on word origins: Despite the opinions that are commonly circulated on university campuses, there is absolutely no connection between the words *statistics* and *sadistics.* Hopefully, you will be convinced of this by the time you finish this book.

The Place of Statistics in the Scientific Method

We have all heard of the scientific method, and most of us have used it, for instance in courses such as biology and physics. From such knowledge and experience we are aware that it is a systematic way of establishing facts based on observation, and it can be applied in many different contexts in a wide variety of disciplines. What may not be as obvious is that, in applying the scientific method, statistical techniques and reasoning play a major role, descriptively and inductively.

The scientific method has been the subject of much discussion among scientists, philosophers, other researchers, and members of the general public. Numerous books have been written about it (see, for example, Hoover and Donovan, 2004), and most science textbooks feature an overview of it in earlier chapters. Yet, despite the large volume of information that is available, the essence of the scientific method can be easily stated in two words: *testing hypotheses*. Now, all we need to know is what "testing" and "hypotheses" mean. Unfortunately this will require more than just two words.

Hypotheses and Theories

Nearly everyone who has ever used the term knows that a hypothesis[2] is an educated guess. Thus, when we hypothe*size* we are guessing about some event or phenomenon; we do not know whether our statement is actually true. On the other hand, it is not a wild guess that is made with absolutely no knowledge about the situation of interest. It is "educated" in the sense that we believe we are right, based upon previously acquired information.

Suppose, for example, that you and a friend are playing a simple game in which your friend puts a coin in a pocket, either the left or the right, in such a way that you cannot see where it has been hidden. Then you try to state the outcome, with a reward given if you turn out to be correct. If you have no idea about which pocket the friend will use, you will select one of the possible outcomes—let's suppose the left pocket—for no particular reason. This is not so much a hypothesis as it is a "stab in the dark." Now, suppose instead that you have played this game before, and you have noted that your friend, who is right handed, puts the coin in the right pocket far more often than in the left one. Knowing this, you state the outcome that would seem to be part of the pattern: that is, the right pocket. *This* is a hypothesis. It is still a guess, and you could be wrong; but under the circumstances it is the most reasonable guess.

Although the example is highly simplified, it is exactly how hypotheses are formulated in scientific research. They are statements scientists use to anticipate what they believe would be the case in a particular situation, if things operate as they have in the past. The previously acquired information that makes their guesses educated could come from any number of sources. Ideally, however, such information comes from a carefully accumulated and well-organized body of knowledge known as a scientific *theory*. Now it may seem strange to refer to a kind of knowledge as a theory, because in ordinary language we often think of knowledge and theory as opposite concepts. We might say to people who are expressing what they think is true something like "Well, that's just theory; what are the facts?" In scientific usage, however, theories contain facts.

To put the matter somewhat formally, a theory is a linguistic entity; it is in the world of language and not "out there" in the world of objects and events. A theory *refers to* objects and events, but it exists only in the minds of people and/or on paper—as books, articles, and so on—in the form of words and sentences. It was indicated above that a theory is "well organized." To be more specific, the sentences that make up a theory are logically organized. Rather than being a collection of statements piled up together, so to speak, they are logically related to one another by the five basic logical operators: "not," "and/but," "and/or," "implication (if . . . then)," and "identity (is the same as)."[3]

Some of the sentences of a theory refer purely to how words are and are not to be employed. Their truth is based on the proper use of deductive logic, not on any characteristics of the object world. An important type of such sentences is a definition. For example, a theory about urbanization might stipulate, "A city plus its suburbs is identical to a metropolitan region." This definition makes no claim about what is the case in reality; it merely indicates that the terms "metropolitan region" and "city and its suburbs" may be used interchangeably without affecting the truth or falsity of sentences in which they are used. Similarly, the phrase "a city is not a suburb" indicates that the terms may *not* be used interchangeably.

In addition to such logical truths, a theory also must contain some "empirical" sentences. These *do* refer to the object world, and they might be true or false depending on what is the case in reality. For instance, one might say, "Boston has fewer suburbs than Chicago." Now whether or not this is a fact is determined not by logical criteria but by an actual count of the suburbs of the two cities. The philosopher of science Karl Popper (2002 [1959]) and others have referred to this criterion as "falsifiability." By this it is meant that the possibility always exists that such a sentence can be proved false; note that this cannot apply to a nonempirical sentence such as "A city plus its suburbs is identical to a metropolitan region." There is one important stipulation in this regard: to be a proper part of a theory an empirical sentence must be *true as far as we know*. That is, it surely might be false, but so far it has proved to be otherwise. It is for this reason that we speak of theories as bodies of *knowledge*—they reflect what is known (at a given moment).

One final, and essential, aspect of a theory is that some of its empirical sentences must refer to a general category of phenomena or events in the real world. This property can be identified by the use of a qualifying adjective such as "all," "every," "any," or "none." Such a sentence is known by several names, including "categorical," "general principle," "law-like generalization," and, rarely today, "law." The reason that the last name is no longer used is that "law" conveys the sense of an absolute truth that can never be false under any circumstances. Of course, from what has just been said about falsifiability, such a sentence could not be part of a theory. Like all empirical sentences in a theory, categoricals must be true as far as we know, but they must also be capable of being proved false under some conceivable circumstances.

This is one of the most important and most widely misunderstood characteristics of the scientific method. The only place where absolute certainty is found in theories is in their logical statements such as definitions. Any other statement—one that would refer to the object world, including even our most firmly established "laws"—is subject to doubt. As we will see at several points in the following chapters, where truth is sought but cannot be absolute, statistics has a major role to play.

Having noted this about theories, it might be clearer why they are viewed as the ideal source for producing hypotheses. When researchers want to learn more about some aspects of urban life, for example, they are wise to turn to the body of urban theory that summarizes what is known, provides logical connections between these facts, and offers generalizations drawn from previous research. In practice, this is easier said than done. Ordinarily, especially in the social sciences, theories of urbanization or of anything else are not to be found in just one book or research report. Instead, relevant theories and parts of theories may be scattered among several different sources (often in several languages). It is for this reason that scientific research typically begins with what is called a *literature search.* This is the activity of locating and examining potentially fruitful sources to discover what is already known about the object of study. This can be quite time-consuming and often frustrating. But because theory is such a powerful part of the research act, it is usually worth the effort. One of the Solution-Centered Applications at the end of this chapter illustrates the procedure of a literature search.

The close ties between theories and hypotheses also underscore the fact that hypotheses, too, are part of the world of language. In fact they are sentences, declarative sentences. You will recall that there are three types of sentences in this respect: declarative, interrogative, and exclamatory. The first type, which includes hypotheses, makes a statement: This is the case. Something is true, etc. The second type, the interrogative, poses a question: Is this the case? Is something true? The exclamatory type of sentence expresses a strong observation, usually with an exclamation mark to stress the point: This book is easy to read! I have found it (*Eureka*)! In indicating that a hypothesis is an educated guess expressed as a declarative sentence, we are saying that it states what is believed to be true: "My boat will float." It does not pose a question: "Will my boat float?" Thus, we speak of a hypothesis as being *accepted* if true and *rejected* if false, rather than saying "yes" or "no" in answer to a question. The final point in connection with seeing hypotheses as sentences is that, like all declarative sentences, they have a subject (noun part) and a predicate (verb part). We return to this feature below.

To summarize this introduction to hypotheses, let us continue with the example of urbanization research and illustrate the main point of our discussion. Suppose that you are interested in the relationship between crime and urbanization. In the course of your studies you find some information about a city (let's call it City D) which apparently has not been included in investigations of the type you are conducting. You learn that it is a large (one million plus) city in the northern industrial, "rustbelt" region of the United States. You are interested in the crime situation in D, and with this in view you refer to existing theories on crime in cities in D's region. You search the literature and find included in the theoretical material a generalization to this effect: "All large cities in the rustbelt have crime rates higher than the national average." With this knowledge in hand, we derive a hypothesis by deductive logic, as follows.

- All large rustbelt cities have higher than average crime rates.
- D is a large rustbelt city.
- ∴ D has a higher than average crime rate.

In the third statement is the hypothesis; the "∴" symbol means "therefore," indicating that you have deduced the hypothesis.

The claim that D has a high crime rate is just that, a claim or guess. You do not at this point *know* that it is true. But you do know that it *ought to be* true if the theory from which you took the categorical statement is sound and if your observation that D is large and in the rustbelt corresponds to the actual situation. The next step is to decide whether to accept the hypothesis or reject it. This procedure is what we referred to in our two-word characterization of the scientific method as "testing," the subject to which we now turn.

Testing Our Expectations

In the formal sense in which we have introduced the concept, a hypothesis is neither true nor false. Rather, it is a statement of a likelihood that is awaiting confirmation. In principle, there are several possible procedures that might be used to help in deciding whether or not a hypothesis is true. For example, the question might be referred to recognized authorities in the field of interest: urban studies, in our example. Those people might then declare that, based upon their knowledge, D does have a high crime rate. Another possibility is to seek to establish what ordinary people have always understood to be the situation: that is, traditional knowledge. If, for example, residents and nonresidents alike have consistently learned from their parents and grandparents that D does *not* have a serious crime problem, then this information would be used to support a decision to reject our hypothesis.

One or both of these bases for determining the truth value of hypotheses, authority and tradition, have been used throughout human history, and in many instances they are still used to this day. However, neither is considered acceptable in contemporary scientific work. Instead, as an aspect of scientific method, the only legitimate means of testing hypotheses is to compare the stated, expected outcome with observable data. In our illustration, this would mean counting the number of crimes committed in D, dividing that number by the population size, and determining whether the quotient is above or below the national average. If it is above, then the hypothesis would be accepted; otherwise, it would be rejected. A result such as this, based upon observable, empirical data, would override both the opinions of authorities and traditional knowledge, if either differed—assuming, of course, our observations and calculations were accurate. Thus, *to test a hypothesis one compares the expectation it states to relevant observable data.*

The rule that only observable data have the "power" to establish the truth or falsity of hypotheses is of primary importance in science generally and in statistical applications in sociology in particular. As noted earlier, when hypotheses are derived from theories, we expect them to be true because of the way theories are constructed. However, the fact that a hypothesis follows logically from a well-established base of knowledge cannot guarantee that it will be accepted when it is tested. If, on the basis of testing, a hypothesis is accepted, then we can conclude that the theory remains sound. But if a hypothesis is rejected—which is often a more interesting outcome of research—then a series of questions must be asked and answered.

- Have the observations, calculations, and other aspects of the testing situation been conducted correctly? If not, then the associated procedures need to be improved and repeated. If so, then
- Were the logical steps taken in deducing the hypothesis followed properly? If not, then the procedure should be corrected and repeated. If so, then
- Were the theoretical principles used in the deductive operation correctly understood and interpreted? If not, then the principles need to be more carefully examined. If so, then the theory has been weakened. New principles need to be established to cover the new, disconfirming evidence.

It is obvious from the foregoing procedure that the act of comparing observations with expectations is far from simple. There are many points at which errors can be made or when our fallible human judgment can lead us astray. One important tool in this process involves the organization of the data we observe in such a way that it becomes informative: clear, unambiguous, and capable of assisting in the process of deciding whether or not to accept a hypothesis. This tool or set of tools for turning observed data into usable information is the concern of descriptive statistics, featured in Part II of this book: Chapters 4 through 6.

Assuming that our observations have been described effectively, we might still wonder how one could be sure that the decision the researcher makes to accept or to reject a hypothesis is the correct one. This very important question is easy to answer: one never can be *sure*. The scientific method is the most effective means for establishing the truth about many things. But the truths it reveals cannot be absolute; they are always subject to doubt because of the complexity of the hypothesis-testing situation. The best that can be said about the results of scientific research is that we are "fairly confident," "very confident," or even "extremely confident" that we are right—but we know that we always could be mistaken. This is reflected in the statistician's use of the term *confidence interval*, as discussed in Chapter 9.

This feature of scientific research may at first seem to be a disadvantage. After all, we would prefer to be certain about our observations and conclusions—especially in social science, when human welfare and even human life might be at stake. Certainty *is* possible in human experience, but only in a subjective sense such as one's faith in God or in the sense of valid deductions. In the latter case, we can be certain that all bachelors are unmarried men; that all unicorns have one horn; and that (1) if all fruit is nourishing, and (2) a banana is a fruit, then (3) a banana is nourishing. The reason we can be certain is that the truth of these statements depends not on observable facts but on the rules of logic. They would be true even if there were no such thing as a bachelor, a unicorn, or a banana. However, once we enter the realm of empirical sentences (which all scientific theories must include), and thus the realm of *inductive* logic, even our most well-established beliefs are still beliefs and subject to disproof.

This situation does have important advantages. Because scientific knowledge is always subject to doubt, we can never be content with yesterday's truths. Instead, the scientist is encouraged to question and challenge the taken-for-granted world, to examine critically what "everyone knows." This is why the sociologist Robert K. Merton (1968) referred to science as "organized skepticism." The scientific method organizes our thinking, and it incorporates the "prove it to me" attitude by calling for fresh observations and new interpretations. When this skepticism fails to refute current knowledge, then such knowledge is reinforced and we are more confident to act on it. But when the doubting and questioning is successful, authentic progress has been achieved.

Were it not for the evidence and argument marshaled by Copernicus and Galileo, we would still be content with the "obvious" understanding that sunset and sunrise are the result of the sun's movement around the earth. Were it not for the findings of Einstein and fellow twentieth-century physicists, we would still believe that subatomic particles and galaxies naturally behaved according to Newton's "laws."

Understanding that one can never be absolutely certain that the decisions to accept or reject hypotheses are correct, scientists therefore depend upon a range of statistical techniques that can at least indicate the *probability* or chances that they have made the right decision. This is where the familiar "margin of error" or "plus or minus 5%" comes from in reports of public opinion polls and the results of other kinds of research. One might think of this parallel: Whereas the rules of deductive logic are used to determine deductive truths, the rules of statistics are used to determine scientific truths. Part III of this book, Chapters 7 through 9, focuses specifically on the principles and techniques of statistical induction. There we will explore in detail such issues as the rules of probability, confidence in our findings, and the errors that are made in accepting or rejecting hypotheses. We will also have the opportunity to elaborate about the place of statistics in the scientific method. Until reaching those chapters, however, we will place such concerns in the background in order to present some fundamental, preliminary topics.

Thus, to review what we have said thus far, the heart of the scientific method is testing expectations, which are derived from theories about an aspect of the world. These expectations, or educated guesses, are formally stated as declarative sentences called hypotheses. These hypotheses are compared to observations. The data that are observed are then organized so that they become information. Based on this information it is determined whether the hypotheses should be accepted as true or rejected as false.

One final point before moving on: You will recall that this procedure has been termed organized skepticism, because any observation or any conclusion based on observation is subject to doubt. In order to ensure that this skeptical orientation is scrupulously maintained, researchers ordinarily do not even overtly attempt to prove their expectations; for this might introduce bias in favor of accepting hypotheses when they should be rejected. Instead, scientists state their expectations in a *negative* form. For example, instead of comparing observations to the sentence "D has a high crime rate," scientists would substitute the sentence "D does *not* have a high crime rate." The former is referred to as the *research* hypothesis because that is what the researcher believes, and the latter as the *null* hypothesis because it is *not* the researcher's expectation. Therefore, in practice it is the null hypothesis that is either accepted or rejected. Researchers then exert maximum effort; they "bend over backwards," to accept the null. But, if this proves all but impossible, then they must, like true skeptics, reluctantly conclude that they were right (until shown otherwise). We return to the role of null hypotheses in research in Part III.

Describing What We Observe: Units, Samples, and Variables

Like all sentences, hypotheses have two main parts: (1) the subject, which states what the sentence is about, and (2) the predicate, which states the action or quality associated with the subject. The subject of a scientific hypothesis is the word or words that refer to the unit of analysis or observation (let us say *unit* for the sake of brevity).[4] In the illustration used in the previous section, the subject of the hypothesis is a specific city, designated by the term "City D."

The predicate of a scientific hypothesis contains one or more *variables*. A variable—one of the most important concepts of scientific research—is an observed characteristic or aspect of a unit that can vary from one unit to another and/or change over the course of time. In our illustration, the variable is "crime rate," which of course might differ from city to city or increase or decrease from year to year. Every variable has at least two *values*—also called "attributes"—which may be qualitative or quantitative. The values are the actual properties between/among which a variable can vary or change. In the crime rates illustration, the pair of attributes is *high/low*. Because there are only two values when crime rate is measured in this way, we refer to such a variable as a *dichotomy*, which is the simplest kind.

If, in a specific context, an observed characteristic does not vary (it has only one value), we refer to it as a *constant*. For example, if I were to collect the ages of a group of 10 students, it would be understood that age is a variable. However, these individuals also have at least one characteristic in common that is not a variable but rather a constant. This is the characteristic "status," with the possible values *student* and *nonstudent*. We stress that this depends on context because one might collect data about status from a group of 10 people of the same age (in years). Suppose that in the process we discovered that 5 were students and 5 were not. In this context, age would be the constant and status would be the variable.

The following two sections explore these matters in greater detail. We begin with the subjects of research, the units; we then return to a further discussion of variables, their values, and how they are measured.

Units and Samples in Social Research

Social scientists study and hypothesize about various aspects of (human) social life. Two types of units used in this kind of research have already been introduced: cities in the crime rate illustration and individual students in the case of finding average age. In addition to these, several other kinds of units can be found in the literature of sociology and related fields. A partial list is shown in table 2.1.

To summarize, social scientists study people (singly and in aggregates), formal and informal organizations, political units, and products of human activity. When we consider the fact that for every type of unit there are numerous (perhaps hundreds of) variables, we can appreciate what a complex task sociologists have taken on. In addition, unlike the objects of study in other fields, those in social science are often quite aware they are being studied, they sometimes object, and they can even dispute or try to alter the findings. With these factors in mind, it is easy to understand why the field has been termed "the impossible science" (Turner and Turner, 1990).

TABLE 2.1   Units of observation in sociology

Typical units

- Individuals with various attributes: students, women, veterans, senior citizens, etc.
- Families, both nuclear and extended
- Households
- Sports teams and work groups
- City blocks, census tracts, and other statistical divisions
- States, provinces, and regions of countries
- Small businesses, corporations, public sector bureaucracies
- Colleges and universities
- Nations and groups of nations (e.g., developed and developing countries)
- Documents such as novels and newspapers
- Works of art, TV programs, music videos

In sociology and in other sciences as well, researchers generally do not observe just one unit at a time, although this is often done with case studies. This fact points to another important and related concept: *sample*. A sample is a set of (usually more than one) units upon which scientific observation focuses. In other words, we observe only the units that form our samples and none other. When we define descriptive statistics as the process of organizing our observations and turning data into information, we are implying that we are describing the sample. Recall that *a* statistic is an indicator that conveys information about a sample. So, although it is somewhat redundant, it would be entirely appropriate to refer to descriptive statistics as *sample* statistics.

One such statistic is very familiar to you; in fact, we have mentioned it already. This is the average—or, to be more exact, the sample mean of a variable. But an even more important statistic—so important that we tend to forget that it is a statistic—is the *size* of a sample. This is nearly always designated by the symbol "*n*" (lowercase), which stands for the *n*umber of units. So when we say, for example, "*n* =10," we are indicating that a particular sample has 10 units—people, households, and so on.

It is generally the case that a sample size is smaller than the total number of units to which our hypotheses refer. That is, we might form a hypothesis to this effect: "The average age of the students in my college is 21.5 years." But in order to test this hypothesis, we ordinarily do not attempt to track down all of the students—of whom there may be thousands—to determine their ages. Instead, we select a sample of, say, *n* = 30 and determine the age of each member of the sample. Thus, as the 30 students in this illustration are part of the entire student body, a sample is always part of a whole.

The whole from which a sample is selected (or "drawn") is referred to as a sampling *universe* or, more commonly, *population*. Both terms convey the idea of being all-inclusive, and both are relative—which is why they are qualified here with the word "sampling." For in this context, a universe is not the entirety of objects and events on the earth and beyond. Nor is a population the sum total of all persons living in a part of the world or in the entire world. Rather, these terms are defined as the entire collection of units to which a hypothesis refers and from which a sample is drawn. In a circular but useful definition, then, a sample is a proper subset of a population. Every unit contained in a sample is also included in the population, but some units in the population are not in the sample.

The procedure that allows us to go from observations of samples to conclusions about populations that we do not observe—especially the conclusion that a hypothesis should be accepted or rejected—is at the heart of inductive statistics. We return to it briefly below and then at length in later chapters. Before doing so, however, let us consider the other main part of hypotheses, the predicate: the part that contains the variable(s).

Variables in Social Research

We have noted that a variable refers to a characteristic of a unit that can change over time or differ from unit to unit. In addition, we have seen that every variable must have at least two values or attributes between which it can vary or differ. The variety of variables used in social research is as great as or greater than the types of units that are studied. A partial listing of the categories of variables one is likely to encounter in this context is shown in table 2.2.

It would be difficult to condense such a list much further, in part because there is a great diversity of units and research interests found in the social sciences. However, survey researchers use an acronym to remind them of the kinds of variables that are

TABLE 2.2   Sociological variables

Typical variables

- Biological characteristics: gender and age
- Stratification variables: wealth, political power, prestige, income
- Group characteristics: ethnic membership, marital status, sexual orientation, occupation, nationality, religious affiliation
- Geographic factors: place of birth, residence, migration history
- Knowledge factors: degree to which one is informed about current issues, history, local affairs, and so on
- Attitudinal features: political orientation, attitudes on issues and events
- Practices: frequency of voting, church attendance, TV watching

---

essential in their work. It is "DKAP." It stands for (1) *D*emographic characteristics, such as age; (2) *K*nowledge; (3) *A*ttitudes; and (4) *P*ractices. This is certainly a useful and easy to remember classification, but of course it refers to only a small part of the enormous number of potentially interesting characteristics of individuals, groups, and products of human activity.

Summary

By this point, you should have a fairly clear idea of what statistics is and why we use it—as phrased in the title of this chapter. According to the concise dictionary definition quoted in the first section, it is the field that focuses on the collection, presentation, analysis, and interpretation of large amounts of numerical data. Social statistics, in particular, is that branch of the field specializing in numerical data that pertain to human units of observation and to variables that refer to the individual characteristics and social relationships among these units.

We use statistics for two broad purposes. One of these, featured in the section on scientific method, is to assist in formulating and testing hypotheses. In the context of testing hypotheses, the procedure is widely known as induction (or inference), and thus the application is referred to as *inductive statistics*. The other purpose to which statistics is put, and the more basic of the two, is description: conveying the meaning of what we observe to others. Several of the key principles of *descriptive statistics* were discussed in the section on units, samples, and variables. An examination of the last of the three, variables, begins our next chapter on measurement and data.

KEY TERMS

Constant: A characteristic or feature of a unit that has only one attribute within a sample and thus does not change, vary, or differ.

Deduction: The logical process in which truth is derived by following set rules, independent of any observations that might be made.

DKAP: *D*emographics, *K*nowledge, *A*ttitudes, and *P*ractices. The principal types of variables used in social survey research.

Falsifiability: The property of a statement that makes it possible for it to be shown false.

Hypothesis: A sentence that states what is believed to be true based on prior knowledge.

Induction: The logical process of generalizing from what is immediately observed.

Law-like generalization: A general statement, usually part of a theory, that has been tested and never (yet) shown to be false. Formerly referred to as a "law."

n (lowercase): The *n*umber of units in a sample.

Null hypothesis: A hypothesis that states the opposite of what the researcher believes to be true, usually indicating "no difference," "no relationship," "no connection," etc.

Parameter: A measure of a characteristic of a population.

Research hypothesis: A hypothesis that states what the researcher believes to be true.

Sample: The collection of units actually observed in science, assumed to be drawn from a larger set referred to as a population (or universe).

Scientific theory: A logically organized set of statements that indicates what is known about a certain subject.

Statistic: A measure of a characteristic of a sample.

Unit (of analysis or observation): the individual item, person, group, etc., two or more of which make up a sample or population.

Values (also called "attributes"): Specific categories, rankings, or numbers between which a variable can vary, change, or differ.

Variable: A characteristic or feature of a unit that has more than one value and can thus vary, change, or differ within a sample.

WEB SITES TO BOOKMARK

At the end of each chapter, the URLs (addresses) of several web sites are listed along with a brief description of their contents. You will find visiting these sites to be a useful and interesting way to expand your knowledge about social statistics. Although these addresses were valid at the time of publication, we know that some will be discontinued and others will have changed by the time you read this section. In that case, please consider these URLs to be suggestions, using the list to begin your own exploration. One of the best search engines for such an exploration is www.google.com. Try it.

1. www.emory.edu/EMORY_CLASS/PSYCH230/psych230.html
   This site has annotated lecture materials and descriptions of statistical methods in psychology by Professor J. J. McDowell of Emory University in Atlanta.
2. math.uc.edu/~brycw/classes/147/blue/tools.htm
   Here is a very comprehensive guide to online resources for elementary statistics, including textbooks, web-based software, data sets, exercises and tutorials, and simulations on the Web.
3. www.mste.uiuc.edu/hill/dstat/dstat.html
   This is an online introduction to descriptive statistics maintained by the College of Education at the University of Illinois at Champaign-Urbana.
4. www.statsoftinc.com/textbook/stathome.html
   This Electronic Statistical Textbook (Statistics Homepage) offers training in the understanding and application of statistics.
5. www.yale.edu/ynhti/curriculum/guides/1985/8/85.08.02.x.html
   Yale University maintains this Introduction to Elementary Statistics by Lauretta J. Fox.
6. www.statsoftinc.com/textbook/esc1.html
   Here is another electronic statistics textbook that allows the user to search for terms and general statistical concepts.

SOLUTION-CENTERED APPLICATIONS

In each chapter you will find a set of exercises intended to help you apply some of the key concepts and techniques featured in the preceding text. Some of these will take you to the library; others—in the later chapters—will ask you to solve statistical problems using a computer, and others will ask you simply to use your imagination. It is also possible that some of these applications will in themselves not seem especially interesting; however, they might suggest to you or your instructor other statistics-related activities that would be more appropriate. Making up your own problems in this way is not only a good idea, but it expands the usefulness of the "Solution-Centered Applications" section, which for reasons of space can provide only a sample of relevant, learning-oriented applications.

1. Social research often focuses on institutions of higher education (see Dentler, 2002: Chapter 6). In fact, many colleges and universities now maintain their own department or office of institutional research. Does your school have such a department? This kind of research examines various aspects of a school: its size, its personnel, its financial condition, its curriculum, attitudes of faculty and students, etc. The results of such studies are used for several purposes, including recruitment of future students and strategic planning. The

following exercise asks you to begin an applied institutional research project. In later chapters we will expand on the work you have done here.

Suppose that you have been asked to contribute to a booklet that is to be sent to prospective students and their parents to help them decide whether your school is right for them. In a brief written report, state a reasonable research hypothesis about a relevant aspect of your college or university. For example, "University X has increased its out-of-state enrollment during the past five years." Then state the associated null hypothesis. Next, indicate the "theory" you used to produce your hypothesis; that is, what information do you have that would suggest that the hypothesis is a good guess? Finally, briefly discuss how you would go about testing the hypothesis.

2. Once a client or a community presents a problem to an applied social researcher, often the first step taken is to examine the scholarly literature to see (1) whether, when, and by whom the problem has been encountered in the past and (2) how the problem was approached by others. One essential place to begin this literature search is in the periodical section of a university or college library. The following exercise will help to acquaint you with this crucial aspect of applied social research by asking you not only to visit the periodical section but also to examine some of the material there with regard to units of observation, sampling, and variables.

Go to the periodical section of your school library and select recent issues of two leading research journals, one in a social science and one in a nonsocial science. Ask the librarian for help in finding these journals, if necessary. From each journal select one article to read that reports a research project. Can you identify, in each article, (1) the units of observation, (2) the sample size, and (3) one or more variables? Write a brief report on the results of your search, and be sure to include the correct citation to the articles you used.

3. The following is a purely logical exercise that focuses on the issue of falsifiability. It is designed to help you understand why applied social researchers insist that the hypotheses they are testing can reasonably be expected to be true but that they might prove false, depending on the observations made in testing them. On a sheet of paper, write two sentences that involve social scientific units and variables. Structure one of the sentences so that it is falsifiable and the other so that it is not falsifiable. Discuss why you categorized the sentences in this way.

4. Survey research studies that employ self-administered questionnaires are among the most important tools in applied sociology and related fields. For this exercise, you are to search the Internet for a questionnaire used in an applied social research project. Study the questionnaire and the accompanying explanation. Write a brief report (including the correct citation to the questionnaire) identifying (1) the unit(s) of analysis, (2) the key variable(s) in the study, (3) the hypothesis that the questionnaire appears designed to be testing, (4) the researcher(s) conducting the study, and (5) the client for whom the research is being conducted.

Measurement in Sociology

Quantity, Quality, and Social Aggregates

Now that we have introduced the uses and the main principles of applied social statistics, our overview continues with a discussion of how researchers formally record, or measure, what they observe. The discussion is divided into three main parts. The first consists of a definition and some illustrations of the important concept of *level of measurement*. This refers to the different types of variables employed in social research, ranging from simple categories to "absolute" quantities. Next we consider the distinction between independent and dependent variables, which is the cornerstone of bivariate and multivariate applications. The third and last section of the chapter focuses on sources of social scientific data. These include both data for which the researcher makes the actual observations employed in descriptive and inductive contexts and those that the researcher uses but that have already been collected by another individual or group.

Levels of Measurement

At the end of Chapter 2, we discussed the classification of variables according to substantive categories: that is, the kinds of characteristics to which they refer, such as the survey researcher's DKAP types. However, a far more manageable and, from the statistical point of view, meaningful way of classifying variables is in terms of their types of attributes. The different types are often called *levels of measurement* because (1) each type of attribute can be measured with different scales and (2) there is a hierarchy among these types, with some considered to be at higher levels than others. Another reason why this is an important way of classifying variables is that some statistical procedures and techniques apply to one or two levels but not to the others. This is true of both descriptive and inductive applications.

BOX 3.1   ## Statistics for Sociologists

Quantity or Quality?

As noted in Chapter 2, a debate has been going on among sociologists for several decades concerning the uses and abuses of quantitative research methods, in general, and statistical approaches, in particular. In a highly controversial book entitled *Fads and Fables in Sociology* (Sorokin, 1956), Pitirim Sorokin, the founder of Harvard University's Department of Sociology, parodied what he considered to be the excessive use of statistics with terms such as "testomania" and "quantophrenia." Some years later, in *The Sociological Imagination* (Mills, 1959), a widely cited book by C. Wright Mills, the terms of the argument were established for decades to come. Indeed, Mills' ideas still resonate among sociologists today. In the book, Mills coined the term "abstracted empiricism" to refer to a style of research in which quantitative facts are gathered for their own sake. He contrasts this with a style that he finds equally troublesome, "Grand Theory": speculation with no reference to facts. The approach that he considers to be the correct combination of the two is "intellectual craftsmanship."

Frequently, the abstracted empiricism style is referred to—with negative connotations—as "positivism," with the suggestion that Henri Saint-Simon and Auguste Comte, who coined the term, believed that statistical analysis in itself can lead to truths about social relations. However, as the contemporary theorist Jonathan Turner (1993: Ch. 1) has clearly demonstrated, the real positivism of Comte assumes that statistical analysis is a necessary part of sociology but not a sufficient one. Qualitative and deductive analysis, as well as a commitment to application, are equally important parts of the scientific enterprise.

In fact, the problem had been discussed centuries before even Saint-Simon took it up by the English philosopher Francis Bacon. In his famous book *The New Science* (Bacon, 2004 [1620]), Bacon speaks of different approaches to science using the metaphors of the ant, the spider, and the bee. The ant, says Bacon, collects sticks and ends up with a pile of sticks. This is the abstracted empiricism of the sociologist who collects facts in the belief that they speak for themselves. The spider, for Bacon, spins elaborate webs out of its own substance, as the grand theorist theorizes for theory's sake. But Bacon views the bee as representing the ideal approach, that of intellectual craftsmanship. For the bee collects nectar (facts) and then combines the nectar with its own substance (qualitative and deductive analysis) to produce honey (scientific truth).

This chapter introduces the principles of measurement of sociological variables. You will note that the first, and clearly a major, type of variable consists of qualitative variables, those at the nominal level: gender, ethnicity, geographic location, political orientation, and so on. These form an essential part of the human experience, yet in themselves they cannot be quantified. Therefore, the statistical techniques that can be applied to

FIGURE 3.1 Sir Francis Bacon (1526–1651), the first modern philosopher of science, who argued that good science must include both theory and empirical observation.

them are limited. But this by no means suggests that they can be ignored.

Similarly, we do not claim that statistical measurement and related techniques can substitute for non-quantitative approaches. Field work (participant observation), interpretation of texts and language, deductive theory building, and the other tools of qualitative analysis are essential aspects of the sociological enterprise. More often than not, sociological research and practice are substantially improved when several types of techniques are incorporated: statistical and qualitative analysis, observation and survey research, sociological generalization and the search for "laws" (also called the "nomothetic" method), as well as the exploration of uniqueness in social situations (the "idiographic" method).

Hopefully, you will find in this and related chapters encouragement to avoid the path of the ant (or the spider for that matter) and to strive to emulate the bee.

Nominal Level

Some variables, such as resident status (in a particular state), have attributes that *simply describe a condition*: "resident" and "nonresident." The same would apply to marital status ("never married," "married," "divorced or widowed") and to student status ("current student," "past student," and "nonstudent"). Because the attributes are names for the condition, they are referred to as *nominal* (from the Latin word for "name"). Nominal-level variables are the simplest type, and only a limited range of techniques can be employed with them. Nominal-level data in our Colleges data set include *control* (public/private) and *state*.

Ordinal Level

Some variables have attributes that not only name conditions but also include an obvious ranking among the set of all attributes. The word *ordinal*, from the same Latin word from which we get "order," means just that: rank-ordered. One familiar example of an ordinal-level variable is class in school: freshman, sophomore, junior, senior, and graduate student. You can see that "freshman" and "sophomore," for example, are different names for different classes; but they also can be clearly ranked: sophomore above freshman, and so on. Other examples include socioeconomic class (high, medium, and low) and results of a competition (first, second, third, . . . , last). All of the statistical techniques that apply at the nominal level also apply at the ordinal, and several additional ones apply at the ordinal but not the nominal. An ordinal-level variable in our Colleges data set is *competitiveness rank*.

Numerical (Quantitative) Variables

Many variables have numbers as attributes. Here we are not referring to the kinds of numbers that indicate rank (1st, 2nd, etc.), because those do not really designate amounts but rather refer to relative positions in a ranking system and are therefore ordinal attributes. The kinds of variables known as *numerical* really do refer to a quantity, such as years of education (e.g., 12), household income (e.g., $45,000), GPA (e.g., 3.5), percentage of something (e.g., 32.6%), and number of siblings (e.g., 3). One attribute for each of the preceding variables is shown in parentheses. These numbers are known as "counting" numbers or "cardinal" numbers—suggesting that they are of basic importance. All of the statistical techniques that apply at the nominal and the ordinal levels also apply to numerical variables, and several additional ones apply to numerical variables but not to the others.

Interval versus Ratio Levels

Often a distinction is made between two types of numerical variables, depending on how the zero point (0.0) is derived. If the zero is merely an arbitrary starting point that is set for the sake of convenience, but does not indicate a complete absence of the variable, the variable is designated *interval level*. If a value of 0 on a variable does mean that no amount has been observed, the variable is understood to be *ratio level*. The ratio level is viewed as the higher of the two, and some operations can be performed with variables at that level that do not apply at the interval level.

One example of an interval-level variable is calendar date. We speak of the year in which Barack Obama was inaugurated as president as 2009 because it was the 2,009th year in the Common (or Christian) Era, which began with the year when, according to medieval scholars, Jesus Christ was born.[1] But we know that there are many other calendars—Muslim, Chinese, Mayan, etc.—and each has its own starting point. For example, the Christian year 2009 is equivalent to the year 5769–5770 in the Jewish calendar, because ancient Jewish scholars set their starting year as what they believed was the year the world was created, and the Common Era began 3,760 years later. So, we might ask, what year is it: 2009, 5769, or some other date? The answer is that the date depends on the calendar used. There is no absolute date because there is no true zero point.

An example that illustrates both the interval level and the ratio level is temperature. On both the Fahrenheit and Celsius scales, temperature is an interval-level variable. Temperatures can be negative, and the two scales have different zero points, so that 20 °C = 58 °F, –20 °C = –4 °F, etc. After these scales had come into wide use, physicists found that there was an absolute zero temperature, than which nothing can be colder. Temperature relative to this absolute zero is measured in kelvins (K), units the same size as Celsius degrees. Measured this way, temperature is a ratio-level variable. For example, an object contains twice as much heat energy at 600 K (= 326.85 °C) as it does at 300 K (= 26.85 °C).

Numerical (ratio-level) variables in our Colleges data set include *tuition* and *enrollment*.[2]

Creating an Index with Numerical Variables

Many research applications in sociology call for the use of variables that are derived from raw sample data, but that refer to characteristics that combine information about two or more of the original variables. These derived variables are known as "indices" (singular, "index") and "scales." Although the two terms are sometimes used interchangeably, there are important technical differences between them (for a good, clear discussion and illustration of these differences, see Babbie, 2005: Ch. 6). Here we consider only the former: indices.

One of the best-known indices in sociology is the Socioeconomic Status, or SES, Index, used to measure the position occupied by an individual or group in a social hierarchy. We are well aware that income is a major factor in determining one's position, but it is also true that other factors, such as level of education, play a role. To account for this fact, we create an index consisting of information about income *and* education (and possibly other variables) and assign a score on this index to each individual or group in a sample. An easy way, although not the best way, would be to add the annual income, say in thousands of dollars, to the years of education completed. We might then divide by 2 to show that the index value is the (unweighted) average of income and education. Table 3.1 shows the procedure for a sample of three individuals.

In creating the index shown in table 3.1, we have produced additional and useful information about each individual in the sample without collecting any new data. The index is not only a convenient and more inclusive way of indicating one's status; it also gives us a different perspective on the relative positions in the hierarchy. Note, for example, that the difference between the incomes of individuals A and B is $17,000, and the difference in their educational attainments is 1 year; their SES index scores differ by 8 points. That is, A ranks above B in income, below B in education, but above B in overall SES.

TABLE 3.1   SES index, first approach

Person	Income in thousands (I)	Education in years (E)	SES index $SES = (I + E)/2$
A	65	15	40
B	48	16	32
C	112	20	66

In Chapter 8, Box 8.1, we discuss and apply the concept of educational diversity for the states of the United States. For each state, we create an index that we call the "diversity level." This uses data on the percentage of minority students enrolled in higher education (P1) and the percentage of minorities in the general population (P2). The index is calculated by simply subtracting the percentage in the population from the percentage of students:

$$\text{Diversity level} = (P1 - P2).$$

An index value of 0 indicates that a state has met the standard of equal percentages of minorities in the schools and in the population. A positive score indicates that the standard has been surpassed, and a negative score indicate that the state has fallen below the standard.

For example, one of the states in the sample, Maryland, has P1 = 37.6 and P2 = 36.0. So its diversity level is 37.6 – 36.0 = +1.6; it has surpassed the standard. In Chapter 8, this index is used to illustrate the use of samples in the study of diversity.

Comparing Levels of Measurement

You have probably noticed at this point that some variables can be measured at more than one level. Formally speaking, this possibility arises because of the differences in the *scale* or the units of measurement we employ.[3] In the income illustration we measured the variable in words ("mine," "yours"), rank order (1st, 2nd), interval numbers (dollars above a given starting point), and ratio numbers (dollars above zero).

Researchers are interested in such a property because, ideally, we would like to use variables at the highest level of measurement possible. As we increase the level from nominal to ordinal and so forth, a wider range of statistical techniques apply. If all variables were at the ratio level, then the entire set of statistical tools could be employed in every research situation. But this is not possible in any science, and in sociology it is especially unrealistic.

In general, a variable at a given level of measurement can be "reduced" to lower levels. A ratio-level variable can be converted to an interval-level variable by shifting the zero point from an absolute value (e.g., total income) to a relative one (e. g., income above the poverty line). An interval-level variable can be converted to an ordinal-level variable by indicating the rank ordering (1st and 2nd, higher and lower). And an ordinal-level variable can be turned into a nominal-level variable by simply designating labels with no order implied ("mine" and "yours").

This principle usually does not apply in the other direction. For example, the variable "gender" has two attributes: male and female. There is no suggestion that one is "above" the other, or that one is more than or a given proportion of the other. It is simply a nominal-level variable and must be treated as such. We can say that male incomes are higher than female incomes, but the variable of interest in such a case is income and not gender. The same is true of most other nominal-level variables: student status (registered or not registered), residency, religious affiliation, and countless others.

Social researchers do make a special, widespread exception to this rule. This is in the case of treating a certain kind of ordinal-level variable as if it were interval-level. The type of variable is familiar to anyone who has participated in a social survey, and it is known as a Likert scale (the first syllable rhymes with "pick"), named after its inventor, Rensis Likert. A Likert scale item presents to the respondent a stimulus, in the form of a statement or phrase. The respondent is then instructed to select one of a set of answers that reflect his or her knowledge, attitudes, or practices and that have a clear ranking. An example of a Likert item and some hypothetical responses are shown in Box 3.2.

Because a Likert scale is clearly an ordinal-level variable, we can easily compare respondents by ranking them on each item. Let us say that you checked "I strongly

---

BOX 3.2   ## Statistics for Sociologists

Likert Scale: Ordinal or Interval?

The Board of the University has proposed dropping the football program. Indicate how you feel about this (check one).

☐ I strongly disagree   ☐ I disagree   ☐ I have no opinion   ☐ I agree   ☐ I strongly agree
        1   2   3   4   5

Outcome

			interval a	*interval b*
You	"strongly disagree"			
I	"have no opinion"	I	You	Other
Other	"strongly agrees"	1	3	5

Does *interval a* equal *interval b*?

disagree," and I checked "I have no opinion." Then it is obvious that I rank below you (moving from left to right) in our feelings toward the proposal: you are more opposed than I am. Now, suppose that we learn of the response of another person, which is "I strongly agree." That person indicates even less disagreement than I do, and among us the other can be ranked lowest, with me in the middle and you the highest. Moreover, we can say that the other person is three positions below me and four below you. But can we say that there is a two-point difference between you and me, a two-point difference between the other person and me, and a four-point difference between you and the other person? If so, then we could also say that the difference (or interval) between you and me is the same as the difference between the third person and me. That is, we would be able to treat an ordinal-level variable as if it were interval-level. So, for instance, we could use the numbers 1, 3, and 5 to stand for the three responses, add them up (1 + 3 + 5 = 9), divide by 3 (9/3 = 3), and refer to 3 as the average of our responses.

In order make this kind of judgment, some basis must be available to indicate that the difference in the intensity of feeling between any two points on the scale, say between "strongly agree" and "agree," is the same as that between any other, say between "disagree" and "strongly disagree." But this is usually not known; nor is an attempt ordinarily made to establish such a basis. Nevertheless, researchers routinely interpret the numbers associated with Likert items as if they referred to amounts. This does create misleading results in some instances, but the problem is not considered to be serious (see Kim, 1971; 1975; Smith, 1978).

Independent and Dependent Variables

Up to this point we have focused on hypotheses with only one variable in their predicate parts, such as a crime rate, income, or response to a Likert scale item. Statistics and statistical techniques that refer to these are, for obvious reasons, called *univariate*. Although much social research is of the univariate kind, it is far more common to encounter studies of units for which data on more than one variable are employed. Hypotheses and statistical techniques that include two variables are, for equally obvious reasons, known as *bivariate*, whereas applications with three or more variables are called *multivariate*. For the most part, the descriptive and inductive statistics featured in this book are of the first two types: univariate and bivariate. Only toward the end of Chapters 4 and 11 through 14 do we briefly consider multivariate approaches.

Among the several concerns associated with using more than one variable, none is more important than the *relationship(s) between and/or among the variables*—an issue that, of course, does not arise with only one variable. In bivariate applications, the researcher must decide which of the two variables is *independent* and which is *dependent*. This decision is usually based on the theory from which the research hypothesis is drawn; that is, if past research has shown or assumed that a particular variable is dependent on another, then current researchers follow that guideline (until observations indicate otherwise). As a general rule, especially when the relevant theory is not known, we say that any change(s) or difference(s) in the attributes of the dependent variable are the result of changes in the independent. This can be symbolized as:

$$\text{Independent} \rightarrow \text{Dependent}$$

Thus, when deciding between variables A and B, we ask whether it makes more sense to say that changes in A depend on B or that changes in B depend on A. That is,

$$B \rightarrow A \text{ or } A \rightarrow B?$$

In the first case B would be the independent; in the second case the independent would be A. An equivalent way to phrase this is that the independent is a "probable cause" of the dependent—although it is not necessary for our hypotheses to imply cause and effect, just "association."

Whether or not a characteristic to which a particular variable refers actually is the cause of another (e.g., whether variation in level of education is the cause of variation in income) is a difficult matter to determine. At least three things must be established before we can conclude that a relationship is causal:

1. The independent variable must precede the dependent in time.
2. The two variables must be clearly associated, in that they vary together in an observed manner (e.g., high education level goes with high income and low education level goes with low income).
3. All other possible causes, direct and indirect, have been eliminated.

None of these criteria is easy to establish, but one can *never* be certain about the third. Thus, the search for newly discovered causes of observed phenomena is a major undertaking that makes science a never-ending enterprise.

The procedure for determining *probable* cause is far less demanding. It can be illustrated with two of the variables already discussed: income and response to the "football" Likert scale item. Suppose (1) your income is higher than mine and (2) you agree with the proposition to end football less than I do. Which (if either) is the more likely possibility: that our difference in income is the result of our difference in attitude toward the proposal, or that our difference in attitude is the result of our income difference? Although the decision is not always so clear, it seems obvious in this illustration that it is the second option—our incomes are affecting our attitudes.

Two points need to be stressed here. First, no variable is, in itself, either independent or dependent. This is always decided by virtue of its theoretical or logical relationship to another variable. For example, suppose that we were considering the variables (1) level of education, as measured by years of school completed, and (2) income in dollars. Now at first thought it would seem obvious that education is the independent variable in this pair. After all, don't we improve our level of education to increase our earning power, and thus our income? This is quite true. But if we were to specify further that by "income" we meant income of our parents and by "education" we meant our own educational level, it would be clear that income is the independent variable: wealthy parents can pay more to educate their children. It is the context that makes a variable independent or dependent, not the variable itself.

The second point to be stressed is that in nearly all bivariate applications, the independent and dependent must be specified, even if there is no clear choice. In such instances, the researcher may need to guess—knowing that it may well be a wrong guess—or make a choice based on convenience. Otherwise, it is usually not possible to proceed with the analysis. Bivariate tables require one to indicate which variable's attributes are shown in the columns (the independent) and which in the rows (dependent). Bivariate graphs require one to indicate which variable is represented along the horizontal or *x* axis (independent) and which along the vertical or *y* axis (dependent).

In multivariate applications, the choices become a little more complex. Ordinarily, we have a fairly good idea (from theory and context) of what the dependent variable should be, although sometimes even this is unclear. But even if the dependent variable can be established, we still must determine how to treat the other two, three, or more variables; and there are several possibilities, some of which are shown in figure 3.2. If we assume that the dependent variable, C, is response to the football proposal, that variable A is education, and that variable B is income, then each part of the figure would be interpreted as follows:

1. Both education and income are independent variables because they affect one's response, but they do not affect one another.
2. Education affects income, and income affects one's response. In this case, income is an *intervening* variable (because it intervenes between the independent and dependent variables).
3. Education affects income, education affects one's response, and income separately affects one's response. In this case, income acts as both an independent and an intervening variable.

We briefly discuss these and other multivariate possibilities, as well as techniques for describing and generalizing about the relationships, in Chapter 4.

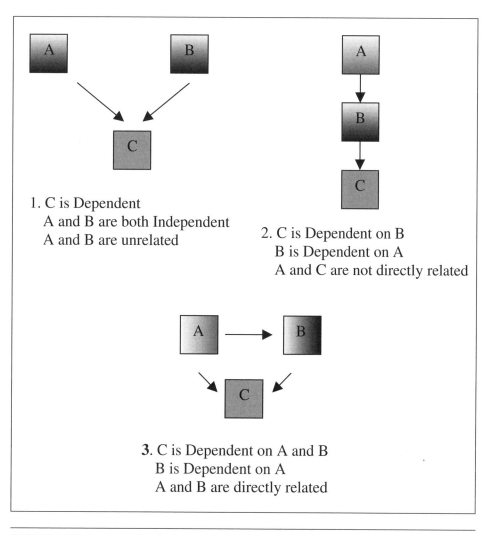

1. C is Dependent
   A and B are both Independent
   A and B are unrelated

2. C is Dependent on B
   B is Dependent on A
   A and C are not directly related

3. C is Dependent on A and B
   B is Dependent on A
   A and B are directly related

FIGURE 3.2   Three types of multivariate relationships.

Where Do Social Scientific Data Come From?

This section discusses the various sources of data used in social research. We begin with a brief summary of the most common techniques of data collection, including the approach that many people equate with social science: survey research. Next, we introduce several useful sources of data that have already been collected and are available online and/or in printed versions. In the following section, we use some of these data to illustrate basic procedures in descriptive and inductive statistics.

Collecting Data

When we refer to samples and units as what we *observe*, we mean more than just casually taking notice, as in "I observed the color of your car." Instead, to observe in the statistical sense involves carefully noting one or more characteristics of each unit and recording what our senses tell us. This act transforms our sense impressions into "raw" data that can be used for descriptive or inductive purposes. Thus, the term *data collection* is synonymous with *scientific observation*, and it more precisely conveys the sense of what actually occurs.[4] As is true in other scientific fields, sociologists employ any of several techniques of data collection, depending on the nature of the problem of interest, practical considerations, and—of special concern in social science—ethical issues. This section summarizes the five major techniques of data collection in sociology: experimental design, surveys, ethnographic research, secondary data analysis, and content analysis.

Experimental Design

A well-known model guides all data collection procedures in every scientific field: the controlled experiment. Although it is not always possible to satisfy all of the conditions of the experimental model, researchers are expected to make as close an approximation as they can.[5] Thus, a brief review of the model can help us better understand most other procedures.

Two features characterize the experimental model: (1) a before/after design and (2) experimental and control samples. The before/after aspect is used to establish a connection between the independent and dependent variables. With additional information, such a connection may help to determine probable cause. The experimental/control feature helps to determine whether the observed association between the variables is real or whether it is actually the result of another, unknown or unmeasured variable. Such a situation, in which the observed association is not authentic, is referred to as a *spurious* (literally, "counterfeit") relationship.

In the illustration shown in figure 3.3, we are testing a hypothesis that stipulates: If work teams watch an instructional film about avoiding errors in the production of microchips, then the performance of the teams will improve. Here the unit of observation (and analysis) is the work team, the independent variable is watching the film, with the attributes "yes" and "no," and the dependent variable is error reduction. The dependent can be measured in any of four ways.

- Nominal: "yes improved" and "no did not improve"
- Ordinal: the teams that do watch the film improved "more" or "less" than the teams that do not watch the film

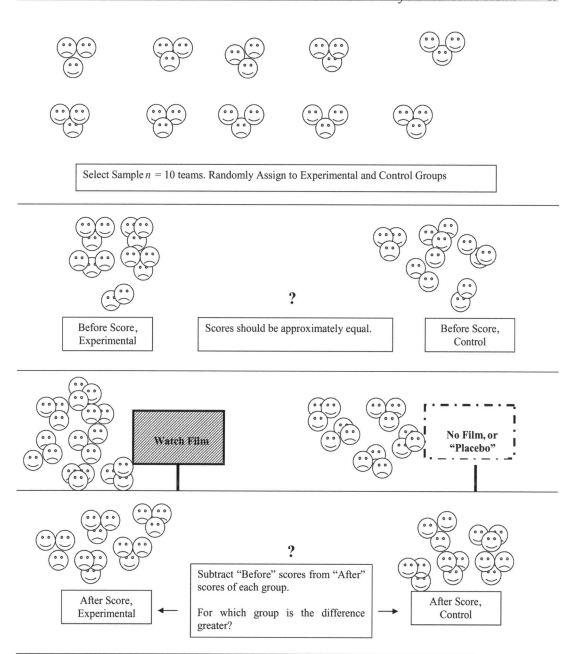

Select Sample *n* = 10 teams. Randomly Assign to Experimental and Control Groups

FIGURE 3.3 The experimental model.

- Interval: measured in the difference in the number of errors above a given level—such as above last week's average
- Ratio, difference in the number of errors after and before the film, from zero on up

For the experiment, 10 work teams of three persons each have been selected from a population of all work teams in a manufacturing facility. With this completed, the sample is divided into two equal-sized subsamples, each with $n = 5$, one of which is to be the experimental group and the other the control group. It is important to ensure that the teams are unaware of the group to which they have been assigned. Also, the two subsamples are to be as much alike as possible so that no difference between them exists that would influence the experimental outcome. This is ordinarily achieved through random assignment, such that chance and only chance determines whether a specific team is placed in one or the other of the two groups.

Next, data are gathered about the performance of each of the teams. This is done so that the experimental and the control group can be given a "before" score, either the total number of errors or an average for each team. At this point, the independent variable (watching the film) can be introduced. Only the experimental group actually watches the instructional material. The control group either watches an entirely unrelated film (such as a documentary on the Grand Canyon) or it watches none at all. If used, the unrelated film plays the role of a *placebo*, the "sugar pill" of medical experiments. This leads those in the control group to believe that they are being "treated," and it preserves the lack of knowledge about which of the groups is the control.

Finally, after the instructional film is shown to the experimental group, each group's performance is tested again. This is done to establish a pair of "after" scores. If the number of errors decreases in the experimental group and either fails to decrease or decreases considerably less in the control group, the researchers can conclude that the hypothesis is supported—or at least that they are on the right track. Any other outcome—for instance, that neither group experiences a decrease—signals that something is wrong, including that the hypothesis does not stand up.

It is important to note that groups, rather than individuals, are being compared. The reasons are discussed further in Box 3.3.

The principal advantage of the experimental model is contained in the name of one of the groups: *control*. The researchers can select their sample, assign units to one or the other group, control how and when the independent variable will enter into the research, measure the dependent variable twice, and rearrange the procedure at will until it is adequate for their purposes. These factors make it the ideal model for scientific data collection.

However, there are several disadvantages. Perhaps the most obvious is that severe legal and ethical constraints apply to experimentation with human subjects. All such

BOX 3.3   Statistics for Sociologists

The Focus on Aggregates

In our discussion of the origins of sociology and statistics in Chapter 1, we stressed that the principal focus of sociological research is not on individuals but on aggregates. You may be familiar with one of the true classic discussions of sociology's concern with aggregates, *The Rules of Sociological Method* by Émile Durkheim (1982). In this book, Durkheim makes a strong case for "social realism," the view that aggregates have a true concrete existence beyond the individuals who make them up. At the same time, he argues against the practice of "reductionism," the attempt to explain aggregate characteristics solely on the basis of individual characteristics—an application of the saying that the whole is always greater than the sum of its parts. This is also the context in which Durkheim introduces the now-famous concept of *social facts*.

Aggregates can range from a two-person relationship, such as a pair of friends, all the way to the entire population of the world, approximately 6.5 billion people. Of course, it is often the case that the units of observation in a research project are individuals. But, as Durkheim pointed out, the sociologist is not concerned with their unique characteristics but rather with the larger categories to which they belong: gender, social class, membership in a particular organization, and so on.

The example of the experimental approach illustrates a common way in which aggregates are treated as units of observation. You will note that the units are work teams (each consisting of three individuals), and it is their performance as teams that is of interest. The data that are collected apply to the teams, not to the individual members; and the variables, watching a film (the independent) and performance (the dependent), are characteristics of the teams as well.

In experimental designs such as this, individual as opposed to aggregate characteristics are not of interest. In fact, procedures are ordinarily employed to nullify or hold constant individual differences. The most common, and typically the most effective, of these is known as "randomization" or "random assignment." With this procedure, individuals involved in the experiment are assigned to a specific aggregate (one of the work groups in our example) based on chance alone. This might involve the toss of a coin or selection of a random number. In this way, an attempt is made to minimize the probability that the assignment is based on whether one is male or female, young or old, skilled or unskilled, etc. In other words, the aggregate's performance is emphasized and the performance of the individuals is discounted.

studies conducted at universities, laboratories, and research institutes in the United States must pass the scrutiny of human subjects committees, formally called Institutional Review Boards (IRBs), established under federal guidelines. Such oversight can modify or even disqualify research that is viewed as harmful to the subjects, that does not ensure confidentiality, or in which informed consent of the subjects is not provided. At the international level, a similar protocol applies under the well-known Nuremberg Convention. The latter was specifically created to abolish the kinds of atrocities inflicted upon prisoners by physicians and scientists during the Nazi era.

Another, more subtle disadvantage of the experimental model is the matter of validity. The results that occur under such controlled situations are often affected by the very conditions that make the model useful. Collectively, these conditions are referred to as the *experimental effect*. These range from the "Hawthorne effect," in which the experience of simply being observed affects "after" performance scores, to the "placebo effect," in which the experience of *believing* that one has been subjected to the independent variable can influence outcomes. Another possibility, referred to as the "testing effect," is that participants in an experiment will learn about the expected outcome (such as performing the task of making microchips) from the "before" test, regardless of any influence of the independent variable. These and many more factors have led social researchers to be skeptical about generalizing from experimental outcomes to what people actually do in the real world. A training film might decrease errors in a laboratory, but the workers and managers are not especially interested in that. They want to know what will happen in the factory.

Because of these and related concerns, most social research does not follow the experimental model to the letter. Of course, social scientists appreciate the advantages of the model. But for practical, ethical, and purely scientific reasons, they are more likely to attempt to simulate experimental controls with the use of *statistical* controls and similar techniques. Clearly, the most frequently employed data collection technique is through the use of face-to-face interviews, telephone interviews, and written questionnaires.

Surveys

Each of these *instruments* has distinctive advantages and limitations, but for statistical purposes they are more or less interchangeable. The procedure for their use begins with the researcher constructing the instrument in such a way that the subjects (who may be units of observation, analysis, or both) are prompted to provide data that are relevant to the hypothesis(es) under consideration. These prompts, or items, may be in the form of a question, "Have you ever watched a microchip production training film?" Or, as in the case of a Likert scale, they are statements to which subjects are to indicate their opinion, attitude, or related fact. For example, "Indicate the number of errors per hour your team made before seeing the training film: (A) None, (B) 1 to 5, or (C) more than 5." An appropriate sample is then selected and each subject, or *respondent,* is interviewed or provided with a copy of the questionnaire to complete. The responses are then recorded and summarized for descriptive and/or inductive applications.

The term *survey research* is applied to interview and questionnaire-oriented studies in which the respondents are part of a large, scientifically selected sample. Ordinarily, the instrument is relatively short and the items can be answered quickly. Some items may be *closed-ended,* in which the respondent must select from among a set of predetermined answers, such as those above. Or they can be *open-ended,* which respondents are to answer in their own words: e.g., "How do you feel about watching training films?" But in either case, the subject is not expected to provide a lengthy, personal narrative. Rather, the goal is to gather somewhat superficial responses from a large number of people.

The use of questionnaires and interviews is often equated with survey research, but this is inaccurate. Although surveys are among the most common contexts in which such instruments are employed, long and short instruments—and those that include in-depth probing—are routinely used in experiments and in other kinds of data collection.

Ethnographic Research

The participant-observer or ethnographic approach has been applied in testing all sorts of social scientific hypotheses. With this technique, the researcher chooses to live among and participate in the lives of people, or to become personally involved in situations, under study. This is accomplished not in the laboratory but in natural settings. A very important aspect of this approach is that the researcher keeps a detailed record of his or her observations, usually in the form of field notes or a journal. Much of this record is in the form of firsthand reports: "today I saw . . . yesterday my neighbor . . . ," and so on. But interviews are routinely used to tap into DKAP-type variables as well as to collect information about the life histories or personal experiences of interviewees.

Secondary Data Analysis

In addition to experimentation and interview/questionnaire (including survey and ethnographic) types of data collection, there is a wide range of techniques for which direct contact with human subjects is not pursued. For this reason, they are often referred to as "unobtrusive," to emphasize the fact that they do not disturb or interfere with the lives of those under study. Perhaps the most widely employed among these is *secondary data analysis.* In this case, the researcher does not seek new data but instead bases description and induction on data collected by others. The U.S. Census Bureau and the census operations of other nations are among the most important sources of secondary data, nearly all of which are collected via large surveys. A related and common source is vital statistics on births, marriages, deaths, illness, and similar life-cycle events. In the United States, these are provided by the National Center for Health Statistics (NCHS).

Another type of secondary data consists of documents and firsthand observations maintained in historical and literary archives. These archives often contain items such as personal letters and diaries of well-known, as well as ordinary, people. This kind of data is especially useful to social historians, historical sociologists, and political theorists. Newspapers are also important sources of data in social research, especially (but not necessarily) research on past events. Combining some of the features of officially collected data and documents are such items as sports records, voting data, and economic indicators (e.g., stock market trends). In brief, any information contained in collections, agency records, and the like that already exists in more or less complete form prior to a given research project would be considered secondary data.

Each of the data sources identified here has special characteristics that separate it from the others: experiments emphasize control, questionnaire/interview approaches use the reports of respondents, ethnographic techniques place the researcher in the midst of the research subjects, and so on. However, each ultimately relies on observing (hearing and seeing) and interpreting the behavior, speech, and/or written reports of human actors.

Content Analysis

In contrast, the last category, known widely as *content analysis*, focuses on the products of human activity, treating them as indicators of sociocultural characteristics of the producer. In such research, the unit is generally not a person, group of people, or organization. Rather, it is all or part of a novel, a movie, a painting, a TV program, or similar item that is not meant especially to *inform* but which researchers observe to understand what it *portrays*. Box 3.4 illustrates this approach to data collection.

Regardless of the type of data collection the researcher uses, from the classical experiment to content analysis, statistics has an important role to play. It is perhaps unnecessary to add that statistical tools cannot substitute for sound theoretical reasoning, good research design, or the appropriate choice of observational approaches. However, the ability to describe one's observations and to generalize correctly from them—that is, to apply descriptive and inductive statistics—supports and enhances these other methodological skills. We often associate social statistics with survey research, and with good reason, considering the extent to which developments in each have depended on the other for so many decades. It would be a mistake to equate the two, however, because the field of statistics has a very wide range of applications; and it does not depend on *any* particular way of collecting data.

| BOX 3.4 | **Statistics for Sociologists** |

Data Collection Using Content Analysis

A study of daytime TV talk shows in which the author of this book was involved illustrates the content analysis procedure. The idea emerged during a casual discussion with a colleague who had spent his youth in the world of carnivals, where both of his parents were employed. We agreed that the old-fashioned carnival "freak show" was more or less dying out, in part because it was considered very offensive. Yet, we speculated, daytime TV now seemed to be fulfilling the same functions—appealing to people's curiosity, satisfying a voyeuristic urge, and so on. This developed into a project in which a sample of daytime talk-show programs would be watched for an extended period and the kinds of guests and problems featured would be recorded. We were ultimately interested in deciding whether an unusually high proportion of time was spent on what could be called "classical freak-show" characters that my colleague recalled from his youth, with such insulting labels as:

- The Fat Man/Lady: extremely obese people
- The Tattooed Man/Lady: people with most of their skin surface covered with tattoos
- The "Hoochie Coochie" Girl: female striptease dancers
- The Thin Man/Lady: people who are extremely underweight
- Bearded Women: women with large amounts of facial hair
- Midgets and Giants: very short or very tall people
- One-Armed Men, etc.: people with missing or malformed body parts
- Sword-Swallowers, etc.: people who can ingest unusual objects

The results of this study indicated that some categories, such as one-armed men, were not represented at all, whereas others—hoochie coochie girls, fat and thin men and ladies—were among the most common types of guests. We also discovered that several other types of "contemporary freak-show" guests and issues were repeatedly featured. These included drug addicts, people who had experienced incest, and prostitutes.

The point of this example is to emphasize that, although many—extremely diverse—people were observed on the TV screens, they were not the units of observation. Instead, our focus was on programs (usually one hour in length) and our main variable was the proportion of each program devoted to "classical freaks." This is typical of the content analysis approach.

Sources of Secondary Data

Researchers typically make the observations on which they base their statistical analyses using one or more of the techniques discussed above. But for the past several decades increasing reliance has been placed on the use of secondary survey data. Because of the difficulty and expense of conducting large-scale social surveys, it is often far more practical to formulate and test hypotheses with data that have already been collected and made available by others. With the help of high-speed downloads and, especially, with the ever-increasing capacity of the Internet, an enormous amount of information is now available and can be accessed with little difficulty by professionals and students. In fact, the data sets used in the SPSS exercises in this book are examples of secondary data.

The most common sources of secondary survey data are the national census operations, now regularly conducted in well over one hundred countries. The sizes of census samples and the number of variables with which they work are so vast that a university or corporation, not to mention a private researcher, cannot manage them. But because the results of census surveys are generally in the public domain, they can easily be used in projects with the most modest budgets. The U.S. Census Bureau has conducted a complete enumeration of the population every 10 years since 1790. In addition, at every census count ever-increasing amounts of data are collected from large samples in every state and county in the nation. This information is now available in hard copy, on CD-ROMs, and online.

The U.S. Census Bureau also provides ongoing estimates of the size and other characteristics of the U.S. population between official decennial counts. These include the monthly current population survey (CPS), which studies such variables as age, household size, occupational characteristics, income, ethnicity, and family structure. The results of the CPS are published in the journal *Current Population Reports* (*CPR*) and online. The Internet address to access the *CPR* and other census data, maps, a complete international database, and news and information about the census operations is: www.census.gov.

Another U.S. government data archive is maintained by the National Center for Health Statistics (NCHS), located in Bethesda, Maryland. The home page for the NCHS web site is at www.cdc.gov/nchwww. Here you will find information on vital statistics, including births, deaths, illness, and related topics. This site contains numerous detailed tables that can be downloaded or printed in whole or in part.

In addition to such official sources, several universities now maintain libraries of data sets collected by social scientists in the course of large-scale government or privately sponsored studies. Among the leading collections in the United States is the one at the University of Chicago's National Opinion Research Center (NORC). NORC is the home of the most widely used database of its type, the General Social Survey (GSS). This study is updated regularly, contains a wide range of variables, and employs a national sample of several thousand respondents. The NORC web site is at www.norc.uchicago.edu.[6]

Similar collections are maintained by the Institute for Research in the Social Sciences (IURC) at the University of North Carolina and the Inter-University Consortium for Political and Social Research (IUCPSR) at the University of Michigan. Each of these organizations makes data sets available to the public, usually for a nominal fee, and each has catalogs available online that describe the sample, the variables, and other features of each set. The relevant web sites are, for the Institute for Research in the Social Sciences, www.iurc.unc.edu, and for the Inter-University Consortium for Political and Social Research, www.icpsr.umich.edu.

Summary

Because data are so central in both major types of applications and, in fact, in all aspects of social statistics, we concluded this chapter with a discussion of the sources of statistical data. On this basis, in the chapters that follow we do not deal directly with the techniques of data collection. There we generally assume that the data we are describing or are employing for inductive purposes already "exist." However, we have in this brief introduction at least provided a framework for understanding that such data do not just appear from nowhere. Rather, a survey, an experiment, a secondary data set, or the like was conducted or accessed to produce the raw material on which we base our analyses.

With this in view, we now move to the part of this book that features the techniques of descriptive statistics. This exploration begins in Chapter 4 with a close and detailed look at the descriptive tool that organizes units, variables, and attributes: the frequency distribution.

KEY TERMS

Bivariate: Hypotheses and statistical techniques that apply to two variables.

Content analysis: A type of unobtrusive research in which books, movies, TV programs, and other cultural artifacts are studied with the aim of understanding those who produced and/or are intended to consume them.

Data collection: Locating and compiling information for descriptive and inductive purposes, synonymous with *scientific observation*.

Dependent variable: The probable or suspected effect in a bivariate hypothesis or application.

Experimental effect: In an experimental design, the change in a dependent variable that is the result of the experiment itself rather than being an authentic effect of the independent variable.

Experimental model: The procedure for gathering data that employs a before/after and experimental-group/control-group design.

Independent variable: The probable or suspected cause in a bivariate hypothesis or application.

Institutional Review Board (IRB): A committee of peer-experts that reviews proposed research involving human subjects. The proposals are ordinarily submitted by colleagues at a university or other research institution.

Instruments: The interview schedules and questionnaires used to gather information directly from the verbal reports of respondents. Instruments are often called "surveys" because of their wide use in survey research.

Interval level: A numerical type of variable whose zero point is an arbitrarily set starting place.

Levels of measurement: A way of classifying variables according to how close or how far their attributes are to being true numbers. The level of measurement determines the range of techniques that can be employed with a given variable. Statisticians generally recognize three or four levels.

Likert scale item: A common ordinal level–type of variable that is often treated as numerical.

Multivariate: Hypotheses and statistical techniques that apply to three or more variables.

Nominal level: The simplest type of variable, whose attributes are names or categories only.

Numerical level: The types of variables whose attributes are actual (cardinal) numbers. Both interval- and ratio-level variables are considered to be numerical.

Ordinal level: The type of variable whose attributes have an inherent rank ordering.

Participant-observer (or ethnographic) approach: A technique of data collection in which the researcher is personally involved (to varying degrees) in the social situation under study.

Ratio level: A numerical type of variable whose zero point literally means complete absence. This is the most complex type.

Secondary data analysis: A type of unobtrusive research in which the researcher works with data that have been collected previously. A familiar application is the use of census data.

Statistical controls: Procedures applied in the collection and analysis of nonexperimental data that simulate the controls that are exercised in an experiment.

Survey research: Interview-and questionnaire-oriented studies in which the respondents are part of a large, scientifically selected sample.

Univariate: Hypotheses and statistical techniques that apply to a single variable.

Unobtrusive research: Any of several research techniques designed so that they do not disturb or interfere with the activities of those under study.

WEB SITES TO BOOKMARK

The following four sites discuss level of measurement.

1. http://trochim.human.cornell.edu/kb/measlevl.htm
    A very complete site supported by Cornell University that includes color graphics.
2. http://courses.csusm.edu/soc201kb/levelof-measurementrefresher.htm
    This is a refresher discussion with a link to a longer discussion. It is maintained by Professor Kristin Bates at California State University, San Marcos.
3. www.okstate.edu/ag/agedcm4h/academic/aged5980a/5980/chp3/CHAPTER3/sld010.htm
    This is a portion of an online text from Oklahoma State University.
4. www.mors.org/EC2000/presentations/polakoff/sld003.htm
    Here is a research site sponsored by the private organization, Novigen Sciences.

The following three sites focus on independent and dependent variables.

1. www.cs.umd.edu/~mstark/exp101/expvars.html
    This site is maintained by the University of Maryland.
2. www.kmsi.org/curriculum/kmsi/sharedconcepts/data/represent/graph/variables/independent.htm
    This site has interactive graphs and downloadable material.
3. http://www-biol.paisley.ac.uk/scicalc/variables.html
    Here is a brief discussion from England that ends with a surprise.

The following five sources of online data were introduced earlier.

1. www.census.gov
    United States Bureau of the Census.

2. www.cdc.gov/nchs
    United States National Center for Health Statistics.
3. www.norc.uchicago.edu
    The National Opinion Research Center, University of Chicago.

4. www.iurc.unc.edu
    Institute for Research in the Social Sciences, University of North Carolina.
5. www.icpsr.umich.edu
    Inter-University Consortium for Political and Social Research, University of Michigan.

SOLUTION-CENTERED APPLICATIONS

1. This application can be done as an individual or a group project. As noted in the latter sections of this chapter, the U.S. Census Bureau is an indispensable source of secondary data to applied social scientists. This exercise introduces you to the vast resources that the Census Bureau now posts online at www.census.gov.

    The allocation of federal funds in the United States is often based on the regional distribution of the population. For example, federal highway funding may be greater for states in some regions than in others. The policies and decisions that affect these kinds of allocations require data on population size and other variables for each of the regions. In this exercise, you are to prepare the kind of data set that is relevant for this type of application. We will use it in several of the solution-centered exercises in this and following chapters.

    The first step is to access the home page of the U.S. Bureau of the Census web site. Explore some of the links to familiarize yourself with the resources that are available. One of the most useful of these links is the "American Fact Finder," whose link is on the left side of the home page. After you have explored this site a little, you are to find values on six variables for the 50 states, recent census data from either 1990 or 2000.

    As one of the variables, select "Region," which is nominal level. The attributes for the main categories of "Region" are Northeast, South, Midwest, and West; and each category is further divided into two or three smaller units such as New England and Mid-Atlantic for the East. Use the larger categories.

    Next, select two variables for which you will create ordinal-level categories.

    *   The first of these is "population ages 25 and above with less than a 9th-grade education." The average for the entire United States for this variable is 7.5%. You are to give each of the states a ranking based upon its specific percentage, as follows: *low* = less than 6.0%; *medium* = 6.0% to 8.9%; and *high* = 9.0% and above.
    *   The second of these is "percent of population ages 21 to 24 with a disability." The average for the entire United States for this variable is 19.2%. You are to give each of the states a ranking based upon its specific percentage, as follows: *low* = less than 15.0%; *medium* = 15.0% to 23.0%; and *high* = above 23.0%.

    The three other variables will be numerical. One of them will be total population size. The other two are of your choosing and might include number of persons below age 5, percentages in various racial/ethnic categories, etc. With these data, and according to the instructions on creating an SPSS data file in Chapter 2 of the *Study Guide*, create an SPSS data file to be used in later exercises.

2. This exercise focuses on using library resources to identify key statistical concepts. It is a continuation of Solution-Centered Application 2 in Chapter 2. Select three recent issues of sociology journals from the periodical section of your school library. Select one article in each that reports the findings of a research project. For each article, identify the main dependent and independent variables, and also note whether there are other (independent or intervening) variables. Next, determine the level of measurement of each of the variables identified. In a brief write-up, list the name of each article, the author(s), the journal, volume, number, and pages. Then name the variables in each, state their levels of measurement, and provide a brief explanation of your reasons for (a) designating the independent, dependent, and—if appropriate—intervening variables as you did and (b) deciding on the levels of measurement.

3. Search the Internet for sources of statistical data not mentioned in this chapter. Select and explore three web sites that you believe to be especially useful for applied social researchers. Based on this exploration, write a brief report in which you provide the URLs, the names of the sites, and the names of the individuals or organizations that maintain the sites. Also include a description of the kinds of data the user can expect to find, and your reasons why you believe that applied social scientists would find it useful.

Tools and Techniques
of Description

The aim of descriptive statistics in sociology is to communicate observations about human experience to an audience. In many ways, this aim is no different from that of other kinds of description, as when we talk about a recent vacation, a fiction writer depicts an event, or an artist conveys impressions of a scene. In all such instances, the challenge is to have the audience understand something as the describer understands it.

The main feature that sets a statistical description apart, in sociology and in all scientific fields, is its steadfast dedication to accuracy. This is not to say that other types of description are unconcerned with accuracy. If we took our vacation on the Great Lakes, for example, it would be unfair to our audience to pretend we were in Florida. Writers, even writers of fiction, want their accounts to be realistic. Even the most abstractly oriented artists strive for a sort of authenticity. Nevertheless, accuracy is neither the sole concern nor, often, the most important consideration in other types of description. In these cases, we also want to be interesting, entertaining, moving, provocative, and the like. For better or for worse, however, statisticians do not especially care about such goals—although they can be achieved unintentionally, provided that their descriptions are as accurate as possible.

This interest in accuracy helps explain why statisticians have developed a set of specialized tools and techniques to help them convey their observations. First and foremost, whenever possible, their observations are quantified. Even in the case of nominal-level variables, whose attributes are by definition *not* numbers, they count the number of times each attribute is observed. This procedure, which is applied at all levels of measurement, is the basis of the *frequency distribution*. It is the most fundamental and most extensively used descriptive tool in social research. As emphasized in Chapter 4, which includes a detailed discussion of frequency distributions, quantification allows us to communicate in (1) unambiguous, (2) uniform, and (3) easily replicated ways. Although not an absolute guarantee, these three features of communication considerably improve the prospects of accuracy.

Equally familiar to statisticians are the concepts of *central tendency* and *dispersion*, the subjects of Chapters 5 and 6, respectively. These are the tools that provide the most powerful summaries of our observations and that help to bridge the gap between descriptive and inductive applications. The main advantage of measures of central tendency and dispersion is that, like frequency distributions, they transform what we observe into numbers. In fact, as we will note in the course of the discussion of these tools, they are in effect doubly quantitative, for they convey in numbers the essence of frequency distributions, which themselves are numerical representations. It is this characteristic that makes it possible for us to proceed to statistical induction armed only with key measures of central tendency and dispersion to stand for our observations, leaving behind the actual frequency distributions from which they are derived.

Frequency Distributions and Public Sociology

If social statisticians were asked to name *the* single most important tool in their repertoire, there is little doubt that most would agree that it is the *frequency distribution*. Once the raw data for a research project are collected, the first step in description is to create frequency distributions. At the very end of the inductive process, the generalizations that the researcher seeks to establish (or challenge) are made with reference to frequency distributions. Moreover, at every step between data collection and generalization, frequency distributions play a pivotal role. These tools come in many varieties: simple and complex; univariate, bivariate, and multivariate; empirical and theoretical; tabular and graphic; and those that differ according to level of measurement. This chapter will introduce all of these types except the theoretical, which we save for later discussion.

Before going into the details, however, it might help to say a few words about frequency distributions in general. First, a formal definition:

A frequency distribution is a means of displaying observations of one or more variables for a sample of units so that each attribute (of each variable) is associated with the number of times that it (the attribute) was observed. The "number of times" is synonymous with "frequency." Frequency distributions can be displayed as tables or as graphs.

In other words, a frequency distribution is a way of indicating how often specific attributes occur in a sample.

Suppose that we are observing students in a sample class of size 30 ($n = 30$), and that we are interested in the dichotomous variable "school experience." As a dichotomy, this variable has two attributes, "new" and "returning." Now, assume that we survey the class, asking the relevant question, and it turns out that there are 16 new students and 14 returning ones. We might stop here, because the phrase "16 new students and 14 returning ones" is a kind of minimal frequency distribution. That is, it reports the frequency with which each attribute was observed.

Although such an account in words is technically a correct frequency distribution, it obviously has limitations. Most important, as the number of attributes increases, the phrases become longer and more cumbersome to write out. Imagine that we had surveyed every U.S. citizen in the entire student body, composed of several thousand individuals, about the variable "state in which you were born." Our verbal frequency distribution might look something like this: "672 from Alabama, 47 from Alaska, 145 from Arkansas, . . . , 23 from Wyoming." Not very tidy, is it? And what would happen if we combined the two variables, so that we could create a bivariate frequency distribution to examine the relationship between school experience and place of birth? Here, use of words alone might make it even *more* difficult to understand the situation. For example: "672 students from Alabama of whom 372 are new and 300 are returning, 47 from Alaska of whom 32 are returning and 15 are new," etc.

It is for reasons such as these that we almost always employ one (or both) of two forms of presentation for our frequency distributions: tables and graphs. These are discussed in the following sections. The use of tables and graphs—as opposed to a verbal statement of our observations—suggests a key feature of frequency distributions: that they convert raw *data,* from which it is difficult to extract any meaning, into *information*—something that can *inform.* This all-important conversion from data to information lies at the core of descriptive statistics, for it allows us to communicate to others what we see and to do so in a way that they can understand as well as we do.

Univariate Frequency Distributions: Common Features

All univariate frequency distributions, regardless of the level of measurement of the variable of interest, have certain features in common. This section focuses on such features. In the following section, we discuss some aspects of frequency distributions that apply only to ordinal and/or numerical variables.

The Structure of a Frequency Table

All tables are made up of *rows*, the horizontal sections, and *columns*, the vertical sections. At the intersection of each row and column is a *cell.* Thus, each column consists of a set of cells equal to the number of rows; and each row consists of a set of cells equal to the number of columns. Finally, every cell contains words, numbers, or other symbols.

The next thing to note is that all univariate frequency distribution tables have at least two columns. The left column is reserved for the variable and its attributes. As illustrated in table 4.1, the first cell of the column contains the name of the variable (or, as we will see in the next section, a word or symbol that stands for the name of the

TABLE 4.1   Frequency illustration 1

Name of variable	School experience
Names of attributes:	New
	Returning

variable). For example, in the case of our dichotomy, it is the variable "school experience." Following this, the remaining cells of the first column contain the name of an attribute: "new" and "returning" in our illustration.

Of course, if a variable has more than two attributes, more than two rows for the variable name are required. For the variable "state in which you were born," 50 rows would be needed, and so on.

The second, right-side, column that is required in all frequency distribution tables, as illustrated in table 4.2, is reserved for the frequencies themselves, that is, the number of times each attribute is observed. The first cell of the column always contains the symbol for "frequency," the italic "*f*." Every other cell, up to the last, contains a number that indicates the appropriate frequency. Here we have placed in parentheses the symbols (f_1) and (f_2) to show that these are the first and second frequencies. These symbols are ordinarily not shown, but they are understood to exist. The very last cell of this column always contains the sum of all the frequencies.

Because the left column includes every possible attribute and the right column contains every observation of each attribute, the sum of all the frequencies is equal to n, the sample size. That is,

$$\sum_{i=1}^{a}(f_i)=n \quad \text{where } f_i \text{ is a frequency and } a \text{ is the number of attributes.}$$

You may recall that this is the symbolism for summation, as represented by uppercase sigma (Σ). It indicates that we are to take each frequency beginning with the first (this is what is meant by the "$i=1$" shown below the sigma) and add it to every other frequency until will have covered all attributes. The actual number of attributes (2, 3, 4, etc.) is

TABLE 4.2   Frequency illustration 2

School experience	f	The frequency symbol
New	16 (f_1)	frequencies
Returning	14 (f_2)	
	$n = 30$	n, sample size; sum of frequencies

indicated by the "*a*" above the sigma. Here the number of attributes is simply 2, so the summation formula would read:

$$\sum_{i=1}^{2}(f_i)=n\,.$$

That is, with $f_1 = 16$ and $f_2 = 14$,

$$\sum_{i=1}^{2}(f_i)\ =16+14=30.$$

Appendix B contains a review of the symbols involved in summation and additional examples.

Let us illustrate these points with another example, this time using a numerical (in this case ratio-level) variable with several attributes rather than a nominal-level dichotomy. Here is the situation: Each member of a group of 15 out-of-state students living on the same floor of a dormitory was asked to indicate to the researcher the number of times he or she traveled back to his or her home town this semester. The raw data are shown are shown in table 4.3, and the corresponding frequency distribution is in table 4.4.[1]

When we compare the two tables, it becomes more obvious how a frequency distribution transforms raw data into information. From table 4.3, it is difficult to see

TABLE 4.3   Raw data on question to dorm residents
about traveling home

Student	Number of trips home
Allison	3
Brenda	2
Charles	0
Dawn	5
Eugene	3
Frank	3
Glen	5
Harriet	2
Ian	1
Janella	1
Kris	3
Leora	2
Mike	0
Nancy	4
On-Kim	4

TABLE 4.4   Univariate frequency distribution based
on table 4.3

Number of trips (x)	f
0	2
1	2
2	3
3	4
4	2
5	2
	$n = 15$

any kind of overall pattern that would help us describe the "going home" practices of the students; we can only say how each individual behaved. But with table 4.4 we can immediately see that the most frequent number of trips for the group is 3 (four students are in this category). In addition, there was a four-way tie for the least frequent number of trips reported: 0, 1, 4, and 5. Thus, relatively few students traveled infrequently and relatively few traveled very frequently, whereas nearly one-half of the students (7 of 15) went home either two or three times. Note, too, how the sum of the frequencies is equal to the sample size ($n = 15$). By the formula,

$$\sum_{i=1}^{a}\left(f_i\right)=n\,.$$

With a (the number of attributes) = 6,

$$\sum_{i=1}^{6}\left(f_i\right)=2+2+3+4+2+2=15.$$

Of course, the descriptive advantage gained by converting raw data into a frequency distribution does come at a price. That is, in the conversion we have lost the details concerning the individual practices. Merely by examining table 4.4, we cannot any longer say how often Allison, or Brenda, or any of the other students traveled. This kind of trade-off is very common in both descriptive and inductive statistics, as we shall see several times throughout this book: Details are sacrificed for comprehension. Such an exchange is usually considered worthwhile.

Proportions, Percentages, and Probabilities

In addition to the first two columns indicating the attributes and frequencies, respectively, most univariate frequency tables also include a third column. This contains the *percentage* of the entire sample that is observed to have a given attribute. The percentage is calculated in two steps:

First we create a *proportion*, symbolized by a lowercase *p*. A proportion is defined as a frequency divided by the sample size, and there are as many proportions in a univariate frequency distribution as there are attributes. The formula is:

$$p_i = f_i/n \,, \quad \text{where } i \text{ ranges between 1 and } a, \text{ the number of attributes.}$$

The lowest possible value for any proportion is 0, which occurs when a frequency is 0. The highest possible value is 1.0, which occurs when a frequency is equal to n (that is, the entire sample has the same attribute). Because of this 0 to 1 property, we can interpret a proportion as "a portion of the whole (1 is the whole)." Table 4.5 shows the proportions associated with the frequency distribution in table 4.4.

With these proportions calculated, we can expand our ability to describe the results of our survey of the 15 dorm students. For example, we can say that a proportion of .267 has taken three trips; the proportion of those who have taken 0 trips is .133, which is the same proportion of those who have taken 1, 4, or 5 trips, etc.

We are treating the calculation of proportions as the first step in the process of finding percentages because proportions, as such, are ordinarily not included in frequency distributions (although there is nothing wrong with including them). We use proportions for many other statistical purposes, however, so it important to remember what they are and how they are derived (and the rule that they range between 0 and 1.0). In most respects, proportions provide exactly the same information as do percentages, but they do so in a slightly different form. In fact, even though there is a technical difference between proportions and percentages, it is useful to think of them interchangeably. Thus, you might be asked a question in percentages but be expected to answer it in proportions, and so on.

TABLE 4.5   Proportions table

Number of trips	f_i	$f_i n$	p_i
0	2	2/15	.133
1	2	2/15	.133
2	3	3/15	.200
3	4	4/15	.267
4	2	2/15	.133
5	2	2/15	.133
Total	$n = 15$	15/15	1.0

The close connection between proportions and percentages is clear when we take the second step, in which we multiply the proportion by 100. That is, symbolizing a given percentage as pct$_i$ (or with the percentage symbol %),

$$\text{pct}_i = p_i \times 100.$$

There are, of course, as many percentages in a univariate frequency distributions as there are proportions, which is also the same as the number of attributes. Just as we can think of proportions as portions of a whole, we can think of percentages as portions of 100. So, there is a very direct and simple equivalence between the two. A proportion of 0 is equal to 0 percent, a proportion of .10 is equal to 10%, a proportion of .27 is equal to 27%, a proportion of .50 is equal to 50%, and a proportion of 1.0 is equal to 100%. Thus, just as we can easily convert proportions to percentages, we can convert percentages to proportions by dividing by 100. That is,

$$p_i = \text{pct}_i / 100 .$$

So, for example, 34.6% is .346 as a proportion.

Table 4.6 is based on table 4.5. Each entry in the third column is derived by applying steps 1 and 2 above to the respective frequencies. This allows us to say that 26.7% of the sample traveled three times, 13.3% did not travel at all, and so on. Of course, the total of the percentages equals 100%.

The use of percentages (and, to a lesser extent, proportions) to describe frequency distributions allows us to put our observations into terms that are familiar and understandable to others. But there is another, even more important advantage. That is, percentages and proportions make it possible to compare, easily and quickly, two or more frequency distributions whose sample sizes differ.

TABLE 4.6   Frequency distribution with a third column
for percentages

Number of trips (x)	f	%
0	2	13.3
1	2	13.3
2	3	20.0
3	4	26.7
4	2	13.3
5	2	13.3
	$n = 15$	100.0

TABLE 4.7   Frequency distribution for the travel
home variable with $n = 28$

Number of trips (x)	f
0	3
1	4
2	6
3	7
4	6
5	2
	$n = 28$

To help illustrate this point, table 4.7 was created to display information about the frequency with which another group of students traveled home during the semester. Here, however, the sample size is 28 rather than 15. Now, according to this table, 3 of the 28 students did not travel at all; whereas in the first sample ($n = 15$) only 2 students did not travel. Based on this comparison alone, it is obvious that more students in the second group made no trips than in the first. But couldn't the difference be a result of the fact that there are more students altogether in the second group?

This question suggests that we are not really interested in the comparison between the frequencies, as such. Rather, we would like to understand—and to measure—the patterns of travel in relation to the total number of travelers. Or, to put it in another, statistically familiar way, we are interested in the travel patterns *controlling for* (that is, removing the influence of) the size of the samples.

Proportions and percentages help us control for sample size. We know that .133 or 13.3% of the group of 15 made no trips home. To find the proportion and percentage with that attribute in the group of 28, we divide 3 by 28 for a proportion of .107, and multiplying by 100 we get 10.7%. This allows us to say that, despite the higher frequency in comparison to the first group, there were *relatively fewer* students in the second group who made no trips. Similarly, we found that 3 students in the first group traveled home twice, compared to 6 who traveled twice in the second group. So, were the students in the second group more likely to have made two trips? Let us compare the proportion and percentage for this attribute in the smaller group, which we found to be .200 or 20.0%, with the proportion and percentage in the second group, 6/28 = .214 or 21.4%. These results allow us to affirm that the students in the second group did have a relatively higher frequency of two-time travelers.

Along with proportions and percentages, statisticians use another "*p*" word to discuss frequency distributions. In fact, we slipped in the concept, though not the term itself, while discussing the comparison between samples of different sizes. This is *probability* (plural *probabilities*). The concept of probability and its application to statistics will be discussed at length in Chapter 7. We introduce it here in order to stress its close connection with proportion and percentage. In fact, as we are reminded by the common use of the symbol "*p*" to stand for probability as well as for proportion, the two are in many important respects identical. Under the most common conditions, they are simply two different ways to express the same thing.[2]

Formally, *probability* is defined as the number of ways a specific "outcome" can occur, divided by the number of all possible "outcomes." Thus, we can easily calculate the probability of getting a head in a single flip of a perfect coin that has a head and a tail. It is 1 (the number of ways a head can occur) divided by 2 (the number of all possible outcomes—1 for the head plus 1 for the tail) or $1/2 = .5$. This is the same as the probability of getting a tail, because there are only two equally likely outcomes. In instances such as this, when the probability of two or more outcomes is the same, it is referred to as *equiprobability*. This concept is discussed further in Chapter 7.

When applied to a frequency distribution, the number of ways a specific outcome can occur is simply the frequency of a given attribute, and the number of all possible outcomes is the sum of the frequencies of all attributes, which is the same as the sample size, or *n*. Thus, using the example of the 15 students and their trips back home, we can ask, "What is the probability that a student takes four trips home?" The answer is derived by dividing the frequency of the attribute "four trips," which is 2, by the sample size, which is 15. This turns out to be $2/15 = .133$. So, the probability of taking four trips is .133. But is not the proportion of students who take four trips also .133? Of course it is, because probability is expressed as a proportion. Only the way of asking and answering the question differ.

The lesson to be taken from this is that percentage, proportion, and probability can be used more or less interchangeably. In fact, they are used interchangeably in many statistical applications. So, although there are minor technical differences, we should feel comfortable when looking at a frequency distribution such as that shown in table 4.4 to say something like the following: "The proportion of students who made three trips is .267; that is, the probability that a student made three trips is .267; that is, 26.7% of the students took three trips."

Graphing Univariate Frequency Distributions

The alternative method of presenting frequency distributions is in the form of graphs. These are as familiar as tables and are often used in conjunction with them. With recent developments in the techniques of computer graphing, the variety of possible ways to show the relationships between attributes and frequencies is limited only by one's imagination. Nevertheless, all such graphics are ultimately based on one or more of the

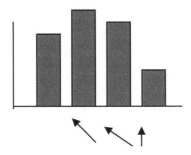

In an ordinary bar graph, there are spaces between the bars.

FIGURE 4.1   Ordinary bar graph.

three types to be discussed in this section: bar graphs, histograms, and line graphs (also known as frequency polygons).

Bar Graphs and Histograms

Bar graphs and histograms are the most common types of graphs used to display univariate frequency distributions. Each bar in a bar graph represents an attribute, and the height of the bars represents the respective frequencies, percentages, proportions, or probabilities. The ordinary bar graph, such as that shown in figure 4.1, is used for non-numerical variables. To indicate this, a space is left between bars, showing that the attributes are not continuous but are merely discrete categories (or ranks).

A histogram, shown in figure 4.2, is used with numerical variables. It is distinguished from ordinary bar graphs in that there is no horizontal separation between bars and all bars must have the same width. In this way, they appear as a "cluster" or a single structure with an uneven top.

As shown in figure 4.3, the horizontal axis of a bar graph or histogram represents the variable, and on it we mark off the attributes (in order). On the vertical axis we mark off, according to scale, the frequencies, percentages, etc. Thus, the horizontal axis corresponds to the first column of a frequency table and the vertical axis corresponds to the second column (or third in the case of percentages).

Each bar is drawn in four steps: (1) Locate the attribute that the bar represents along the horizontal axis and sketch in (actually or in your imagination) a reference line parallel to the vertical axis. (2) Locate the frequency (percentage, etc.) associated with the attribute along the vertical axis and sketch in a reference line parallel to the horizontal axis. (3) Mark the point at which the two reference lines meet as the center of the top line of the bar. (4) Draw the top and then draw the two sides parallel to the vertical axis and all the way down to the horizontal axis. Fill in or color as appropriate.

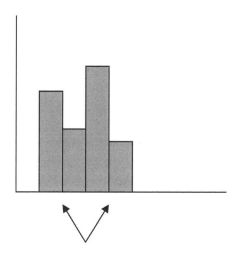

A histogram has no spaces between the bars.

FIGURE 4.2   Ordinary histogram.

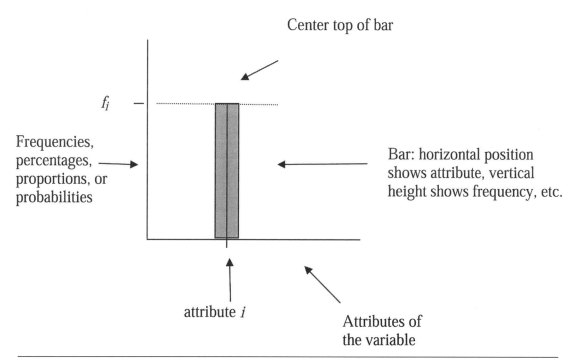

FIGURE 4.3   Anatomy of a histogram.

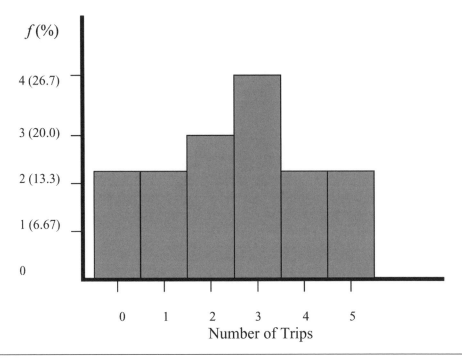

FIGURE 4.4   Histogram for number of trips.

Figure 4.4 shows the histogram for table 4.5. As in the case of the pie chart, the graph portrays the distribution of attributes in a clear and easy to understand manner.

Line Graphs or Frequency Polygons

The third and last graphic method to be considered here is the line graph. When this type of chart is used to show a frequency distribution it is often referred to as a *frequency polygon*.[3] It is used widely in descriptive applications, and, as we shall see, it is a very effective visual aid in inductive statistics a well. Its basic meaning and method of construction are essentially the same as those that apply to histograms. In fact, one way (but not the most efficient way) to construct a line graph is to begin with a histogram.

If we begin with a histogram, the first step in transforming it into a line graph is to connect the midpoints of the tops of adjacent bars (the points created by the intersection of the two reference lines). Next, erase the bars and, voilà! You have a frequency polygon. The reason that this is not the most efficient way to make a line graph is that it is not even necessary to draw bars. Rather, following the step of locating the point at which the two reference lines intersect, go on to the next attribute, until all the points are marked. When they are joined, the line graph is completed. Both methods are shown in figure 4.5, and figure 4.6 contains the line graph that corresponds to tables 4.3 and 4.4.

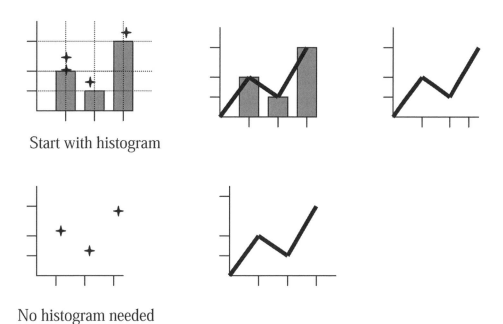

Start with histogram

No histogram needed

FIGURE 4.5   Creating a line graph.

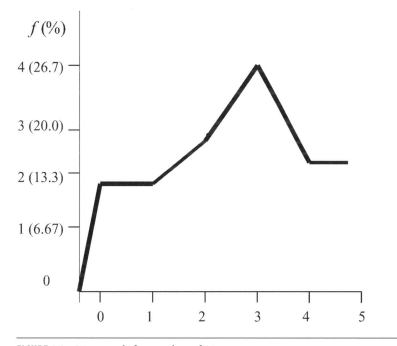

FIGURE 4.6   Line graph for number of trips.

Univariate Frequency Distributions: Ordinal and Numerical Variables

The rules concerning the basic structure of frequency distributions and the calculation of proportions, percentages, and probabilities discussed above are applied consistently, regardless of whether the variable of interest is nominal, ordinal, or numerical. However, certain procedures are applied *only* to ordinal-level and/or numerical variables. This is because the attributes of such variables are more than simple categories.

Order of Attributes

At the nominal level, the order in which the attributes are listed does not matter. The illustration in the preceding session for the variable "student status" listed the attributes in the left column with "new" in the first row for the variable name and "returning" in the second row. This seems reasonable because new students have been on campus a shorter time. But it is equally reasonable to list "returning" first and then "new" (because returning students were on campus first). In fact, with this variable and all other nominal-level variables—dichotomies or other types—*any* order in which attributes are listed is as reasonable as any other, as long as all are listed in the appropriate column. They might be listed in alphabetical order, such as the set of states, beginning with Alabama and ending with Wyoming. They might be listed in order of frequencies, so that the attribute with the highest frequency is listed first and the attribute with the lowest frequency listed last. Or they might be listed according to the researcher's personal preferences. There is no statistically meaningful reason why one ordering should be preferred over another.

That is not the case, however, with ordinal and numerical variables. Here, order matters, not only because a frequency distribution is easier to follow when attributes are listed in order but also because certain statistical techniques require it. Returning to our example of 15 students in the dorm, table 4.8 shows the raw data for the

TABLE 4.8   Raw data for the variable "year in school" for 15 students

Student	Year in school	Student	Year in school
Allison	Soph	Jomo	Fresh
Brenda	Fresh	Kwame	Fresh
Carlos	Senior	Len	Senior
Davida	Senior	Mahmood	Junior
Eunice	Fresh	Nora	Soph
Gopal	Junior	Oshu	Junior
Harry	Soph	Perry	Junior
Israel	Junior		

TABLE 4.9   Frequency distribution based on table 4.8

Year in school	f	%
Fresh	4	26.7
Soph	3	20.0
Junior	5	33.3
Senior	3	20.0
Total	15	100.0

variable "year in school," with the attributes "fresh," "soph," "junior," and "senior." The frequency distribution in table 4.9 and the histogram in figure 4.7 list the attributes in this exact order, which is correct. This is because the ranking associated with year in school is accurately reflected in the ordering. It would be a mistake, on the other hand, to list them in alphabetical order: "fresh," "junior," "soph," senior." Similarly, a listing according to the frequencies of the attributes from high to low, such as "soph," "senior," " fresh," "junior," would also be incorrect. Such "disordered" listings make it difficult to see whether certain important patterns exist in the overall distribution.

This same rule of ordering applies to numerical variables. This is in keeping with the principle, discussed in Chapter 3, that any rule that holds at a given level of measurement also holds at higher levels. Recall that in table 4.4 the attributes indicating the number of trips taken by each of the 15 students took during the semester are correctly listed in order from "0" to "5." It would be wrong to list them according to frequency (e.g. 3, 2, (4-way tie) 0, 1, 4, 5) or any other criterion. On the other hand, as long as the attributes of ordinal or numerical variables are listed in order, then *it makes no difference at all, in terms of understanding or as it affects statistical techniques, whether the order is ascending or descending*. A listing of year in school with the order "senior,"

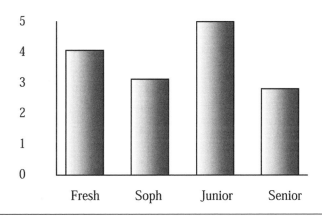

FIGURE 4.7   Bar graph based on table 4.8.

"junior," "soph," "fresh" is as valid as the order listed in table 4.8. Similarly, a listing of the attributes for number of trips with the order "5, 4, 3, 2, 1, 0," is perfectly acceptable.

Cumulative Frequencies and Percentages

One common measure that is used to help describe frequency distributions at the ordinal or numerical level, and that clearly illustrates why attributes must be listed in order, is *cumulative frequency*. Each attribute in an ordinal or nominal frequency table has a cumulative frequency, symbolized by the italic "*cf*." The cumulative frequencies are ordinarily listed in the fourth column following percentages. The definition of a cumulative frequency is:

The cumulative frequency of a given attribute is the number of times that that attribute and every attribute with a value following it in the table is observed.

Attributes may be listed in either ascending order (from low values/ranks to high values/ranks) or descending order (from high to low). For this reason, we speak of values "beneath" a given attribute, which can either be high or low depending on how the attributes are listed. The formula for cumulative frequency is

$$cf_i = \sum_{j=\text{last}}^{i} \left(f_j \right),$$

where cf_i is the cumulative frequency associated with the ith (1st, 2nd, 3rd, etc.) attribute (the one we wish to calculate); f_j is the frequency of attribute j, which is at or beneath attribute i; and "last" is the attribute (value/rank) listed last on the table. Tables 4.10a and 4.10b, the first in ascending and the second in descending order, are derived from table 4.8. The tables show the cumulative frequencies recorded in the fourth column. Note that the "*cf*" symbol is placed in the top cell of that column.

The number 15 in the next cell of table 4.10a is associated with the attribute "fresh"; the next number in the column, 11, is associated with the attribute "soph," and so on. Because the order is descending, the 15 indicates that in the sample, 15 students are freshmen or one of the classes listed below it, 11 are sophomores or a class listed below, eight are juniors or a class listed below it, and three are seniors (no class is listed below it). The actual calculation of these cumulative frequencies begins at the top. For "fresh," we add its frequency, 4, to all the frequencies with lower attributes. Thus, *cf*(fresh) = 4 + 3 + 5 + 3 = 15. For "soph," we take its frequency, 3, and add it to the frequency for juniors and sophomores. Thus, *cf*(soph) = 3 + 5 + 3 = 11. For "junior," we take its frequency, 2, and add it to the frequency for seniors. Thus, *cf*(junior) = 5 + 3 = 8. Finally, for "senior," we take its frequency, 4, and use it as its cumulative frequency as well (because there are no attributes listed beneath it). Thus, *cf*(seniors) = 3.

TABLE 4.10   Cumulative frequencies

(a) Calculated from low to high

Year in school	f	%	cf
Fresh	4	26.7	15
Soph	3	20.0	11
Junior	5	33.3	8
Senior	3	20.0	3
Total	15	100.0	

(b) Calculated from high to low

Year in school	f	%	cf
Senior	3	26.7	15
Junior	5	20.0	12
Soph	3	33.3	7
Fresh	4	20.0	4
Total	15	100.0	

This same procedure is followed in calculating the cumulative frequencies shown in table 4.10b. Because in this distribution the attributes are listed in descending order, the 15 in the first cell of the fourth column, beneath the "*cf*" symbol, indicates that 15 students are in the senior class or a class listed below senior. The number 12 in the cell beneath the 15 indicates that 1 of the students are juniors or below, and so on.

You can see that in this table and in table 4.10a the cumulative frequency for the attribute with the lowest value/rank matches its (noncumulative) frequency, and the cumulative frequency for the attribute with the highest value (or rank) matches the sample size, *n*. This is always the case with cumulative frequency distributions, because the entry for the attribute with the highest value/rank refers to the frequency with which all attributes were observed—that at the top and all others beneath it. The entry for the attribute with the lowest value/rank refers to the frequency with which this and only this, the last-recorded, attribute occurs.

This and the other features of cumulative frequency distributions can be seen in table 4.11, which is based on table 4.4 for the numerical variable "number of trips." All 15 students took zero or more trips, 13 took one or more trips, and so on. You will also note that no total is ever shown for cumulative frequencies. It makes no sense to add cumulative frequencies together, so any such total would be a meaningless number.

Figure 4.8 displays the information about the cumulative frequency for "number of trips" as a bar graph, and figures 4.9a and 4.9b display the information as line graphs

TABLE 4.11   Number of trips for 15 students showing cumulative frequencies

Number of trips	f	cf
0	2	15
1	2	13
2	4	11
3	4	7
4	1	3
5	2	2
Total	15	

(note the identical shapes of the curves regardless of whether we cumulate from low to high or high to low). This special cumulative frequency polygon occurs in many statistical and scientific applications. Accordingly, it has several names. Statisticians often refer to it as the *ogive* (from a medieval French word for "diagonal arch"). Mathematicians know it as an "S" curve, for obvious reasons. In the physical sciences, this curve represents the phenomenon of *saturation*. When a dry sponge begins to soak up water, the absorption rate increases with time until a turning point is reached at which the absorption process slows. Ultimately, the sponge becomes saturated, as shown by the upper limit reached by the curve. This is also how cumulative frequency works: rapidly at first, then slowing, then reaching the maximum of the total sample size. Finally, the curve is known to social scientists as "Pareto's curve," after the Italian economist and sociologist who discovered the principle at work in certain market situations.[4]

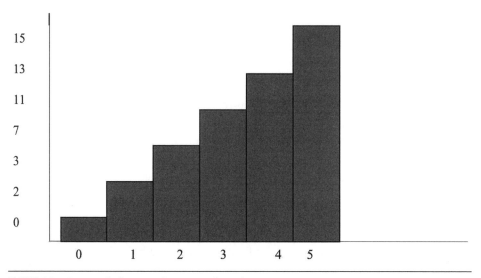

FIGURE 4.8   Bar graph for cumulative number of trips.

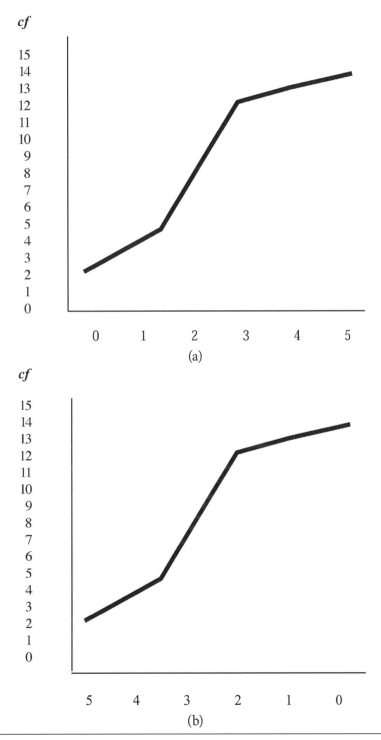

FIGURE 4.9   Cumulative frequency polygon for number of trips, cumulating (**a**) from low to high and (**b**) from high to low.

Just as we can associate a percentage with each frequency shown in a distribution, each cumulative frequency can be expressed as a percentage. This is referred to as the *cumulative percentage*, symbolized by *c%* and ordinarily listed in the fifth column of a frequency table. The formula for the cumulative percentage is

$$c\%_i = \left(cf_i/n\right) \times 100, \quad \text{where } cf_i \text{ is a given cumulative frequency and}$$
$$n \text{ is the total sample size.}$$

Table 4.12 extends table 4.11 with the addition of the cumulative percentage column. The first cell in that column, below the *c%* symbol, is 100, indicating that 100 percent of the sample made 0 or more trips. The 86.7 in the next cell down indicates that this is the percentage of the students who made one trip or more. The 39.3 in the following cell down is the percentage of those who made two trips or more, and so on. The calculation for zero or more trips was $c\% = (15/15) \times 100 = 100$; for one or more trips it was $(13/15) \times 100 = 86.7$; for two or more trips, it was $(11/15) \times 100 = 39.3$, etc.

Grouping

A final, and very useful, special feature of frequency tables for variables beyond the nominal level is *grouping* of attributes. Ordinarily this technique applies only to numerical data, although one occasionally sees it used at the ordinal level. A table that employs grouping is referred to as a *grouped frequency distribution*. It is similar to all of the others we have been considering except that individual attributes are not listed in the first column. Instead, as the name suggests, sets of consecutive attributes are grouped together into what are called *class intervals*. You have surely seen such frequency distributions, but you may not have examined how they are constructed.

TABLE 4.12   Number of trips for 15 students showing cumulative percentages

Number of trips	f	cf	c%
0	2	15	100.0
1	2	13	86.7
2	4	11	39.3
3	4	7	25.0
4	1	3	10.7
5	2	2	7.1
Total	15		

TABLE 4.13   Monthly incomes for 75 households

Income			
$ 725	$2,388	$ 6,500	$10,745
$ 940	$2,412	$ 6,530	$11,015
$1,074	$2,509	$ 6,730	$11,088
$1,095	$2,592	$ 7,050	$11,172
$1,100	$2,684	$ 7,087	$11,190
$1,174	$3,210	$ 7,090	$11,362
$1,191	$3,380	$ 7,200	$11,637
$1,460	$3,700	$ 7,330	$11,680
$1,559	$4,200	$ 7,500	$11,836
$1,585	$4,600	$ 7,625	$11,950
$1,717	$4,790	$ 7,700	$12,120
$1,731	$4,800	$ 7,790	$12,474
$1,780	$4,980	$ 7,804	$12,890
$1,787	$5,110	$ 7,900	$13,350
$1,816	$5,550	$ 7,985	$13,380
$1,840	$5,720	$ 8,710	
$1,890	$6,020	$ 8,850	
$1,995	$6,140	$ 9,200	
$2,066	$6,175	$ 9,787	
$2,230	$6,290	$10,203	

Table 4.13 lists the monthly incomes of a sample of 75 households residing in a midwestern suburb. These range from $725 to $13,380. Although this table contains some interesting facts, it does not allow the reader to understand clearly how incomes are distributed among these households: How many of them have very high incomes? Are there several households whose income is below $1,000? What is the most common range of incomes? To help in these matters, an ungrouped frequency distribution was created, as shown in table 4.14. Unfortunately, because no two incomes are exactly the same, the frequency distribution is essentially no different from the listing of raw data. All we learn from it is that every income has the same frequency of 1 and the same percentage of 1.3%. It is in instances such as this that grouping of attributes is appropriate.

Table 4.15 shows this distribution with the attributes grouped into intervals of $2,000 for all but the topmost interval, and in the " . . . or above" format for the topmost interval. The latter is referred to as an *open interval* because it does not state a specific endpoint. This term also applies to intervals with the " . . . or below" format. You will immediately notice several things about this type of frequency distribution. First, the

TABLE 4.14   Ungrouped frequency distribution based on table 4.13

Income (x)	f	%	cf	Income (x)	f	%	cf
$ 725	1	1.3	1	$ 6,175	1	1.3	39
$ 940	1	1.3	2	$ 6,290	1	1.3	40
$1,074	1	1.3	3	$ 6,500	1	1.3	41
$1,095	1	1.3	4	$ 6,530	1	1.3	42
$1,100	1	1.3	5	$ 6,730	1	1.3	43
$1,174	1	1.3	6	$ 7,050	1	1.3	44
$1,191	1	1.3	7	$ 7,087	1	1.3	45
$1,460	1	1.3	8	$ 7,090	1	1.3	46
$1,559	1	1.3	9	$ 7,200	1	1.3	47
$1,585	1	1.3	10	$ 7,330	1	1.3	48
$1,717	1	1.3	11	$ 7,500	1	1.3	49
$1,731	1	1.3	12	$ 7,625	1	1.3	50
$1,780	1	1.3	13	$ 7,700	1	1.3	51
$1,787	1	1.3	14	$ 7,790	1	1.3	52
$1,816	1	1.3	15	$ 7,804	1	1.3	53
$1,840	1	1.3	16	$ 7,900	1	1.3	54
$1,890	1	1.3	17	$ 7,985	1	1.3	55
$1,995	1	1.3	18	$ 8,710	1	1.3	56
$2,066	1	1.3	19	$ 8,850	1	1.3	57
$2,230	1	1.3	20	$ 9,200	1	1.3	58
$2,388	1	1.3	21	$ 9,787	1	1.3	59
$2,412	1	1.3	22	$10,203	1	1.3	60
$2,509	1	1.3	23	$10,745	1	1.3	61
$2,592	1	1.3	24	$11,015	1	1.3	62
$2,684	1	1.3	25	$11,088	1	1.3	63
$3,210	1	1.3	26	$11,172	1	1.3	64
$3,380	1	1.3	27	$11,190	1	1.3	65
$3,700	1	1.3	28	$11,362	1	1.3	66
$4,200	1	1.3	29	$11,637	1	1.3	67
$4,600	1	1.3	30	$11,680	1	1.3	68
$4,790	1	1.3	31	$11,836	1	1.3	69
$4,800	1	1.3	32	$11,950	1	1.3	70
$4,980	1	1.3	33	$12,120	1	1.3	71
$5,110	1	1.3	34	$12,474	1	1.3	72
$5,550	1	1.3	35	$12,890	1	1.3	73
$5,720	1	1.3	36	$13,350	1	1.3	74
$6,020	1	1.3	37	$13,380	1	1.3	75
$6,140 (mdn)	1	1.3	38				

TABLE 4.15   Grouped frequency distribution for incomes of 75 households

Class interval	*m*	*f*	%	*cf*	*c%*
$12,700 and above	—	3	4.0	75	100.0
$10,700 to $12,699	$11,699.50	12	16.0	72	96.0
$8,700 to $10,699	9,699.50	5	6.7	60	80.0
$6,700 to $8,699	7,699.50	13	17.3	55	73.3
$4,700 to $6,699	5,699.50	12	16.0	42	56.0
$2,700 to $4,699	3,699.50	5	6.7	30	40.0
$700 to $2,699	1,699.50	25	33.3	25	33.3
Total		75	100.0		

variable itself is not named in the first cell of the farthest left column. In grouped distributions this is replaced by *class interval* to indicate that the attributes that follow are not actual values but ranges: $700 to $2,699, and so on. The ranges are specified by the smallest possible attribute in the interval, called the *lower limit (ll)*, and the largest value is *the upper limit (ul)*. Thus, the second interval from the top in table 4.15 has a $ll = \$10,700$ and an $ul = \$12,699$. Because the topmost interval is open, it has no upper limit. Similarly, an interval with the label " . . . and below" has no lower limit.

The column following the list of class intervals is headed with a lowercase *m*. This stands for the *midpoint* of the respective intervals. Midpoints are often included in grouped frequency distributions. This is because in certain calculations, such as that for the mean, in the absence of the frequencies for each attribute in the interval range the midpoint is assumed to be the specific value of every attribute. As the name suggests, the midpoint is the value halfway between the lower and upper limits of an interval. Its formula is:

$$m = (ll + ul)/2.$$

Thus, the midpoint for the $10,700 to $12,699 interval is $11,699.50 because (10,700 + 12,699)/2 = 23,399/2 = \$11,699.50. The same procedure is followed to find the midpoint of each interval except the open one, which has no midpoint. If it is necessary to determine a midpoint for an open interval, an upper limit (or, in the "and below" format, a lower limit) is created that includes the highest value observed. For example, in the distribution shown in tables 4.13 and 4.14, the upper limit might be $13,380.

The next thing to note in table 4.15 is the column of frequencies. These are derived by adding together the frequencies of all of the attributes that lie within a given interval. The following formula shows how this is done:

$$f_{(ll-ul)} = \sum_{i=ll}^{ul} f_i,$$

where $f_{(ll-ul)}$ is the frequency for the interval between the lower limit (ll) and upper limit (ul) and f_i is the frequency of a given (ungrouped) attribute.

This means that an ungrouped frequency distribution is required in order to create the associated grouped frequency distribution, because the frequencies included in the latter are taken from the former. So, for example, the frequency of 3 shown in table 4.15 for the "$12,700 and above" interval is the sum of

the frequency of 1 for the attribute $12,890

plus 1 for the attribute $13,350,

plus 1 for the attribute $13,380,

all listed in tables 4.13 and 4.14. Once the frequencies have been determined for a grouped frequency distribution, the calculation and interpretation of percentage, cumulative frequency, and cumulative percentage are identical to those that apply to an ungrouped distribution.

Frequency Distributions with Two Variables

Thus far we have examined univariate frequency distributions, emphasizing that they are the primary tools for descriptive statistics. But statisticians also make considerable use of frequency distributions for bivariate and even multivariate description. This section introduces some of the main features of such distributions in table form. Tables that display information for more than one variable have a familiar name which, as we will soon see, is self-explanatory: *cross-tabulations* or, for short, *crosstabs*. We begin with bivariate applications and then move to situations in which three or more variables are involved.

Bivariate Crosstabs

As we mentioned in Chapter 3, when two (or more) variables are used together for descriptive purposes, the procedures used are referred to as measures of *association*. It was also noted that it is often necessary to decide, in bivariate applications, which of the two is the independent and which is the dependent variable. Often this is an easy decision to make; but sometimes it is a matter of guesswork. Because the independent variable is the "probable cause" of the variation of the dependent, the researcher must determine which of the variables occurs first in time. The other criteria, correlation and the absence of other causes, are not applicable in this decision because only a probable, and not an actual, cause-and-effect relationship is sought. It may be necessary to guess about which the independent variable is, but,

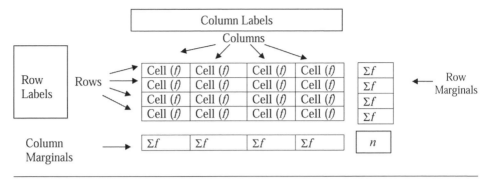

FIGURE 4.10   Structure of a bivariate crosstab.

in this situation, a bad guess is better than no guess at all. For, without some kind of determination as to which of the two variables is the independent, it is not possible to create a crosstab.

The Structure of the Crosstab

The reason why the independent and dependent variables must be identified lies in the structure of a crosstab table. As indicated in the model table in figure 4.10, a crosstab, like any other table, consists of *rows* and *columns*. At the intersection of each row and column is a *cell*. And in each cell we find a *frequency* (and possibly other information). The most widely used convention is to use the horizontal direction for the independent variable and to have each column represent an attribute of that variable. Similarly, the vertical direction is used for the dependent variable, with each row representing one of its attributes. The column and row labels are used to name the two variables and their respective attributes. This is why one must designate an independent and a dependent variable without going any further.

The frequencies contained in each cell of a crosstab show the number of units in the sample observed to have a combination of the attributes of the column and the row of its cell. In other words, each frequency indicates how many times the combination of a given attribute of the independent variable and a given attribute of the dependent occurs in the sample.

In addition to the cells that contain the frequencies, all crosstabs include an extra row, column, and cell, referred to as *marginals* because they are on the margins of the table. These are used to show totals. The column marginals contain the sum of the frequencies for each column, and the row marginals contain the sum of the frequencies for each row. The cell at the lower right contains the sum of all column totals, which equals the sum of all row totals, which is the *grand total,* equal to the *sample size, n.* As we know from balancing a checkbook, if the sum of the column totals does not equal the sum of the row totals, we have made a mistake. Another way to understand the marginals is to notice that each column total is the sum of all units in the sample with a given attribute on the independent variable and that each row total is the sum of all units with a given attribute on the dependent variable.

What the Crosstab Tells Us

To illustrate these points, let us return to our survey of 15 dorm students. Table 4.16 contains data derived from table 4.3 plus the year in school for these students, who constitute a different group from those shown in table 4.8. For the sake of simplifying the example, we have changed the two variables "number of trips home" and "year in school" into dichotomies. In the first case, a nominal-level variable, we assigned a "Yes" to those students who took more than two trips and a "No" to those who took two or fewer trips. For the other variable, still ordinal level, we assigned an "L" to those in one of the lower classes, freshman and sophomore, and a "U" to the upper classes, junior and senior. This is not to suggest that crosstabs can be used only with such variables. In fact, they can be used with variables at any level of measurement and with any number of attributes. However, beyond a certain point, tables that show numerical variables become difficult to interpret and require some method of grouping attributes.

TABLE 4.16   Trip and class data for the 15 students
listed in table 4.3

Student	*More than two trips?*	*Class*
Allison	Y	L
Brenda	N	L
Charles	N	L
Dawn	Y	U
Eugene	Y	L
Frank	Y	U
Glen	Y	U
Harriet	N	U
Ian	N	L
Janella	N	L
Kris	Y	U
Leora	N	L
Mike	N	U
Nancy	Y	L
On-Kim	Y	L

TABLE 4.17   Univariate frequency distribution for number of trips based on table 4.16

More than two trips?	f
Yes	8
No	7
Total	15

TABLE 4.18   Univariate frequency distribution for class based on table 4.16

Class	f
Lower	9
Upper	6
Total	15

Tables 4.17 and 4.18 contain the univariate frequency distributions for each of the variables, respectively. We can see that 8 of the 15 students took more than two trips and the other 7 did not. Moreover, 9 of the students are in a lower class and the other 6 are in an upper class. The next table, table 4.19, shows the crosstab for the two variables. First, note that we have decided that "lower or upper class" would be the independent variable because the students were in their classes before any traveled home. For this reason, the columns are labeled with the attributes of class, "lower" and "upper," and the rows are labeled "yes" and "no," indicating whether or not they traveled home more than twice. Reading off the frequencies in each cell, we see that 4 students are in a lower class and traveled more than twice; 5 are in a lower class and did not travel more than twice; 4 are in an upper class and traveled more than twice; and, finally, 2 are in an upper class and did not travel more than twice. The marginals indicate that 9 of the students are in a lower class, 6 are in an upper class, 8 traveled more than twice, and 7 did not travel more than twice. The sum of the rows and the sum of the columns add to n, which equals 15, as they should.

By comparing tables 4.17, 4.18, and 4.19 you can see that the column marginals exactly match the univariate frequency distribution for the independent variable and the row marginals match the univariate frequency distribution for the dependent variable. This is always the case with a crosstab, because the marginals actually *are*

TABLE 4.19   Crosstab based on table 4.16

More than two trips?	Class		Row total
	Lower	Upper	
Yes	4	4	8
No	5	2	7
Col. total	9	6	$n = 15$

the univariate distributions in a slightly different format. This means that once the decision is made about which of two variables of interest will be the independent and which will be dependent, the marginals of their crosstab can be directly determined. However, and this is an interesting and an important point, the *frequencies* of a crosstab cannot be directly determined from the univariate distributions. In the example of the dorm students, from the two univariate distributions we can learn how many students traveled more than twice (8) and how many are in a lower class (9). But we cannot know how many of the 9 lowerclass students are among the eight students who traveled more than twice. For this information, and, in general, in order to create any crosstab, we need to return to the original raw data, here shown in table 4.16.

Crosstabs and Association

Once the crosstab has been completed, it is possible to use it descriptively, as a tool for understanding the association between the variables. Most simply put, we do this by seeking to discern "interesting" patterns in the data. Because we have distinguished between independent and dependent variables, one reasonable way to begin this task is to ask whether the former does in fact seem to affect the latter. For example, does the fact that a student is a member of a lower or an upper class make any difference in terms of how often that student travels? From table 4.19 we can see that four lowerclass and four upperclass students took more than two trips home. So by this criterion there seems to be no difference. However, there are more—three more—students in the lower class than in the upper class, which is reflected in the greater number of lowerclass students who did not travel two or more times: 5 versus 2. Thus, it appears that lowerclass students do travel less often (perhaps because they spend more time studying).

This sort of conclusion is easy enough to draw if a crosstab is simple—for instance, if it has two dichotomous variables, the simplest crosstab possible. But, as the number of attributes in either or both of the variables increases beyond two or three, a direct comparison of frequencies becomes increasingly difficult. It is at this point, as is the case with univariate distributions, that percentages (or proportions) play an important role. We return to the use of percentages in measuring association following a brief comment on graphic presentation of crosstabs.

Graphing Crosstabs

The bar graphs, histograms, and line graphs discussed earlier can all be adapted to bivariate applications. The general procedure is to display separately each attribute of one of the variables, usually the independent. This can be done with positioning, labels, shading, or colors. Then the frequencies of the other (dependent) variable are shown for each attribute. Figure 4.11 contains a simple bivariate bar chart based on table 4.19. Here the two attributes of the independent variable, "class rank," are separated and identified by the shading of their respective bars. The nine lowerclass students are represented by solid bars, and the six upperclass students are represented by patterned bars. Each pair of bars is then positioned on the horizontal axis according to the attributes on the dependent variable, "number of trips." The frequency with which each attribute was observed is indicated on the vertical axis, as usual. One can instantly see that four students from each group traveled two or more times, whereas five from the lower class and two from the upper class traveled of fewer two times.

Percentages in the Crosstab

As we will discuss in a moment, there is more than one way to calculate percentages in a crosstab. However, because we are usually interested in determining the impact of the independent on the dependent variable, the most obvious way is to express each frequency as a percentage of the total for the respective attributes of the *independent* variable, which are listed as the *column* totals. Thus, in table 4.20 we see that the frequency of 4 for the lowerclass/yes cell can be divided by 9, the total of all lowerclass students, and then multiplied by 100 to create a percentage. That is, $(4/9) \times 100 = .444 \times 100 = 44.4\%$. A little over 44% of the lowerclass students

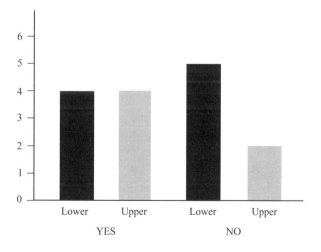

FIGURE 4.11   Bivariate bar graph using frequencies from table 4.19.

TABLE 4.20   Crosstab shown in table 4.19 with column percentages

More than two trips?	Class rank		
	Lower	*Upper*	
Yes	4 (44.4%)	4 (66.7%)	8
No	5 (55.6%)	2 (33.3%)	7
Col. total	9 (100%)	6 (100%)	$n = 15$

took two or more trips. Similarly, the percentage of upperclass students who took more than two trips is $(4/6) \times 100 = .667 \times 100 = 66.7\%$. Using the same procedure, we find that 55.6% of the lowerclass students did not take more than two trips and 33.3% of the upperclass students did not take more than two trips. These results, which confirm our impression that lowerclass students travel less often, are shown in table 4.20.

The percentages shown here are known as *column percentages* because the frequencies are divided by the column totals. The formula, though somewhat complicated looking at first, is straightforward:

$$col\%_{i,j} = \left(f_{i,j} / total_{colj} \right) \times 100,$$ where $col\%_{i,j}$ is the column percentage for the frequency in row i and column j, $f_{i,j}$ is the frequency in that row and column, and $total_{colj}$ is the total for column j.

Thus, in table 4.20, the column percentage for lowerclass students who did travel more than twice, those in the cell in row 1 and column 1, is calculated as follows.

$$col\%_{1,1} = \left(\frac{f_{1,1}}{total_{col1}} \right) \times 100 = \left(\frac{4}{9} \right) \times 100 = .444 \times 100 = 44 \ 4\%.$$

Figure 4.11, which shows the percentage bar chart, has this same effect—especially when compared to figure 4.9, which is based upon frequencies only. Looking quickly at figure 4.9, it first seems that the likelihood is the same that lower-and upperclass students will take two or more trips. This is because the absolute number from each class who travel this often is the same (four students each) and the bars are thus the same height. This interpretation is misleading because there are more lowerclass students in the sample. Figure 4.11 does take this difference into account in showing that lowerclass students do travel less often.

Column percentages are the most common and the most useful type. But you might occasionally see one or both of two other ways to represent percentages in a bivariate frequency distribution. These are *row percentages* and *total percentages*. The first is a percentage of the total for the respective attributes of the *dependent* variable. It is calculated by dividing each frequency by the total of the row in which it is located and then multiplying by 100. Its formula is:

$$row\%_{i,j} = \left(f_{i,j} / total_{rowi} \right) \times 100, \quad \text{where } row\%_{i,j} \text{ is the row percentage for the frequency in row } i \text{ and column } j, f_{i,j} \text{ is the frequency in that row and column, and } total_{rowi} \text{ is the total for row } i.$$

Table 4.21 shows the same crosstab as in table 4.20 except that the column percentages have been replaced by row percentages according to the above formula. Note that the percentage entries have changed because the frequencies are divided by a different denominator (the row total) before multiplying by 100. So, the 50% in the lowerclass/yes cell (first row, first column) is derived as follows:

$$row\%_{1,1} = \left(\frac{f_{1,1}}{total_{row1}} \right) \times 100 = \left(\frac{4}{8} \right) \times 100 = .500 \times 100 = 50.0\%.$$

The 71.4% in the lowerclass/no cell (second row, first column) is derived as follows:

$$row\%_{2,1} = \left(\frac{f_{1,1}}{total_{row2}} \right) \times 100 = \left(\frac{5}{7} \right) \times 100 = .714 \times 100 = 71.4\%.$$

The other type of percentage, the total percentage, is based on the entire sample size. It is calculated by dividing each frequency by the size of the sample, *n*.

$$total\%_{i,j} = \left(f_{i,j} / n \right) \times 100, \quad \text{where } total\%_{i,j} \text{ is the total percentage for the frequency in row } i \text{ and column } j, f_{i,j} \text{ is the frequency in that row and column, and } n \text{ is the sample size.}$$

TABLE 4.21   Crosstab shown in table 4.19 with row percentages

More than two trips?	Class rank		Row total
	Lower	Upper	
Yes	4 (50.0%)	4 (50.0%)	8 (100.0%)
No	5 (71.4%)	2 (28.6%)	7 (100.0%)
Col. total	9	6	$n = 15$

TABLE 4.22   Crosstab shown in table 4.19 with total percentages

More than two trips?	Class rank		Row total
	Lower	Upper	
Yes	4 (26.7%)	4 (26.7%)	8 (53.4%)
No	5 (33.3%)	2 (13.3%)	7 (46.6%)
Col. total	9 (60.0%)	6 (40.0%)	$n = 15$ (100.0%)

Table 4.22 shows the same crosstab as in table 4.21 except that the row percentages have been replaced by total percentages according to the above formula. Note that the percentage entries have changed because the frequencies are now divided by n before multiplying by 100. So, the 26.7% in the lowerclass/yes cell (first row, first column) indicates that 26.7% of all 15 students are in this cell. It is derived as follows:

$$total\%_{1,1} = \left(\frac{f_{1,1}}{n}\right) \times 100 = \left(\frac{4}{15}\right) \times 100 = .267 \times 100 = 26.7\%.$$

The 33.3% in the lowerclass/no cell (second row, first column) is derived as follows:

$$total\%_{2,1} = \left(\frac{f_{1,1}}{n}\right) \times 100 = \left(\frac{5}{15}\right) \times 100 = .333 \times 100 = 31.3\%.$$

You can see that when total percentages are used, the marginals are also expressed as percentages. That is, 60.0% of the 15 students are in a lower class, 53.4% of the students took more than two trips, and so on.

All three methods of finding percentages are legitimate. However, because some readers may not be aware that there are three different approaches, those who produce a table are obliged to indicate just *what* a particular number is a percentage *of*: column totals, row totals, or the entire sample size. Otherwise, misleading conclusions can be drawn about the relationship between the two variables of interest. In any case, the column percentages provide the clearest and most informative measures of association.

As noted, it is possible to apply the general principles of crosstabs to instances in which three or more variables are involved. For more on this topic, see the online Chapter 15 at http://www.rowmanlittlefield.com/RL/Books/WeinsteinStats.

BOX 4.1   Statistics for Sociologists

Public Sociology and an Illustration Using Bivariate Crosstabs

One of the main premises of our approach to introductory statistics is that, although sociology is a science, it is also a technology for promoting positive social change. As we discussed in Chapter 1, the invention of the field coincided with the incorporation of then-current innovations in mathematical statistics *and* a desire to use such positive knowledge to create a better world. In every generation, from the days of Comte, to C. Wright Mills' era in the 1950s and 1960s, to the present, sociologists have sought to develop the applied side of the field and to increase public awareness of its practical value—often in the face of resistance by those who believe that sociology should be a "pure" science. Applied sociologist Douglas Klayman (2007: 36) made this point in a recent article: "Sociology has a long history of applying social theory and methods to the identification of the causes and consequences of social problems."

The Call for a Public Sociology

In a recent effort to advance sociology on both the scientific and the practical fronts, the American Sociological Association (ASA) President for 2003–2004, Michael Burawoy (2004: 104–105), introduced an initiative he labeled *Public Sociology*. He defined the approach as "a sociology that seeks to bring [the discipline] to publics beyond the academy, promoting dialogue about issues that affect the fate of society, placing values to which we adhere under a microscope." Commenting on this initiative, Klayman (2007: 40) argued that "By educating decision makers in government and the non-profit sectors, and through the rigorous practice of sociology, sociologists can make a better world a reality."

In just a few short years, the program for a *Public Sociology* has moved to the forefront of the field. Several books and articles have been written on the subject, and courses on its principles and practices have been introduced into the curricula at colleges and universities throughout the world. Among these recent curriculum innovations, American University in Washington, DC, has introduced a Master's of Arts Concentration in Public Sociology, under the leadership of Dr. Klayman.

In July 2005, the ASA Task Force on Institutionalizing Public Sociology submitted a report to the ASA Council with the title "Public Sociology and the Roots of American Sociology: Reestablishing Our Connections to the Public" (available at http://pubsoc .wisc.edu/e107_files/public/tfreport090105.doc). In response to this report and in recognition of the importance of the program, the ASA soon established a new section on Sociological Practice and Public Sociology. Several web sites are now dedicated to Public Sociology, including a comprehensive site with many relevant links at http://pubsoc.wisc.edu/news.php.

An Illustration Using a Bivariate Frequency Distribution

This chapter focuses on the most basic of statistical tools, the frequency distribution. Yet, even at this elementary level, the connection between social statistics and applied/public sociology is apparent. To illustrate this point, let us consider an issue of widespread public interest and concern: regional migration in the United States and its economic causes and consequences.

By the time of the 2000 U.S. Census count, it had been well documented that a clear trend was under way involving the migration of individuals and households from the northeastern and midwestern states (the "snow belt") to the southern and western regions (the "sun belt"). Extensive research based on surveys and secondary data analysis has been conducted in an attempt to understand this demographic movement; for example, see William Frey (shown in figure 4.12), "Snow Belt to Sun Belt: The Migration of America's Voters," *Brookings Report Online*, posted June 2005.[*]

One apparently obvious factor is economics. That is, for a variety of reasons, including deindustrialization, the snow belt was becoming poorer and the sun belt was becoming more prosperous. Thus, people were seeking opportunities in more affluent regions. Now, although this explanation may be valid to some degree, the situation is far more complex than it would first appear. For at the moment, the snow belt states as a whole have substantially *lower* rates of poverty than most of the sun belt States.

The following two tables contain information drawn from the 2000 Census (at www.census.gov). Table 4.23 contains is a listing of the 50 states plus the District of Columbia. For each state, information is given on the region: "E" for East, "M" for Midwest, "S" for South, and "W" for West. In addition, each state is given a value of "L" or "H" to indicate whether its percentage of persons living below the poverty level is low or high in comparison to the national average of 12.4%. Although the relationship between the two variables is not immediately obvious from these raw data, table 4.24, a bivariate frequency distribution, makes a clear statement.

---

[*] At www.brookings.edu/speeches/2005/0606demographics_frey.aspx

FIGURE 4.12 William Frey, a demographer at the Brookings Institution, has conducted extensive statistical research on snow belt to sun belt migration. Day Walters/ Photographic Illustration, used with permission.

Of the 50 states plus DC, 32, or nearly 63%, are below the national average, whereas 37% have higher than average poverty levels. Nearly 90 and 92% of the snow belt states of the East and Midwest, respectively, are below the national average. In contrast, about 69 and 47% of the sun belt southern and western states, respectively, are above the national average. By these measures, the sun belt has a higher incidence of poverty than the snow belt.

Of course, this may change; but for many years to come, families, local governments, the states, the federal government, and private sector companies and industries will need to take this reality into account in their decision making. The sun belt may be sunny, but it remains relatively poor.

TABLE 4.23   Regions and poverty levels of the states and DC

State	Region	Poverty level	State	Region	Poverty level
Maine	E	L	North Carolina	S	L
New Hampshire	E	L	South Carolina	S	H
Vermont	E	L	Georgia	S	H
Massachusetts	E	L	Florida	S	H
Rhode Island	E	L	Kentucky	S	H
Connecticut	E	L	Tennessee	S	H
New York	E	H	Alabama	S	H
New Jersey	E	L	Mississippi	S	H
Pennsylvania	E	L	Arkansas	W	H
Ohio	M	L	Louisiana	W	H
Indiana	M	L	Oklahoma	W	H
Illinois	M	L	Texas	W	H
Michigan	M	L	Montana	W	H
Wisconsin	M	L	Idaho	W	L
Minnesota	M	L	Wyoming	W	L
Iowa	M	L	Colorado	W	L
Missouri	M	L	New Mexico	W	H
North Dakota	M	L	Arizona	W	H
South Dakota	M	H	Utah	W	L
Nebraska	M	L	Nevada	W	L
Kansas	M	L	Washington	W	L
Delaware	S	L	Oregon	W	L
Maryland	S	L	California	W	H
District of Columbia	S	H	Alaska	W	L
Virginia	S	L	Hawaii	W	L
West Virginia	S	H			

TABLE 4.24   Crosstab showing the association between region and poverty level

Poverty level	Region				Totals
	East	Midwest	South	West	
Low	8 (88.9%)	11 (91.7%)	4 (30.8%)	9 (52.9%)	32 (62.7%)
High	1 (11.1%)	1 (8.3%)	9 (69.2%)	8 (47.1%)	19 (37.3%)
Totals	9	12	13	17	51

Summary

We have now covered most of the basic features of frequency distributions, from distributions displaying a univariate dichotomy to those describing relationships among several variables with several attributes each. We have seen that in some instances the attributes of interest are ungrouped, and in other instances they are grouped into categories or class intervals. We have also compared frequency tables with their corresponding graphic forms, such as histograms and line graphs.

To put these apparently complex matters into a simple perspective, let us recall our earlier definition of frequency distributions. That is, they are objects that indicate how often the different attributes of a variable or variables are observed in a sample. Although the varieties and examples of frequency distributions considered here have ranged widely, they all share this key feature.

It is obvious that as the number of variables, their level of measurement, and the number of attributes increases, the amount of information contained in a frequency table or graph increases as well. In fact, at some point we are inclined to wish that all of the information could be summarized into one or two especially relevant items. Well, it might help to know that statisticians feel the same way. It is for that reason that they often do not try to comprehend *everything* that a frequency distribution might tell us. Rather, as suggested earlier in this chapter and in Chapter 3 as well, they are willing to ignore some details in order to achieve a better overall understanding of what has been observed. The most important "overall understanding" of a frequency distribution is its *central tendency*. Thus, we continue our discussion with a closer look at central tendency, which is the main topic of Chapter 5.

KEY TERMS

Cells: The intersections of the rows and columns of a frequency table. Cells contain the frequencies in bivariate tables.

Column percentages: In a crosstab, frequencies divided by column totals multiplied by 100.

Columns: The vertical sections of a frequency table.

Crosstab: Short for "cross-tabulation." A frequency distribution showing observations and combinations of observations for two or more variables.

Cumulative frequency: For ordinal and numerical variables, the number of observations of a specific attribute and all attributes above or below it.

Cumulative percentage: A cumulative frequency multiplied by 100.

Data: Observations in their unprocessed or "raw" form.

Dichotomy: A variable (usually nominal-level) with two and only two attributes.

Frequency: The number of times a specific attribute or combination of attributes is observed in a sample.

Frequency distribution: A table or graph that displays the frequencies for one or more variables for a sample.

Frequency polygon: A graphic frequency distribution displayed as a line graph.

Grouped frequency distribution: For numerical (and possibly ordinal) variables, a distribution showing the number of observations for a range of values rather than a single value.

Histogram: A graphic frequency distribution that displays attributes along the horizontal axis and frequencies along the vertical.

Information: Data that are organized to be "informative," for example as tables or graphs.

Marginals: The set of row, column, and grand totals (sample size, *n*) in a crosstab.

Percentage: A proportion multiplied by 100.

Probability: A means of expressing a proportion in terms of chances of occurrence.

Proportion: A frequency divided by the sum of all frequencies (sample size, *n*).

Row percentages: In a crosstab, frequencies divided by row totals multiplied by 100.

Rows: The horizontal sections of a frequency table.

WEB SITES TO BOOKMARK

1. http://www.geostatistics.com/GSWin/GSWIN-FrequencyDistribution.html
   These are interactive frequency distribution exercises for environmental scientists.
2. http://www.ats.ucla.edu/stat/stata/faq/clstab.htm
   This site, from UCLA, has instructions on creating grouped frequency distributions, including histograms.
3. http://davidmlane.com/hyperstat/A26308.html
   These are Hyperstat presentations of frequency tables, histograms, and frequency polygons.
4. http://www.geostatistics.com/GSWin/GSWIN-CumulativeFrequency.html
   Here are interactive cumulative frequency distribution exercises for environmental scientists.
5. http://www.citadel.edu/citadel/otherserv/psci/courses/kuzenski/crosstab.htm

The Citadel maintains this discussion of crosstabs.
6. http://cain.ulst.ac.uk/sutton/selecttabs.html
   This tutorial on crosstabs from the University of Ulster allows readers to create their own tables with data on political conflict.
7. http://erc.msh.org/quality/pstools/pspchrt.cfm
   These instructions for creating a pie chart, with a direct link to histograms, are maintained by a branch of the United Nations Children's Fund.
8. http://193.61.107.61/volume/vol0/pie.htm

This discussion of pie charts from Coventry University has links to several other graphics, including histograms and frequency polygons.

SOLUTION-CENTERED APPLICATIONS

1. Using the U.S Census data set on regional distribution created in Application 1 of Chapter 3, perform an SPSS run that will produce the univariate frequency distribution for the nominal- and ordinal-level variables. For each variable, create bar charts, histograms, and line graphs. Next create two crosstabs and histograms. Each consists of region and one of the ordinal-level variables (less than 9th-grade education and percent with disabilities). Assuming that your client is interested in policies that may affect the regional allocation of federal funds, write a brief result describing your results.

The SPSS instructions you will need are found in Chapter 4 of the study guide.

2. Find an article in a recent issue of a sociology journal in which crosstabs are used. Select two or three of these crosstabs. Copy the tables, the titles, any descriptive notes, and the relevant text. With this information (1) describe how the tables fit into the study reported in the article and (2) interpret the tables, indicating the independent and dependent variables and the degree to which they are associated. What types of percentages did the authors use? Finally, indicate the uses to which

the author(s) believe their findings can be put. Do these tables seem to be useful for such purposes?

3. Go to the web site from the University of Ulster listed in web Sites to Bookmark (http://cain .ulst.ac.uk/sutton/selecttabs.html), and use its interactive feature to create a set of crosstabs. For this application we will create and print three tables. Each of the three will have the same dependent variable, one that appears to you to be an aspect of the situation in Ireland worth explaining. Then, for each table, select a different likely independent variable. With this output, write a brief comparative analysis of the findings. Summarize the frequencies and percentages and indicate which of the independent variables appears to be most closely related to the dependent. Conclude with a brief discussion of how these results may be applied in policy, community research, or other contexts.

Central Tendency in Microsociology

The preceding chapter ended with a brief discussion of how statisticians seek to summarize relatively large amounts of information with a single measure. In this way, it is possible to grasp and convey the essence of our observations while avoiding the problem of becoming disoriented in a flood of unimportant details. As we have mentioned several times, it is true that, in the process of summarizing, some information is lost. But this loss is generally not a serious matter, especially when the information can be recovered—for instance, in the form of a complete frequency distribution.

In this and the following chapter, our attention is turned to two sets of measures that summarize the information contained in frequency distributions. The first set, measures of *central tendency*, is the focus of this chapter. In Chapter 6 we introduce the complementary set, measures of *dispersion*. This chapter begins with a series of definitions, descriptions, and illustrations of the three principal measures of central tendency. Following this, the chapter concludes with the key, linking concept of *deviation*. At that point we can move on to our discussion of dispersion.

What Is Central Tendency?

Just as the frequency distribution is the single most important tool of descriptive statistics, central tendency is the single most important summary measure of a univariate frequency distribution.[1] As the name suggests, a measure of central tendency is the attribute of a variable of interest that is in the "center" of a distribution. Once this measure is known, we also know that most of the other attributes are distributed more or less evenly either above this "center" or below it. It is true that with access only to a measure of central tendency, we have lost sight of all other specific attributes and their frequencies. However, we still have a fairly clear idea of the general shape of the distribution.

Strictly speaking, the concept of central tendency applies only to variables at the ordinal and numerical levels. This is because we really cannot have a "center" unless there is at least a rank order in which a clear "high" and a clear "low" can be identified. Furthermore, in one sense of the word "center," numerical data are required because the operations of addition and division must be performed (we can't legitimately add, subtract, multiply, or divide ranks). Thus, how—and even whether—a measure of central tendency can be found for a particular univariate distribution depends on the level of measurement of the variable. So, let us consider each level and the associated measure(s).

Nominal Level and the Mode

As just noted, nominal-level distributions cannot have a "center" and, therefore, cannot have a central tendency. Instead, the usual practice is to summarize such a distribution with the single best measure available for this type of data, which is the *mode*. The mode is defined as the *attribute with the highest frequency*. Once this is found, we can at least say that no other attribute has a frequency this high.

Table 5.1 contains the nominal-level frequency distribution illustrated in table 4.2. From the above definition, it should be obvious that the mode of the following distribution is "new." That is because the higher frequency (16) is associated with this attribute.

Sometimes one can forget that the mode (along with the more literal measures of central tendency) is an attribute, not a frequency, and conclude in this illustration that the mode is "16." This is understandable because when looking to identify the mode, one first must find the highest frequency. So we do begin with the "*f*" column. However, once the highest frequency is found, the next step is to look over in the variable (here it is "school experience") column and find the associated attribute.

Using this same type of example, let us expand the sample of 30 students to include 20 recent grads, as shown in table 5.2. In that case, the mode would change to "recent grad" (not "20"). The bar graph in figure 5.1 contains this same information for the new

TABLE 5.1   Mode table

School experience	f	
New	16	
Returning	14	Mode = "new"
	$n = 30$	

TABLE 5.2   Mode table 2

School experience	f	
New	16	
Returning	14	Mode = recent grad
Recent grad	20	
Total	$n = 50$	

sample of $n = 50$. Such a graph makes it especially easy to identify the mode, because it is the attribute with the highest bar.

Finally, let us revise the sample once more by adding another group of 20, those who are incoming ("Inc."). This group is represented by the bar at the left in figure 5.2. Now we have a situation in which there is more than one mode. Is this possible? The answer is yes, it is possible to have two or even more modes, as long as the criterion is met that they be the attributes with the (same) highest frequency. A distribution with one mode is referred to as *unimodal*, one with two modes is *bimodal*, and with more than two modes it is *multimodal*.

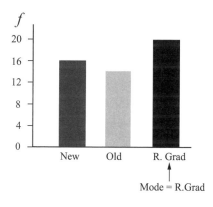

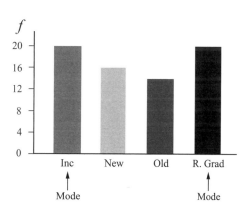

FIGURE 5.1   Mode bar graph.

FIGURE 5.2   Bimodal bar graph.

The Median: The Value of the Middle Case

The mode can be used with univariate frequency distributions at any level of measurement. But, for the reason mentioned above, the next measure of central tendency to be considered, the *median* (symbolized as *mdn*), requires that the variable involved be ordinal or numerical. Unlike the mode, the median actually does represent a "center." In fact, its definition is *the attribute that divides a frequency distribution into two equal parts.* By "equal parts" we mean here an equal number of units above and below. An alternative, but equally accurate, way of defining the median is *the attribute associated with the middle unit(s).*

The procedure used to find the median of a frequency distribution has two steps. First, we must locate the middle unit, the point at which the distribution is divided into equal parts. Then we identify the attribute associated with that unit, the one at the dividing point.

You probably know that if n is the size of a sample, the *middle* unit is found by the formula $(n + 1)/2$. Thus, if $n = 3$, the middle unit is $(3 + 1)/2 = 4/2 = 2$, or the second. If $n = 25$, the middle unit is $(25 + 1)/2 = 26/2 = 13$, or the 13, and so on. You have probably also noticed that if n is an even number, and thus $n + 1$ is odd, there is no true middle *unit* (in the sense of one whole number). Instead, the formula produces a number ending in ".5" or "1/2." So, for example, if $n = 4$, the middle "unit" is the $(4 + 1)/2 = 5/2 = 2.5$, or the second and one half. If $n = 26$, the middle "unit" is the $(26 + 1)/2 = 27/2 = 13.5$, or 13 and one half.

In such a situation, we have one of two options:

1. When the variable is ordinal level, we first find the attribute of unit $n/2$. Next, we find the attribute associated with unit $(n + 2)/2$ and treat it as a *second* middle unit. For example, if $n = 26$, $n/2 = 26/2 = 13$; and $(n + 2)/2 = (26 + 2)/2 = 28/2 = 14$. So, the two middle units are the 13th and 14th. If they have the same attribute, then it is the median. But if the attributes are different, then we say that the median is "between" the two.
2. When the variable is numerical, we can either follow this option or we can find the average between the two attributes (e.g., of the 13th and 14th units). This is done by adding the attributes together—which, unlike the situation with ranks, is legitimate because they are numbers—and dividing by 2. In this way we derive a fictitious, but reasonable, attribute for the fictitious unit number 13.5, 2.5, and so on. We illustrate these options as we discuss the median further.

At times, one can find the middle case(s) of a frequency distribution simply by inspection. But the correct, and always reliable, way is to use the cumulative frequency distribution. Table 5.3 is similar to the table used in Chapter 4 to illustrate ordinal-level

TABLE 5.3   Median table

Year in school	f	%	cf
Freshman	3	20.0	15
Sophomore	6	40.0	12
Junior	2	13.3	6
Senior	4	26.7	4
Total	$n = 15$	100.0	

frequency and cumulative frequency. The variable is "year in school" and the sample size is 15.

Notice that the distribution is unimodal and that the mode is "sophomore." Can you see why? Next we need to be sure that the attributes are ordered. Here they are in ascending order, so that the first attribute has the lowest rank, the last has the highest rank, and others fall in between in order. Now, to find the median we first must identify the middle unit, or student. Because $n = 15$, an odd number, we know that there will be a unique middle and that it is student $(15 + 1)/2 = 16/2 = 8$. So the attribute of the 8th student is the median. But where is the 8th student? Here is where the cumulative frequencies come in. Looking at the "*cf*" column, we can see that the first three students are freshmen, so that can't be the median. The next six students (the 4th, 5th, 6th, 7th, 8th, and 9th) are sophomores. Among these is the 8th, which we have been seeking. Therefore, mdn is "sophomore."

The information shown in table 5.4 and figure 5.3 is taken from the sample of suburban households introduced in Chapter 4. The variable selected is "length of residence," for which 72 of the 75 households provided data. With $n = 72$, we can illustrate the procedure used when n is even. You can quickly note that the mode is "less than 1 year," with a frequency of 21 households. The cumulative frequencies,

TABLE 5.4   Length of residence for 75 households

Length of residence	f	cf	c%
Less than 1 year	21	21	29.2
1 to 5 years	14	35	48.6
6–10 years*	20	55	76.4
11–15 years	12	67	94.4
More than 15 years	5	75	100.0
	$n = 72$		

*mdn

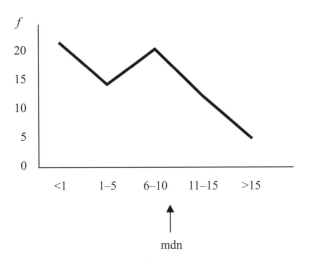

FIGURE 5.3   Line graph of length of residence for 72 households (in years).

as well as the cumulative percentages, have been calculated to assist in finding the median.

The first step is to locate the middle household(s). The formula says that it would be household number $(n + 1)/2 = (72 + 1)/2 = 73/2 = 36.5$. Thus, we must locate the 36th and 37th households. Looking at the cumulative frequencies, we see that the first 35 households have the attributes "less than 1 year" and "1 to 5 years." The next 20, numbers 36 through 55, have the attribute "6–10 years." This means that the 36th and the 37th have both resided in the suburb "6–10 years," and that is the median. You might have noticed that the cumulative percentages could also be used to identify the household(s). We are seeking the 36th unit, which has a cumulative percentage of $(36/72) \times 100 = 50.0\%$, and the 37th, which has a cumulative percentage of $(37/72) \times 100 = 51.4\%$. Looking down the "$c\%$" column, we see that 48.6% of the households are in the "less than 1 year" or "1 to 5 years" category, and the next category, which brings the cumulative frequency up to 76.4% and therefore includes 50.5% and 51.4%, has the attribute "6–10 years," which is the median.

Numerical Variables and the Mean

When our variable of interest is numerical, central tendency can be measured not only by the mode and the median but also by the *mean*.[2] This is the technical term for a measure with which you are certainly familiar: the average. In recognition of its importance, some statisticians note that from this point forward we will be focusing almost exclusively on the statistics of the mean. For example, we will soon see that the chief measure of dispersion, the standard deviation (which incorporates the mean), is considered to be the *second* most important measure of numerical frequency distributions.

The mean, universally symbolized as $\bar{x}$, is the center of a distribution, but not in the same sense as the median. We have just seen how the median divides the set of units in a distribution into two equal parts. But in the case of the mean, the number of units above does not necessarily equal the number of units below. Instead, the mean is at the center of the units *accounting for the numerical values of their attributes*. To calculate the mean, we add together the values of the attributes for all of the units and divide by the number of units.

Following this definition, the basic formula is

$$\bar{x} = \frac{\sum_{i=1}^{n}(x_i)}{n}.$$

The $\bar{x}$ on the left is the sample mean. You may recall from Chapter 4 that the lowercase x is commonly used to denote a numerical variable. In the above formula, x stands for the attribute or value of a specific unit. The summation from $i = 1$ to n indicates that every unit is included in the sum. Then the sum is divided by n, the sample size.

To illustrate, suppose that we have given a quiz to 11 students ($n = 11$) and that the possible scores are between 1 and 7. The results, for each student respectively, were 5, 3, 3, 4, 4, 4, 4, 4, 4, 4, 4. Thus, the mean is

$$\bar{x} = \frac{\sum_{i=1}^{a}(x)}{n} = \frac{5+3+3+4+4+4+4+4+4+4+4}{11} = \frac{43}{11} = 3.91.$$

Although this is a perfectly legitimate formula, and it works every time, it is a bit awkward to use with a frequency distribution. This is obvious when we present the set of 11 scores in the form of a simple distribution table in table 5.5. Note that the mode is 4 (with a frequency of 8), and that the median is also 4. Do you see why mdn = 4?

In this situation, which is by far the more common one, we find the mean by adding the scores *weighted* by the frequencies and then divide by n as follows.

1. To achieve the weighting, we find the product of each attribute multiplied by the frequency with which the attribute occurs. Thus, the attribute, or score, "5" is observed

only once; then (5 times 1) = 5 is the weighted value. The score 3 is observed twice; then (3 times 2) or 6 is the value. The score 4 is observed eight times; then (4 times 8) or 32 is the value.

2. When all of these products are found we then add them together. In this example, the sum would be 5 + 6 + 32 = 43.

3. When the weighted values are added together, we then divide by the sum of the frequencies, which is the same as the sample size, *n*. The result is the mean.

The following formula incorporates these steps:

$$\bar{x} = \frac{\sum_{i=1}^{a}(f_i x_i)}{n}$$

Here, f_i refers to the frequency of a given score, x_i is the score, and the summation from 1 to *a* indicates that every value from the lowest to the highest (rather than every unit) is included in the sum. So, using this formula, the mean of the distribution is

$$\bar{x} = \frac{\sum_{i=1}^{a}(f_i x_i)}{n} = \frac{(3 \times 2) + (4 \times 8) + (5 \times 1)}{11} = \frac{6 + 32 + 5}{11} = \frac{43}{11} = 3.91.$$

The results of the two formulas agree exactly because the formulas are just slightly different ways to achieve the same result.

At this point we can easily illustrate how the median and the mean are each centers of a distribution but not in the same sense. To find the median of the frequency distribution above, we must first locate the middle student. This is $(n + 1)/2 = (11 + 1)/2 = 6$. The next step is to find the sixth student's score. The cumulative frequencies show that the first two students have the score "3," and then students 3 through 10—including the sixth—have a 4. Therefore 4 is the median.

TABLE 5.5   Mean table

Score (x)	f	cf
3	2	2
4	8	10
5	1	11
	n = 11	

Now, suppose that we increase the score of one of the students—perhaps because we made a mistake in grading—from 5 to 7. This would change the frequency distribution to that shown in table 5.6. This increase would not change the median, but the mean would change. Do you see why? Let us calculate the new mean.

$$\bar{x} = \frac{\sum_{i=1}^{a}(f_i x_i)}{n} = \frac{(3 \times 2) + (4 \times 8) + (5 \times 0) + (7 \times 1)}{11} = \frac{6 + 32 + 0 + 7}{11} = \frac{45}{11} = 4.1.$$

The mean is now a little higher because *one* of the students received a higher score than in the first example.

What happens to the median? Because the n is unchanged, the position of the median remains the sixth student. And because there were no changes in the frequencies for the scores of students 1 through 6, the median remains 4. This shows that the value of the mean depends not only on the number of units (students) above and below the middle case; it is also affected by the actual values (scores) of the units.

The Relationship between Measures of Central Tendency

When we describe a univariate frequency distribution of a numerical variable, it is of interest to note the relationship between the median and the mean. As mentioned, they are both measures of central tendency, but they refer to different types of centers. The median literally splits the distribution in half, so with it we can quickly identify which attributes are associated with the lower and which with the upper half of the distribution. Recall the incomes (ungrouped) of the 75 households in our example in table 4.4. The median, $6,140, determines that households earning less are among the lower 37 and households earning more are in the upper 37.

TABLE 5.6   Changed frequency distribution

Score (x)	f	cf
3	2	2
4	8	10
5	0	10
7	1	11
	$n = 11$	

The mean also divides the distribution into two equal parts, but the parts do not necessarily contain the same number of units. Instead, the two parts are equal with respect to *the sum of all of the values of the units in each part*. Thus, in the example of the 75 households, whose (ungrouped) mean is $6,032.87, the sum of all of the incomes of the households whose earnings are below the mean is equal to the sum of the incomes of the households whose earnings are above the mean.

In this example, although the values of the median and the mean are close, they are not identical. If we subtract the value of the median from that of the mean, we see that the difference is just over $107:

$$(\bar{x} - \mathrm{mdn}) = (\$6{,}032.87 - \$6{,}140.00) = -\$107.13.$$

The "–" sign here indicates that the mean is less than the median. The size of the difference, $107.13, is a measure of the distance between the two. What this indicates is that possibly more than one half of the households have an income that is above average. Obviously all households whose rate is above the median of $6,140 have an income that is higher than $6,032.87. But if any household has an income in that $107.13 range between the mean and the median, it would also be above the average yet below the middle as measured by the median.

In addition to the situation in which the value of the median is higher than that of the mean, there are two other possible relationships. One is that the mean is greater than the median, in which case the difference would be positive (+). The other possibility is that the two might be equal, in which case the difference between them would be zero (0). Statisticians refer to the difference between the mean and the median as *skew* (from an Old English word for twist or slant),[3] and to the three possibilities as follows: When the mean is less than the median, the distribution is said to have *negative* skew; when

TABLE 5.7   A negatively skewed distribution

Number of trips (x)	f	cf	
0	2	2	
1	2	4	
2	5	9	mean = 3.42, mdn = 4
3	6	15	
4	7	22	
5	6	28	
6	3	31	
	n = 31		

TABLE 5.8   A symmetrical distribution

Number of trips (x)	f	cf	
0	2	2	
1	4	6	
2	6	12	mean = 3.0, mdn =3
3	7	19	
4	6	25	
5	4	29	
6	2	31	
	n = 31		

the mean is greater, it has *positive* skew; and when they are equal it has zero skew, or more commonly, it is said to be *symmetrical*.

Tables 5.7, 5.8, and 5.9 and the accompanying histograms display these relationships with data from our model study of the travel patterns of dorm students. In these illustrations the sample size is 31, and the possible attributes range from 0 to 6 trips. Table 5.7 shows a distribution with a negative skew, in which the mean is less than the median. As in the household income example, more units (that is, students) are above average (in the number of trips). Table 5.8 shows a symmetrical relationship, in which the mean and the median are the same (both equal 3 trips).[4] The symmetry is evident in the accompanying histogram. If you draw a line down the middle, each side will be a mirror image of the other. This is an important factor in inductive statistics, as we shall see. For if one knows that a distribution is symmetrical, then all of the measures that apply to one half also apply to the other, except that the positive and negative signs are reversed. Table 5.9 shows positive

TABLE 5.9   A positively skewed distribution

Number of trips (x)	f	cf	
0	2	2	
1	9	11	
2	6	17	mean = 2.32, mdn =2
3	9	26	
4	2	28	
5	2	30	
6	1	31	
	n = 31		

skew, in which the mean is greater than the median. In this case, less than one-half of the schools are above average.

The histograms highlight another aspect of skew and symmetry. That is, they show the *tails* and *body* of frequency distributions. In figure 5.4, for example, you can see that the left end, which is known as the *negative tail*, is flattened and drawn out, whereas the right end, the positive tail, is raised and shortened. Between the two tails is the body of the distribution. This is a typical picture of negative skew, showing relatively small frequencies for low values and relatively large frequencies for high values. The opposite is the case for positive skew, as shown in figure 5.6. Here the negative tail is elevated and shortened (showing large frequencies for low values) and the positive tail is flattened and drawn out (because there are small frequencies for high values). In a symmetrical distribution, as shown in figure 5.5, neither tail is especially flattened nor especially elevated; and they are mirror images of each other. Thus, not only can we calculate a distribution's skew—or its absence—by subtracting the median from the mean, we can *see* it in the shape of the body and tails of the graph of the distribution.

Deviations from the Mean

Before concluding this discussion of central tendency, we introduce one more measure associated with the mean. It is the *deviation from the mean*, or simply the *deviation*; and it underscores a natural link between central tendency and our next main topic, dispersion. A deviation is actually an alternative way of expressing a unit's value in a numerical-level frequency distribution, for instance, the number of trips a specific student takes or the tuition rate of a specific university. We should now be familiar with the common symbol x_i, which stands for the attribute or value of the

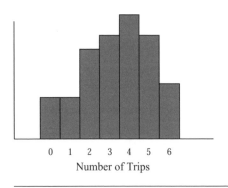

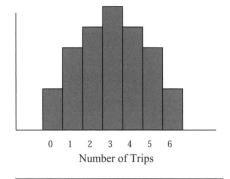

FIGURE 5.4   A negatively skewed distribution.   **FIGURE 5.5**   A symmetrical distribution.

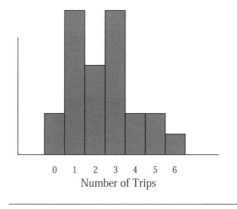

FIGURE 5.6   A positively skewed distribution.

*i*th unit (student, university, etc.). For the sake of comparison, from this point on we will also refer to x_i as the *i*th *raw score*. This indicates that it is the value or attribute itself, not changed or transformed in any way. A deviation, in contrast, *is* a value that is changed or transformed. Because it is not a raw score, we can unofficially call it a "cooked" score.

A raw score is transformed into a deviation by subtracting the value of the sample mean from it. Thus, if x_i is a given raw score, $x_i - \bar{x}$ is its associated deviation. For example, in the distribution shown in table 5.8 and figure 5.5, the mean is 3.0 trips, and the two students whose frequencies are shown at the top of the table took 0 trips. Their raw scores are, thus, $x_1 = 0$ and $x_2 = 0$. Transforming these scores to deviations, we see that $x_1 - \bar{x} = -3$ and $x_2 - \bar{x} = -3$; that is, each has a deviation of –3. This is another way of saying that each has a raw score that is 3 (trips) *below* the mean. In fact, a negative deviation always indicates a raw score below the mean. If you asked these students their value on the variable "number of trips," they might say "zero." But it would be just as correct to say "minus three," as long as they indicated that this score was expressed as a deviation. Similarly, we see at the bottom of the table that two of the students have a raw score of 6 trips. As deviations, these would be expressed as (6 – 3) = +3, or 3 (trips) *above* the mean. A positive deviation indicates a raw score above the mean. Finally, note that the seven students who took 3 trips have raw scores equal to the mean. Their deviations are, thus, (3 – 3) = 0. That is, if a raw score is equal to the mean of its sample, then its deviation is 0, because it is 0 (trips) above and 0 below the mean.

We can apply this procedure to any numerical frequency distribution for which the mean is known. To illustrate further, let us return to the sample of incomes for 75 households. Using the ungrouped frequency distribution, we found that $\bar{x}$ = $6,032.87.

| BOX 5.1 | **Statistics for Sociologists** |

Using Central Tendency in Microsociology

Because of the complexity of social relations, the field of sociology has evolved into three partly overlapping branches, which specialize in the study of three different levels or scales of interaction. Although the divisions between these categories are sometimes arbitrary, they allow researches to make observations and develop theories that are more manageable and easier to comprehend. From the highest (largest) to the lowest (smallest), these are the macro-, meso-, and micro- levels. *Macrosociology* focuses on institutions, societies, and inter-society (e.g., international) relations. *Mesosociology* focuses on large groups and organizations, and *microsociology* deals with interpersonal relations and small groups.

The German sociologist (and contemporary of Max Weber) Georg Simmel is often credited with establishing the foundations for microsociology through his theories of the dyad (two-person interaction) and triad (three-person interaction). The collection by Kurt Wolff (1950) includes this and related aspects of Simmel's contributions. The study of microsociology today consists of several subfields, including symbolic interactionism, the sociology of emotions, social psychology, phenomenology, and ethnomethodology. An important reference in this branch of sociology is Thomas Scheff's *Microsociology* (Scheff, 1994). The leading journal on the subject is *Social Psychological Quarterly: A Journal of Microsociologies*.

The following example, based on recent study at a university in the United States, illustrates the microsociology approach and applies the concept of central tendency as introduced in Chapter 5. The study was conducted in conjunction with a project examining the use and value of student evaluations of faculty performance. In reviewing these evaluations, a fairly obvious hypothesis emerged, suggesting that faculty members who receive highly positive ratings tend to encourage classroom interaction, whereas those whose ratings are negative tend to emphasize one-way communication ("straight lecturing," etc.).

Ten instructors were selected at random, and the researchers observed a sample of the classes taught by those instructors over the course of one semester. The observers received permission to attend the classes, but, to avoid any experimental effect, the instructors were not aware of exactly what was being observed. Among the data that were recorded was a count of the number of times a student interacted with the instructor and/or responded to the comments of other students for each (50-minute) class period. If the instructor responded to a student's comment or question, that counted as an additional interaction. If the instructor did not acknowledge the comment, it was not counted.

TABLE 5.10   Number of Interactions for Instructor KA

Class	No. of interactions
1	3
2	7
3	2
4	4
5	6
6	1
7	3
8	8
Total	34

Table 5.10 contains a log of interactions for one of the instructors ("KA") over the course of eight classroom observations. You will note that the number ranged between 1 (for the 6th class) and 8 (for the 8th class). With a total of 34 interactions, the mean is 34/8 = 4.25.

$$\bar{x} = 4.25$$

Table 5.11 lists the results for all 10 of the instructors, showing the mean number of interactions for each set of eight classroom observations, along with an indication of whether the instructor was among the five most highly rated in the sample ("H") or among the lowest ("L").

Table 5.12 summarizes this information by listing separately the mean of the interactions for each of the two groups of instructors: those with high and those with low evaluations. At the bottom of the table the separate means (the "means of the means") are shown for each of the groups. Based on these results, the hypothesis that

TABLE 5.11   Mean interactions and evaluation ratings for 10 instructors

Instructor	Mean number of interactions	Evaluation rating
KA	4.25	L
RK	3.50	L
MM	8.13	H
DR	6.75	L
FT	10.00	H
RW	7.25	H
LC	7.00	H
RO	9.63	H
GB	2.00	L
PL	3.00	L

TABLE 5.12   Mean interactions and combined means for the two groups

Mean number of interactions	
Low-rated instructors	*High-rated instructors*
4.25	8.13
3.50	10.00
6.75	10.00
2.00	7.25
3.00	9.63
Total $= 19.5; \bar{x} = 3.5$	Total $= 45.01; \bar{x} = 9.0$

higher-rated instructors have more classroom interaction is strongly supported: The instructors with low evaluations averaged 3.5, whereas the instructors with high evaluations have an average of 9.0, more than twice as many interactions.

This example provides a very basic perspective on the vast field of microsociology; yet it does represent the main concerns of the approach. Although universities, students, instructors, classrooms, and student evaluations are involved, the major emphasis is on *interaction* and the role it plays in the classroom. It might not have been immediately apparent how the concept of central tendency can be applied in micro-level research such as this. But it should now be clear that it is applied just as it is at any level of sociological analysis. It provides us with the single most important piece of information about how variables vary in a sample. In Chapter 6, we return to this illustration in considering the role played by the *second* most important piece of information: dispersion.

We have selected three representative households: one at the lower range of incomes, one at the middle, and one at the higher range: $1,890, $6,140, and $12,890. Their respective deviations $x_i - \bar{x}$ are $(1,890 - 6,032.87) = -\$4,142.87$; $(6,140 - 6032.87) = +\$107.13$; and $(12,890 - 6,032.87) = +\$6,857.13$. You might recall the +$107.13 figure from the previous section because that income is exactly at the (ungrouped) median. As mentioned in the example of students' trips home, it would be perfectly correct to refer to the highest income, for example, as +$6,857.13, which might at first seem relatively low until you added the necessary qualification that this is its deviation and not its raw score.

Deviations, and in particular the entire set of deviations for a given sample, have a property that is both interesting and, as we will see in the discussion of dispersion, bothersome. We illustrate with the raw scores for "trips home," first shown in table 4.3. First, let us calculate the mean:

$$\bar{x} = \frac{\sum_{i=1}^{n}(x_i)}{n} = \frac{(3+2+0+5+3+3+5+2+1+1+3+2+0+4+4)}{15} = \frac{38}{15} = 2.53.$$

Next, we subtract 2.53 from each student's raw score, and record these as the deviations in the third column of table 5.13. So, for example, Allison (who took 3 trips) has a deviation of +0.47, or 47/100 trips above the mean; Charles (who took no trips) has a deviation of −2.53; and Glen (who took 5 trips) has a deviation of +2.47.

When we add these deviations together (and account for rounding error) we find that:

$$\sum_{i=1}^{n}(x_i - \bar{x}) = +.47 - .53 - 2.53 + 2.47 + .47 + .47$$

$$+ 2.47 - .53 - .53 - 1.53 - 1.53 + .47 - 2.53 + 1.47 + 1.47.$$

Grouping the positive values and the negative values together, we see that the total equals (9.75 − 9.75) = 0. The reason may be obvious. That is, the sum of the positive values (+9.75) exactly balances out the sum of the negative values (−9.75), with the result that the sum is *zero.*

TABLE 5.13   Raw scores and deviations for number of trips home, $n = 15$

Student	Number of trips home	
	Raw score	*Deviation $x_i - \bar{x}$*
Allison	3	3 − 2.53 = +0.47
Brenda	2	2 − 2.53 = −0.53
Charles	0	0 − 2.53 = −2.53
Dawn	5	5 − 2.53 = +2.47
Eugene	3	3 − 2.53 = +0.47
Frank	3	3 − 2.53 = +0.47
Glen	5	5 − 2.53 = +2.47
Harriet	2	2 − 2.53 = −0.53
Ian	1	1 − 2.53 = −1.53
Janella	1	1 − 2.53 = −1.53
Kris	3	3 − 2.53 = +0.47
Leora	2	2 − 2.53 = −0.53
Mike	0	0 − 2.53 = −2.53
Nancy	4	4 − 2.53 = +1.47
On-Kim	4	4 − 2.53 = +1.47

This zero sum is not just a peculiarity of the frequency distribution for "number of trips." It occurs with *every* distribution of numerical-level variables. The reason is clear when we restate what we have just seen. That is, total of the values (the attributes weighted by their frequencies) below the mean exactly equals the total of the values above the mean. Now, recall our definition of the mean. It is the attribute that divides the distribution into two parts such that the sum of the values in the part above it is equal to the sum of the values below it. In other words, the sum of the deviations from the mean always equals zero *by definition*, because the mean is that attribute which, when subtracted from every other attribute, produces a sum equal to zero![5] This, then, is the property of the deviation that is interesting. Early in the next chapter we will see what makes it so bothersome.

KEY TERMS

Bimodal: Having exactly two modes.

Body: The portion of a frequency polygon that is at or near the center.

Deviation: An individual value (of a numerical variable) in a sample, or raw score, minus the mean value of that variable for the entire sample. This is an alternative to a raw score.

Mean: The central value of a distribution, in which cases are weighted by their values.

Median: The attribute associated with the middle unit(s) of a frequency distribution.

Modal interval (modal category): The interval in which the mode occurs in a grouped frequency distribution.

Mode: The attribute of a variable with the highest frequency in a sample.

Multimodal: Having three or more modes.

Negative skew: The type of skew in which the mean is less than the median.

Positive skew: The type of skew in which the mean is greater than the median.

Skew: The characteristic of a frequency distribution in which the number of cases whose values are above the mean is not equal to the number of cases whose values are below the mean, and therefore the mean does not equal the median; the opposite of symmetry.

Symmetry: The characteristic of a frequency distribution in which the number of cases whose values are above and below the mean are equal, and therefore the mean equals the median; the opposite of skew.

Tails: The portions of a frequency polygon that are at the extreme left (negative) and extreme right (positive) ends.

Unimodal: Having one and only one mode.

WEB SITES TO BOOKMARK

1. http://davidmlane.com/hyperstat/A39322.html
   This is the Hyperstat discussion of central tendency. The first three links—"mode," "median," and "mean"—take you to topics covered in this chapter.
2. www.mste.uiuc.edu/hill/dstat/centtend.html
   This site at the University of Illinois has great interactive color graphics.
3. http://research.med.umkc.edu/tlwbiostats/mmm01.html

This site, from the University of Missouri–Kansas City, has specific medical applications.

4. www.statcan.ge.ca/edu/Power_Pouvoir/ch11/exer/5214866_eng.htm
   "Digitalbrain" presents an introduction to central tendency that includes self-grading exercises.
5. www.osc.edu/education/webed/Projects/model_and_statistics/measures.shtml

Maintained by the Ohio Supercomputer Center, this site has several links to additional information on central tendency. Among these are sites that discuss the "stem and leaf" and "box and whiskers" learning tools that many statisticians use to illustrate the principles of central tendency.

SOLUTION-CENTERED AND SPSS APPLICATIONS

The solution-centered and SPSS Statistics applications for central tendency are combined with the applications for dispersion, because the two types of measures are so closely related. These are found at the end of Chapter 6.

Dispersion and the Analysis of Social Deviance

This chapter continues and concludes our discussion of descriptive statistics with a further look at the techniques used to summarize frequency distributions. In Chapter 5 we focused on the single most important characteristic of frequency distributions: central tendency. Here we consider the *second* most important feature: dispersion. In ordinary language, to *disperse* means to spread out. Something that is dispersed is spread out over a wide area rather than concentrated in one place. So the noun *dispersion* means "spread-out-ness."[1]

As in Chapter 5, three alternative measures will be introduced. However, unlike the case of central tendency, in which some measures can be used with nominal and/or ordinal level as well as numerical variables, measures of dispersion apply *only* to numerical variables. The reason for this limitation lies in the technical definition of dispersion as *the degree to which the attributes, or values, of the units in a (univariate) distribution differ from one another.* Thus, if the units are colleges and universities, and the variable is tuition in dollars, the dispersion of such a distribution is the degree to which—the amount of dollars by which—tuition rates of the schools differ from one another.

The terms *differ* and *degree* tell us why dispersion applies only to numerical variables. For one can determine the difference between attribute values only by subtracting one from another, which, in turn, is possible only when such attributes are numbers. Under these conditions, a measure of dispersion will be expressed as a number ranging from 0, indicating no difference, to some large quantity, indicating a great difference. The three measures discussed below all do have this characteristic, although each provides a different perspective on how "spread out" a distribution is.

The Range

The most familiar and simplest measure of dispersion is the range. Its symbol is a capital *R*, and it is derived by subtracting the smallest attribute observed in a distribution from the largest attribute observed. That is,

$$R = \text{(highest value – lowest value)}.$$

Although it has serious limitations, which we will discuss shortly, the range does provide useful information. As is true of all measures of dispersion, it does have a minimum value of 0, with higher values indicating greater degrees of dispersion. Most relevant, perhaps, it is a valuable supplement to the picture of a frequency distribution that is revealed by the mean and the other measures of central tendency.

Figure 6.1 contains information about the performance of a class of 26 students in social statistics based on three exams. According to the frequency distributions, the mean for each of the first two exams was 82.5 points. In this respect, student performance was the same. But on the third exam, the mean rose to 86.0, or an overall improvement of 3.5 points.

When comparing the first two sets of scores, we do see that, although the means are equal, there are some differences. For one thing, the distribution for the first exam is symmetrical, with a median of 82.5, and it is bimodal, with a frequency of 6 students for the scores of 80 and 85. Measuring its dispersion, we see that its range is $R = (100 - 65)$ = 35 points. In contrast, the distribution for the second exam has a negative skew, with a median of 85, and although it is bimodal as well, its modes are at 85 and 90. Finally, it has a smaller range of $R = (95 - 65) = 30$ points. With this in mind, we can say that, although the students averaged the same on the first two exams, differences between student performances narrowed between the first and second.

When comparing the first and third exams, we see that the ranges are equal (30 points). This indicates that differences in student performance were the same for the first and third exams and that, in fact, they widened between the second and third. It is clear from the means that performance improved on the average between the first and third exams. However, the distribution for the third exam has a positive skew, indicating that less than one half of the students scored above average. Moreover, the distribution is unimodal. With this in mind we can say that, although the distributions of the first and third exams are equally dispersed, there are notable differences in their central tendencies.

These comparisons indicate that dispersion, as measured by the range, adds to our descriptive powers, because, in combination with central tendency, it allows a more complete and more revealing description of frequency distributions than central tendency alone. In addition, we can see that dispersion is a separate aspect of distributions, which

x (score on exam 1)	f	cf
65	1	1
70	2	3
75	4	7
80	6	13
85	6	19
90	4	23
95	2	25
100	1	26
	n = 26	

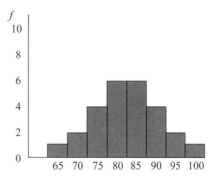

$\bar{x} = 2145/26 = 82.5$; mdn = 82.5; modes = 80, 85; range = $(100 - 65)$ $s^2 = 67.87$

x (score on exam 2)	f	cf
65	1	1
70	2	3
75	4	7
80	5	12
85	6	18
90	6	24
95	2	26
100	0	26
	n = 26	

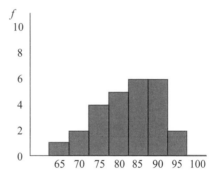

$\bar{x} = 2145/26 = 82.5$; mdn = 85; modes = 85, 90; range = $(95 - 65) = 30$

x (score on exam 3)	f	cf
65	3	1
70	4	3
75	4	7
80	6	12
85	5	17
90	4	23
95	1	26
100	1	26
	n = 26	

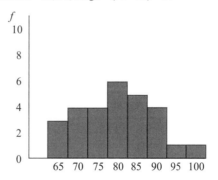

$\bar{x} = 2235/26 = 86$; mdn = 85; mode = 80; range = $(100 - 65) = 35$

FIGURE 6.1   Three frequency distributions comparing central tendency and dispersion.

does not depend directly on central tendency. Two distributions may have the same mean but different ranges, etc.

With that noted, we will quickly add that the range is not the most effective measure of dispersion. The following section demonstrates why this is so.

Variance and Standard Deviation

Figure 6.2 contains a frequency table and associated histogram for a hypothetical distribution of exam grades comparable to the distribution for the first exam. This table has been arranged so that the means, medians, modes, and ranges of the two exams are identical. Yet the two are obviously different. The table in figure 6.2 indicates that the frequencies for the scores of 70, 75, 90, and 95 are each 1 (compared to 2, 4, 4, and 2, respectively, for exam 1), and the frequencies for 80 and 85 are each 7 (compared to 6 each for exam 1). Just considering the little we have said so far about dispersion, it is clear that this distribution is more dispersed than that for the first exam, even though their ranges are equal.

Finding a More Complete Measure of Dispersion

The key to this discrepancy is that the range measures dispersion by using only *two* attributes: the highest and the lowest values. If two distributions should agree in these respects but differ in other ways—as in the case of that for the first exam and that shown in figure 6.2—the range cannot detect the difference. This suggests that a more adequate measure of dispersion is needed—one based on more than two values. Ideally, it should be based on *all* values and all frequencies.

This is the main advantage of the two measures of dispersion featured in this section; that is, they do account for all of the values observed in a univariate frequency

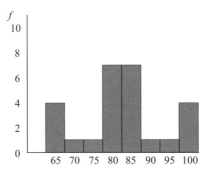

x (score on alternative model exam 1)	f	cf
65	4	4
70	1	5
75	1	6
80	7	13
85	7	20
90	1	21
95	1	22
100	4	26
	$n = 26$	

FIGURE 6.2 Scores on alternative exam to compare with exam 1, showing equal means and ranges but unequal variances and standard deviations.

distribution. We can see how this is accomplished by extending the logic of the range. In calculating the range, we select two observations, the score of one unit (e.g., a student) with the highest observed value (his/her score), x_{hi}, and the score of one unit with the lowest value, x_{lo}. Then, $R = (x_{hi} - x_{lo})$. However, we ignore the scores of all of the other students with the highest or the lowest score, as well as the scores of all of the students whose score is neither the highest nor the lowest.

One way to use all of the scores would be to calculate the difference between the first student's score and the second student's score, then calculate the difference between the first student's score and the third student's score, then the difference between the first student's score and the fourth student's score, and so on. That is, we would create the set of differences: $(x_1 - x_2), (x_1 - x_3), \ldots, (x_1 - x_n), \ldots, (x_{n-1} - x_n)$. Next, we might add all of these differences together to get a measure of total dispersion and divide by n to derive an average of the differences. Although this approach would be on the right track, it would also be awkward to calculate, especially when the sample size is large. For $n = 3$, there would only be $1 + 2 = 3$ pairs.[2] For $n = 4$, there would be $1 + 2 + 3 = 6$ pairs. But for $n = 26$, there would be $1 + 2 + 3 + \cdots + 24 + 25 = 325$ pairs!

Fortunately, there is a much easier way to achieve the same goal. This is to use the deviations, $x_i - \overline{x}$. Each deviation represents the difference between the value of a unit (the score of a specific student) and a single value, the sample mean. Thus, the number of pairs is greatly reduced to just n. So, for $n = 4$, there are 4 pairs: $(x_1 - \overline{x})$, $(x_2 - \overline{x})$, $(x_3 - \overline{x})$, and $(x_4 - \overline{x})$; and for $n = 26$, there are only 26. In this way, we *might* add all of the deviations together to derive a measure of the total dispersion:

$$\sum_{i=1}^{n}(x_i - \overline{x}).$$

This *might* then be divided by n to produce the average of the deviations:

$$\frac{\sum_{i=1}^{n}(x_i - \overline{x})}{n}.$$

Unfortunately, this doesn't solve the problem. You may already have caught on that, although we are very close to ending our search for the "ideal" measure of dispersion, the approach of adding deviations and dividing by n *won't* quite work. Nevertheless, a simple illustration will make the point clearly.

Table 6.1 shows a frequency distribution for the variable "number of trips" for a sample of only five students. Because the sample mean is 1 trip, each of the two students who did not travel at all has a deviation of –1, or a total of –2 for both students combined. This is shown in columns 3 and 4. The frequency of 2 is multiplied by –1 to get the –2 shown in column 4, labeled $f(x_i - \overline{x})$. Because 1 is also the mean, the student who traveled once has a deviation of 0. Finally, each of the two students who traveled twice has a deviation of +1, for a total of +2 in column 4.

Looking at the bottom entry of column 4, you will now certainly recall that the sum of the deviations is zero here because the sum of the deviations is *always zero*. Therefore, the formulas given above are not very helpful. That is,

$$\sum_{i=1}^{n}(x - \bar{x}) = 0,$$

and therefore

$$\frac{\sum_{i=1}^{n} f_i(x_i - \bar{x})}{n} = 0,$$

regardless the values of the attributes, the mean, or *n*. You probably also recall why this is true: because the mean is defined in such a way that deviations above it (those that are positive) cancel out the deviations below it (those that are negative).

How, then, can we derive a valid measure of dispersion based on the use of all deviations? Obviously, the cancellation between the negative and positive deviations must be eliminated. And how can this be done? Well, if we multiply a positive number by itself—square it—the result is positive; and if we square a negative number the result is also positive. Thus, the most direct way to get around the problem of the positives and the negatives canceling each other out is by squaring every deviation.[3] This will produce the set of squared deviations $(x_i - \bar{x})^2$. The sum of these terms (where *n is* the sample size),

$\sum_{i=1}^{n}(x_i - \bar{x})^2$, or $\sum_{i=1}^{a} f(x_i - \bar{x})^2$ (where *a* is the number of attributes), will not always

equal zero. In fact, although it can equal zero in the special case that *every value* in a distribution equals the mean (e.g., all students in the sample take exactly the same number of trips), the sum is otherwise always a positive number. The sum of the

TABLE 6.1   Simple frequency distribution illustrating the sum of deviations

(Col. 1)	*(Col. 2)*	*(Col. 3)*	*(Col. 4)*	*(Col. 5)*	*(Col. 6)*
X *(number of trips)*	*f*	*Deviations* $(x_i - \bar{x})$	*Frequencies times deviations* $f(x_i - \bar{x})$	*Deviations squared* $(x_i - \bar{x})^2$	*Sum of deviations squared* $f(x_i - \bar{x})^2$
0	2	−1	−2	1	2
1	1	0	0	0	0
2	2	+1	+2	1	2
	n = 5		$\Sigma = 0$		$\Sigma = 4$

Mean = 1, mdn = 1, *R* = 2, and variance (s^2) = 4/5 = .80.

squared deviations is often abbreviated as "the sum of squares," or—even more brief-ly—as "SS."

Let us return to our illustration in table 6.1. Note that column 5 contains the squared deviations, which are all either positive or zero. Column 6 contains the fre-quencies multiplied by the squared deviations, and the total, $\Sigma = 4$, is entered in the last cell. The final step is to divide 4 by n to derive the average of the squared deviations: $4/5 = 0.80$. This, at last, is our "ideal" measure of dispersion. The 0.80 is the average of the squared deviations, and it is known as the *sample variance*. It is symbolized by a lowercase s squared: s^2. Thus, the sample variance,

$$s^2 = \frac{\sum_{i=1}^{a} f_i (x_i - \bar{x})^2}{n},$$

where f_i is the frequency for the ith attribute and a is the number of attributes.

By applying this formula we can now demonstrate the difference between two frequency distributions whose means are equal and whose ranges are equal but that differ in other ways. Returning to figure 6.1, we focus on the distribution for exam 1. The calculation worksheet shown in table 6.2 is based on the data for "score on exam 1" shown in figure 6.1. Column 3 of the worksheet contains the deviations—each value minus the mean of 82.5. Column 4 lists the squared deviations, and column 5 contains the frequencies multiplied by the squared deviations. The last

TABLE 6.2   Worksheet for calculating variance for exam 1

(Col. 1)	*(Col. 2)*	*(Col. 3)*	*(Col. 4)*	*(Col. 5)*
x	f	$(x_i - \bar{x})$	$(x_i - \bar{x})^2$	$f(x_i - \bar{x})^2$
65	1	−17.5	306.25	306.25
70	2	−12.5	156.25	312.50
75	4	−7.5	56.25	226.00
80	6	−2.5	6.25	37.5
85	6	+2.5	6.25	37.5
90	4	+7.5	56.25	226.00
95	2	+12.5	156.25	312.50
100	1	+17.5	306.25	306.25
	$n = 26$			$\Sigma = 1764.50$

$$s^2 = \frac{\sum_{i=1}^{a} f_i (x_i - \bar{x})^2}{n} = \frac{1764.50}{26} = 67.87$$

entry in column 5 is the sum of the frequencies times the deviations squared, and in the last row that sum is divided by n (26) to produce the variance, 67.87 points (squared). That is, the average of the squared differences between the scores and the mean is nearly 68 points (squared).

This variance can be compared to the distribution for scores on another exam, given as an alternative to exam 1, shown in figure 6.2. We have seen that the means of the two exams are equal (82.5), as are the ranges (35). Yet it only takes a quick look at the histograms to see that the alternative has a higher degree of dispersion. A comparison of the respective variances will verify that.

The worksheet for calculating the variance of the alternative exam is shown in table 6.3. As in the worksheet for exam 1, columns 3, 4, and 5 show the deviations, the squared deviations, and the frequencies times the squared deviations, respectively. The sum at the bottom of the fifth column, 2,962.50, is greater here than the corresponding sum for exam 1. It is obvious that the source of the difference is in the distribution of the frequencies. In the alternative case, the frequencies are higher for extreme values and near the center, whereas in the case of exam 1 the frequencies are more evenly spread out. This situation creates a higher degree of dispersion in the alternative case. When we divide the sum of 2,962.50 by the same n (26), the result is therefore a larger variance: 113.94, approximately twice as large as the variance for exam 1. Clearly, then, although the means and ranges are the same in each case, student performances in the hypothetical situation are less consistent.

TABLE 6.3   Worksheet for calculating variance for alternative exam

(Col. 1)	(Col. 2)	(Col. 3)	(Col. 4)	(Col. 5)
x	f	$(x_i - \bar{x})$	$(x_i - \bar{x})^2$	$f(x_i - \bar{x})^2$
65	4	−17.5	306.25	1225.00
70	1	−12.5	156.25	156.25
75	1	−7.5	56.25	56.25
80	7	−2.5	6.25	43.75
85	7	+2.5	6.25	43.75
90	1	+7.5	56.25	56.25
95	1	+12.5	156.25	156.25
100	4	+17.5	306.25	1225.00
	$n = 26$			$\Sigma = 2962.50$

$$s^2 = \frac{\sum_{i=1}^{a} f_i (x_i - \bar{x})^2}{n} = \frac{2962.50}{26} = 113.94$$

The Standard Deviation: Rescaling the Variance

Variances are much larger in absolute value than the deviations that are being compared, and often larger than the actual quantities, such as 113.94 for test scores that can never themselves exceed 100. From the point of view of a computer or a scientific calculator, such numbers are, of course, no trouble at all. But it is often difficult to envision how such amounts relate to the actual measured quantities. For this reason, most of the time (in about three fourths of the applications in sociology), the variance is actually converted to a measure of dispersion that is easier to manage and more comparable to the range. This is done by taking the square root of the variance. The procedure is based on the fact that the square root of any number greater than 1.0 is smaller in absolute value than the number itself. For example: $\sqrt{1.10} = \pm 1.05$; $\sqrt{25} = \pm 5$; $\sqrt{100} = \pm 10$, and so on. You will recall that the "$\pm$" sign is a reminder that a number has two square roots, one positive and the other negative;[4] however, this "scaling-down" procedure for variance uses only the positive root.

So the variance has an important role to play in the measurement of dispersion, but its *positive square root* $\left(\text{symbolized as} +\sqrt{}\right)$ is more familiar to statisticians and nonstatisticians alike. This measure is known as the *sample standard deviation,* and its symbol is a lowercase *s.* As indicated, its formula is

$$s = +\sqrt{s^2}\,.$$

Taken together, the sample size (n), the sample standard deviation (s), and the sample mean ($\bar{x}$) provide all of the information about a sample that is necessary to perform most operations of elementary inductive statistics.

We can easily convert a known sample variance to a standard deviation by finding the positive square root of the former. This is also the easiest way to calculate the standard deviation; that is, first find s^2 by one of the methods discussed above and then solve for s. Thus, in the examples of exam 1 and the alternative distribution, we found the following variances:

exam 1: $$s^2 = \frac{\sum\limits_{i=1}^{a} f_i (x_i - \bar{x})^2}{n} = 67.87, \text{ and}$$

alternative exam: $$s^2 = \frac{\sum\limits_{i=1}^{a} f_i (x_i - \bar{x})^2}{n} = 113.94.$$

Therefore, the respective standard deviations are

$$s = \sqrt{\frac{\sum\limits_{i=1}^{a} f_i (x_i - \bar{x})^2}{n}} = \sqrt{67.87} = 8.24$$

and

$$s^2 = \sqrt{\dfrac{\sum\limits_{i=1}^{a} f_i (x_i - \overline{x})^2}{n}} = \sqrt{113.94} = 10.67.$$

The standard deviations give a more realistic sense of the respective "averages" of the differences between scores than do the variances, although we need to remember that they are special kinds of "averages"[5]—equal to 8.24 and 10.67 points, in this example.

Standard Score: Deviation Divided by Standard Deviation

The deviations of a frequency distribution $(x_i - \overline{x})$, which are used in calculating the variance and the standard deviation, were introduced in Chapter 5 as a set of alternative, or "cooked," scores that can be substituted for "raw" scores. In the example of exam 1 (shown in figure 6.1), for which the mean $\overline{x} = 82.5$ points, a student whose raw score is $x = 80$ has a deviation of $(x_i - \overline{x}) = (80 - 82.5) = -2.5$. A student whose raw score is $x = 85$ has a deviation of $(x_i - \overline{x}) = (85 - 82.5) = +2.5$, and so on.

Often in descriptive and, especially, in inductive applications it is necessary to compare deviations based on different samples. At times, the samples may be related, as in figure 6.1, where we compare a series of exam scores for a particular course. At other times, the samples may be very different, as when we compare a sample of exam scores of 26 students with a sample of tuition rates of 75 colleges and universities. For such comparisons, statisticians create another set of alternative scores based on the deviations. These are "cooked" twice, so to speak. The procedure adjusts the deviations to a standard—specifically, the standard deviation—that controls for sample dispersion. The procedure is called *standardization*, and the results, the "twice-cooked" scores, are referred to as *standard scores*.

Calculating Standard Scores

The goal in creating standard scores is to express each deviation not merely as the number of points, dollars, etc., by which a specific unit lies above or below the mean of the distribution, i.e., $(x_i - \overline{x})^2$. Rather, it is to express this quantity as a proportion of the standard deviation. Because, in general, every distribution has a distinct standard deviation, its set of standard scores reflects the distribution's degree of dispersion as well as the individual differences from the mean.

Thus far we have focused on the means and standard deviations of samples—the collection of observed units, symbolized as $\overline{x}$ and s. However, we shall soon deal with other kinds of collections of units, those that are unobserved and/or unobservable, for which different symbols need to be employed to avoid confusion. For this reason, it is best to learn the formula for standard scores first with words, and then with the appropriate symbols. The symbol for a standard score, itself, is always the same. It is z_i, which reads "the standard score for the *i*th unit." Because of this universally employed symbol, standard scores are often called, simply, *z scores*. Thus, the formula in words is

$$z_i = \text{deviation}_i \div \text{standard deviation}.$$

When referring to sample values, this is expressed as

$$z_i = \frac{(x_i - \bar{x})}{s} \quad.$$

In every sample, there is one standard score for each deviation, and one deviation for each raw score. This means that the value associated with each unit can be expressed in any of three ways: the raw score, the "once-cooked" deviation, and the "twice-cooked" standard or *z*-score. Consider our example of the distribution of scores on exam 1, shown in table 6.4, for which $\bar{x} = 82.5$ and $s = 8.24$. A student who received a grade of 65 (column 1) can also be said to have a score that is 17.5 points below the mean expressed as a deviation (column 2), and a standard score of –2.12 (column 3). This standard score can also be stated as "2.12 standard deviations below the mean." A student who received a grade of 90 would have a deviation of 7.5 points above the mean and a standard score of +0.91—just over 0.9 of a standard deviation above the mean.

The main advantage of a standard score is that it controls for the values of both the central tendency *and* the dispersion of the distribution from which it is taken. This allows us to make comparisons between samples without regard to their means and standard deviations. Let us illustrate with the distribution of alternative exam scores (figure 6.2), shown in table 6.5. In this distribution, as in that for exam 1, a student with a raw score of 65 would have deviation of –17.5. This is because the means of the two distributions are

TABLE 6.4 Comparing raw scores, deviations, and *z* scores for exam 1

(Col. 1)	*(Col. 2)*	*(Col. 3)*
x (raw score exam 1)	*Deviation*	*Standard score (z)*
65	–17.5	–2.12
70	–12.5	–1.52
75	–7.5	–0.91
80	–2.5	–0.30
85	+2.5	+0.30
90	+7.5	+0.91
95	+12.5	+1.52
100	+17.5	+2.12

$\bar{x} = 82.5; s = 8.24.$

equal (82.5), so that for both exam 1 and the alternative exam, a raw score of 65 has a deviation of (65 − 82.5) = −17.5. However, a student with a 65 on the alternative exam would have a different *standard score* than would one with a 65 on exam 1 because the standard deviations (by which we divide the deviations) are different: 10.67 and 8.24, respectively.

As shown in table 6.5, a raw score of 65 on the alternative exam corresponds to a standard score of $z_i = (x_i - \bar{x})^2/s = 17.5/10.67 = -1.64$, that is, 1.64 standard deviations below the mean. By this criterion, we can say that a score of 65 on the alternative exam is "better" than the same score on exam 1, because the former is closer to the class average in terms of the number of standard deviations below the mean. In fact, a 65 in the alternative exam case is almost as "good" as a 70 on exam 1 (whose standard score is −1.52). By the same reasoning, a raw score of 90 on the alternative exam is not as "high" as a 90 on the first exam because the former represents a standard score of only +0.70 compared to +0.91.

We can likewise convert each of the 75 household monthly incomes, introduced in table 4.13, to a standard score. This is done using the mean and standard deviation, as shown in table 6.6 (with the calculations of $\bar{x}$ and s omitted).

The following are some interesting observations that can be drawn from the distribution of standard scores for the incomes:

1. Household 01 has a standard score that is nearly 1.4 standard deviations below the mean.
2. Households 19 and 20 have a standard score of approximately −1.0.
3. Households 37 and 38 have a standard score of approximately 0, indicating that their incomes are average for the sample.

TABLE 6.5 Comparing raw scores, deviations, and *z* scores on the alternative exam

(Col. 1) *x (raw score alternative exam)*	*(Col. 2)* *Deviation*	*(Col. 3)* *Standard score (z)*
65	−17.5	−1.64
70	−12.5	−1.17
75	−7.5	−0.70
80	−2.5	−0.23
85	+2.5	−0.23
90	+7.5	+0.70
95	+12.5	+1.17
100	+17.5	+1.64

$\bar{x} = 82.5$; $s = 10.67$.

TABLE 6.6   Standard scores for monthly incomes of 75 households

Household	Raw score	z score	Household	Raw score	z score
01	$ 725	−1.37386	39	$ 6,175	0.03679
02	940	−1.31821	40	6,290	0.06655
03	1,074	−1.28353	41	6,500	0.12091
04	1,095	−1.27809	42	6,530	0.12868
05	1,100	−1.27680	43	6,730	0.18044
05	1,174	−1.25764	44	7,050	0.26327
07	1,191	−1.25324	45	7,087	0.27285
08	1,460	−1.18362	46	7,090	0.27362
09	1,559	−1.15799	47	7,200	0.30209
10	1,585	−1.15126	48	7,330	0.33574
11	1,717	−1.11709	49	7,500	0.37974
12	1,731	−1.11347	50	7,625	0.41210
13	1,780	−1.10079	51	7,700	0.43151
14	1,787	−1.09898	52	7,790	0.45481
15	1,816	−1.09147	53	7,804	0.45843
16	1,840	−1.08526	54	7,900	0.48328
17	1,890	−1.07232	55	7,985	0.50528
18	1,995	−1.04514	56	8,710	0.69293
19	2,066	−1.02676	57	8,850	0.72917
20	2,230	−0.98431	58	9,200	0.81976
21	2,388	−0.94342	59	9,787	0.97170
22	2,412	−0.93720	60	10,203	1.07937
23	2,509	−0.91210	61	10,745	1.21966
23	2,592	−0.89061	62	11,015	1.28955
25	2,684	−0.86680	63	11,088	1.30844
26	3,210	−0.73065	64	11,172	1.33018
27	3,380	−0.68665	65	11,190	1.33484
28	3,700	−0.60383	66	11,362	1.37936
29	4,200	−0.47441	67	11,637	1.45054
30	4,600	−0.37088	68	11,680	1.46167
31	4,790	−0.32170	69	11,836	1.50205
32	4,800	−0.31911	70	11,950	1.53156
33	4,980	−0.27252	71	12,120	1.57556
34	5,110	−0.23887	72	12,474	1.66719
35	5,550	−0.12498	73	12,890	1.77486
36	5,720	−0.08098	74	13,350	1.89393
37	6,020	−0.00333	75	13,380	1.90169
38	6,140	0.02773			

Mean = $6,032.87; standard deviation = $3,863.47.

4. Households 59 and 60 have a standard score of approximately +1.0.

5. Household 75 has a standard score that is nearly 2.0 standard deviations above the mean.

BOX 6.1   ## Statistics for Sociologists

Deviance and Dispersion

The Study of Deviance

Deviance[*] is one of the most important concepts in the sociologist's vocabulary. Courses on the subject or on "deviant behavior" or "deviancy," as it is often called, are among the most popular classes on university campuses in the United States and throughout the world. And more theories of deviance have been developed than of practically any other sociological phenomenon. (For more details, see http://sociologyindex.com/deviant.htm.)

In order to discuss how the concept of deviance is used, it is necessary to consider the closely related concepts of *norm* and *conformity*. When we speak of behavior as deviant, there is always the understanding that it deviates *from* something. This something is a norm. Behavior that is *not* deviant is said to conform to or be in conformity with the norm; it is *norm*al. Norms are rules intended to govern the behavior of members of a group. They function to promote conformity and social control. Norms can exist as part of informal folk culture, transmitted by word of mouth and passed down from generation to generation. They can also be formalized in writing as part of normative codes of rules, such as constitutions and operating procedures for religious groups, universities, corporations, and other organizations. An important subset of these formalized rules consists of the *laws* that exist as part of legal codes. In most cultures, a further distinction is made between civil and criminal laws.

In all of these cases, the norm has two parts: the first defines or stipulates the correct or incorrect behavior; the second part is the *sanction*, which indicates the consequences of conforming (a positive sanction) and/or deviating (a negative sanction). For example, most universities have a formal norm stipulating that students cannot register for credit in classes unless they pay their tuition. If they pay, then the positive sanction is that they will receive credit (if they pass the course!). If they deviate and do not pay, the negative sanction is that they will not receive credit.

---

[*] The word literally means "differing" (from the main trend), and is from the Latin *de* meaning "from" + *via* meaning "road," that is, "off the road."

Although we tend to think of deviant behavior as "bad," strictly speaking, deviancy can be either negative or positive. Negative deviancy is behavior that fails to conform in a way that falls short of normative expectations. Not paying tuition is negative deviancy in this sense. Positive deviancy is behavior that not only conforms to the norm but exceeds normative expectations. For example, if a student not only paid tuition but also gave a voluntary contribution to the university's endowment fund when the tuition bill came, this would certainly not be normal behavior. It would be deviancy, but of the positive type.

There seems to be little controversy over these definitions. It might at times be diffi-cult to determine with certainty whether a specific behavior deviates or conforms (that is one reason why we have courts and due process); but deviancy and conformity are real types of behavior. On the other hand, a serious problem arises when we attempt to label an *individual or a group* as "deviant." At this point, the act of attaching such a label to a person or group (as opposed to a behavior) takes on a political character. It involves a power struggle over who is entitled to do the labeling and who has the authority to make it stick. We know that everyone deviates for some norms at some point in their lives. By that criterion, *everyone* is a deviant. We also know that some acts of deviancy—probably most—are never detected. Thus, some people who should by this criterion be considered deviant avoid the label.

Many norms are so widely ignored or so rarely enforced that they do not have any effect. Yet, at times, individuals or groups are singled out for personal or political reasons for violating such "mock rules."** For example, some instructors announce an attendance policy in their classes that includes the provision that the student must provide a written note from the doctor in case of illness. But in practice, they never ask for a note, and stu-dents eventually catch on that it really isn't necessary. Then, a student whom the instruc-tor doesn't like for some reason receives a lower-than-expected grade. The student is told by the instructor that points were deducted because an absence was not explained by a doctor's note. In such a situation, the student's behavior was deviant; but then so was that of every other student. Why was this one labeled "deviant" and no one else?

Complexities in the study of deviance such as these make it a challenging and fas-cinating field of applied research. Several theoretical perspectives in microsociology, some mentioned in Chapter 5, deal specifically with the issue of labeling individuals or groups as "deviant." Perhaps the most popular and fruitful of these is the "labeling theory" approach (see http://www.apsu.edu/oconnort/crim/crimtheory14.htm).

** The observation that organizations can have "mock" rules was first made by Alvin Gouldner (1964). He noticed that workers in a gypsum plant that had a strict no-smoking policy obeyed the rule throughout the premises where fire posed a real danger. But everyone, including the supervisor, routinely ignored it in the front office, where they felt the rule made no sense (despite the conspicuously posted "No Smoking" signs). The only time they conformed in the office was when the fire marshal paid a visit.

An Application to the Classroom Interaction Study

It may have already occurred to you that a close parallel exists between the concepts of deviance from a norm and deviation from the mean. That is, both refer to how behavior may differ from a set standard. In the case of deviance from a norm, which we can refer to as "social deviance," the difference is generally qualitative: either behavior conforms or it doesn't. In the case of deviation from a mean, which we will call "statistical deviance," on the other hand, the difference is always quantitative. This is to say that, in principle, social deviance is not necessarily statistical deviance, and vice versa. However, if (1) we can quantify a norm and (2) establish or assume that the norm coincides with a mean, then the two are identical. The familiar normal ("bell") curve represents this overlap between norm and mean, as will be discussed in Chapter 7.

In the example of the study of classroom interaction introduced in Chapter 5, we recorded the average number of interactions occurring in the classes of 10 instructors. These are reproduced in table 6.7 along with additional information. The third column shows each instructor's score as a deviation from the mean; the fourth column lists the squares of these deviations, and the last column shows their standard (z) scores. The graph in figure 6.3 shows the distribution of z scores from low to high, with those below the mean indicated by the lighter shading.

Some of the instructors scored close to the mean, such as DR, who had a $z = +0.22$. In this respect, DR's performance was about average. But can we call it "normal"? We return to this question in a moment. The performance of others, however, deviated by large

TABLE 6.7   Number of interactions and z scores for 10 instructors

Instructor	Mean number of interactions	$(x_i - \bar{x})$	$(x_i - \bar{x})^2$	z scores
KA	4.25	−1.9	3.60	−0.71
RK	3.50	−2.65	7.02	−0.99
MM	8.13	1.96	3.92	+0.73
DR	6.75	0.60	0.36	+0.22
FT	10.00	3.85	14.82	+1.44
RW	7.25	1.20	1.44	+0.45
LC	7.00	0.85	0.72	+0.32
RO	9.63	3.48	12.11	+1.30
GB	2.00	−4.18	17.40	−1.57
PL	3.00	−3.15	9.92	−1.18
Total	61.51		71.31	
	mean $= 6.15$		$s = 2.67$	

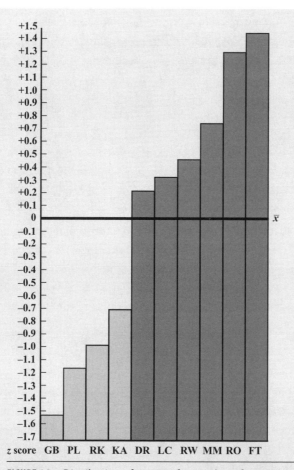

FIGURE 6.3   Distribution of *z* scores for number of interactions.

amounts, as indicated by their *z* scores: GB (*z* = −1.57, or more than one and one-half standard deviations below the mean), PL (*z* = −1.18), RO (*z* = +1.30), and FT (*z* = +1.44, or nearly one and one-half standard deviations above the mean). In this respect, their performance was well below, or well above average. But can we call it "deviancy"?

The issue of whether or not we can refer to the performance of DR as "normal," that of GB and PL as "negative deviance," and that of RO and FT as "positive deviance" depends on whether or not we are willing to count the *mean* of the distribution as a *norm*. Clearly, there is an expectation that instructors should encourage a certain amount of classroom interaction. But it is highly unlikely that the expectation (as an informal norm) is so specific that "a certain amount" means an average of 6.15 interactions per class session. It is possible that "a certain amount" simply refers to one or more interactions per class. By this standard, the performance of all 10 of our instructors would be in the normal range or positively deviant. It is also possible that "a certain amount" refers to at least 15 interactions per class. In this case, the performance of *all* of the 10 instructors would be negatively deviant.

Lacking the information necessary to decide whether and to what extent the norm in question coincides with the observed mean, it would be wise to reserve judgment about whose performance conformed and whose was deviant. But if, for the sake of illustration, we are willing to assume that approximately six interactions per class is not only average but is also normal, the results of the study reveal a close relationship between the statistical concept of dispersion and the sociological concept of deviance.

Three other properties of standard scores are worth noting here, in part because at least two of them come up again in our discussion of inductive applications.

First, *the standard score of the mean is always equal to zero.* For example, if a student happens to receive a grade on an exam that is exactly equal to the value of the mean, then the student's $z = 0$. This follows directly from the formula for the standard score. Because

$$z_i = \frac{(x_i - \overline{x})}{s},$$

it follows that if $x_i = \overline{x}$, then $z_i = (\overline{x} - \overline{x})/s = 0$. If someone scored 82.5 on exam 1, then the z score would be $(82.5 - 82.5)/8.24 = 0$. Using this formula, a student may tell a roommate about receiving a "0" in statistics and that it wasn't too bad. Once the roommate recovers from the shock, it can then be made clear that the "0" is a z score and that it indicates an average grade.

Second, *if a deviation is exactly equal to +1 standard deviation (s) or –1 standard deviation (–s), then the standard score is +1.0 or –1.0.* Again, this can be seen from the formula. Because

$$z_i = \frac{(x_i - \overline{x})}{s},$$

it follows that if $(x_i = \overline{x}) = \pm s$, then $z_i = \pm(s/s) = \pm1.0$. Thus, if someone happened to receive a grade of 90.29 on exam 1, this would translate to a z score of

$$\frac{(90.29 - 82.5)}{8.24} = \frac{8.24}{8.24} = +1.$$

Third, because the negative values of the standard scores cancel out the positive ones, *the sum of the standard scores for a given distribution is always 0.* As just shown, 0 is always the standard score of the mean. This verifies the definition of the mean as the attribute that divides a distribution into two parts, one of which is the total of all scores above it and the other the total of all scores below it. Recall that the reason we decided to use squared deviations $(x_i - \overline{x})^2$ instead of deviations $(x_i - \overline{x})^2$ to find an "ideal" measure of dispersion is that the sum of deviations always equals zero. Because $\sum(x - \overline{x}) = 0$ and $z_i = (\overline{x} - \overline{x})/s$, the formula for the sum of standard scores is just an extension of the formula for the sum of the deviations.

$$\sum_{i=1}^{n} z_i = \sum_{i=1}^{n} \frac{(x_i - \overline{x})}{s} = \frac{0}{s} = 0.$$

Summary

Now that we have seen how the standard score is defined and applied, we should note that it combines three of the major elements of descriptive statistics. These are: (1) an observation, as represented by a raw score; (2) central tendency, as represented by the mean; and (3) dispersion, as represented by the variance and standard deviation. Although these are not the only components of descriptive statistics, they do provide the necessary foundations for the other main type of statistics: induction, which is the focus of the following several chapters.

KEY TERMS

Dispersion: The tendency of values in a frequency distribution to "spread out," or disperse. It is the second most important property of a frequency distribution, after central tendency.

Range: The measure of dispersion calculated as the difference between the highest and lowest observed values in a frequency distribution.

Variance: The measure of dispersion calculated as the average of the squared deviations.

Standard deviation: The most commonly used measure of dispersion, the (positive) square root of the variance.

WEB SITES TO BOOKMARK

1. www.quickmba.com/stats/dispersion/
   This site has a brief definition of "dispersion" and discussions of the main measures, including the mean deviation.
2. www.uwsp.edu/PSYCH/stat/5/CT-Var.htm
   A psychology statistics site, posted at the University of Wisconsin at Stevens Point, that brings together the main concepts of central tendency and dispersion (here referred to as "variability").
3. mathworld.wolfram.com/StandardDeviation.html
   This site, aimed at the physical sciences, discusses and illustrates the concept of standard deviation. It explains why the term "root-mean-square" is used as a synonym for standard deviation.

SOLUTION-CENTERED APPLICATIONS (FOR CHAPTERS 5 AND 6)

Using SPSS for These Applications: The following two exercises ask you to find means, standard deviations, and standard scores. This can be done in several ways, but, especially when *n* is large, PASW Statistics is the easiest. Here is a guide.

Once you have created and/or opened an already-created data file, the SPSS commands are:

1. Click Analyze.
2. On the drop-down menu, click Descriptive Statistics.
3. On the side menu, click Descriptives.
4. From the list of the variables on the left, click the variable(s) of your choice.
5. Click the arrow in the center to direct it into the "Variables" box to the right.
6. Click the box to the lower left that reads "Save standardized vales as variables."
7. Click OK.

The output will appear on the screen, and the set of standard scores will appear in what was the first empty column in the data view.

Application 1: For decades, the Federal Bureau of Investigation (FBI) and other law enforcement agencies have maintained a database on crimes that are reported by local agencies. This Solution-Centered Application uses some of these data to answer a few questions that have important policy implications.

Some researchers have claimed that the rates of violent crimes in the United States are declining and that they are declining most rapidly in states that have had high rates in the past. If true, this is interpreted as evidence that increased funding for local law enforcement is having a positive effect. If this is not true, then it is possible that other strategies need to be employed.

To shed light on this issue, suppose that you have been asked by a representative of the Department of Justice to track the rates of violent crimes for a one-year period (2004–2005) for each of the 50 states. The procedure will be to (1) access the relevant data; (2) perform some calculations of central tendency and variability; (3) analyze your findings; and (4) write a brief report on your findings.

1. The data: Go to the web site of the Disaster Center, an organization that posts official crime statistics, at http://www.disastercenter.com/crime/US_States_Rate_Ranking.html. Make a copy of the table entitled "US States Crime 2004–2005 Crimes per 100,000 and Ranking." This table contains information on several variables, some of which you may want to use in other assignments or even in other courses. We will focus here only on the violent crime rate for each state for each of the two dates.

2. Calculations: You might want to create a PASW Statistics data file with the table by cutting and pasting or hand copying. These calculations can also be done with an Excel spreadsheet or with a hand calculator. Find:
   A. The means, medians, and modes for the 50 states for each of the two years
   B. The ranges and standard deviations for each year
   C. The set of 50 *z* scores for each of the two years.

3. Analysis:
   A. Compare the measures of central tendency for each year and decide whether there is an overall decline in the rates.
   B. Compare the measures of dispersion and decide whether the distributions are becoming more or less "spread out."
   C. Compare the *z* scores state by state and identify the states that showed relative declines, those that experienced increases in their rates, and those that exhibited little or no change. Did the states that had high crime rates in the earlier year experience declines during the period?

4. The report: In your report, discuss your procedure and your findings. State your conclusion concerning the trends you observed and indicate whether or not you believe that increased funding does make a difference. Include a table or two that support(s) your conclusion.

Application 2: According to the Union of Concerned Scientists (UCS), "The world's countries contribute different amounts of heat-trapping gases to the atmosphere. . . . The picture that emerges from [comparative] figures is one where—in general—developed countries lead in total carbon emissions and carbon emissions per capita, while developing countries lead in the growth rate of carbon emissions" (from the UCS web site at http://www.ucsusa.org/global_warming/science/each-countrys-share-of-co2-emissions.html).

With this in mind, you are to collect data on the CO_2 emissions (an important, but not the only, source of "greenhouse" gases) for the 10 countries that have the highest per-capita emissions and the 10 countries with the lowest per-capita emissions. There are many sources for these data in books, periodicals, and online (e.g., http://www.nationmaster.com/graph/env_co2_emi_percap-environment-co2-emissions-per-capita).

Once you have identified your countries, determine whether the countries with the highest emissions are in fact the most developed and the countries with the lowest emissions are the least developed. Again, this can be accomplished in any of several ways. For example, you can use the PRBWorldPopulationData set that you downloaded and determine the level of development for each of the 20 selected countries. It is generally agreed that the best single measure of level of development is average life expectancy at birth, which is included in that data set. If you select that variable, find its mean and standard deviation and create standard (z) scores on it.

If the UCS statement is true, then the 10 countries with the highest per-capita emission rates should have large, positive z scores: +1.0 and above. The 10 countries with the lowest rates should have large, negative z scores: −1.0 and below.

Once you have collected your data and combined the two sets of results, write a brief report of your findings. Include the data you used and one or more tables.

Testing Your Skills

Practice Quizzes for Chapters 3–6

The following four practice quizzes test your skills with topics covered in Chapters 3–6. They focus on level of measurement, frequency distributions (univariate and bivariate), central tendency, and dispersion.

QUIZ 1: An application to the sociology of education

Instructions: Table 1 contains information about a sample of U.S. colleges and universities. Using these raw data, answer each of the 10 following questions (plus one extra credit).

1. What does n equal? Name each of the variables in the table and state the level of measurement of each.
2. Create a univariate, ungrouped frequency distribution for each variable, in table form. Include frequencies and percentages, and, for one variable of your choosing, create a bar graph (or histogram if appropriate).
3. For each variable to which it applies, find the mode.
4. For each variable to which it applies, find the median.
5. For each variable to which it applies, find the mean.
6. For the two variables represented in columns I and III of the table, create a crosstab containing frequencies in each cell and the marginals (percentages will be calculated in question 8).
7. Indicate which is the independent and which is the dependent variable used in question 6. Explain why you made that choice.
8. Using the crosstab in question 6, calculate the correct set of percentages that will best show whether or not the independent variable does have an effect on the dependent. Redraw the crosstab here with the percentages now included. Based on these, would you accept or reject the hypothesis that there is an effect? Explain your decision.

TABLE 1   Characteristics of U.S. colleges

Column	I	II	III
School	**Admin**[1]	**Sports**[2]	**Comp.**[3]
College A	Church	12	2
College B	State	10	2
University A	State	10	2
University B	State	8	3
University C	Church	6	1
College C	Church	4	2
College D	Church	7	1
University D	Private	4	3
College E	Private	8	1
University E	Church	7	2
College F	Private	5	2
University F	Church	9	3
College G	Church	8	4
University G	Private	12	3
University H	Private	12	4

1. "Admin " refers to the kind of organization that administers the school.

2. "Sports" refers to the number of varsity sports teams the school has.

3. "Comp." refers to how competitive the school is: 1 = "not," = "2 somewhat," 3 = "moderately," and 4 = "very."

9. Select the subsample consisting of only the *state* schools and indicate its *n*. Using only these, create the univariate frequency distribution for the variable in column II.

10. For the new frequency distribution created in question 9, find the mean, the range, and the standard deviation.

Extra credit: Create the frequency polygon for a variable for which you calculated the mean. Is it symmetrical or skewed? If skewed, what type of skew is it?

QUIZ 2: An application to urban sociology

Instructions: Table 2 contains a set of raw data for a sample of large U.S. cities. Using these data, answer each of the 10 following questions (plus one extra credit).

1. What does *n* equal? Name each of the variables in the table and state the level of measurement of each. What do we call the special kind of variable in column III (in addition to naming it by its level of measurement)?

TABLE 2   Information about U.S. cities

Column	I	II	III
City	Age of city	No. of hospitals	Has a major university
A	Young	10	No
B	Middle-aged	8	No
C	Young	9	Yes
D	Old	7	Yes
E	Young	9	No
F	Old	7	Yes
G	Middle-aged	8	Yes
H	Middle-aged	7	No
I	Old	7	Yes
J	Old	8	No
K	Young	10	No
L	Middle-aged	8	Yes
M	Middle-aged	9	No
N	Old	8	No
O	Middle-aged	9	No
P	Old	7	No
Q	Young	10	Yes

2. Create an ungrouped frequency distribution for each variable, in table form. Include frequencies and percentages.
3. For the variable in column II, create a bar graph and a frequency polygon.
4. For each variable to which it applies, find the mode.
5. For each variable to which it applies, find the median.
6. For each variable to which it applies, find the mean.
7. Is the frequency polygon created in question 3 symmetrical or skewed? If skewed, which type of skew is it?
8. Using a crosstab that includes frequencies, marginals, and the appropriate percentages, indicate whether you think that there is a relationship between a city's age and whether or not it has a major university. Be sure you consider which variable should be the independent.
9. Select the subsample consisting of only the *old* cities and indicate its *n*. Using only these, create the univariate frequency distribution for the variable "number of hospitals."
10. For the frequency distribution created in question 9, find the mean, range, and standard deviation.

Extra credit: Evaluate the following expression, where n is the sample size, x is an individual value of the interval-level variable, and $\bar{x}$ is the mean of that variable. Explain your answer.

$$n \div \sum (x - \bar{x})$$

QUIZ 3: An application to medical sociology

Instructions: Table 3 contains a set of raw data for a sample of patients at a nearby clinic. Use these data to answer the following 10 questions.

1. What does n equal? Name each of the variables in the table and state the level of measurement of each. What do we call the special kind of variable in column III (in addition to naming it by its level of measurement)?
2. Create an ungrouped frequency distribution for the variables in columns I and III, in table form. Include frequencies and percentages.
3. For the variable in column II, create a bar graph and a frequency polygon.
4. For each variable to which it applies, find the mode.
5. For each variable to which it applies, find the median.

TABLE 3 Information about clinic patients

Column	I	II	III
Patient ID #	Health of patient	No. of annual visits to clinic	Residence
1	Fair	2	Urban
2	Fair	1	Rural
3	Good	3	Rural
4	Fair	2	Urban
5	Poor	0	Urban
6	Fair	2	Rural
7	Poor	1	Urban
8	Good	2	Rural
9	Good	2	Rural
10	Fair	3	Urban
11	Poor	1	Urban
12	Fair	0	Urban
13	Good	3	Rural

6. For each variable to which it applies, find the mean.

7. Is the frequency polygon created in question 3 symmetrical or skewed? If skewed, which type of skew is it?

8. Using a crosstab that includes frequencies, marginals, and the appropriate percentages, indicate whether you think that there is a relationship between a patient's health and his/her residence. Be sure you consider which variable should be the independent.

9. Select the subsample consisting of only the *patients with "good" health* and indicate its *n*. Using only these, create the univariate frequency distribution for the variable "number of annual visits."

10. For the new frequency distribution created in question 9, find the mean, the range, and the standard deviation.

QUIZ 4: An application to the sociology of education

Instructions: Table 4 contains a set of raw data for a sample of U.S. colleges. Use these data to answer the following 10 questions (plus one extra credit).

TABLE 4   Information about 15 colleges and universities

Column	I	II	III
College	Type of administration	Size of student body	No. of students (per faculty)
A	Private	Small	20
B	Public	Medium	19
C	Public	Medium	20
D	Religious	Large	24
E	Public	Medium	20
F	Private	Small	24
G	Religious	Large	22
H	Public	Large	22
I	Public	Medium	24
J	Private	Medium	24
K	Private	Small	19
L	Public	Large	22
M	Religious	Small	20
N	Public	Medium	19
O	Religious	Medium	20

1. Name each of the variables in the table and state the level of measurement of each.
2. Create a univariate, ungrouped frequency distribution for each variable, in table form. Include frequencies and percentages, and, for one variable of your choosing, create a bar graph.
3. For each variable to which it applies, find the mode.
4. For each variable to which it applies, find the median.
5. For each variable to which it applies, find the mean.
6. For the two variables represented in columns I and II, create a crosstab containing frequencies in each cell and the marginals (percentages will be calculated in question 8).
7. Indicate which is the independent and which is the dependent variable used in question 6. Explain why you made that choice.
8. Using the crosstab in question 6, calculate the correct set of percentages that will best show whether the independent variable has an effect on the dependent. Based on these, would you accept or reject the hypothesis that there is an effect? Explain.
9. Select the subsample consisting of only the *small* schools and indicate its *n*. Using only these, create the univariate frequency distribution for the variable "number of students (per faculty)."
10. For the new frequency distribution created in question 9, find the mean, the range, and the standard deviation.

Extra credit: Create the frequency polygon for a variable for which you calculated the mean. Is it symmetrical or skewed? If skewed, what type of skew is it?

III

The Logic of Statistical Induction

Because we have mentioned inductive statistics several times in earlier chapters, you probably have a good idea of what this approach is about. Chapters 7, 8, and 9 build upon these introductory comments. Here the technical details are provided to help you understand the steps involved in statistical induction and appreciate what it can (and cannot) tell us.

We have already noted that induction is essentially the same mental process as generalization. There are three main steps:

1. We observe the characteristics of specific objects or events.
2. We organize our observations (as when we turn data into information).
3. Finally, we provisionally conclude that all objects or events that are of the same type as those observed, including those of which we have no direct knowledge, have the same characteristics.

For example, as was true of Europeans before they visited Australia, one might have observed several swans, noting that they are all white. The next step is to generalize by stating that all swans, including those never observed, are white. This conclusion was drawn inductively, as the observer generalized from a few cases to every case. As is true of all such generalizations, one cannot be certain that the conclusion is true. Rather, one can say only that it is likely to be true until proved otherwise. In the present example, Europeans eventually viewed the black swans of Australia, and the fallibility of induction (or at least that act of induction) was proved.

The following discussion formalizes this familiar way of thinking as it applies to statistical reasoning. In doing so, three main tools are introduced: probability theory, the concept of a sampling distribution, and the useful procedure of creating confidence intervals. Each of these is based upon the key premise of induction: we seek to use our observations to understand something we have not observed—not with absolute certainty but with a reasonable chance (probability) of being correct. These tools are then applied in the final chapters in the defining feature of inductive statistics: testing hypotheses.

Generalizations and Social Justice

This chapter begins our exploration of inductive applications. For this reason, our attention now turns from techniques for describing samples to the logic of generalization. At this point, you should know much about frequency distributions—univariate, bivariate, and multivariate—and about their role in organizing data so that they can be used as information. In addition, you should understand what central tendency and dispersion are and why they are so important in summarizing frequency distributions. With this in mind, we now ask: What can be concluded about the populations from which our samples are drawn based on our knowledge of the samples' frequency distributions and measures of central tendency and dispersion? The answer to this question comes in several steps. The first few of these are provided in the main sections of this chapter. The latter steps are featured in the remaining chapters of this part of the text.

Why Do We Sample?

Before turning to these technical matters, it might help to reflect on why scientists (and nonscientists as well) use samples at all. Wouldn't it be preferable, one might wonder, to deal with the larger populations directly? Wouldn't our knowledge be more accurate if we observed the whole rather than just a part? Clearly, the answer is "yes"—if we could observe populations directly, our knowledge *would* be more accurate. However, there are many situations in which it is simply too costly, in time, labor, and money, to attempt to study entire populations. For some research projects, the additional knowledge that would be gained is not worth the additional effort required to go beyond the findings achieved with a good sample. This is why sampling theory is part mathematics and part economics, and why statisticians are famous (or notorious) for seeking to get "the most bang for the buck."

Another and perhaps more serious obstacle to working with populations is that many populations of interest to social researchers and other scientists simply cannot be observed. In these instances, the best we can ever do is to generalize from samples. Every 10 years, the U.S. Bureau of the Census attempts to count every individual person residing in the nation. But if you think about it, this is an impossible undertaking, and the Census Bureau is well aware of it. Even if the Bureau could get an accurate count on the fictitious "Census Day" of April 1, the total would be obsolete the moment the count was concluded. That is, thousands of people would have died, tens of thousands of babies would have been born, and migration (in and out of the country) would have occurred as the census takers were doing their work. And, of course, all of the enumerating does not take place on one day. Rather, it is stretched out over months—during which the size and composition of the U.S. population is continually changing.

Even apparently more manageable populations raise problems. Suppose that you wanted to learn something about the career aspirations of students at your university, whose enrollment is generally in the range of 20,000. Unless you specified *current* students, your population would include all students who ever attended (including some who are no longer alive) as well as students who will attend in the near future. In this case, you would never be able to observe the population, whether by telephone, e-mail, in person, etc. But, such tricks aside, could you observe even the current enrollees? Would you use a list? Can you be sure that such a list is up to date? Might there not be students who dropped out after the list had been composed? Would you count them? Could you find them? You probably get the point. Such questions are endless. In all such cases, including the Census enumeration, we *are* dealing with samples, even when we aim to observe populations.

It is not too far-fetched to say that we all, expert and layperson alike, draw conclusions from samples all of the time. We walk or drive home from class every day, "knowing" that our house will be where we left it based on a sample of observations (after all, we did not run home at lunchtime to check whether it was still there). And we realize that such "knowledge" is partial only when the seemingly impossible occurs. We arrive home and, as occurred in Turkey in the spring of 2000, discover that an earthquake had swallowed up the house during the morning hours (perhaps we should have "expanded" our sample by coming home for lunch).

Speaking of lunch, did you ever make soup for a friend or relative? And while it was cooking, didn't you stir it, dip in a spoon, and taste it to see whether it had enough salt or pepper or whether it was ready in other ways? Perhaps it did need a little salt, so you added some, washed the spoon (of course), stirred again, . . . and then dipped in the spoon and took another taste, and so on. At some point, you were satisfied and let it simmer, "knowing" how it would taste—*all* of it. You might have taken 5 or 10 or even 20 spoonfuls, but at some point you decided you were satisfied. You certainly did not eat the entire contents of the pot just to be absolutely sure that your friend would like it.

What you were doing was sampling. In this case you sampled because to "observe" the entire population would be self-defeating; there would be nothing left for your friend. You were even taking a *random* sample (described later in this chapter), for in stirring the soup before every taste you were ensuring that each portion of the mixture—top, bottom, sides, middle—was the same as every other.

Sometimes we get the impression that only social scientists sample, and that non-social scientists study all units of interest. A chemist, for example, knows that when one combines certain sodium compounds with chlorine compounds, under the proper conditions, one will produce sodium chloride. Is the chemist basing this knowledge on the experience of working with all sodium and all chlorine in the universe? Obviously not. This kind of knowledge, like most knowledge in any of the sciences, social and non-social, is derived from the observation of samples. Fortunately for the chemist, samples of chemicals can be made pure and uniform, unlike samples of people.

For better or worse, we are destined to base our knowledge largely on the observation of samples. With this granted, it is especially important to learn as much as possible about how far we can generalize and about what the limits of generalization are. The purpose of the remainder of the chapter is to begin this learning process in a formal way.

BOX 7.1   ## Statistics for Sociologists

Social Justice and Capital Punishment

It is tempting to pretend that minorities on death row share a fate in no way connected to our own, that our treatment of them sounds no echoes beyond the chambers in which they die. Such an illusion is ultimately corrosive, for the reverberations of injustice are not so easily confined.

Supreme Court Justice William Brennan (figure 7.1)

The Field of Social Justice Studies

The study of *social justice* is an interdisciplinary field that applies theory and research in sociology, criminology, and related disciplines. Its main premise is that the concept of justice refers not only to the legal system but to political institutions, the economy, and all other realms of human relationships. Proponents argue that if we are going to employ standards of equity and fairness in the courts of law, we should do the same wherever social norms and values are in question. Thus, in creating positive social change, we should seek to establish a just *society*, not merely a just system of formal civil and criminal law.

FIGURE 7.1   U.S. Supreme Court Justice William Brennan [courtesy of the Library of Congress].

The philosophical framework for social justice studies was established over the centuries and can be traced back to the work of ancient thinkers such as Aristotle and classic European philosophers such as Baruch Spinoza and Immanuel Kant. The contemporary ethicist John Rawls has been especially influential in the revival of interest in the subject with his view of *distributive justice* (Rawls, 1971)—a concept that goes back through Thomas Aquinas to Aristotle. Among Rawls's many key contributions is the view, which is now shared by most practitioners, that the rights of individuals must be safeguarded against unjust social practices, even if such practices are very widespread. In fact, the rights of individuals must be protected even if such practices are *legal* in the formal sense. Thus, the fact that certain behavior is considered legal—such as arresting and deporting a person with no warrant or trial, as in totalitarian regimes—does not make it just.

The field of social justice is among the most popular and fastest growing specializations in sociology. Courses and degree programs in the field are offered at colleges and universities throughout the United States, and a scholarly journal in the field, *Social Justice,* which has been published for more than 30 years, is now available online at www.socialjusticejournal.org/. A recent publication by the Society for the Study of Social Problems (SSSP), *Agenda for Social Justice, Solutions 2008,* is specifically addressed to applied sociologists. The entire volume can be downloaded from the SSSP web site at www.sssp1.org/index.cfm/m/323.

Is Capital Punishment Just?

The topic of capital punishment is of special interest in the field of social justice studies. It also demonstrates better than most other topics how the principles and concepts in the field, including distributive justice, are applied. The question of whether the death penalty is—or can be—just has been debated for centuries. It has been abolished in nearly all of the industrialized countries; but it remains legal although, opponents argue, immoral in more than 40 of the United States. The Supreme Court has taken up the issue hundreds of times, including 214 cases since 1991.[*]

On January 1, 2000, Illinois Governor George Ryan declared a moratorium on the death penalty, stating that "I have grave concerns about our state's shameful record of convicting innocent people and putting them on death row. I cannot support a system, which, in its administration, has proven to be so fraught with error and has come so close to the ultimate nightmare, the state's taking of innocent life."[**]

---

[*] For online references, see: www.aclu.org/capital/index.html; www.deathpenaltyinfo.org/article .php?did=184&scid; www.law.cornell.edu/supct/search/search.html.
[**] www.deathpenaltyinfo.org/timeline.pdf, also www.deathpenaltyinfo.org/article.php?did=483.

One of the most common concerns among social justice researchers involves the issue of race and ethnicity. Considering the fact that members of minority groups are subject to prejudice and discrimination in other realms of society, is it possible that these biases carry over into the criminal justice system with the consequence of what Governor Ryan calls "the ultimate nightmare"?

Data collected by the Death Penalty Information organization from official state and federal records provide some insight into this issue. Table 7.1 contains information on 33 states that carried out at least one execution between 1991 and 2007. Along with the total number of executions for each state, we have listed the percentage of all executions and the percentage of the general population of the state represented by whites. Texas tops the list with 379 inmates executed, of whom 183 (about 48%) were white, which means that 196 (about 52%) were nonwhite. This can be compared to 71% white and 29% nonwhite in the general population. In other words, for this state 52%/29% = 1.8 times as many nonwhites were executed as would have been the case if the percentage executed were the same as in the population. The ratio for whites is about 48%/71% = 0.68 to 1. These ratios are indices (see Chapter 3) that measure a group's over- or under-representation among those executed. A low value on the index is evidence of bias in favor of the group; a high value is evidence of bias against the group. We need to add quickly that "bias" in this sense is a statistical term and does not prove racial discrimination; whether the statistical bias is due to racial discrimination depends on several other factors. But this type of bias is obviously a concern when we consider the larger issue of social justice.

Of course, neither Texas nor any other single state necessarily reflects the national pattern. Each state has unique social and cultural characteristics and its own legal system. In order to get a better understanding of the national situation, and also to illustrate the logic of sampling and sampling distributions, we have selected a random sample, "sample A," of 10 states from the list in table 7.1. For each state, we have calculated the index of bias for the white group (0.68 in the example of Texas).

For sample A, the mean $\bar{x} = 0.837$ and the standard deviation $s = 0.687$. This indicates a bias in favor of the white group (whites are underrepresented among executions); but the standard deviation also suggests that there is considerable dispersion, even in this small sample. The indices ranges from a high of 1.17 for Pennsylvania and 1.10 for Montana—states in which whites are *over*represented among executions—to 0.67 in Delaware and, as noted, 0.68 in Texas. The latter two execute substantially fewer whites relative to their concentration in the population.

TABLE 7.1   Executions of white prisoners by state, 1991–2007

State	Total	White	% white in executions	% white in population
Alabama	35	19	54.29	71.1
Arizona	22	17	77.27	75.5
Arkansas	27	19	70.37	80
California	13	8	61.54	59.5
Colorado	1	1	100.00	82.8
Connecticut	1	1	100.00	81.6
Delaware	14	7	50.00	74.6
Florida	64	39	60.94	78
Georgia	39	26	66.67	65.1
Idaho	1	1	100.00	91
Illinois	12	7	58.33	73.5
Indiana	17	14	82.35	87.5
Kentucky	2	2	100.00	90.1
Louisiana	27	14	51.85	63.9
Maryland	5	2	40.00	64
Mississippi	8	5	62.50	61.4
Missouri	66	39	59.09	84.9
Montana	3	3	100.00	90.6
Nebraska	3	1	33.33	89.6
Nevada	12	9	75.00	75.2
New Mexico	1	1	100.00	66.8
North Carolina	43	29	67.44	72.1
Ohio	24	15	62.50	85
Oklahoma	83	52	62.65	76.2
Oregon	2	2	100.00	86.6
Pennsylvania	3	3	100.00	85.4
South Carolina	36	24	66.67	67.2
Tennessee	2	2	100.00	80.2
Texas	379	183	48.28	71.0
Utah	6	4	66.67	89.2
Virginia	98	51	52.04	72.3
Washington	4	4	100.00	81.8
Wyoming	1	1	100.00	92.1
Totals	1054	605	57.40	76.43

Source: http://www.deathpenaltyinfo.org/article.php?did=483

TABLE 7.2 Comparison table

Statistic	Sample A	Sample B	Sample C	Average of $\bar{x}$'s
$\bar{x}$	0.837	0.737	0.821	0.798
s	0.229	0.107	0.170	

We can now ask to what extent we can generalize from this result, based on a very small sample, to the mean index, μ, for the entire United States. The exact answer will have to be postponed until Chapter 7, when we present the techniques for establishing a *confidence interval*. At this point, however, we can feel more "confident" with a sample of $n = 10$ than with information about one state. We would conclude, with only these data in mind, that an estimate for μ is closer to 0.88 than it is to 0.68.

For the sake of comparison, we have drawn two additional samples, samples B and C, from the set of states in table 7.1. Their respective means and standard deviations are shown in table 7.2. You can see that the mean for sample B is smaller than that of sample A, and for sample C it is slightly smaller.

Granting that a sample mean provides a better estimate of μ than does the value for a single state, we are now faced with another question: Which sample mean? From the discussion in this chapter, the answer should be fairly clear. Any sample mean, if the sample was selected randomly and if n is large (which, unfortunately, is not the case here), will give a reasonable estimate of the population mean, but we cannot expect any particular $\bar{x}$ to equal μ exactly. In other words, referring to $(\bar{x} - \mu)$ as *error*, we cannot expect error to equal 0.

Now recall that the mean of the sampling distribution of means is the same as the mean of the population, μ. If we could calculate all possible sample means, then their average would be μ. Of course, this is rarely if ever possible. But if we were to take the average of a set of sample means, even just a few, we would probably (but not necessarily) have an estimate of μ that is better than any single sample mean. In table 7.2, the average of the three sample means is listed as 0.798. Although researchers do not ordinarily work with more than one sample, we have done so here for the sake of illustration. Under these circumstances, we would say that the value 0.798 is our best estimate, although we can't know that for certain unless we also happen to know the population mean.

As it happens, again for the sake of illustration, we do know μ, which can be calculated from table 7.1. We see that for all of the states combined, the proportion of executed inmates who were white is 0.544, and the proportion who are white in the population of the states is 76.43. The mean index for the population is thus

0.544/0.764 = 0.712. The average of the three sample means, 0.798, is closer than any of the individual sample means. And, of greater importance, no matter which index value we use, it is clear that a racial bias exists, at least in statistical terms. As noted, whether or not this indicates social injustice is another matter.

To extend this example one further step, table 7.3 contains information about the racial and ethnic characteristic of inmates sentenced to be executed but who are still alive on death row.

Among the many specific facts revealed by these data, the most pertinent from a social justice perspective is, again, the relative proportions of black and white inmates on death row in comparison to their respective concentrations in the general U.S. population. Whereas 41.3% of death row inmates are black, the group represents only 12.3% of the total U.S. population. This is more than a 3-to-1 ratio of inmates to members of the general population. In contrast, 45.5% of death row inmates are white, but the group makes up more than 75% of the total population, or a ratio of 0.6 to 1.

Now, if the group of 3,292 death row inmates were a random sample of the U.S. population—which, of course, we know is almost certainly *not* the case—we would expect about 2,470 members to be white and about 400 to be black. Compare these to the actual totals of 1,498 and 1,359, respectively.

Using the logic of the sampling distribution (although the assumptions do not quite hold here and the mathematics is inexact), we could ask what a reasonable expectation for a random sample of $n = 3,292$ would be. With a sample percentage for whites of 45.5%, more than two-thirds of all possible population percentages would lie within one standard error unit of the sample percentage; and well over nine-tenths of the population percentages would lie within two standard error units. Even using the most generous estimate of a standard error unit (about 3.0 percentage points), we would expect the population percentage for whites to be between 42.5% and 48.5% for one standard error and between 39.5% and 51.5% for two standard error units. The actual population percentage of 75.1 is far above even the wider range. It is remotely possible that the death row sample was selected randomly from the general population, but it is *extremely* unlikely.

Thus, the question remains the same as it was following examination of table 7.1: Was the sample selected with a bias—conscious or not—against blacks? We know, by definition, that it was selected with a bias against people convicted of capital crimes. Are blacks far more likely to be convicted of such crimes? We know that the set of people convicted of capital crimes is based on the determination that indicted defendants actually committed those crimes. Is there a bias against blacks in the indictment or determination process? And finally, we know that not everyone who commits a capital

TABLE 7.3   Racial and ethnic characteristic of inmates sentenced to be executed but still alive on death row

State	Total	Black No.	Black Prop.	White No.	White Prop.	Latino No.	Latino Prop.	Asian (prop.)	Native Am. (prop.)
Alabama	195	93	0.477	100	0.513	2	0.010	0	0
Arizona	124	13	0.105	88	0.710	20	0.161	0.024	0
Arkansas	37	23	0.622	14	0.378	0	0.000	0.000	0
California	660	235	0.356	254	0.385	136	0.206	0.033	0.0197
Colorado	2	1	0.500	0	0.000	1	0.500	0.000	0
Connecticut	8	3	0.375	3	0.375	2	0.250	0.000	0
Delaware	18	7	0.389	8	0.444	3	0.167	0.000	0
Florida	397	139	0.350	221	0.557	35	0.088	0.003	0.003
Georgia	107	50	0.467	53	0.495	3	0.028	0.009	0
Idaho	20	0	0.000	20	1.000	0	0.000	0.000	0
Illinois	11	3	0.273	5	0.455	3	0.273	0.000	0
Indiana	23	7	0.304	16	0.696	0	0.000	0.000	0
Kansas	9	4	0.444	5	0.556	0	0.000	0.000	0
Kentucky	41	9	0.220	31	0.756	1	0.024	0.000	0
Louisiana	88	55	0.625	30	0.341	2	0.023	0.011	0
Maryland	8	5	0.625	3	0.375	0	0.000	0.000	0
Mississippi	66	35	0.530	30	0.455	0	0.000	0.015	0
Missouri	51	21	0.412	30	0.588	0	0.000	0.000	0
Montana	2	0	0.000	2	1.000	0	0.000	0.000	0
Nebraska	9	1	0.111	5	0.556	3	0.333	0.000	0
Nevada	80	29	0.363	42	0.525	8	0.100	0.013	0
New Mexico	2	0	0.000	2	1.000	0	0.000	0.000	0
North Carolina	185	98	0.530	72	0.389	4	0.022	0.005	0.054
Ohio	191	96	0.503	88	0.461	3	0.016	0.010	0.010
Oklahoma	88	33	0.375	48	0.545	3	0.034	0.000	.045
Oregon	33	3	0.091	26	0.788	2	0.061	0.000	0.030
Pennsylvania	226	137	0.606	68	0.301	19	0.084	0.009	0
South Carolina	67	38	0.567	29	0.433	0	0.000	0.000	0
South Dakota	4	0	0.000	4	1.000	0	0.000	0.000	0
Tennessee	107	43	0.402	59	0.551	1	0.009	0.019	0.019
Texas	393	161	0.410	121	0.308	107	0.272	0.010	0
Utah	9	1	0.111	6	0.667	1	0.111	0.000	0.111
Virginia	20	12	0.600	8	0.400	0	0.000	0.000	0
Washington	9	4	0.444	5	0.556	0	0.000	0.000	0
Wyoming	2	0	0.000	2	1.000	0	0.000	0.000	0
Totals	3292	1359	0.413	1498	0.455	359	0.109	0.042	0.010
U.S. proportions			0.123		0.751		0.125	0.036	0.009

Source: www.deathpenaltyinfo.org/article.php?did=483.

crime is arrested and indicted. Is there a bias against blacks at this point in the process; are they more likely than whites to be arrested?

Interestingly, an important factor enters into the process at several stages. Arrest, indictment, conviction, sentencing, and carrying out the sentence are all affected by the group to which the alleged *victim* belongs. A situation in which a white person is believed to have murdered a black person is least likely to end in a death sentence or execution. In contrast, the chances of a death sentence or execution are the greatest when a black person is convicted for murdering a white person.

Most of these issues are unresolved, although much research in this area has been conducted and continues to the present. We certainly cannot give a definite answer to the question of whether or not capital punishment has a racial bias. Much of the evidence suggests that it does, although many critical questions remain unanswered. Regardless of the outcome, however, the entire debate sheds light on the fact that *criminal* justice cannot be understood without also examining the more general problems of *social* justice.

Statistics, Parameters, and Generalization

In Chapter 2, we defined a *statistic* as a characteristic of a sample, and we contrasted it with a *parameter*, a corresponding characteristic of a population. The statistics to which we have been introduced so far are the sample size (n), the mean ($\bar{x}$), the median (*mdn*), the mode, the range (R), the set of deviations ($x_i - \bar{x}$), the variance (s^2), the standard deviation (s), and the set of standard (or z) scores. Because a sample represents only a part of the population from which it was drawn, we would expect that the parameters such as population size, population mean, population median, and so on, might differ from the corresponding statistics (see figure 7.2 for the symbols for the major statistics and parameters). In some cases this is obvious. The sample size is, by definition, smaller than the population size. In other cases, such as the mean, we may not be able to be absolutely certain. This is especially true when we do not have direct knowledge of the parameters—which in practice is most of the time.[1]

The purpose of the inductive applications we are considering here is first to derive statistics such as—and especially—the mean using the techniques introduced in previous chapters. Then, with other tools to be discussed soon, we create an estimate of the corresponding parameter. These procedures take us from part (the sample) to whole (the population) and from statistic to parameter (see figure 7.3). It is for this reason that we sometimes refer to inductive logic as "going from particular to general." However, most logicians view this as an inexact way of describing induction and prefer the more common and better-understood term *generalization*. In any case, in order to get

Measure	Sample statistic	Population parameter	Comment
size	n	ν	Parameter is pronounced "new." Rarely used but helpful when discussing size of sampling frame (see text below).
mean	$\bar{x}$	μ	Parameter is pronounced "mew." Widely used for population and other nonsample distributions.
proportion	p_i	π_i	Parameter is the Greek "pi." This is ordinarily used when comparing attributes of nominal- and ordinal-level variables.
deviation	$x_i - \bar{x}$	$x_i - \mu$	The statistic indicates the difference between a raw score and its sample mean; the parameter indicates the difference between a raw score and the population mean.
variance	s^2	σ^2	The parameter is the Greek lowercase "sigma" (Σ) squared.
standard deviation	s	σ	The parameter is the Greek lowercase "sigma" (Σ).

Note. All symbols are lowercase letters. Letters from the Roman alphabet are used to stand for statistics, and letters from the Greek alphabet are used to stand for parameters.

FIGURE 7.2   Common symbols for statistics and parameters.

a clearer idea of how this procedure works, it is necessary to look more closely at the relationship between a sample and a population.

Sampling Techniques

Effective generalization in statistics requires that our samples be as *representative* as possible of the populations from which they are drawn. In other words, the sample should reflect as closely as possible the relevant features of the population. If, for example, a population has a very high proportion of home owners, yet our sample has relatively few, the latter would be a poor representation of the former if the question

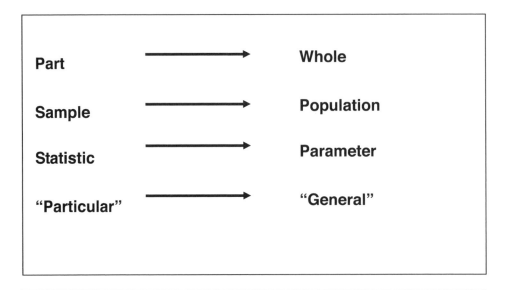

FIGURE 7.3   The procedure of inductive logic.

being investigated had anything to do with home ownership. Achieving a representative sample, in turn, depends very much on (1) the manner in which a sample is selected from a population and (2) the size of the sample. These requirements are listed in order of importance because, as we shall see, a small sample that is selected correctly is far more useful than a large sample that is not properly selected. A sample is selected, or "drawn," in such a way that some units from the population occur once and only once in the sample. For example, the 26 students whose scores on three exams were discussed in previous chapters were selected from the population of all students who took the three exams over the past several semesters. The set of 75 households whose incomes were also discussed earlier was selected from a population of approximately 1,000 households in the community. And, of course, your sample of 50 colleges and universities used in the IBM SPSS Statistics Base exercises was selected from the population of 384 schools (see figure 7.4).

Although its importance is secondary, in practice the first thing that must be determined in selecting a sample is its size (n). This decision is made on the basis of several factors, including cost and the degree of accuracy required. In the social sciences, such decisions can often be very complex, largely because of the money involved in selecting and observing samples. In fact, an entire field of sampling theory has developed to help researchers negotiate the many obstacles associated with the seemingly simple question "How large should my sample be?"[2] Once the sample size determined—for example, 75 households—the next step is to decide on the procedure that will identify which units (e.g., households) in the population will be part of the sample and which will not.

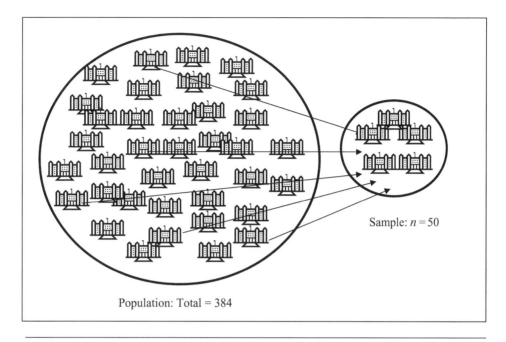

Sample: $n = 50$

Population: Total = 384

FIGURE 7.4   Selecting units (colleges) from the population into the sample.

There are basically two broad options in this regard. The one that is much preferred is to select a *probability sample.* This is defined as a sample for which *the probability that a unit from the population will be selected into the sample is known.* Several types of samples, to be discussed soon, are included in this category. The other option, the one that is viewed as less than entirely acceptable for scientific purposes, is a *non-probability sample.* As the name indicates, with this procedure one does not know the probability that a given unit in a population will be selected. When using samples to generalize about populations, there is always the possibility of error. The problem with non-probability sampling is that most of the error is unknowable and uncontrollable. In contrast, the error that occurs with probability sampling has been well studied and understood. Thus it can be explicitly taken into account in making generalizations.

Non-probability Samples

Non-probability sampling is often referred to as "convenience" sampling, because the units are selected into a sample in a convenient but usually unscientific manner. One of the most familiar types is that employed by interviewers and pollsters who stand outside a large store in a shopping mall and ask passers-by to respond to a set of questions. These interviewer-samplers might have a quota of, say, 100 interviews per day, but it is also likely that they simply stop as many people as possible until the store closes.

In any case, there is nothing wrong with this procedure, provided that the researcher involved is willing to be very cautious about making generalizations from the 100 or so interviews. Suppose, for example, that one of the questions asked is "Do you believe that our city needs more parks?" Further, let us assume that 75% of those who responded said "yes." It is fair and accurate to report that 75% of the respondents gave an affirmative answer, but it cannot be concluded that 75% of the residents of the town believe that there should be more parks. Nor is it even accurate to say that 75% of all persons who visited the mall on the day in question believe that there should be more parks. In fact, it is even unfair to conclude that 75% of all people who passed by the interviewer on that given day believe in more parks.

These limitations apply because, in the absence of further information, the interviewer has no idea of the chances that a resident of the town, a mall visitor, or a passer-by was actually interviewed. Thus, it is possible that an unusually high proportion of park lovers in these populations happened to be interviewed whereas most of those not interviewed think that there are enough parks. We simply cannot know these things.

Other examples of non-probability sampling include selections based on friendship, proximity of residence, respondents most likely to be articulate, and "experts." All of these are legitimate means to gather data, but the information created from such data cannot be accurately generalized beyond a very limited range. If one is interested in learning about one's relatives, one's neighbors, articulate people, or experts, then these are the sorts of people who *should* be contacted. If one wishes to know about "the average citizen," "the man or woman on the street," and so on, however, it is very unlikely that such information can be derived from these kinds of convenience samples.

Probability and Probability Samples

Probability sampling, in which the probabilities of selection are known, requires a tool known as a *sampling frame*. This is an actual list or other representation of the set of units from which the sample is drawn. It may not be, and usually is not, identical to the population of interest—the "study population"—which is ordinarily inaccessible, but it is meant to come as close as possible to containing all of the population's units.

For example, suppose that we were interested in selecting a sample of $n = 26$ from the population of all students who registered for a course in statistics at your college during the past five years. For this purpose, we would need to know which students did and which did not take statistics. But how could we know that? Well, the obvious approach would be to obtain a list of registrants for the statistics classes that included the name, ID number, and an address, e-mail address, or phone number for each student. Of course, we would need to check the names to see whether the information was complete. We would also have to assume that no student registered who is not on the list and that everyone on the list actually registered. Based on these assumptions, we could produce a revised set of names that, although unlikely to be absolutely identical to the study population, would nevertheless serve as the sampling frame. Obviously, samples taken at the mall, along with other non-probability samples, lack a sampling frame.

The most basic type of probability sampling is *random sampling*, known more technically as *pure random sampling with replacement*. It is defined in terms of the concept of *equiprobability* first mentioned in Chapter 4. You will recall that the subject of probability was introduced in that context in relation to proportion, with the comment that under certain common conditions the two are simply different ways to express the same idea. These include the conditions of equiprobability.

A proportion for a specific attribute is the frequency associated with the attribute divided by n (f/n). The probability of a specific attribute occurring is the number of times that attribute occurs divided by the total number of ways that any attribute can occur. Thus, if in a class of 26, 10 students had the attribute "70–100" (i.e., they scored between 70 and 100), the *proportion* with a score in that range is $10/26 = 0.38$. Alternatively, we could say that the *probability* that any given student in that class has a score in the 70–100 range is $10/26 = 0.38$. Both are valid ways of describing the situation.

The essence of equiprobability is implied in the phrase "any given student." By using this phrase, we are assuming that every student has the same chance as any other to be that "given" one. In general, equiprobability refers to a situation in which *the probability of a unit being selected is equal to the probability of selection of any other unit*. A random sample, then, is one in which units are drawn from a sampling frame into a sample on the basis of equiprobability. We stress that the units are drawn from a sampling frame rather than from a study population. This is because there might be units that are part of the latter but are not included in the former (e.g., students who did register but whose names were erroneously omitted from the list). They would have no chance at all of being included in the sample.

The mechanics of drawing a random sample are what ensure equiprobability. These include use of a computer (IBM SPSS Statistics Base will select a random sample of any size) and drawing a sample from a table of random numbers. One illustrative method is to print unique numbers for the units, such as the student ID numbers of those listed as statistics class registrants, on small, equally weighted balls such as table tennis balls. Then we place the balls in a rotating basket such as those used at lottery drawings. After they have been thoroughly tumbled, *so that none has a better chance of being selected than any other*, we choose one and record the number. Next—and this is an important but often-overlooked step—we replace the ball. We repeat the process until n different numbers have been chosen.

The reason that a ball is replaced after it is chosen, and the reason we stress that this is a random sample *with replacement*, is to keep the probabilities equal. If, for instance, the total number of units in the sampling frame, symbolized as ν, is 1,000 and we seek an $n = 26$, then we want to be sure that the probability of any ball being selected is $1/1,000 = .0010$ on each and every one of the 26 draws. But if we were to forget to replace the ball on the first draw, then the probability of any one being selected on the second draw would be $1/999 = .0011$ for the balls still in the basket but 0 for the one selected, and so forth. The principle of equiprobability would have been violated.

Incidentally, the ratio of the sample size to the total number of units in the sampling frame ($n/ν$), assuming that the latter is known, is referred to as the *sampling fraction*. It represents the probability that a given unit will occur in a sample once the entire sample has been drawn. Because in our example each student has a .001 chance of being selected on any specific draw and because there are 26 draws altogether, the probability of occurring in the sample is $.001 + .001 + \cdots + .001$, out to 26 terms. This equals $26/1,000$ or .026 (2.6 times in 100). The inverse of the sampling fraction, $π/n$, is called the *sampling interval* (SI) because it represents the interval in the sampling frame between one selection and another. In our example, it is $1,000/26 = 38.46$. That is, 1 in every 38.46 students in the sampling frame is selected into the sample.

The calculation of the sampling fraction follows a principle of probability theory known as the *addition rule* (see figure 7.5):

If the probability of an outcome is p_1 and the probability of another, mutually exclusive outcome is p_2, then the probability of either the first or the second on one draw, selection, etc., is $p_1 + p_2$. (Note the "either/or" wording.)

Suppose that we are to select one student out of three—Joan, Dave, and Kwame—to turn off the lights after class. Now, given the assumption of equiprobability, the probability of selecting any one is $1/3 = .33$. But, we ask, what is the probability of selecting *either* Joan *or* Kwame? According to the addition rule, it is $.33 + .33 = .67$. In the case of random sampling from a sampling frame of 1,000 students, if the probability of a given student being selected on any one draw is .001, then the probability of being selected on one of the 26 draws is the same as the probability of being selected on the first, *or* the second, *or* the third, and so on. That is, $.001 + .001 + \cdots = 26/1,000 = .026$.

Two related principles of probability are worth considering at this point. The first is just another extension of the concept of proportions, the *converse rule* (see figure 7.6). It states that if the proportion of units in a sample with a specific attribute is f/n, then the proportion that does *not* have the attribute is $1.0 - f/n$. You can see why this is so if you recall that a proportion of 1.0 is the same as 100%, or all units in the sample. If 10 of 26 students have a grade in the 70–100 range, then the proportion in this range is $10/26 = .38$ (or 38%). This means that the proportion of students who fall below this range is $1 - (10/26) = 16/26 = 1 - .38 = .62$.

If p_A is the probability that outcome A will occur,

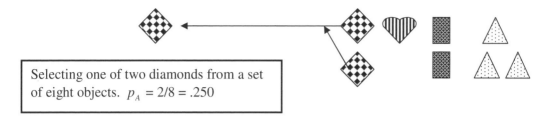

Selecting one of two diamonds from a set
of eight objects. $p_A = 2/8 = .250$

and p_B is the probability that outcome B will occur,

Selecting one of three triangles from a set
of eight objects. $p_B = 3/8 = .375$

Then $p_A + p_B$ is the probability that *either* outcome A *or* outcome B will occur.

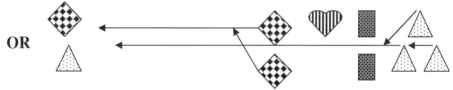

OR

Selecting one of two diamonds **or** one of
three triangles from a set of eight objects.
$p_A + p_B = .250 + .375 = .625$

FIGURE 7.5   The addition rule of probability theory.

If p_A is the probability that outcome A will occur,

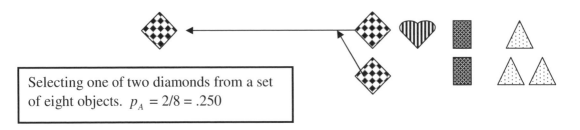

Selecting one of two diamonds from a set of eight objects. $p_A = 2/8 = .250$

then q_A is the probability that outcome A will **not** occur, where $q_A = 1 - p_A$

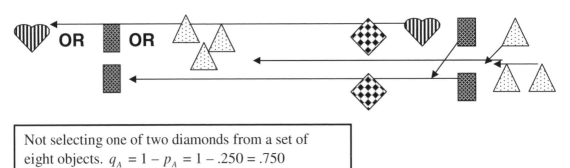

Not selecting one of two diamonds from a set of eight objects. $q_A = 1 - p_A = 1 - .250 = .750$

FIGURE 7.6   The converse rule of probability theory.

By the very same reasoning,

If the probability of a given outcome is p, then the probability that the outcome will not occur is 1 – p.

We often use q to stand for $1 - p$, so that $p + q$ *always equals 1.0*. Thus, if the probability that a given student among the 1,000 in the sampling frame will be included in a sample with $n = 26$ is $p = .026$, then the probability that the student will *not* be included is $q = 1 - p = (1 - .026) = .974$, or 97.4 times out of 100. With $p = .026$ and $q = .974$, $p + q = 1.000$.

The final principle is the *multiplication rule* (see figure 7.7). This applies not to one draw, selection, etc., but to two or more. In this case, we ask what the probability is that one thing will occur and also another and another, and so on. The rule states:

If p_A is the probability that outcome A will occur,

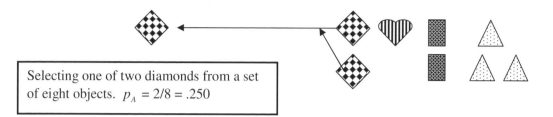

Selecting one of two diamonds from a set
of eight objects. $p_A = 2/8 = .250$

and p_B is the probability that outcome B will occur,

Selecting one of three triangles from a set
of eight objects. $p_B = 3/8 = .375$

Then $P_A \times P_B$ is the probability that *both* outcome A *and* outcome B will occur in two
tries (with replacement).

Selecting one of two diamonds **and** one of three
triangles in two tries from a set of eight objects.
$P_A \times P_B = .250 \times .375 = .094$

FIGURE 7.7   The multiplication rule of probability theory.

If p_1 is the probability of one outcome and p_2 is the probability of another, mutually exclusive outcome, then the probability that both the first and the second outcomes will occur (in that order) is $p_1 \times p_2$.

In the illustration in which we select one of three students to turn out the lights, we saw that the probability of selecting any one is .33. Similarly, the probability of selecting one *or another* is .33 + .33 = 0.67. Now, in applying the multiplication rule, we ask, what is the probability of selecting any one (e.g., Dave) two days in a row? The answer here is $(.33) \times (.33) = .109$. What is the probability of selecting him three days in a row? Obviously, it is $(.33) \times (.33) \times (.33) = .036$. Applying this rule to random sampling, we might ask, what is the probability of randomly selecting two specific individuals (who, for instance, may happen to be good friends) into a sample with a known sampling fraction of .026? The small chance that this can occur may surprise you. It is only $(.026) \times (.026) = .0007$ (7 times in 10, 000)!

Other Kinds of Probability Samples

In addition to random sampling, there are three other types of probability sampling procedures that are commonly used. These are the *systematic* (list), *stratified*, and *multistage cluster* methods. Although none of these produces a strict equiprobability sample, they each include a random aspect, and they do allow the user to know the exact probability that a unit in the population will be selected into the sample.

Systematic or List Sampling

Systematic or list sampling is used when the sampling frame is a physical list, as opposed to a set of ID numbers or the like. With this procedure, the listed units (individuals, schools, etc.) are divided into two groups. Members of one group, whose size is n, are selected one at a time into the sample. Items from the other group, whose size is equal to the total number of units on the list minus n $(\pi - n)$, are not selected. The sampling interval (SI), which equals σ/n, represents the number of units that are skipped between one selection and another. So, for example, if we sought to draw a sample of 26 students from a list of 1,000, the sampling interval of 38.5—rounded to 39—would indicate that we are to select a student, skip down the list 39 places and select the next, and so on.

Before the first selection is made, however, a starting point must be established. It might be the first unit, in which case the next unit selected would be unit 1 + SI = 40. However, it might be the second, which would make the next selection the 2 + SI = 41st entry. In fact, any of the first SI (39) units would be appropriate for a starting point. Under these circumstances, in order to introduce an element of equiprobability, the starting point is selected at random, usually from a random number table. For the example in which 26 students are selected, we generated a random start of 33. Thus, the sample includes the 33rd student, the $(33 + 39) = $ 72nd, the 105th, the 138th, and so on.

Systematic sampling assigns the following probabilities. For the first SI units on the list, 39 in our example, the probability of being selected (at random) is 1/SI, or .026, which is the sampling fraction. For each unit in the interval that is skipped, the probability is 0; they cannot be selected. And for each unit beyond the starting point whose place corresponds to the starting point plus $1 \times SI$, $2 \times SI$, $3 \times SI$, and so on (the 72nd, 105th, 138th, . . . in the example), the probability is 1.0; they must be selected. With this said, you can understand why systematic samples are often treated as if they were pure random samples, with no serious consequences.

Stratified Sampling

Stratified sampling is undertaken when the researcher wants to ensure that the sample contains a specific proportion of relevant groups that are found in the population, e.g., public and private universities; male and female students; or freshman, sophomore, junior, and senior dorm residents. With a random or a systematic sample the probabilities of any unit being chosen are more or less equal. A stratified sample is needed in some instances because there is no guarantee that relevant groups will be represented in a random or systematic sample in any specific proportion. For example, a sampling frame may contain an equal number of male and female students, but a random or systematic sample taken from such a sampling frame could easily consist of more males than females or more females than males, although it is possible but unlikely that the proportions would be vastly different. It all depends on chance.

To ensure that proportions in the sampling frame are preserved in the sample, the stratified sampling procedure follows these steps:

1. Select a sample size, n.
2. Determine the groups whose proportions in the sample are to be fixed, and select the appropriate proportions. If two groups are used, then the proportions would be symbolized as p_1 and p_2. The two quantities, which we designate n_1 and n_2, are the sizes of the two subsamples, respectively.
3. Divide the sampling frame into two parts, each consisting of members of only one of the groups. If v represents the number of units in the entire sampling frame, then v_1 is the number in the first group and v_2 is the number in the second.
4. Each part of the original sampling frame is then treated as a smaller sampling frame, and n_1 and n_2 units are selected, at random or systematically, from each part, respectively. The sampling intervals are $[v_1/n_1]$ and $[v_2/n_2]$, and the sampling fractions, which are also the probabilities of selection in a given random draw, are $[n_1/v_1]$ and $[n_2/v_2]$, respectively.

For example, suppose that we wished to have equal proportions of male and female students in our sample of 26. Then the proportions p_1 and p_2 would equal 0.5 and 0.5, and the size of each subsample would be $(0.5 \times 26) = 13$. Now, suppose further that the sampling frame of 1,000 students consisted of 400 males and 600 females. Then the respective sampling intervals would be $400/13 = 30.8$, rounded to 31, and $600/13 = 46.2$, rounded to 46. Thus, the probability of a male being selected randomly is .032, and that for a female is .022. You can see that with stratified sampling, the probabilities of selection are known, but they are equal only when the desired sample proportions happen to correspond exactly with the proportions in the sampling frame.

Multistage Cluster Sampling

This method, which is often used with natural geographic areas such as states, cities, and neighborhoods, selects units at two or more levels of aggregation. In essence, this means that two or more sampling frames are used. The first consists of the larger units, which are the *clusters* or *primary sampling units*, and a sample of these is selected randomly, systematically, or by another method.[3] For example, the clusters might be states in the United States. Then, once a set of clusters is selected, each cluster is treated as a sampling frame made up of the units within it. These latter units are *secondary sampling units*. If states are the primary sampling units, the secondary sampling units might be cities within the states. The procedure may stop here, or it might continue to a third stage, in which the *tertiary* or (if this is the last stage) *final sampling units* are selected. If the secondary sampling units are cities, the tertiary units might be neighborhoods (by ZIP code) or households within cities. It is the number of final sampling units (e.g., households) that determines the final sample size n.

Here is an illustration. A researcher wishes to take a sample of 5,000 urban households in the United States. The first sampling frame is the set of 50 states, of which 5 are selected. Then, within each state, a list of all large cities is created, and 5 of these cities are chosen. This produces a total of 25 cities. Then, in each city, a list of all households is created, from which 200 are selected. The final sample size is thus $5 \times 5 \times 200 = 5,000$.

Multistage cluster sampling is adopted for the sake of convenience and cost, because only a small set of the clusters is used to select the final sample. In addition, because the clusters are selected by a procedure that favors the most populous areas, it tends to give all final sampling units a fairer chance of selection. The probability that any final unit will be included in the sample is determined by the multiplication rule, in which we find the product of the probabilities of selection at each stage.

To emphasize a point made earlier, the purpose of all of these techniques of probability sampling is to ensure the highest possible degree of *representativeness*. We understand that drawing conclusions about a population (or sampling frame) based on observations of a sample involves compromise and estimation. So we sample with care so that we can minimize the error that would be introduced if the characteristics of the population were poorly reflected in that segment of the population we actually study.

Sampling Distributions

An often poorly understood aspect of generalizing from a sample to a population is that the procedure is *indirect* and accomplished in *two* steps. We do not merely determine a statistic, such as the mean score on an exam taken by 26 students, and then directly generalize to the parameter, e.g., mean score for all 1,000 students who ever took the exam. Instead:

- We compare our statistic to the set of *all possible* statistics of that type, e.g., sample means.
- Then we compare the set of all possible statistics to the parameter.

The set of all possible statistics to which we refer is called a *sampling distribution*, and it plays a crucial role in inductive applications.

A sampling distribution is just another kind of frequency distribution, which can be expressed as a table or as a frequency polygon. However, it differs from the frequency distributions discussed thus far in that it is *not* based on observations. Rather, it is based on theoretical probabilities. It is a statement of what *would be the outcome if certain conditions were achieved.* You are probably familiar with another sort of theoretical probability distribution, so it might help to take a quick look at one of these before continuing with our exploration of sampling distributions. As shown in figure 7.2, when describing frequency distributions based not on sample observations but on populations and probability distributions, the symbol for the sample mean, $\bar{x}$, is replaced by μ, and the symbols for the standard variance and standard deviations, s^2 and s, are replaced by σ^2 and σ, respectively.

Theoretical Probability Distributions

Perhaps in an elementary math class or, if you are so inclined, at a gambling casino you have already seen the distribution of possible outcomes on a pair of dice. Each single die is, of course, a cube; so it has six faces. On each face a number of dots are embossed, from 1 to 6. Now, here comes the "if certain conditions" part. If:

1. The die is perfectly balanced so that each side has an equal chance of being on top after a toss;

TABLE 7.4   The 36 possible outcomes of tossing two dice

Die 1	Die 2	Total	Die 1	Die 2	Total
1	1	2	5	2	7
1	2	3	3	4	7
2	1	3	4	3	7
1	3	4	2	6	8
3	1	4	6	2	8
2	2	4	3	5	8
1	4	5	5	3	8
4	1	5	4	4	8
2	3	5	3	6	9
3	2	5	6	3	9
1	5	6	4	5	9
5	1	6	5	4	9
2	4	6	4	6	10
4	2	6	6	4	10
3	3	6	5	5	10
1	6	7	5	6	11
6	1	7	6	5	11
2	5	7	6	6	12

2. No matter how many times or under what conditions the die is tossed, the balance remains the same—unaffected by wear and tear, atmospheric effects, or disturbing vibrations;

3. Each time the die is tossed, it clearly and unambiguously shows an "up" side—it never lands on a corner, never rolls away without being seen again, etc.

Then $p_1 = p_2 = p_3 = p_4 = p_5 = p_6 = 1/6 = .167$ (where p_1 is the probability of showing a 1, p_2 is the probability of showing a 2, and so forth. In other words, if the die were perfect, then there would be an equiprobability of each face showing up.

In craps and other casino games, two dice thrown together. When this occurs, the pair can show any of 36 possible combinations, as listed in table 7.4: $1 + 1, 1 + 2, \ldots, 6 + 6$. Now, with two "perfect" dice, thrown under equally ideal circumstances, each of these combinations would have the same chance, $1/36 = .028$, of showing up. Now, we know that certain combinations have the same total, from 2 to 12, as shown in the third column of table 7.4. For example, both $1 + 2$ and $2 + 1$ add to 3. Using the addition rule, table 7.5 and figure 7.8 indicate the probabilities of showing each of the 11 sums. You can see why 7 is considered a lucky number in craps (especially if you bet on it!), because it is the

TABLE 7.5   Probabilities of the possible outcomes of tossing two dice

Col. 1	Col. 2[a]	Col. 3	Col. 4	Col. 5[b]
X	$ncomb_X$	Cumulative combinations	p_X	$(ncomb_X)(X - \mu)^2$
2	1	1	.028	25
3	2	3	.055	32
4	3	6	.083	27
5	4	10	.111	16
6	5	15	.138	5
7	6	21	.167	0
8	5	26	.138	5
9	4	30	.111	16
10	3	33	.083	27
11	2	35	.055	32
12	1	36	.028	25
Total = 36			1.000	210

[a]Number of combinations adding up to X.

[b]Terms in the summation under the radical in the numerator of the expression for the standard deviation of this distribution.

most likely total. On the other hand, 2 and 12, affectionately known as "snake eyes" and "boxcars," respectively, are considered to be losers. They are the least likely totals.

Table 7.5 and figure 7.8 depict the associated theoretical probability distribution. They indicate that if conditions were ideal, in every 36 tosses of a pair of perfect dice you should expect one 2, two 3s, three 4s, and so on. Notice that the X at the top of column 1 of the table does not indicate the value of a numerical variable but rather a possible sum on a given throw. Also, the third column is not headed by "f" for "frequency." Rather, it uses "p" for probability (the sum of the entries in this column is, of course, 1.0, or 100%). This is because the values are not frequencies. No one actually threw any dice before the table was created; no observations were made or recorded; and no sample was used at all. The distribution is derived from probability theory, nothing more or less.

Although distributions such as these are not based upon actual observations, they nevertheless do have central tendencies and dispersions, as measured in the usual way by modes, medians, means, ranges, variances, and standard deviations. Figure 7.8 shows quite clearly that the distribution of dice tosses is unimodal and symmetrical. In fact, the mean, median, and mode all coincide at the value 7. The position of the median is found by taking the total number of combinations, 36, adding 1, and dividing the result by 2. That is, $(36 + 1)/2 = 37/2 = 18.5$. Looking down the column that shows the cumulative

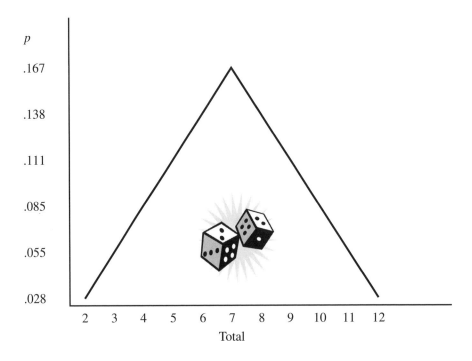

FIGURE 7.8   Theoretical probability distribution for a toss of two dice.

number of combinations to find the median, we see that the 18.5th outcome (that between the 18th and 19th) has the value 7. The mean, μ, is calculated using the formula

$$\mu = \frac{\sum_{i=1}^{k}(ncomb_i)(x_i)}{t},$$

where k is the number of possible outcomes, $ncomb_i$ is the number of combinations that add to a given sum, x_i is the sum of two dice on a given toss, and t is the total number of possible combinations.[4] Therefore,

$$\mu = \frac{\begin{array}{c}(1 \times 2) + (2 \times 3) + (3 \times 4) + (4 \times 5) + (5 \times 6) + (6 \times 7)\\ + (5 \times 8) + (4 \times 9) + (3 \times 10) + (2 \times 11) + (1 \times 12)\end{array}}{36} =$$

$$\frac{2 + 6 + 12 + 20 + 30 + 42 + 40 + 36 + 30 + 22 + 12}{36} = \quad 252/36 = 7.$$

The range of the distribution is $(12 - 2) = 10$, and the standard deviation of the probabilities, σ_p, is found using the formula

$$\sigma_p = \sqrt{\frac{\sum_{i=1}^{k}(ncomb_i)(x_i - \mu)^2}{t}}.$$

Column 5 of table 7.5 lists the terms of the sum in the numerator and, in the last cell, the total is 210. Thus,

$$\sigma_p = \sqrt{\frac{210}{36}} = \sqrt{5.83} = 2.42.$$

With these values of the theoretical distribution in mind, let us now suppose that you actually do throw a pair of dice 36 times and record the outcome. In this way, you could create an actual frequency distribution, indicating how many times you threw a 3, a 4, a 9, and so on. Your distribution would have a mode, a median, a mean, and a standard deviation, calculated according to the formulas used for sample means and other statistics introduced in Chapters 5 and 6.

But how closely do you think your actual distribution would agree with the theoretical one? Try it if you like, or you can take it on faith that your distribution would vary somewhat and possibly even a great deal from the theoretical distribution (for example, as shown in figure 7.9). Why? Because reality is never perfect, of course. No dice are absolutely fair; atmospheric conditions do play a role in the outcomes, etc. Now imagine that you repeated the trial for another 36 tosses, and recorded the proportions of all 72 tosses combined. Would this distribution be closer to the theoretical one? Perhaps it would, but perhaps it would not.

Now, let us really stretch our imaginations and suppose that you threw the dice not 36 or 72 times, but *one million* times. Do you think *these* proportions, mean, and standard deviation would come close to the theoretical distribution? It is a good bet (as long as we are in the casino mood) that you do think so. And most statisticians would very much agree with you. But why are you so confident that the outcome of one million tosses would be better, as measured by how close the actual distribution comes to the theoretical one, than the outcome of 36 tosses? If the phrase "law of averages" is coming to mind, you are definitely on the right track.

Here is the idea: *As the number of actual tosses increases, the observed frequency distribution of the outcome gets closer and closer to the theoretical probability distribution.* When, we might ask, does the actual become *identical* to the theoretical—the same

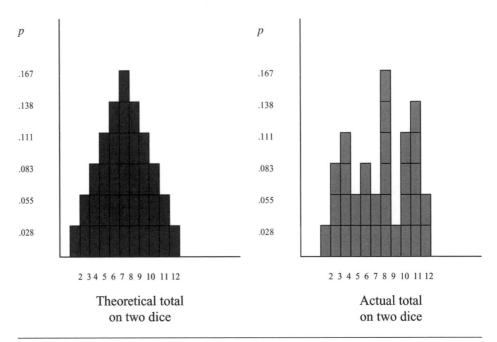

FIGURE 7.9   Comparison of theoretical and actual outcomes in 36 tosses of two dice.

proportions, the same mean, the same standard deviation, etc.? Well, naturally, when the number of tosses is infinite—this is to say, never in reality but certainly in theory.

As noted, most of us know this as the law of averages. However, statisticians prefer to call it *the law of large numbers*, for two reasons. First, this emphasizes that we can expect to see the theoretical distribution approach the real one only when the number of tosses, tries, samples, or whatever is being observed gets very large—so large that it approaches infinity. This happens because the theoretical probability distribution assumes conditions that cannot possibly prevail—for instance, that all faces of the die are always perfectly balanced. As the number of tosses increases, however, these "disturbing factors" tend to cancel each other out. And when the number is huge, their effects become minuscule.

The second reason for preferring the phrase "law of large numbers" is that the notion of a law of "averages" gives us false hope (or false pessimism, as the case may be) that things will "even out."[5] Things are definitely bound to even out, but unfortunately it might take an eternity or two. Some dice players find themselves in a situation in which they have thrown three "snake eyes" (1+1) in a row (this is an automatic losing toss in most games of craps). They then get ready for the next toss, saying: "Well, I can't get a 'snake eyes' this time, the law of averages is against it." Actually, the law of large numbers tells us nothing about a single toss. The probability of getting another 2 after throwing three of them in a row is the same as the probability of getting a 2 on your first toss of the evening, which is .028. In fact, it is the same probability as getting another 2 after throwing sixty-five 2s in a row, .028. The law of averages will not save a gambler on a bad streak (nor doom one on a good streak). However, don't we still wonder why such streaks occur? The technical statistical terms for these streaks are "bad luck" and "good luck." Not very helpful, is it?

Sampling Distributions as Theoretical Probability Distributions

Like the distribution of possible outcomes from tossing a pair of "perfect" dice, a sampling distribution is based on probability theory alone, not on actual observations. In particular, the sampling distributions to be employed in this and later chapters assume that all samples are of the pure random type.[6] In addition, they assume that all samples are independent (all units are replaced in the population each time a sample is drawn) and that infinitely many are selected from a population of unlimited size. In reality, of course, one cannot be assured of perfectly pure random samples, just as one cannot be entirely certain that a die is perfectly balanced. Nor can one attain an infinite number of samples in a finite amount of time. Nor are the populations from which we draw our samples unlimited in size. With this understood, however, sampling distributions do provide a useful—in fact, a crucial—tool to which we can compare our actual, imperfect, finite, and limited observations.

The "outcomes" and probabilities that make up a sampling distribution are derived from the assumption that once the size, n, of a random sample is determined, one can draw (with replacement) an unending succession of samples with n units from a never-exhausted population of such units. The population can be described by its parameters for any given variable—for instance, the average tuition of a large number of colleges and universities, or the standard deviation of their tuition rates.

Under these circumstances, each sample drawn can be described by its corresponding statistics, such as the average tuition for the n colleges and universities in your particular sample or the standard deviation of their tuition rates. These are symbolized as $\bar{x}_1, \bar{x}_2, \bar{x}_3, \ldots$, and $s_1, s_2, s_3, \ldots$, respectively, for each sample.

A sampling distribution, then, includes the set of all possible statistics of a certain type (all means, standard deviations, and so on) for samples of size n (see figure 7.10). As with other frequency distributions, this information is listed in the first column of a frequency table or along the horizontal axis of a frequency polygon. The other component of a sampling distribution, the one that occupies the second column of the table or is assigned to the vertical axis of the line graph, is the set of probabilities. These are the probabilities that a given sample mean will occur in any of an unlimited number of random samples of size n. Sampling distributions, like other probability distributions

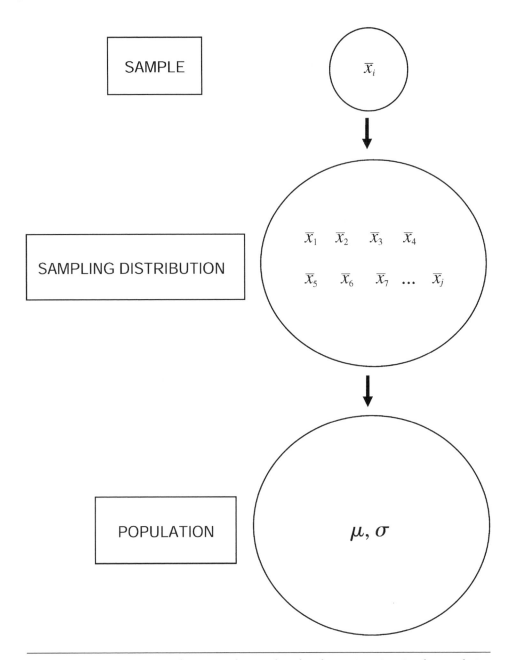

FIGURE 7.10   Comparing a sample mean to the sampling distribution in estimating the population parameters.

tossing dice, etc.), have central tendencies and dispersions, which are represented by means, standard deviations, and other parameters.

We begin our discussion with univariate distributions, focusing on one variable at a time. For most of the applications to follow, the statistic of greatest interest is the mean. Thus, for practical purposes, our attention is first directed to *the sampling distribution of means* (as opposed to the sampling distribution of other statistics, such as the standard deviation or the variance). Combining these stipulations with the previous general comments, we can define the sampling distribution of means as follows:

The set of all possible means of random samples of size n, and the probabilities of their occurrence, drawn from a population with a mean of μ and a standard deviation of σ.

A model of such a distribution is shown in table 7.6.

The sampling distribution of means that applies when these conditions hold has some very interesting and some very important properties that assist in the procedure of generalizing from sample to population. As we shall see in the next chapter, these properties depend to some extent on the size of *n*, with one version of the distribution used when *n* is large and another when *n* is small (below 30 or so). Before discussing these, however, let us first get an overview of how the sampling distribution is used.

Although the sampling distribution of means refers to an enormous number of samples and their means, the typical researcher can observe only one or, at most, a few

TABLE 7.6　A model sampling distribution of means

$\bar{x}$ *(sample means)*	p
$\bar{x}_1$	p_1
$\bar{x}_2$	p_1
$\bar{x}_3$	p_1
.	.
.	.
.	.
$\bar{x}_i$	p_1
.	.
.	.
.	.

The left column contains the set of means for a specific variable (e.g., tuition rate) of all possible samples of size *n* drawn from a single population. The right column lists the probabilities that the corresponding means will occur.

samples and means. However, if one can know where the value of his or her single mean lies relative to the value of all possible means, then the job of generalizing to the population from which all means (including the researcher's) are derived is made much easier. Moreover, if one can know not only the relative value of the observed mean, but also the probability with which it (and all other possible means) is likely to occur, then a major part of the inductive puzzle is solved. That is, the probability that the observed sample mean is equal to or at least close to the population mean can, with a little more information, be determined. And, as we have seen, with access to the sampling distribution of means, one can indeed know the relative value and the probability of occurrence of the observed mean. This, in greater detail, is what we meant when we said earlier that the often misunderstood aspect of induction is to go from the sample to the population indirectly, using the sampling distribution as an intermediate step. This is illustrated in figure 7.11.

To show how specifically this is done, we now need to examine the properties of the sampling distribution of the mean, beginning with the case of large samples. To help visualize these properties, we have taken several random samples of household incomes. In this illustration a small part of the sampling distribution was created by selecting not one or two samples but first 10, then 20, then 30, and finally 40 (see tables 7.7 and 7.8 and figure 7.12). This is certainly not the huge number of samples stipulated for the theoretical distribution, but it is enough to shed some further light on the relationship between populations, samples, and sampling distributions. Each sample in the illustration has an $n = 50$, and each was chosen randomly from the set of all householders residing in the suburb. The histogram for the population is shown in figure 7.12(a), and, as footnote noted in the table 7.8, the population parameters are $\mu = \$5,452.54$ and $\sigma = \$3,843.78$.

The tables and figure 7.12(b)–(e) show the partial sampling distributions as the number of samples depicted increases from 10 to 40. Perhaps the first thing to note is that in each case there are relatively few samples with very small means (low incomes) and relatively few with very large means (high incomes). On the other hand, as the size of the means approaches the center of each distribution, the number of samples with such means increases steadily. This is reminiscent of the distribution of tosses of dice as the outcomes approach 7 from both the high and the low sides. The reason for this is that in any given sample, the lower individual values (e.g., the incomes of the lower-earning households among the 50 selected) balance out the higher values (the rates of the higher-earning households among the 50). Thus, sample means tend to be less extreme than individual values. Similarly, sample means that are of moderate size are the most likely to be observed.

The result of this "few low, few high, many in the middle" pattern is a distribution that—as in the case of dice throws—is unimodal and symmetrical: the single mode, the median, and the mean coincide. In addition, because of the tendency for

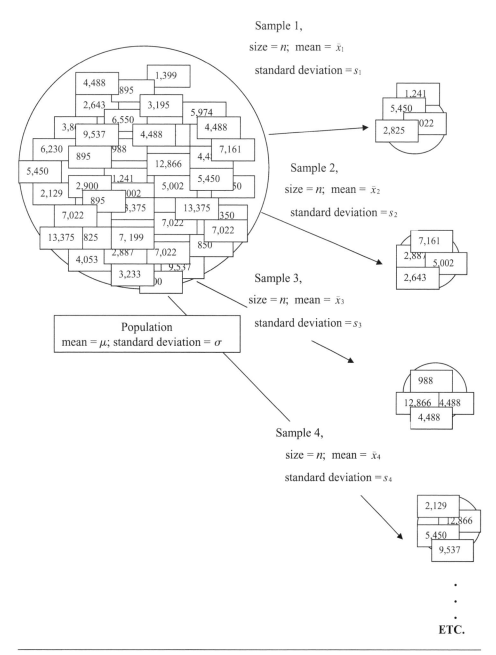

FIGURE 7.11   Drawing several samples of size *n* from a single population. Units are households and the variable is monthly income.

TABLE 7.7   Mean incomes of 40 random samples ($n = 50$) of households drawn from the same population

Sample number	$\bar{x}_i$	Sample number	$\bar{x}_i$
1	5756.08	21	5279.54
2	5851.70	22	5439.26
3	5259.40	23	5285.92
4	5857.12	24	5251.66
5	5874.88	25	5452.54
6	5688.60	26	6277.80
7	5207.53	27	5423.60
8	5378.06	28	6501.40
9	5559.36	29	5051.56
10	5317.48	30	6182.86
11	5555.96	31	6122.76
12	5465.34	32	4353.86
13	5002.33	33	5242.92
14	6130.00	34	4902.24
15	6012.76	35	5261.22
16	5776.47	36	4994.50
17	5797.74	37	5527.67
18	5580.62	38	4523.08
19	6297.92	39	4874.44
20	5960.70	40	5292.92

TABLE 7.8   Means and standard deviations of groups of sample means, taken 10, 20, 30, and 40 at a time

Number of samples	Mean of $\bar{x}_i$	Standard deviation of $\bar{x}_i$
10	5575.02	264.94
20	5666.50	329.75
30	5649.21	389.32
40	5514.30	477.22

Population parameters: $\mu = 5452.54$; $\sigma = 3843.78$; $\sigma / \sqrt{n} = 543.59$

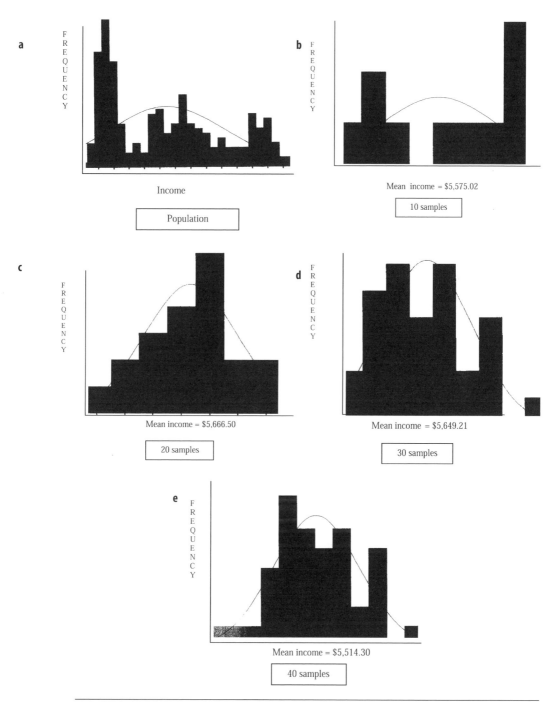

FIGURE 7.12 (a) Population distribution; (b–e) sampling distributions with different sizes.

low values to balance out high values, the sampling distribution is less dispersed than the population and therefore has a smaller variance and standard deviation. In fact, it is known that the standard deviation of the entire sampling distribution is smaller than the standard deviation of the population by a factor of $\sqrt{n}$. The larger the n, the greater the difference between the standard deviation of the population and the standard deviation of the sampling distribution. In our example with samples of $n = 50$ households, this indicates that the sampling distribution of means is only $1/\sqrt{50} = 1/7.07 = .141$, or 14.1%, as dispersed as the population from which the samples were drawn.

The standard deviation of the sampling distribution of means is known by a special name, which helps to avoid confusion with the standard deviation of the population and the standard deviations of all of the separate samples. It is called the *standard error of the mean*, and it is symbolized as $\sigma_{\bar{x}}$. By virtue of its relationship to the standard deviation of the population (σ),

$$\text{Standard error of the mean, } \sigma_{\bar{x}} = \frac{\sigma}{\sqrt{n}}.$$

Thus, the complete distribution of samples with $n = 50$ from the population of household incomes has a standard error of the mean equal to

$$\frac{\$3843.78}{\sqrt{50}} = \frac{\$3843.78}{7.07} = \$543.67.$$

You can see from table 7.8 that the standard deviation of the distribution of sample means does approach this amount as the number of samples increases, although with only 40 samples there is a still a difference of about \$66.00 (\$543.67 compared to \$477.22).

In examining the histograms in figure 7.12, you have probably noticed the smooth curve that is overlaid on each. You may also have recognized it as the familiar "bell curve," also known as the *normal curve,* which depicts the *normal distribution.*[7] This is meant to indicate that as the number of samples increases, the distribution comes closer to taking on the shape of the bell curve (see figure 7.13). Again, with only a tiny fraction of all possible samples depicted in these graphs, the shape is not very evident. But you can clearly see that the histograms approximate it more closely as the number of samples increases. This is a very important property of the sampling distribution of means:

When n is very large the distribution is normal.

This fact makes it possible to employ the sampling distribution in a very precise manner when generalizing from only one of the samples of which it is composed to the population from which all of the samples are drawn.

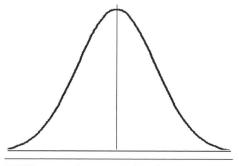

FIGURE 7.13   The normal distribution.

    The final property of the sampling distribution of means should not come as much of a surprise. With the complete distribution consisting of many, many samples—using k to stand for the total number of samples, we can sum all of the sample means in the distribution:

$$\bar{x}_1 + \bar{x}_2 + \cdots + \bar{x}_k = \sum_{i=1}^{k} \bar{x}_i.$$

If we then divide the sum by the total number of samples (k), we get the *mean of all sample means*:

$$\frac{\sum_{i=1}^{k} \bar{x}_i}{k},$$

where k is the (large) number of samples. This quantity, "the mean of means," will in fact equal the mean of the population from which the samples were drawn:

$$\frac{\sum_{i=1}^{k} \bar{x}_i}{k} = \mu.$$

    Table 7.8 shows that as the number of samples in the partial distribution increases, the mean of the distribution does indeed approach the population mean. We see at the bottom of the table that the population mean, $\mu = \$5,452.54$. This can be compared to the mean of the distribution of 40 samples, which is \$5,514.30. They are not identical; but even with so few samples, the difference is only about \$60.00.

    The reason that the mean of all sample means is equal to μ is that the small sample means balance out the large ones (just as small values in an observed frequency distribution balance out large ones). This occurs in such a way that the sum of the sample means smaller than the population mean will exactly equal the sum of sample means larger than the population mean. Thus, even when we have no direct knowledge about the population, if we can know something about the mean of the sampling distribution, then we can reliably assume that the same is true of the population mean. This, too, is an important key in using the sampling distribution in inductive applications.

Let us briefly review the properties of the sampling distribution of means before moving on to Chapter 8, where we put it to use in inductive statistics.

1. It is a theoretical frequency distribution based on the laws of probabilities.
2. It consists of the means (for a given variable) of samples of a fixed size (usually $n > 30$).
3. The samples are assumed to be randomly and independently selected.
4. The number of samples is extremely large, approaching infinity.
5. The distribution has the "few small means, many middle-sized means, few large means" shape. In fact, it is normal, as represented by the bell-shaped curve.
6. The mean of the distribution is equal to μ, the mean of the population from which the samples are drawn.
7. The standard deviation of the distribution is known as *the standard error of the mean*, symbolized as $\sigma_{\bar{x}}$. It is always smaller (indicating less dispersion) than the standard deviation of the population. In fact, it is equal to the standard deviation of the population divided by the square root of the sample size: $\sigma_{\bar{x}} = \sigma / \sqrt{n}$.

KEY TERMS

Addition rule: The rule of probability theory that applies to finding the probability of one outcome, A, *or* another, B. That is, the probability of A is *added* to the probability of B.

Converse rule: The rule of probability theory that applies to find the probability of an outcome, A, *not* occurring. That is, the probability of A is subtracted from 1.0.

Equiprobability: The method of sampling that seeks to ensure that the probability of any unit of a population being selected into the sample is the same as that of all other units.

Law of large numbers: The so-called law of averages. As the number of samples taken from a given population increases, and as the sizes of the samples increase, the distribution of sample statistics (especially the mean) becomes increasingly normal, or bell-shaped.

Multiplication rule: The rule of probability theory that applies to finding the probability of one outcome, A,

and another, B. That is, the probability of A is *multiplied* by the probability of B.

Multistage cluster sample: A type of probability sample in which units of a population are grouped into subpopulations referred to as "clusters" (usually geographically defined). These may, in turn, be subdivided into subclusters, etc. A sample of the clusters is chosen (and possibly a sample of subclusters chosen from these), and then a sample of units is selected from the chosen clusters (subclusters).

Non-probability sample: A type of sample in which units are selected from the population for the sake of convenience, to serve a specific purpose, or haphazardly. With this procedure, the probability of a given unit in the population being selected into the sample is unknown (and possibly unknowable).

Probability sample: A type of sample in which the probability that a given unit in the population will be selected into the sample is known.

Pure random sample: A type of probability sample that satisfies the conditions of equiprobability (see above).

Sampling distribution: The set of all statistics (especially the mean) of all possible samples of a given size drawn from the same population. Thus, *the sampling distribution of means* is the set of all possible sample means.

Sampling fraction: The size of a sample divided by the size of the population from which the sample is drawn. The reciprocal of sampling interval.

Sampling frame: The physical object such as a list or set of file cards that contains the names or symbols assumed to represent every member of a population. Technically, samples are drawn from sampling frames, not from populations directly. Statisticians are aware that sampling frames may include names or symbols that do not correspond to any member of the population, and that some members of the population may not be represented by a name or symbol in the frame.

Sampling interval: The size of a population divided by the size of a sample drawn from that population. The reciprocal of sampling fraction.

Standard error of the mean: The standard deviation of the sampling distribution of means, symbolized as $\sigma_{\bar{x}}$.

Stratified sample: A type of systematic sample for which the sampling frame is divided into subpopulations, or strata, in accord with attributes of a variable of interest (e.g., a stratum of all males and one of all females in the case of the variable "gender"). A random sample is then drawn from each stratum, usually to preserve the population proportion in each stratum.

Systematic sample: A sample that is selected from a sampling frame according to a desired sampling fraction. The first unit is usually selected randomly from the first sampling interval.

Theoretical probability distribution: A frequency distribution that is based not on observation but on an application of the rules of probability. The law of large numbers indicates that under certain conditions observed frequency distributions can approximate theoretical probability distributions.

WEB SITES TO BOOKMARK

1. http://link.springer.de/link/service/journals/00440
   The link to the leading journal *Probability Theory,* published in German and English. Online versions and an electronic sample copy are available.
2. www.math.niu.edu/~rusin/known-math/index/60-XX.html
   A great resource with dozens of links to probability topics, from the widely acclaimed *Mathematical Atlas.*
3. www.probabilitytheory.info
   "An in-depth but easily readable guide on probability theory, covering various aspects of the theory with a bias to gambling games and strategies. Includes working examples in an Excel spreadsheet."
4. www.probability.net

   A set of tutorials on probability, many of them at the advanced level.
5. http://trochim.human.cornell.edu/kb/sampling.htm
   An introduction to sampling posted by Cornell University. It includes a discussion of the distinction between probability and non-probability sampling methods.
6. http://trochim.human.cornell.edu/tutorial/mugo/tutorial.htm
   Another Cornell site, this consisting of a set of tutorials on sampling theory. This is a basic introduction and goes well with the discussion in this chapter.
7. http://www2.chass.ncsu.edu/garson/pa765/sampling.htm
   An excellent introduction to the logic of sampling posted by North Carolina State University.

SOLUTION-CENTERED APPLICATION

Using the library and/or Internet sources, gather some biographical information on the applied sociologist and statistician Leslie Kish (1910–2000). Be especially alert to material about his discovery of what we now call "margin of error." Using the information you have gathered, write a brief essay on Kish and his contributions to sampling theory.

Additional Solution-Centered Applications are combined with the SPSS Applications for this chapter in the *Study Guide*.

Induction

Using Sample Means in the Study of Diversity

A researcher interested in how a single, numerical-level variable is distributed in a population begins the exploration with a description of the characteristics of a sample of units drawn from that population. These characteristics include the frequencies of the variable's attributes and associated proportions or percentages, as presented in frequency distribution tables and graphs, and measures of central tendency and dispersion—especially the sample mean and sample standard deviation, $\bar{x}$ and s, respectively.

Let us review some relevant points about sampling made in Chapter 7: The size of the sample, designated as n, is ordinarily determined in advance on the basis of many considerations—scientific, practical, and financial. It was also emphasized that the method by which the n units are selected from the population into the sample is very important, more so even than n itself.

The method of selecting the sample is important because the goal of sampling is to select a set of units that is as representative of the population as possible. For, although we do observe the sample, it is almost always the case that our primary interest is in the population. Thus we would like to believe that what is true of the sample is (more or less) also true of the population and vice versa. In order to determine the extent to which a sample is representative, it is necessary to use one of the methods of selection categorized as *probability sampling*. As we have seen, the most direct way to achieve this aim is to pursue pure random sampling.

When we can assume that our sample of size n has been randomly selected, then we are able to use the sampling distribution of means introduced at the end of Chapter 7. The purpose of this sampling distribution is to "locate" our sample mean, $\bar{x}$, in relation to all possible means of all possible random samples of size n. Then, based on this location, we determine (more or less) the value of μ, the population mean. Our focus is first on the mean, and thus on its sampling distribution, because it is the single most important characteristic of a distribution of a numerical-level variable.

This chapter demonstrates and illustrates this process of moving from a statistic, in particular the sample mean, to a parameter, in particular a population mean, with the use of a sampling distribution. We begin with a close look at the normal or bell curve, whose shape the sampling distribution of means takes as the number of samples becomes very large, and a discussion of its role in inductive statistics. We then move on to consider another, closely related sampling distribution: the near-normal distribution of means of small samples. In these contexts, the central concept of the *confidence interval* is introduced and employed. Finally, once the basic principles relating to the role of the sampling distribution and the confidence interval are established, we conclude with the techniques of hypothesis testing. This last topic, which might be considered the "backbone" of inductive statistics, is then revisited in Chapter 9 and in each chapter that follows.

The Sampling Distribution of Means as Normal

As we saw in Chapter 7, for a single numerical-level variable, the sampling distribution of means of random samples with $n > 30$ has three key properties: (1) Its mean is equal to μ, the mean of the population from which the samples were drawn. (2) Its standard deviation (the standard error of the mean, or $\sigma_{\bar{x}}$) is equal to the standard deviation of the population, σ, divided by the square root of n, $\sigma_{\bar{x}} = \sigma/\sqrt{n}$. (3) It is a normal distribution—it has the shape of the bell curve. In this section we examine this third condition, the fact that the distribution is normal.

Properties of the Normal Distribution

The normal distribution is a very important theoretical probability distribution that occurs in numerous contexts in the physical, biological, and social sciences. As a theoretical distribution, one can never expect to find an exact replica of it in any actual observations of empirical phenomena. In fact, most of the phenomena studied by scientists do not exhibit anything like a normal distribution. On the other hand, some real-world variables do tend to have distributions close to that of the ideal normal one, and these include the means of random samples as the number of samples becomes very large.

Two points need to be stressed here before continuing. First, we want to be clear about the difference between (a) the *size* of *a specific* sample, n, which must be greater than 30 for the assumption of normality to hold, and (b) the *number of samples* of a given size, which must be very large indeed before the normal shape is clearly approximated. Second, because it is theoretical, the sampling distribution for a variable is normal whether or not its distribution in the population or in any of the individual samples is approximately normal. In fact, depending on the variable involved, it is highly unlikely that the population or any sample will be even remotely normal, but that is irrelevant to the shape of the sampling distribution (see figure 8.1).

Like all normal distributions, the sampling distribution of means is symmetrical, with the mean, median, and mode all coinciding at the value of the population mean (μ). Therefore, exactly 50% of all possible sample means (the $\bar{x}$'s) equal or are greater than μ, and 50% equal or are less than μ. Because the mode and mean of the sampling

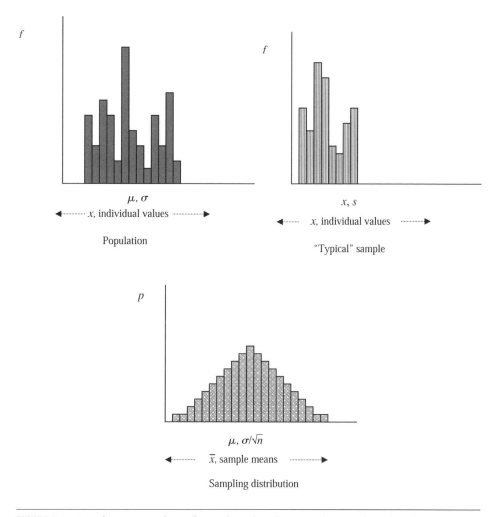

FIGURE 8.1   Population, sample, and sampling distribution. The sampling distribution is normally distributed regardless of the shape of the population distribution or the distribution of any sample.

Few very low values   **Few very high values**

Frequencies increase as values approach the mean

FIGURE 8.2   The shape of the normal distribution.

distribution coincide, the value of the sample means with the highest frequency is, in fact, μ. Expressing this in probability terms, the mean of any given random sample drawn from the population (for instance, the mean of *your* selected sample), has an equal chance, $p = .5$, of being above or below the population mean, and the most likely value of your mean is μ. Looking at figure 8.2, we can extend this assessment even further. The probability is very low that your sample mean will be very much smaller than the population mean, and the probability is equally low that it will be very much larger. But the probability that the value of your sample mean will occur increases the closer it gets to the population mean, from either the low or the high end of the distribution.

Estimation and Error

Knowledge of your sample mean, thus, allows you to make a fairly good guess about the value of the population mean. Without any information other than the value of your sample mean, what do you suppose would be the best guess—or, technically, "estimate"—about the value of the population mean? Obviously, the best estimate is that the two are equal: $\mu = \bar{x}$. If you are very lucky and it happens to turn out that the sample and population means are equal, then you could say that there was *no error* whatever in your estimation.

This difference between a sample mean and the mean of the population from which the sample is drawn, is called

$$(Sampling)\ error = \bar{x} - \mu.$$

If the two means were equal, then the error would be 0.

Of course, we cannot realistically expect no error at all. Yet it is unlikely that the population mean will be much greater than or much less than your sample mean. For example, selecting the 10th random sample from the population of households discussed in Chapter 7 (see table 7.7), $\bar{x} = \$5,317.48$. Based on this, your best single value estimate of μ would be $\$5,317.48$, and, in any case, you would expect it to be about $\$5,300$. You would surely not want to estimate μ to be something as low as $\$1,500$ or as high as $\$10,000$, because (1) such population means are next to impossible and (2) the expected error, $\bar{x} - \mu$, would be unreasonable. As table 7.8 shows, the actual $\mu = \$5,452.54$. The error using the 10th sample is thus ($\$5,317.48 - 5,452.54) = -\$135.06$; the estimate is about $\$135$ too low. Would you agree that this is a good guess?

The Concept of Confidence Interval

Now, we might ask, is it possible to be more precise about such estimates than simply using such phrases as "good guess," "far off," and "about"? The answer is yes. One can be more precise about estimating parameters from statistics and, in particular, population means from sample means, using a sampling distribution. To do so, however, one must be willing to accept two conditions.

Condition 1: The first condition is that we can never be absolutely sure—in other words, never 100% confident—about the characteristics of the whole (the population) given knowledge only about a part (the sample). The best we can do in this regard is to be 95% confident or 99% confident or some other *level of confidence* less than 100%. With this, of course, we are also admitting that if we are only 95% confident, then we could be wrong 5% of the time; if we are 99% confident, then we could be wrong 1% of the time; and so forth.

The phrase "level of confidence" is commonly used to describe estimates of the mean, as discussed below. The degree to which we might be wrong (e.g., 100% – 95% = 5% or 100% – 99% = 1%) is expressed as a probability rather than a percentage: e.g., .05 and .01. It is referred to as the *level of significance* and is symbolized by the lowercase Greek alpha, α. We return to this later.

You can see that the estimation procedure does not provide us with *certain* knowledge about the value of the parameter, μ in our case. Rather, it indicates what is most likely to be its value at a stated level of confidence. In fact, common practice in social statistics—which will be followed from this point on—is to employ the 95% confidence (.05 significance) and 99% confidence (.01 significance) levels exclusively (although technically speaking any other level is legitimate).

Condition 2: The second condition that relates to estimating a parameter (μ) from a statistic ($\bar{x}$) is that one can never be very confident in stating an *exact* value of the parameter. Instead, it is more sensible to indicate a range of values, or an *interval* within which the parameter is likely to occur. Moreover, the larger the interval, the more confident we are. If, as illustrated above, our sample mean = $5,317.48, it would be difficult to say that we were very confident that there was no error if we were to state that the exact value of μ is $5,317.48. That is why we are inclined to say "about $5,300."

Defining "Confidence Interval"

We can make this a little more exact, and we can feel more confident, by suggesting that μ is likely to lie within a specific interval—for example, the interval between $5,000 and $5,500. As with grouped data in frequency distributions, the smaller value is called the "lower limit" and the larger value is the "upper limit." We could also choose a wider interval, say between $4,500 and $6,000, and feel even more confident. In fact, if we could choose a huge interval, e.g., between $1,500 and $10,000, we would be almost certain that the value of μ is somewhere between these generous lower and upper limits.

Unfortunately, the more confident we are, the less exact we can be; and the more exact we must be, the less confident we are. This is as much the situation in daily life as it is in statistical applications. If someone asked you to estimate the starting annual income of your next job, you would be hard-pressed to blurt out a figure such as $48,345.75. You would be somewhat more confident to estimate something between $40,000 and $55,000. And you could be all but certain about an interval between $1.00 and $1 million.

Taking these comments together, we can now introduce the central concept of the *confidence interval*. First, a definition:

A confidence interval, abbreviated CI, is a *range of values above and below a sample mean within which one is confident that a given percentage or proportion of all possible means lie.*

As noted, this given percentage is, for our purposes, either 95% or 99%. If the population mean turns out to be exactly equal to the sample mean, then there is no error. But as one moves closer to the lower and to the upper limits of the interval, the amount of error increases to the point at which it surpasses the allowable 95% or 99% boundaries.

It is for this reason that the quantity used to determine this range of values around $\bar{x}$ was first referred to by L. Kish (see Chapter 7) as the *margin of error*, or ME. This quantity is subtracted from the sample mean to determine the lower limit of the range and added to the sample mean to determine the upper limit. Thus,

$$\text{The 95\% or 99\% CI} = \bar{x} \pm \text{ME},$$

where the 95% and 99% intervals each have their own ME. With a mean score ($\bar{x}$) on an exam equal to 75 points, and the ME for 95% calculated to be 5 points, the 95% CI would be $75 \pm 5 = (75 - 5)$ to $(75 + 5) = 70$ to 80. We would be 95% confident that the population mean (μ) has a value between 70 and 80 points. Next, we see how the appropriate margin of error is determined.

Finding the Margin of Error

With the concept of confidence interval in mind, let us now return to the sampling distribution of means. Because it is a normal distribution, the sampling distribution of means has an "architecture" that is completely and exactly known. This knowledge comes from the formula for the function and curve introduced in Chapter 7, which translates the value of any given sample mean, $\bar{x}$, into the probability that such a value will occur (using the mathematical constants $\pi = 3.14159\ldots$ and $e = 2.71828\ldots$). To make matters easier, this knowledge has been incorporated into a table well known to statisticians and reproduced as table A.1 in Appendix A.

Because the formula and tables of the normal distribution are used for so many different applications, one cannot take advantage of them merely by using the raw score of our sample mean. After all, some sampling distributions refer to tuition in dollars, others to exam scores in percentages, others to educational attainment in years attending college, and so forth. However, as we saw in Chapter 6, if one has access to a raw score, the mean of the distribution in which the raw score occurs, and the standard deviation of the distribution, one can translate it into a "twice-cooked" score known as the standard or z score. Fortunately, the formula and tables for the normal distribution are always arranged to accommodate z scores. In this way, the units used or the scale of values for our sample means are irrelevant, because the "cooking" process (standardization) cancels them out. That is, to use the formula or table for values of the normal curve, raw scores must be translated into z scores.

Recall the two steps for finding the z score:

1. Subtract the raw score from the mean. This produces the deviation.
2. Divide the deviation by the standard deviation. This translates the deviation into standard deviation units.

These steps allow you to compare your scores with any other set of standard scores regardless of the variables or units of measure employed. This follows from the observation that the best definition of the standard score is in words rather than symbols, because symbols change depending on the application:

$$z = \text{deviation/standard deviation.}$$

In Chapter 6 this procedure was applied to convert individual raw scores (x_i) into z scores in a sample where the sample mean, $\bar{x}$, and standard deviation, s, were known. In that case, the *deviation/standard deviation* formula was symbolized as $z = (x - \bar{x})/s$. Now we can apply this procedure to convert sample means into z scores in a sampling distribution whose mean (μ) and standard deviation, the standard error of the mean ($\sigma_{\bar{x}} = \sigma/\sqrt{n}$), are known. Here, the formula is:

$$z = \frac{x - \mu}{\sigma_{\bar{x}}}.$$

The z produced in this formula expresses the sample mean as a certain *number of standard error units from the mean* of the sampling distribution (which is always equal to the population mean). Recall that, as a standard deviation, a standard error unit is a kind of average: the "average" difference between sample means in the distribution and the mean of the distribution (which equals μ).[1] If a sample mean and the population mean are equal, then $\bar{x} - \mu = 0$ and $z = 0$. That is, a sample mean whose value is the same as the population mean is zero standard error units from the population mean.

If the difference between a sample mean and the population mean happens to equal the standard error of the mean, that is, if $\bar{x} - \mu = \sigma_{\bar{x}}$, then $z = \sigma_{\bar{x}}/\sigma_{\bar{x}} = +1.0$. Such a sample mean is exactly one standard error unit *above* the population mean. If the difference between a sample mean and the population mean happens to be negative and equal to the standard error of the mean, that is, if $\bar{x} - \mu = -\sigma_{\bar{x}}$, then $z = -\sigma_{\bar{x}}/\sigma_{\bar{x}} = -1.0$. Such a sample mean is exactly one standard error unit *below* the population mean. If $\bar{x} - \mu = \pm 2\sigma_{\bar{x}}$, then $z = \pm 2$. If $\bar{x} - \mu = \pm\frac{1}{2}\sigma_{\bar{x}}$, then $z = \pm 0.5$, and so on.

Table A.1 can be used to find the probabilities for the occurrence of $z = 0$, $z = \pm 1.0$, $z = \pm 2.0$, $z = \pm 0.5$, and every other possible value of z from 0 and above. (Like other tables of this type, table A.1 ends at a relatively large z value—in this case ± 3.09, because higher z values are rare and the probabilities of their occurring are small, although they can be calculated if necessary.) Values of z to one decimal place (tenths) are found in the first column. Each entry in the top row allows us to find z to two decimal places (hundredths): 0.00, 0.01, 0.02, etc. The entries in the body of the table indicate the probability that a score lies between the mean and a given z value either added to or subtracted from the mean. All z values in the table are positive, but the table is equally valid for negative values, because the normal distribution is symmetrical. Thus, the probability associated with a specific *z* value that lies above the mean (e.g., *z* = +1.5), with exactly the same as the probability associated that *z* value below the mean, e.g., *z* = –1.5.

The table represents one-half or 50% of the entire distribution, from the mean to the upper limit or from the mean to the lower limit. Thus, to find the probability that a value lies *beyond* a given *z* (to the right/above or left/below), we subtract the entry corresponding to that *z* value from .50. Suppose, for example, that we have calculated a *z* value of 1.31. To find the probability that a score lies between the mean and *z* = 1.31, first locate 1.3 in the first column (1.3 is in the 14th row). Then, note from the top row of the table that 0.01 is in the third column. The entry in the 14th row, third column is .4049. This indicates that the probability of a score lying between the mean and 1.31 standard deviation units above is a little more than 0.4 (4 chances in 10). The probability that a value lies above 1.31 (or below –1.31) units is equal to .5000 – .4049 = .0951. The probability is just under 1 in 10. Note that .4049 and .0951 add to .50

The entries in table A.1 can be expressed in several different ways. Because they are probabilities, they can easily be stated as proportions and/or when multiplied by 100 as percentages. In the first case, they represent the proportion of all sample means in the sampling distribution whose values lie between *z* and *μ* or whose values lie beyond *z* (subtracting the table entry from 0.5). In the second case, they represent the percentage of all sample means in the sampling distribution whose values lie between *z* and *μ* or whose values lie beyond *z* (subtracting the table entry from 0.5) will be selected randomly. And, perhaps most informative of all interpretations, the entries represent the percentage or proportion of the entire area under the bell curve that lies between *z* and *μ*, or beyond *z*.

To illustrate, if we go down the first column until we reach *z* = 1.0 and locate the entry in the second column (for *z* = 1.00), we find the number .3413. Subtracting .3413 from .5 we find .1587. Read as percentages, these indicate that

- 34.13% of all sample means lie between the mean of the population and a given sample mean with a standard score of *z* = +1.0 or *z* = –1.0
- 15.87% of all sample means lie beyond a given sample mean with a standard score of ±1.0.
- Also, 68.26% (34.13% + 34.13%) of all sample means lie *between* sample means with *z* scores between –1.0 and +1.0.

Stated as probabilities, these entries indicate that the probability of selecting a sample whose value lies between the population mean and a *z* score of +1.0 is .3417. Also, the probability of selecting a sample whose value lies between the population mean and a *z* score of –1.0 is .3413. And the probability of selecting a sample whose mean lies beyond a *z* of ± 1 is .1587. Stated in relation to area under the bell curve (see figure 8.2), these entries indicate that 34.13% of the area lies between the mean and a *z* score of +1.0. The same percentage lies between the mean and a *z* score of –1.0, and 15.87% of the area lies beyond a *z* score of ±1.0.

TABLE 8.1   Finding confidence intervals with σ known

	Proportion or percentage		
z^a	*Between z and μ*	*Between –z and +z*	*Beyond z*
±2.00	.4772 or 47.72%	.9544 or 95.44%	.0228 or 2.28%
±0.50	.1915 or 19.15%	.3830 or 38.30%	.3085 or 30.35%
±0.33	.1293 or 12.93%	.2586 or 25.86%	.3707 or 37.07%
±1.96	.4750 or 47.50%	.9500 or 95.00%	.0250 or 2.50%
±2.58	.4951 or 49.51%	.9900 or 99.00%	.005 or 0.50%

$^a z = (\bar{x} - \mu) / \sigma_{\bar{x}}$.

The table can also be used in the other direction. That is, if we are given the probability, proportion, or percentage between an unknown z score and μ, or beyond an unknown z score, the z score can be determined. This is done by finding the given probability in the body of the table or by subtracting the entry for the corresponding z score from .50. By going across to the first column, we find z to one decimal place. By moving up to the first row, we find the second decimal place. For example, if we are told that .224 of all sample means lie between the mean and z, we can see that $z = \pm 0.59$. If we know that .115 of the sample means lie beyond z, we subtract .115 from .500, which equals .385. Locating the proper row and the proper column, we can see that for the entry .3849 (which rounds to .385) $z = \pm 1.2$.

Finally, if we know that .95 of all sample means lie between $-z$ and $+z$, we also know that one-half of .95 = .475 lies between μ and $+z$, and the same proportion, .475, lies between μ and $-z$. Finding .475 in column (b), we see that the corresponding z =1.96. Thus, .95 of all sample means lie between $-1.96z$ and $+1.96z$. Table 8.1 shows some additional sets of z scores and the corresponding proportions, probabilities, or percentages—all derived from table A.1.

Of special interest are the last two rows in table 8.1, that for ±1.96 and that for ±2.58. As the third column of each of the rows indicates, these two z scores encompass 95% and 99% of all possible sample means, respectively. It is from these rows that we obtain the information necessary to create the corresponding 95% and 99% confidence intervals. The arithmetic is straightforward. Let us begin with the 95% CI.

From the table and the curve itself we see that 47.5% of all possible sample means lie between μ and a z score of 1.96 standard error units ($\sigma_{\bar{x}}$) above μ, or in the interval ($\mu + 1.96\sigma_{\bar{x}}$). Similarly, 47.5% of all sample means lie between μ and a z score that is 1.96 standard error units ($\sigma_{\bar{x}}$) below μ, or in the interval ($\mu - 1.96\sigma_{\bar{x}}$). Combining the two, (47.5 % + 47.5%) = 95% of all possible sample means lie between $+1.96\sigma_{\bar{x}}$ and $-1.96\sigma_{\bar{x}}$.

Recalling that our purpose here is to estimate an (ordinarily) unknown population mean from a sample mean, this application of the normal curve to the sampling distribution of means requires one further logical step. The value of the population mean is equal to the value of at least one possible sample mean. In fact, we know that the population mean is equal to the sample mean with the highest frequency, because it coincides with the mode of the distribution. Thus the interval that includes 95% (or any other percentage) of all possible sample means also includes 95% of all population means.[2] With this noted, we see that $\pm 1.96\sigma_{\bar{x}}$ is the ME for the 95% CI. By the formula CI $= \bar{x} \pm$ ME,

The 95% confidence interval around $\bar{x}$, a known sample mean $= \bar{x} \pm 1.96\sigma_{\bar{x}}$.

This same reasoning applies to the 99% CI, except that the correct number of standard error units is 2.58 rather than 1.96. In this case, ME $= \pm 2.58\sigma_{\bar{x}}$, and

The 99% confidence interval around $\bar{x}$, a known sample mean $= \bar{x} \pm 2.58\sigma_{\bar{x}}$.

To illustrate the use of confidence intervals, let us return once again to our set of household incomes. Earlier we had assumed that our selected sample was the 10th from table 7.7, whose mean $\bar{x} = \$5,317.48$. We observed that with this information alone, our best estimate of the population mean (μ) would of course be $5,317.48. However, it is unlikely that this will be an "error-free" estimate, so it would be more appropriate to state a reasonable range of population means within which the actual μ is likely to fall. To achieve this, we now determine the 95% CI around the sample mean. As the note to table 7.8 indicates, we happen to know the value of σ, which is $3,843.78.

It will not always be the case that σ is known. In fact, it is most *un*likely that π will be known in real-world applications. After all, our purpose in using confidence intervals is to estimate μ. But if σ is known, then μ must also be known (it is required for calculating σ), so why estimate it? We shall soon make adjustments for this reality, but for the moment let us continue to assume that we know the exact value of σ. Of course, we always know n, the sample size, because we selected the sample. Thus, under these conditions it is easy to derive the standard error of the mean, $\sigma_{\bar{x}}$. That is, $\sigma_{\bar{x}} = \$3,843.78/\sqrt{50} = \$3,843.78/7.07 = \$543.59$.

We can now calculate the 95% CI by the formula $\bar{x} \pm$ ME. First find the margin of error:

$$\text{ME} = 1.96\sigma_{\bar{x}} = 1.96(\$543.59) = \$1,065.44.$$

Substituting in the formula, the 95% CI $= \bar{x} \pm$ ME $= \bar{x} \pm \$1,065.44$. Next, we subtract the margin of error from and add it to the sample mean of $5,317.48:

$$\$5,317.48 - \$1,065.44 = \$4,252.04$$

$$\$5,317.48 + \$1,065.44 = \$6,382.92.$$

Our 95% CI = $4,252.04 to $6,382.92. We are confident that 95% of the time, the mean of the population from which our sample was drawn will lie in this range. Conversely, we are also aware that 5% of the time (or, expressed as a proportion, .05) the population mean will lie outside of this range: it will be higher .025 of the time and lower .025 of the time. Because we are in the unusual position of actually knowing the population mean, which is $5,452.54, we can verify that in this case our estimate is correct (see figure 8.3).

The 99% CI is similarly found using 2.58 as our *z* value. First find the margin of error:

$$ME = 2.58\sigma_{\bar{x}} = 2.58(\$543.59) = \$1,402.46.$$

The margin of error in this case is $1,402.46, which is larger than that for the 95% CI, which was $1,065.44. As we noted earlier, this is because when we seek to be more confident, we also need more leeway.[3] Thus, the 99% CI will always be wider than the 95% CI.

Next, we subtract the margin of error from and add it to the sample mean of $5,317.48:

$$\$5,317.48 - \$1,402.46 = \$3,914.54$$

$$\$5,317.48 + \$1,402.46 = \$6,719.94.$$

Our 99% CI = $3,914.54 to $6,719.94. We are confident that 99% of the time, the mean of the population from which our sample was drawn will lie in this range. Comparing this to the population mean of $5,452.54, we see that it falls within the 99% CI as well. This will always be the case. That is, if a population mean falls within the 95% CI, then it will certainly fall within the 99% CI, because the 95% CI as a whole falls within the 99% CI. However, it is possible for a given *μ* to fall outside of the 95%

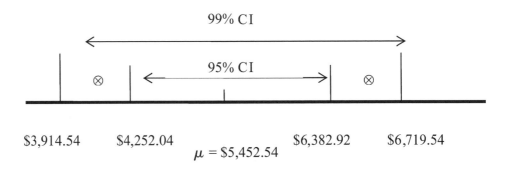

FIGURE 8.3   95% and 99% confidence intervals.

but inside the 99% CI. This possibility is denoted by the hypothetical values marked with an ⊗ in figure 8.3.

Because the illustration using household incomes is based on a series of 40 random samples drawn from the same population (for which the mean is known), we can make an interesting experiment by reversing the procedure used to derive the formulas for the 95% and 99% confidence intervals.

Looking at the data from table 7.7, we see that only one sample mean out of 40 (sample 30, with $\bar{x}$ = $6,182.86), or 2.5% of all of the sample means, falls outside of the 95% CI, and none of them fall outside of the 99% CI. This result is even better than what could be expected by chance, and it verifies—not absolutely, but with 99% confidence— that the samples shown in the table were in fact selected at random.

Additional discussion of using the normal distribution to establish confidence intervals around proportions can be found in Chapter 15 online at http://www.romanlittlefield .com/RL/Books/Weinsteinstats/.

Estimating Confidence Intervals When σ Is Not Used

There are two conditions, mentioned briefly above, under which we may not assume that the sampling distribution of means is distributed normally or that its standard error does equal $\sigma / \sqrt{n}$. The first is when the size of the sample, n, is small, usually considered to be less than 30. With samples this small, there is likely to be more error (a greater difference between sample means and μ) than is estimated by standard error of the mean. Thus, the confidence intervals that would be created if $\sigma_{\bar{x}}$ were employed would be too narrow, and too many population means would fall outside such intervals than is allowable by probability theory. However, as n increases to 30 and above, this problem becomes negligible.

The second condition that rules out the assumption of a normal distribution having a standard error of $\sigma / \sqrt{n}$ is both more common and more obvious. It arises when the standard deviation of the population, σ, is not known. In this case, the researcher has no choice but to avoid using $\sigma_{\bar{x}}$. Because the numerator of $\sigma_{\bar{x}} = \sigma / \sqrt{n}$ is σ, the standard error of the mean simply cannot be calculated. The reason that this condition is so common is that researchers rarely do know σ, unless they have information from an outside source (for instance, about another, very similar population).

If we are faced with either or both of these conditions, certain conventional substitutions are made in calculating the margin of error that, in turn, affect the size of the confidence intervals. The first substitution comes in determining an alternative to $\sigma_{\bar{x}}$. Because it is used in place of the standard error of the mean, the alternative is known as the *estimated standard error of the mean*, and it is symbolized as $s_{\bar{x}}$. As you may have gathered from this symbol, it is not based on σ, as is the standard error of the mean.

Because we do not have access to the value of σ, the estimated standard error is based on s, the standard deviation of the sample that is being observed and around which we wish to create the confidence intervals. This, of course, is always known or can be easily calculated, along with the mean and all other features of the sample. The formula for the estimated standard error of the mean is similar but not identical to that for the standard error itself. Let us compare them.

1. Standard error of the mean: $\sigma_{\bar{x}} = \sigma / \sqrt{n}$.

2. Estimated standard error of the mean: $s_{\bar{x}} = s / \sqrt{n-1}$.[4]

In the numerator of $s_{\bar{x}}$, s is directly substituted for σ. In the denominator of $s_{\bar{x}}$, we see that $n - 1$ is substituted for n (in each case the square root is taken). Recall that the effect of the denominator is to reduce the size of the error in relation to the standard deviation in the numerator. The effect of using $n - 1$ instead of n in the second equation the second is to make the denominator smaller and the whole fraction larger.[5] This adjustment is made, in part, because the standard deviation of a sample, the numerator of $s_{\bar{x}}$, is virtually always smaller than the standard deviation of the population from which the sample was drawn. Subtracting 1 from n brings the value of $s_{\bar{x}}$ closer to that of $\sigma_{\bar{x}}$, thus making the former a more accurate estimator of the latter. The $(n - 1)$ factor is obviously an adjusted sample size. It is referred to as the degrees of freedom, or *d.f.* (this important statistical concept is defined in the "Key Terms" section of this chapter and, in greater detail, in Chapter 10). Thus, in the application under discussion, if $n = 50$, *d.f.* = 49; if $n = 34$, *d.f.* = 33, etc.

At this point, it *appears* that we can redefine the 95% and 99% confidence intervals when n is small and/or σ is not known:

$$95\% \text{ CI} = \bar{x} \pm 1.96(s_{\bar{x}})?$$

$$99\% \text{ CI} = \bar{x} \pm 2.58(s_{\bar{x}})?$$

Before we take these formulas too seriously, let us quickly note the "?" after each. These indicate that the formulas, although seemingly logical, are *not* correct. Here the problem is that the z or standard scores of 1.96 and 2.58 are based on the normal distribution, as mapped out in table A.1.

However, with a small n and/or lacking knowledge of σ, we can no longer assume that the sampling distribution of means is perfectly normal (although it is obviously close to being normal). Thus, neither these nor any other z scores are appropriate. As was the case with σ and n in the standard error of the mean, the standard (z) scores need to be replaced in the estimated standard error. In particular, they are too small. Because the standard error is being estimated, we want to *increase* the margin of error—to give ourselves more leeway. And to do this, we want to substitute *larger* values for 1.96 and 2.58, respectively.

This is accomplished through the use of an alternative theoretical probability distribution, well known to statisticians as the *t*, or Student's *t*, distribution.[6] The formula for this distribution is similar to the one for the normal distribution, as indicated by these common features:

1. The means of the normal (*z*) distribution and the *t* distribution are both equal to the means of the populations from which the samples were drawn.
2. Both distributions are symmetrical.
3. Both have the characteristic "few low scores, many middle scores, few high scores" shape.

Values of the *t* distribution are shown in Appendix table A.2. Consequently, using table A.2, we substitute *t* scores for the *z* scores. The *t* scores, too, are "twice-cooked" in that they are deviations divided by standard deviations. However, they reflect the fact that we are using the estimated as opposed to the actual standard error of the mean. Let us compare them:

(1)
$$z = \left(\frac{\bar{x} - \mu}{\sigma_{\bar{x}}} \right)$$

(2)
$$t = \left(\frac{\bar{x} - \mu}{s_{\bar{x}}} \right)$$

Based on formula (2), we can now state properly the formula for confidence intervals when *n* is small and/or σ is not known:

The CI around $\bar{x}$, a known sample mean $= \bar{x} \pm ts_{\bar{x}}$.

where the *t* is derived from table A.2 (not table A.1). The same formula is used for the 95% and the 99% CIs, but the value of *t* will be different depending on which CI we are calculating.

All that is necessary now is to determine how these *t* values are derived from table A.2. The first thing to be noticed is that in this table, and in each table that follows, we focus not on the levels of confidence (95% and 99%) but on the complementary *levels of significance*, .05 and .01. These are indeed equivalent, except that instead of emphasizing the *percentage* of the time we expect to be correct (to have a population mean lie *within* the interval) we emphasize the *probability* of being incorrect (of having a population mean that lies *outside* of the interval). As mentioned earlier, the universally recognized symbol for level of significance is the lowercase Greek alpha: α. So, we can make the following translations: The 95% CI is the same as α = .05; the 99% CI is the same as α = .01. The first step in using table A.2, then, is to select the desired CI and the corresponding α and go to that column.

The next step in finding the correct t value for our confidence interval is to determine a number known as *degrees of freedom*, symbolized as *d.f.*[7] This allows us to adjust the t value based on the size of the sample. For these applications,

Degrees of freedom, or d.f. = $n - 1$.

Note that *d.f.* is the same value as the $(n - 1)$ in the denominator of $s_{\bar{x}}$.

Once we calculate *d.f.*, we can select the appropriate row. Because this is an abridged table, not every possible value of *d.f.* is shown. If the value we seek is not listed, the rule is to round to the closest *lower* number on the table: e.g., if our *d.f.* is 47 and only 40 and 50 are given, we round *down* to 40. The effect of this is, once more, to increase the margin of error. The entry that is at the intersection of the proper column for α and the proper row for *d.f.* (rounding considered) is the t value we seek. This value will always be larger than 1.96 for α = .05 and larger than 2.58 for α = .01. Notice, however, that as you move down the .05 or .01 column, the closer the table t value gets to 1.96 or 2.58, respectively. In the last row, indicating a very large $n - 1$, t *does* equal 1.96 and 2.58.

In other words, as $n - 1$ increases, the closer the table t values are to z values. This is because there is actually a different t distribution for each value of *d.f.*; and the larger the *d.f.*, the closer the distribution is to being normal. As shown in figure 8.4, we can think of each row of a t table as a single probability distribution. Although selected values of α are listed, the complete row actually includes every value of α from 0.5 down to 0.

As $n - 1$ increases, the curve of the theoretical frequency distribution, which is symmetrical, becomes less and less "spread out." This is because its dispersion as measured by the standard error $(s_{\bar{x}})$ is becoming smaller. You can also see that its shape is becoming less and less flat and increasingly peaked. This property, the degree to which a distribution's shape is flat or peaked, is referred to as *kurtosis*.[8] A flat distribution is called *platykurtic* (from the Greek word for "flat"; think of a "plateau"); a peaked distribution is called *leptokurtic* (from the Greek word for "thin"). A distribution whose shape is somewhere in between is called *mesokurtic (meso* meaning "middle"). In these terms, as the t distributions increase in degrees of freedom, they become less platykurtic and more leptokurtic. Similarly, a sampling distribution is more leptokurtic than the associated population distribution.

Illustration When σ Is Not Known, for Any Sample Size

To illustrate the procedure for finding confidence intervals with the t distribution, we use two examples from earlier discussions. The first is based on the assumption that

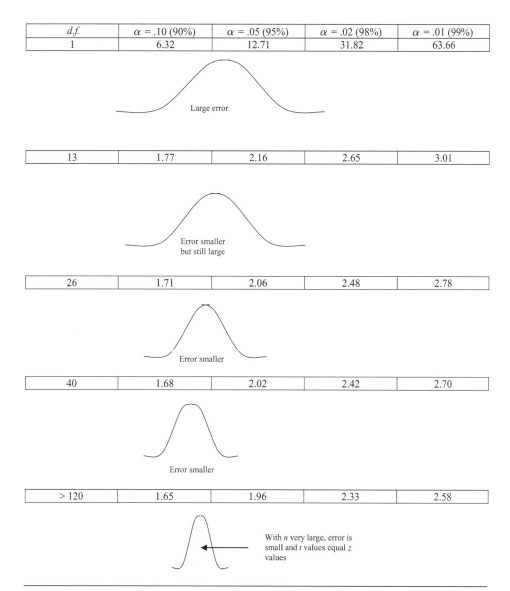

d.f.	α = .10 (90%)	α = .05 (95%)	α = .02 (98%)	α = .01 (99%)
1	6.32	12.71	31.82	63.66

Large error

13	1.77	2.16	2.65	3.01

Error smaller
but still large

26	1.71	2.06	2.48	2.78

Error smaller

40	1.68	2.02	2.42	2.70

Error smaller

> 120	1.65	1.96	2.33	2.58

With *n* very large, error is small and *t* values equal *z* values

FIGURE 8.4   Table *t* values. Table *t* values are large when *d.f.* is small. The *t* values measure standard error, which has *n* in the denominator. Thus, when *n* (and therefore *n* – 1) is small, the error is large. As *n* increases, standard error decreases and the *t* values get smaller as they approach the standard error of the normal distribution.

the standard deviation of the population is not known, although the sample size is not especially small. The second uses a small sample.

You will recall that one of the samples, the 10th, from the set of household incomes was used to create the 95% and 99% CIs with σ known. It will be instructive to use the same sample, but to disregard σ (pretending we never saw it). This will allow us to use the sample standard deviation, s, and the t distribution. The mean of the sample, whose $n = 50$, was calculated to be $5,317.48. We also calculated the standard deviation, which turned out to be $3,750.80.

With this information alone, we can create the two confidence intervals. First, we calculate the estimated standard error of the mean, $s_{\bar{x}}$. With $s = \$3,750.80$,

$$s_{\bar{x}} = \frac{s}{\sqrt{n-1}} = \frac{\$3750.80}{\sqrt{50-1}} = \frac{\$3750.80}{\sqrt{49}} = \frac{\$3750.80}{7} = \$535.84 \;.$$

Next, we calculate the margin of error:

$$\text{ME} = ts_{\bar{x}}.$$

At this point we need to find the value of t from table A.2. For the 95% CI, we look down the $\alpha = .05$ column, and with $d.f. = n - 1 = 50 - 1 = 49$, we round to 40. The entry at $\alpha = .05$, $d.f. = 40$, is 2.021, somewhat larger than 1.96, as expected. It is this value that we substitute for t in the equation for ME. That is,

$$\text{ME} = 2.021(\$535.84) = \$1,082.93.$$

The 95% CI $= \bar{x} \pm \text{ME} = \bar{x} \pm \$1,082.93$. With $\bar{x} = \$5,317.48$, subtracting and then adding ME gives us

$$\$5,317.48 - \$1,082.93 = \$4,234.55 \quad \text{and}$$

$$\$5,317.48 + \$1,082.93 = \$6,400.41.$$

The 95% CI is $4,234.55 to $6,400.41. We estimate that 95% of all possible population means lie in this interval.

Because we also used the same sample to create confidence intervals with σ known, we can make some direct comparisons. As calculated above, the margin of error with σ known is $1,065.44, and the 95% CI is $4,252.04 to $6,382.92. As figure 8.5 indicates, there is really not very much difference between the actual margin of error and the CI derived from the normal distribution and those estimated using the t table. The estimate errs on the side of lower confidence, which is to be expected, so that some sample means that actually lie outside of the interval under the normal

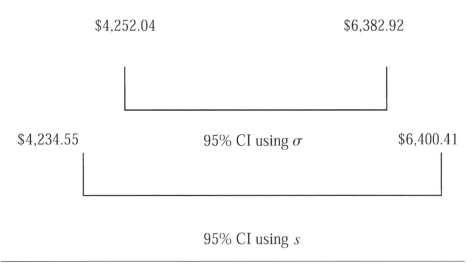

FIGURE 8.5   Comparative CIs.

curve fall within the interval created with the *t* distribution. But the difference is only about $18.00 on each end.

To calculate the 99% CI around the sample mean, $\bar{x}$ = $5,317.48 (assuming that σ is not known), all that is required is to select a new *t* value from table A.2, because we have already found the value of $s_{\bar{x}}$ to be $535.84 in establishing the 95% CI. Thus, the 99% CI = $5,317.48 ± *t*($535.84).

The correct *t* value now comes from the .01 column of table A.2, again at *d.f.* = 49 (rounded to 40). This turns out to be 2.704 (which is greater than 2.58). The margin of error in this case is, thus,

$$\text{ME} = 2.704 \times \$535.84 = \$1{,}448.91.$$

Subtracting this amount from and adding it to the sample mean, we get $5,317.48 − $1,448.91 = $3,868.57 and $5,317.48 + $1,448.91= $6,766.39.

The 99% CI is $3,868.57 to $6,766.39. We estimate that 99% of all possible population means lie in this interval.

We can once more compare this outcome with the margin of error and, here, the 99% CI with σ known. As calculated above, these are ME = $1,402.46 and 99% CI = $3,914.54 to $6,719.94. In this case the difference between the actual margin of error derived from the normal distribution and that estimated using the *t* table is about $46 on either side. Again, the estimate errs on the wide side, but here too it is quite close to the actual value.

Illustration with a Small Sample

Whether or not σ is known, when the size of our sample is small, the correct procedure for establishing confidence intervals is to use the estimated standard error of the mean, $s_{\bar{x}}$, and the t distribution (table A.2). For our illustration, we use the example introduced in Chapter 4 in which 15 dorm students, who (we assume) were selected randomly, were asked to indicate the number of times they traveled home during the semester. The table of responses is reproduced as table 8.2.

These data can be used to answer a question concerning the most likely average number of trips taken by the population of all dorm students from which the sample was drawn. First, we calculate the sample mean and standard deviation:

$$\bar{x} = \frac{\sum_{i=1}^{6} f_i x_i}{15}$$

$$s = \sqrt{\frac{\sum_{i=1}^{6} f_i (x_i - \bar{x})^2}{15}}$$

Note the "6" at the top of the summation sign, indicating the number of attribute values rather than the number of students.

$$\bar{x} = \frac{0 + 2 + 6 + 12 + 8 + 10}{15} = \frac{38}{15} = 2.53$$

$$s = \sqrt{\frac{\sum_{i=1}^{6} f_i (x_i - 2.53)^2}{15}}$$

TABLE 8.2   Table of responses

Number of trips (x)	*f*
0	2
1	2
2	3
3	4
4	2
5	2
	$n = 15$

$$= \sqrt{\frac{35.73}{15}} = \sqrt{2.38} = 1.54.$$

With this information, we can now calculate the ME.

$$ME = ts_{\bar{x}} = t\left(\frac{s}{\sqrt{n-1}}\right) = t\left(\frac{1.54}{\sqrt{14}}\right) = t\left(\frac{1.54}{3.74}\right) = 0.41t.$$

With $d.f. = 14$ and $\alpha = .05$, the value of t from table A.2 is 2.145. Thus,

$$ME = 2.145(0.41) = 0.88.$$

$$95\% \text{ CI} = \bar{x} \pm ME = 2.53 \pm 0.88.$$

Subtracting the ME from and adding it to the sample mean, we get

$$2.53 - 0.88 = 1.65$$

$$2.53 + 0.88 = 3.41.$$

The 95% confidence interval is 1.65 to 3.41. We can be confident that 95% of all population means lie within this range.

The corresponding 99% CI is calculated similarly, except that a different value of t is required. Looking down the $\alpha = .01$ column of table A.2, at 14 degrees of freedom, we see that the value is 2.977. This number replaces the 2.145 in the calculations above. Thus, the new margin of error = 2.977(0.41) = 1.22 (as expected, larger than the ME for the 95% CI). The 99% CI = (2.53 − 1.22) to (2.53 + 1.22) = 1.31 to 3.75. We can be confident that 99% of all population means lie within this range.

BOX 8.1   ## Statistics for Sociologists

Diversity and Induction Using Sample Means

As a sociological concept, *diversity* refers to the extent to which a group, organization, or other aggregate consists of individuals with a variety of social characteristics. The opposite of "diversity" is uniformity. In this sense, a university whose student body includes minorities of different backgrounds (African American, Latino, and others) as well as non-minorities, women as well as men, etc., is said to be more diverse than one made up only of white males.

Diversity in Higher Education

In the view of most sociologists, and as expressed in the official policy of the American Sociological Association,[*] the effectiveness of a society's democratic political system can be judged by the diversity of its institutions. Since the landmark *Brown v. Board of Education* Supreme Court decision in 1954, the major focus of applied research in this area has been on race and gender in the educational institution, especially in the United States.[**] The most commonly used standard for measuring diversity is adapted directly from sampling theory: The student body of a school, including a college or university, should achieve a level and type of diversity that accurately represents the diversity of the general population from which the student body is drawn. Thus, if students come from a population that is about 50% male and 50% female, the student body should also be one-half male and one-half female.

Anyone who follows the news is well aware that there are numerous unresolved issues surrounding diversity in higher education, especially with regard to race and ethnicity. Questions have been raised about whether or not such diversity should be sought, about how it can or should be achieved, and about several related matters. The lawsuit and subsequent decision concerning the University of Michigan's admissions policy (*Gratz v. Bollinger* and *Grutter v. Bollinger*) constitute perhaps the most widely publicized example of this controversy.[***]

An Example Using the Sample Mean (σ Not Known)

Policies and programs intended to address issues of diversity in higher education are bound to be complex and controversial for many years to come. Regardless of the outcome, they will require a base of knowledge that includes a measure of how diverse the student bodies of our colleges and universities actually are and how far they differ from the "general population" criterion. In the following example, the procedure for estimating a population mean (μ) from a sample mean ($\overline{x}$) is used to provide such information.

Table 8.3 lists diversity data for a sample of $n = 10$ randomly selected states. Included for each state are the percentages of all minorities and of the two largest minority groups: African American and Latino. Columns 2, 3 and 4 list the percentages in the general population of each state, and columns 5, 6 and 7 list the percentages enrolled

---

[*] See www.asanet.org/cs/root/leftnav/governance/diversity_statement.
[**] The ruling by Chief Justice Earl Warren is online at www.nationalcenter.org/brown.html. The study on which the ruling is substantially based was conducted by an interdisciplinary team led by Nobel Prize–winning sociologist and economist Gunnar Myrdal (1944). It established the foundation for subsequent applied research in this field to the present, and it continues to be widely cited.
[***] A summary of the events is at www.lib.umich.edu/govdocs/affirm.html.

TABLE 8.3   Minority college and university enrollment for 10 states

State	% in population			% enrolled		
	All minorities	African American	Latino	All minorities	African American	Latino
California	40.5	6.7	32.4	53.0	7.7	25.7
Florida	22.0	14.6	16.8	39.6	18.1	17.8
Iowa	6.1	2.1	2.8	9.5	4.4	2.5
Louisiana	36.1	32.5	2.4	35.8	30.7	3.4
Maryland	36.0	27.9	4.3	37.6	27.1	3.7
Montana	9.4	0.3	2.0	13.0	0.6	1.5
New York	32.1	15.8	15.1	33.4	14.1	11.2
Oregon	23.4	1.6	8.0	15.3	2.3	5.1
Tennessee	19.8	16.4	2.2	22.3	19.4	1.7
Washington	18.2	3.2	7.5	20.7	4.2	5.3
$\bar{x}$	24.4	12.1	9.4	28.0	12.9	7.8

Sources: Snyder, T., S. Dillow, and C. Hoffman 2007. *Digest of Education Statistics, 2006*. NCES Number: 2007-017. Washington, DC: National Center for Education Statistics; United States Census Bureau.

in the colleges and universities of each state. The last row contains the means for the sample on each of the variables.

As the means indicate, the average minority enrollment for the 10 states is 28.0%, compared to 24.4% in the general populations. For African Americans, the respective averages are 12.1 and 12.9. For these two groups in the sample, the criterion of representativeness appears to have been achieved or surpassed. The only exception is the Latino group, whose average percentage enrolled is 7.8 but whose average percentage in the general populations is 9.4.

Table 8.4 summarizes these comparisons in showing the diversity levels of each state. These are differences between the percentages of the groups enrolled and the percentages in the general populations. Here a level of 0 would indicate that the percentage enrolled and that in the general population were exactly equal: diversity is achieved according to the criterion of representativeness. A level above 0 indicates that the enrollment percentage exceeds the standard, and a level below zero indicates that enrollment is below the standard.

Looking at the individual states in table 8.4, we see that every state in the sample but Louisiana and Oregon has achieved or surpassed diversity with respect to all minority groups. All the sample states but Louisiana and New York have done so with respect to the African American group. Only Louisiana, however, has done so with respect to the Latino group. Based on these sample findings alone, we might conclude that, on

TABLE 8.4   Differences between diversity in higher education and general population diversity

State	All minorities	African American	Latino
California	+12.5	+1.0	−6.7
Florida	+17.6	+3.5	−1.0
Iowa	+3.4	+2.3	−0.3
Louisiana	−0.3	−1.8	+1.0
Maryland	+1.6	+0.8	−0.6
Montana	+3.6	+0.3	−0.5
New York	+1.3	−1.7	−3.9
Oregon	−8.1	+0.7	−2.9
Tennessee	+2.5	+3.0	−0.5
Washington	−2.5	+1.0	−2.2
$\bar{x}$	+4.5	+1.3	−1.9
10 states	+3.6	+0.8	−1.6

the whole, the 50 states of the United States do have diverse enrollments in higher education, with the possible exception of Latino enrollments.

Yet we do, or can easily, derive additional information that will allow us to make a better-informed generalization. Not knowing the standard deviations (σ) for all 50 states, we can still calculate the sample standard deviations (s) and the estimated standard errors of the mean ($s_{\bar{x}}$), and, using $n = 10$, create the 95% and 99% confidence intervals.

Table 8.5 lists the respective deviations and squared deviations in the diversity levels for the "all minorities" category. As shown at the right of the bottom row, the sum of the deviations squared, $\sum_{i=1}^{n}(x_i - \bar{x})^2 = 439.0$. The sample variance, $s^2 = \sum_{i=1}^{n}(x_i - \bar{x})^2 \Big/ n$ $= 439.0/10 = 43.9$. The standard deviation is thus $s = \sqrt{s^2} = 6.63$. The estimated standard error of the mean $s_{\bar{x}} = s/\sqrt{n-1} = 6.63/\sqrt{9} = 6.63/3 = 2.21$.

To create the 95% confidence interval, symbolized as $\bar{x} \pm \text{ME}$, we first must calculate ME, the margin of error. Because σ is not known (and also because n is less than 30), we will use the formula $\text{ME} = ts_{\bar{x}}$. Therefore, we need to use table A.2 in the Appendix at the appropriate α and degrees of freedom, *d.f.* A 95% CI corresponds to an $\alpha = .05$. The *d.f.* $= (n - 1) = (10 - 1) = 9$. We see that the table t value at $\alpha = .05$ and *d.f.* = 9 is 2.26. Thus, $\text{ME} = ts_{\bar{x}} = (2.26) \times (2.21) = 4.99$.

With $\bar{x} = 3.66$, the 95% CI $= \bar{x} \pm \text{ME} = 3.66 \pm 4.99$. Subtracting and adding ME, the interval ranges from −1.33 to +8.65.

To find the 99% CI, the ME must be recalculated based on the table t value with α at .01 (*d.f.* and all of the other values are unchanged). At $\alpha = .01$ and *d.f.* = 9, the table t

TABLE 8.5   Diversity levels: raw scores and deviations

State	All minorities	$\left(x_i - \overline{x}\right)$	$\left(x_i - \overline{x}\right)^2$
California	+12.5	+8.8	78.2
Florida	+17.6	+13.9	194.3
Iowa	+3.4	+0.3	0.1
Louisiana	−0.3	−4.0	15.7
Maryland	+1.6	−2.1	4.2
Montana	+3.6	−0.1	0.0
New York	+1.3	−2.4	5.6
Oregon	−8.1	−11.8	138.3
Tennessee	+2.5	−1.2	1.3
Washington	+2.5	−1.2	1.3
	$\overline{x} = +3.66$		439.0

value is 3.25. The new ME is (3.25) × (2.21) = 7.18, so the 99% CI is $\overline{x} \pm$ ME = 3.66 ± 7.18. Subtracting and adding ME, the interval ranges from −3.52 to +10.84.

We can now say that we are confident that 95% of all possible mean diversity levels for the 50 states lie between −1.33 and +8.65 and that 99% lie between −3.52 and +10.84. Recall that a score of 0 would indicate exact agreement between the percentage of minorities in the general population of the states and the percentage enrolled in higher education; a positive or negative score would indicate diversity in higher education that is above or below the state standard, respectively. Based on the confidence intervals, we would conclude that the set of 50 states probably have achieved diversity in education, although there are scores within the range (0 to −1.33 for the 95% CI and 0 to −3.52 for the 99% CI) that are below standard.

If it is decided that programs to improve diversity are desirable, our findings suggest that they are not needed uniformly in all 50 states, at least not for the "all minorities" category. It is likely that, as a whole, the set of 50 states are close to or even above the standard. Yet, as we have seen, some of the states in our sample are below the standard for this category, and several are below for the Latino group.

Postscript

Data are available that allow for a comparison, although not a perfectly exact one, between our sample results and the relevant population characteristics. For the United States as a whole (not broken down by state), the percentage of all minorities in the general population is 24.9. Similarly, the percentage of all minorities in the student bodies of colleges and universities is 30.4. Thus, the diversity level is 30.4 − 24.9 = +5.5. This is an above-standard level, and it falls within our confidence levels.

Summary

The procedure for creating a confidence interval around a population mean is the foundation of inductive statistics. In the preceding discussion, we have examined and illustrated this procedure, with a special emphasis on the following points:

- A characteristic of the sample, a statistic—in this chapter it was always the mean—is used to estimate the value of a corresponding characteristic (mean) of the population from which the sample was drawn. This corresponding characteristic is a parameter.
- We generally estimate a likely range within which the parameter (the population mean) lies. This range is the confidence interval.
- The confidence interval is derived by adding and subtracting a margin of error (ME) to and from the statistic.
- The margin of error differs according to (a) whether the sample is small and/or (b) whether the standard deviation of the population is known.
- One can never be absolutely sure that the parameter falls within a given confidence interval. Instead, conventional levels of confidence/significance have been established: (a) 95% or $\alpha = .05$ and (b) 99% or $\alpha = .01$ (where α stands for level of significance).

In the chapters that follow, these basic principles are applied to a wide variety of research situations the social statistician is likely to encounter. You may find it useful to return to the preceding discussion to remind yourself of these principles.

KEY TERMS

Confidence interval (CI): A range of values above and below a sample mean within which one can expect the mean of the population (from which the sample is drawn) to lie a certain percentage of the time. The most common percentages are 95% and 99%.

Degrees of freedom (d.f.): The number of pieces of information needed to determine the probability that a parameter of interest (such as a population mean) will occur. This is based on n in all applications to numerical variables.

Estimate: A measure of a parameter that is based on sample information and used when population information is unknown.

Estimated standard error (of the mean): The estimate of the standard deviation of a sampling distribution, used when σ is not known.

Level of confidence: The percentage that defines a confidence interval, such as 95% and 99%. It is the percentage of time the researcher expects to be correct in making decisions about parameters.

Level of significance: The proportion that defines the part of the sampling distribution that lies outside of a confidence interval. It is the maximum proportion of time the researcher is willing to be incorrect in making decisions about parameters. It is symbolized as α and is equal to (100 – level of confidence)/100.

Margin of error (ME). The value that is added to and subtracted from a sample mean to determine a confidence interval. Its value depend on the value of the standard error (or estimated standard error) and the appropriate z or t value for the given CI.

Normal (Gaussian) distribution: A theoretical probability distribution whose graph is the familiar bell curve. The sampling distribution of means approaches normal as the number and size of samples increase.

Student's t: The statistic used to estimate population means when σ is not known and/or when n is small (designated by the pen name of its inventor).

WEB SITES TO BOOKMARK

1. www.stat.sc.edu/~west/javahtml/ConfidenceInterval.html
   An interactive site maintained by the University of South Carolina. "By changing alpha, students can see how the confidence intervals are affected by this parameter. Also, students can get a good idea of what a confidence interval really means in terms of covering the true mean."

2. www.ruf.rice.edu/~lane/stat_sim/conf_interval
   Another interactive site: "simulates sampling from a population with a mean of 50 and a standard deviation of 10. For each sample, the 95% and 99% confidence intervals on the mean are created."

3. www.cas.lancs.ac.uk/glossary_v1.1/confint.html
   This site, at the University of Lancaster, England, provides definitions of "confidence interval" and related terms.

4. www.ncspearson.com/research-notes/sample-calc.htm
   Calculation of confidence intervals that also works in reverse to determine n if the CI is given.

5. http://davidmlane.com/hyperstat/A42408.html
   See this site for a clear definition of "degrees of freedom" and how they are related to the estimation of parameters from statistics.

SOLUTION-CENTERED APPLICATIONS

1. Using the discussion and tables in Box 8.1, create the 95% and 99% CIs for the African American and Latino diversity levels, following the procedure used for the "all minorities" groups. What would you conclude about the performance of the 50 states with respect to these two groups?

2. From your regional census data set, select a random sample of $n = 10$ (you may use one of the samples created in the applications in Chapter 7). For one of the numerical variables, such as total population size, find the sample mean. Construct both the 95% and 99% confidence intervals around this mean, $\bar{x}$, and determine whether the population mean, μ, lies within or outside of this interval. Based on these results, indicate what this says about the representativeness of your sample.
   (*Hint*: You already know s, or you can calculate it).

3. A Midwestern state recently completed a study of its community policing (CP) programs in medium-sized cities. There are approximately 850 cities of this type. They encompass an average of 24 square miles, with a mean population size of approximately 65,000. The study suggested that, despite the fact that these are not major metropolitan areas, there were frequent complaints about response times for CP calls. In considering several possible solutions to this problem, the researchers decided to explore the option of purchasing two-way cellular systems for foot and bicycle patrols and for off-duty personnel (in addition to the traditional car police radios). One important factor to consider was the cost of these new systems. If they decreased response time by less than 5 minutes, then they were not worth purchasing. If they decreased the response time by more than 10 minutes, then an alternative and more powerful system was justified. However, any improvement between 5 and 10 minutes would make the new system cost-effective.

   To test this option, a random sample of 16 cities was chosen from throughout the state and an experimental two-way cellular system was begun in each. Following the initial trials, three pieces of information were collected for each city: (a) its

TABLE 8.6   Table for Solution-Centered Application 3

City	Population (thousands)	Geographic area (sq. mi.)	Response time improvement (minutes)
A	68	18	4.0
B	82	14	−3.8
C	35	42	10.5
D	44	20	12.0
E	80	26	7.0
F	46	12	9.0
G	60	32	15.0
H	70	34	7.5
I	90	40	−2.0
J	47	19	12.3
K	66	25	11.5
L	37	30	4.3
M	62	20	0
N	73	18	6.8
O	41	31	8.2

[a]Negative response time improvement indicates an increase in response time.

total population size, (b) its geographic area, and (c) its improvement (or increase, as designated by a − sign) in response time. The data collected are shown in table 8.6.

The researchers sought to answer three questions—two about the sample and one about the performance of the new system.

- Was the average population size of the sample cities representative of the state average?
- Was the average geographic area of the sample cities representative of the state average?
- Did the outcome of the experiment suggest that the system would be cost-effective for all of the medium-sized cities of the state?

Using the data in the table and the techniques introduced in this chapter, indicate how the researchers should have answered these questions and their reasons.

Hypothesis Testing

The Foundation of Sociological Theory

The procedure for testing hypotheses lies at the very heart of inductive statistics. It provides the researcher with a set of formalized steps for generalizing from observations made of a sample of units, assumed to be randomly drawn from a population, to the population itself. The procedure can be applied to a broad range of topics in sociology and in many other fields as well. The three chapters that follow this one (10 through 12) focus on hypothesis testing, with each featuring a certain type of hypothesis. However, all of these types share some important common features that are best understood when presented and illustrated in a separate, general discussion. Thus, the next few pages outline the basic hypothesis-testing procedure to be applied in later chapters. In this way, some of the rules, symbols, and the like need only to be introduced once. For the sake of illustration, we draw on the concept of univariate confidence intervals, covered in Chapter 8, and extend their use to hypothesis-testing situations.

Because of its theoretical emphasis, this chapter does not include Solution-Centered or IBM SPSS Statistics Base Applications.

Stating Hypotheses

You will recall from Chapter 1 that a hypothesis is a declarative sentence that states an educated guess about the attributes of one or more variables, and that the variable or variables describe a sample of units under observation. We also noted that the testing process involves establishing whether or not a hypothesis is supported by comparing it with observations. If it is supported, we say we "accept" it; if not, we "reject" it.

Because hypotheses ideally are derived from theories, researchers usually have some clues—beyond the sentences themselves—concerning why they might be supported, how to go about establishing whether or not they are supported, which of the variables is the dependent and which is/are independent, and so on. However, when learning about the testing procedure, as we are doing in this book, we often need to make assumptions about such matters without adequate knowledge to guide us. The rule of thumb that we will follow in such circumstances is that it is better to make a bad assumption than to make none at all. Often when we have made our decision to accept or reject a hypothesis under such conditions, we can correct inappropriate assumptions with the new information gained.

All of the hypotheses to be considered in the following chapters state that something is (or is not) true of the population from which the sample is drawn. Yet the data upon which we base our decisions to accept or reject are derived from the sample we observe. That is, we observe the statistic and we come to a conclusion about a parameter. As we learned in Chapters 7 and 8, this inductive "leap" is accomplished by relying on sampling distributions. Thus, all of the hypothesis-testing procedures to be considered employ sampling distributions such as the normal (z) and t distributions, for which values are listed in the tables in Appendix A.

Researchers state hypotheses because they believe that a certain outcome would occur if data were available to substantiate the belief. For example, as in the illustration in Chapter 1, social scientists might have reason to believe that a certain type of city in the United States (large, industrial, and northern) has a relatively high crime rate. But until they actually determine the crime rates of a set of such cities, their hypothesis remains a guess. The type of hypothesis that indicates what the researcher expects to find is, accordingly, called a *research hypothesis*, and it is symbolized as H_r.

As the sociologist of science Robert K. Merton (1968) famously characterized it, scientific research is "organized skepticism" (the concept was introduced in Chapter 2). In the spirit of organized skepticism, researchers are encouraged to be as skeptical as possible about their own beliefs, and to go out of their way to prove themselves wrong. If, after questioning as rigorously as possible their own assumptions and observations, they find that they simply cannot conclude that they were mistaken, then they "reluctantly" admit that they may be right. It is this spirit that is embodied in the procedure of testing hypotheses. We do not directly test the research hypothesis we believe to be true. Rather, we examine evidence that would support the very opposite hypothesis, referred to as the *null hypothesis*, symbolized as H_0. If a research hypothesis states that "students prefer evening classes," the null hypothesis would state "students *do not* prefer evening classes."

All of the techniques and tables used in the remainder of this book—and throughout the field of statistics—are arranged to test the null rather than the research hypotheses, with the following understanding. If the null hypothesis is accepted, then the research hypothesis is rejected and the researcher's expectations are shown to be unsupported. If the null hypothesis is rejected, then the research hypothesis is accepted and the researcher's expectations are shown to be supported. For example, the null hypothesis that would actually be tested in the study of cities mentioned above is "H_0: Large, industrial northern cities do *not* have relatively high crime rates."

Decisions and Probabilities

Hypothesis testing in statistically oriented social research depends on the use of confidence intervals. The convention introduced in Chapter 8 of using the 95%/.05 or the 99%/.01 level of confidence/significance is thus applied to this procedure. One can never be absolutely certain of being right in accepting or rejecting a null hypothesis. One cannot say, "I have proved this null hypothesis to be correct." Rather, the most that can be said is "I believe that my conclusion will be correct 95% (or 99%) of the time, but there is a .05 (or .01) chance that my decision is wrong." For example, after urban researchers examine a set of cities in order to make an accept-or-reject decision, their conclusion would be something along these lines: "We reject the null hypothesis at the $\alpha = .01$ level. We are 99% confident that, based on our sample, the large, industrial, northern cities of the country do have relatively high crime rates."

Because of the inability of researchers to be certain in hypothesis-testing situations, statisticians recognize four possible outcomes that bear on our decisions. As shown in table 9.1, the researcher either accepts or rejects a null hypothesis about a population that is not observed. The decision is based on sample statistics. Now, in the actual population, the parameters of interest may or may not accord with the decision. Although we might wish that the parameters and statistics would always agree in this manner (the situation of zero error), we know that the use of samples inevitably introduces an element of doubt.

We see in table 9.1 that cells (1) and (4) indicate correct decisions. In the first cell this is because the null hypothesis is accepted and it should be accepted. In the fourth cell it is because the null hypothesis is rejected and it should be rejected. Cell (2) represents an error referred to as a Type I error or α (alpha) error. It is the mistake of rejecting the null when it should be accepted. It is this type of error that we control by establishing confidence intervals or levels of significance. By indicating that we select $\alpha = .05$ or .01, we are saying that we are willing to reject a null mistakenly 5% or 1% of

TABLE 9.1   Decision table: accepting and rejecting hypotheses

Actual situation	*Decision based on statistics*	
Population parameters	*H_0 is not rejected*	*H_0 is rejected*
Support the null	(1) Correct decision	(2) Type I, α error
Do not support the null	(3) Type II, β error	(4) Correct decision

the time, but no more. Cell (3) represents Type II or β (beta) error. This occurs when we accept a null hypothesis when it should be rejected. Techniques for controlling this type of error, via the application of the concept of the "power" of a test, are discussed in more advanced statistics texts.

In recognition of the important role that probability plays in hypothesis testing, statisticians have developed a set of simple and consistently applied steps to be used in the procedure. We present these steps here and illustrate them in the following section. We then apply them in each chapter from this point on.

1. We first state the null and research hypotheses in symbols and also in words. For example, if we believe that the population mean for a given variable such as crime rate has a nonzero value, our research hypothesis in symbols would be:

    H_r: $\mu \neq 0$. Or, in words, "The mean crime rate in the population is not zero."

    The null hypothesis would be:

    H_0: $\mu = 0$. Or, in words, "The mean crime rate in the population is zero."

2. We calculate a statistic based on $\bar{x}$ and other observed data such as n, s, and s_x. Ordinarily this statistic is a standardized or other kind of "cooked" score. This is the *calculated* statistic. Conversion from a raw to a "cooked" score is necessary to control for the measurement units (dollars, rates, exam scores) and the scale of the variable's attributes. This allows us to refer the data to a standard distribution such as z and t.

3. We then consult the appropriate table and decide whether to use $\alpha = .05$ or $.01$. Once this choice is made, we calculate the appropriate degrees of freedom, which is usually based on n. Recall that $d.f. = n - 1$ when we use the t distribution to create a confidence interval around a sample mean. The selected α and the correct $d.f.$ allow us to identify a *table* statistic.

4. We then *compare the calculated statistic to the table statistic.* Our decision to accept or reject H_0 follows this rule: If the calculated statistic is smaller in absolute value than the table statistic, we accept the null hypothesis. If the calculated statistic is greater than the table statistic, we reject the null hypothesis, as shown in table 9.2.

TABLE 9.2   Decision based on
calculated and table values

Result of calculation	*Decision*
Calculated < table	Fail to reject H_0
Calculated > table	Reject H_0

5. When the null hypothesis is rejected, we say that the calculated statistic is *significant.* This is because it has proved to be large enough (in absolute value) to surpass or "beat" the corresponding table value. When we accept the null hypothesis, we say that the calculated statistic is *not significant,* for it has failed to surpass or "beat" the table value. For this reason, the test of a hypothesis is alternatively referred to as a significance test.

The Critical Region and One- and Two-Tailed Tests

The curve of a sampling distribution, such as z (normal) and t, has a body and two tails (see figure 9.1). The tails are the portions of the curve that lie at the extreme ends along the horizontal axis. One of these is the left or *negative* tail. In a sampling distribution of means it encompasses the lowest possible values of sample means that can be drawn from the designated population. The other is the right or *positive* tail, and it encompasses the highest possible values that can be drawn from the designated population. The body is the portion of the curve that lies between the tails.

Nearly all of the tests we will be performing are two-tailed, with the important exception of the one-tailed t-test, to be discussed in Chapter 10. Yet even in the one-tailed situation, we are not saying that the curve has only one tail. Rather, it indicates that our interest is focused on only one of the tails, the negative or the positive, according to the

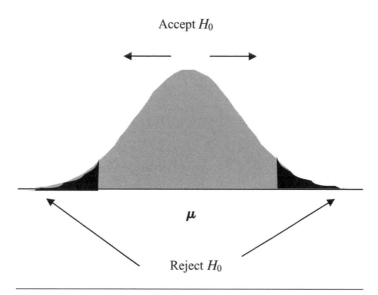

FIGURE 9.1   Body and tails of a sampling distribution indicating acceptance and rejection regions.

hypothesis being tested. The role played by the tails in hypothesis testing is summed up in the concept of *critical region*.

The Critical Region for Two-Tailed Tests

We have already touched upon the idea of a critical region, without using the term, in the context of our discussion of confidence intervals in Chapter 8. We can now make the connection. When we lay out the 95% or 99% confidence interval along the horizontal axis of the curve of a sampling distribution, as shown in figure 9.2, the mean of the distribution divides the interval in half. A small portion of the curve lies beyond the interval at both the left and right ends. Taken together, these portions that are outside of the confidence interval constitute the *critical region*. Added together, and stated as proportions, they make up either .05 or .01 of the total area under the curve. These, of course, are our two commonly used levels of significance, the α's. When we divide these equally between the two tails, we get .025 and .005, or 2.5% and 0.5%, respectively. These principles guide us in testing two-tailed hypotheses.

It might already be obvious that the critical region contains those values of the variable (means, proportions, etc.)—expressed as a z, t, or other kind of "cooked" score—that indicate that we reject the null hypothesis. Conversely, the values that do not fall within the critical region, because they lie within the confidence interval, indicate acceptance of the null hypothesis. Thus, when we compare the calculated statistic (z, t, etc.) with the corresponding table value at a given α, we are determining whether or not

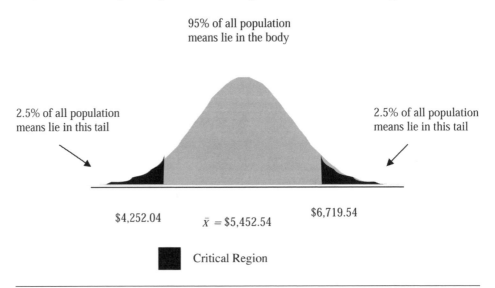

95% of all population
means lie in the body

2.5% of all population
means lie in this tail

2.5% of all population
means lie in this tail

$4,252.04 $\bar{x} = \$5,452.54$ $6,719.54

Critical Region

FIGURE 9.2   A 95% confidence interval along the horizontal axis of a sampling distribution.

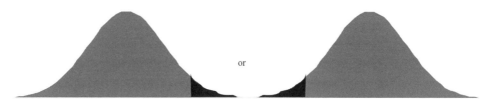

FIGURE 9.3 One-tailed test.

the calculated value falls in the critical region. If so, we reject; if not, we accept. When we refer to this as "beating" the table, we are asking whether the calculated statistic is so large in absolute value that it surpasses the standard set by the table and curve at that specific α.

One-Tailed Tests

The main difference between this procedure and that for one-tailed tests is that the critical region is not divided into two equal parts, one for the lowest and the other for the highest values. Instead, the entire .05 or .01 is placed all in one or the other of the tails, as diagrammed in figure 9.3. We consider further details of one-tailed tests in the next chapter.

An Illustration

Although hypothesis testing is generally employed in bivariate and multivariate applications, the basic steps in the procedure can be adapted to the principles of univariate confidence intervals discussed in the preceding chapters. To illustrate this, let us recall our earlier example of the travels of a sample of dorm students. In considering a policy that would allow a small travel allowance for visits home during weekends and holidays, the administration set a target of (and a budget based on) three trips per semester. However, to be realistic, they were willing to assume that three trips was atypical and, based on supporting or disconfirming evidence, they would adjust their target and allocation.

Because surveying the several thousand dorm students who would be affected was unrealistic, they decided to take a random sample of $n = 75$ students. They determined the mean number of trips actually taken by the students during the prior semester and the standard deviation of the distribution. These turned to be $\bar{x} = 3.55$ trips and $s = 1.8$ trips. They then set up the following hypotheses:

$H_r: \mu = 3.0.$ The observed sample mean could have come from a population with a mean of 3.0, and thus the target number of trips is accurate.

BOX 9.1   **Statistics for Sociologists**

Generalizing about Diversity with Hypothesis Testing

In our discussion of education diversity in Box 8.1, we used confidence intervals to generalize from a sample of 10 U.S. states to the population (the set of 50 states). There we used a "diversity level" index calculated from sample data to determine whether we could conclude that the 50 states had achieved a standard of diversity. This was defined as having percentages of minority students attending higher education equal to the percentages of minority members in the general population—where a score of 0 indicates that the two percentages are equal and the standard is achieved. The sample mean on the index was calculated to be $\bar{x} = +3.66$, indicating that the states in the sample had surpassed the standard by 3.66 points. The sample standard deviation was $s = 6.63$, and the sample standard error of the mean was $s_{\bar{x}} = 2.21$.

This allowed us to calculate the 95% CI as $\bar{x} \pm \text{ME} = 3.66 \pm 4.99$: from -1.33 to 8.65. The diversity level of 0 as the target for the mean for all 50 states does lie within this interval. This led to the conclusion that, with some exceptions, the 50 states are likely to have achieved the standard.

To illustrate the close connection between confidence intervals and testing hypotheses, we can use a *t*-test with the same data. We should come to the same conclusion. Suppose the researchers are seeking to establish that the set of all 50 states had either failed to achieve the standard or exceeded it. We state our hypotheses as follows.

$H_r: \mu \neq 0$.   The observed sample mean could not have come from a population with a mean of 0, and thus the standard was either not achieved or exceeded.

$H_0: \mu = 0$.   The observed sample mean could have come from a population with a mean of 0, and thus the standard is being achieved under present policies.

First we find $t_{calculated}$:

$$t_{calculated} = \frac{\bar{x} - \mu_0}{s_{\bar{x}}},$$

where μ_0 is the mean assumed under the null hypothesis (i.e., 0), and

$$s_{\bar{x}} = \frac{s}{\sqrt{n-1}} = 6.63/\sqrt{10-1} = 6.63/3 = 2.21.$$

So,

$$t_{calculated} = \frac{3.66 - 0}{2.21} = 1.66.$$

Next, we find t_{table}. At $\alpha = .05$ and $d.f. = n - 1 = 9$, the two-tailed $t_{table} = 2.26$. We see that $t_{calculated} < t_{table}$ and therefore fail to reject the null hypothesis. We can conclude that the mean for the 50 states could be zero.

$H_0: \mu \neq 3.0.$ The observed sample mean could not have come from a population with a mean of 3.0, and thus the target number of trips is inaccurate.

1. Because σ is not known, our statistic is t (not z). Thus, we find a *calculated* t value, using $\mu_0 = 3.0$ as the hypothetical population mean, with $n = 75$, $d.f. = (n - 1) = 74$, $\bar{x} = 3.55$, and $s = 1.8$:

$$s_{\bar{x}} = \frac{s}{\sqrt{d.f.}} = \frac{1.8}{\sqrt{74}} = 0.21$$

$$t_{calculated} = \frac{\bar{x} - \mu_0}{s_{\bar{x}}} = \frac{3.55 - 3.0}{0.21} = 2.62.$$

2. For the 95% level of confidence, we look up the two-tailed table value of t in table A.2 at $75 - 1 = 74$ for $d.f.$ and $\alpha = .05$. There is no row in the table for $d.f. = 74$, so we round down to the next lower level for which there is a row, $d.f. = 60$.

$$t_{table} = 2.00,$$

$$t_{calculated} > t_{table}.$$

3. By the rule, because the calculated t is greater than the table t (in absolute vale) we have beaten the table, and we reject the null hypothesis. It is *un*likely that the population mean is 3.0.
4. To test this null hypothesis at the 99% level, we return to step 2 and, instead of selecting 2.00 for our table value, we move to the .01 (two-tailed) column at $d.f. = 60$:

$$t_{table} = 2.66.$$

5. In this case the calculated t, 2.62, is less than the table value (although the difference is quite small). We failed to fall into the critical region, and the null hypothesis should not be rejected.

This result indicates that although the administrators can be 95% confident that 3.0 is an inappropriate target, they cannot be 99% confident. What should they do? If they do not take another sample, and if their goal is to ensure that the allowance covers at least the mean number of trips, they probably should raise the target number of trips to the next whole number, which is 4.0.

This reasoning is supported when we test the null hypotheses using confidence intervals. The decision rule that applies to this situation is that if the hypothesized $\mu = 3.0$ falls within the confidence interval, we fail to reject the null hypothesis, But if $\mu = 3.0$ falls in the critical region, then the null is rejected. Failure to reject the null means that the target number of trips can stand because the administration can be 95%

confident that the observed sample mean could have come from a population with a mean of 3.0 trips. Rejection means that a new target should be considered because the observed sample mean could have come from a population with a mean of 3.0 trips only 5% of the time or less.

$$\text{The 95\% CI (with } \sigma \text{ not known)} = \bar{x} \pm ts_{\bar{x}}.$$

The value of t at $\alpha = .05$ and $75 - 1 = 74$ degrees of freedom comes from the two-tail $\alpha = .05$ column in table A.2. With no *d.f.* entry for 74, we round back to 60 and find the t value of 2.00. The values of $\bar{x}$ and s are given above. Thus

$$\text{ME} = 2.0s_{\bar{x}} = 2.0(0.21) = 0.42.$$

The 95% CI $= \bar{x} \pm \text{ME} = 3.55 \pm 0.42$. Subtracting the margin of error from and adding it to the mean, we get

$$3.13 \text{ to } 3.97.$$

Because 3.0 does not fall within this interval, we must reject the null. It is unlikely that the population mean is 3.0. As it must, this agrees with our test that compared t values directly.

We already know from earlier results that if we increase our margin of error we can accept the null hypothesis. That is, if we wish to be more than 95% confident that 3.0 is an inappropriate target, we can expand the CI. As we saw above, at $\alpha = .01$ and *d.f.* $= 74$ (rounded to 60), the table t value is 2.66. Thus,

$$99\% \text{ CI} = 3.55 \pm (2.66)(0.21) = 3.55 \pm 0.56.$$

Subtracting this margin of error of 0.56 from and adding it to the mean, we see that

$$99\% \text{ CI} = 2.99 \text{ to } 4.11.$$

We see again that the hypothesized population mean of 3.0 now does lie within the confidence interval, although just barely. On this basis, our advice that the administration should raise the target allocation to four trips appears no longer to be statistically supported.

This demonstration indicates that the procedure of testing hypotheses, in which we compare a *calculated* and a *table statistic*, will always yield the same results as do tests that employ confidence intervals. But because the former approach is usually simpler and more "automatic," it will be employed exclusively in the following chapters. As you apply this procedure to a wide variety of hypothesis-testing situations, it will become second nature to you. But if you should need a quick refresher course on the logic of testing hypotheses and/or on the role played by confidence intervals in the procedure, you are invited to return to this general introduction.

WEB SITES TO BOOKMARK

1. http://davidmlane.com/hyperstat/hypothesis
_testing_se.html
This is a self-study module on testing hypotheses
with links to several related sites.

2. www.orst.edu/Dept/philosophy/resources/guide/
Hypoth.html
This site explores the basic philosophical principles
of hypothesis testing.

3. www.stats.gla.ac.uk/steps/glossary/hypothesis
_testing.html
Definitions related to hypotheses and hypothesis
testing are provided here.

4. www.wileyeurope.com/cda/product/0, ,0471611360
%7Cdesc%7C2626,00.html
This introduction to hypothesis testing includes an
interesting application to the Operation Head Start
early education program.

TESTING YOUR SKILLS

PRACTICE QUIZZES FOR CHAPTERS 7–9

The following three practice quizzes test your skills with topics covered in Chapters 7–9. They focus on probability, sampling, and hypothesis testing.

QUIZ 1: An application to comparative sociology

Use table 1 for questions 1–4.

1. Table 1 lists 12 countries and the continents they are on. Answer the following questions based on the table. (a) In selecting a country at random, what is the probability it is from the continent of S. America? (b) What is the probability that it is *not* from Asia?

TABLE 1 Selected countries and their continents

Country	Continent
Argentina	S. America
Brazil	S. America
Canada	N. America
Colombia	S. America
Congo	Africa
Ghana	Africa
Kenya	Africa
Liberia	Africa
Nigeria	Africa
Pakistan	Asia
Peru	S. America
United States	N. America

2. Using the table, (a) what is the probability that a country chosen at random will be either from N. America or S. America? (b) What is the probability that the country will be from any continent other than N. America or S. America?

3. Using the table, if we select a country at random, replace it back in the pool of 12, and select a country again, (a) what is the probability that in both selections the country will be from Africa? (b) Under these circumstances, what is the probability that one country will be from Africa and the other will be from N. America? (*Hint:* In how many ways can this happen?)

4. The hypothetical situation in question 1 was actually tested in three experiments. In the first experiment, 100 researchers selected a country at random. It turned out that 20 of the 100 countries selected were from S. America. In the second experiment 1,000 researchers selected a country at random. It turned out that 370 of the countries selected were from S. America. In the third experiment, 10,000 researchers selected a country at random. Which of the following is the *most likely* result of the third experiment: (a) fewer than 3,700 of the 10,000 selections were from S. America; (2) exactly 3,700 were from S. America; or (3) more than 3,700 were from S. America? Explain your answer.

5. A recent study of several thousand towns and cities examined the total number of hospitals in these places. It turned out that the distribution was approximately normal with $\mu = 15$ hospitals and $\sigma = 8$ hospitals. Express a raw score of 19 hospitals as (a) a deviation and (b) a standard, or z, score.

6. Using the information in question 5, express a raw score of 13 hospitals as (a) a deviation and (b) a z score.

7. Using the information in question 5, what is the probability that a city has a raw score of 17 hospitals or above? What is the probability that a city has a raw score between 13 and 17 hospitals?

8. A sample of $n = 25$ was selected from the thousands of cities and towns whose numbers of hospitals are as described in question 5. Its $\bar{x} = 16$ hospitals, and its $s = 6.0$ hospitals. (a) Calculate the difference between the sample mean and the population mean. (b) Calculate the standard error of the mean, with σ *known* to be 8 hospitals. (c) Convert the sample mean to a standard score.

9. Construct the 95% and 99% confidence intervals around the sample mean in question 8.

10. In the situation given in question 5, assume that you now do not know σ. Under this new condition, construct the 95% and 99% confidence intervals around the sample mean in question 8.

Extra credit (up to 5 points): The (a) distribution of sampling error and the (b) sampling distribution of means are identical. That is, both are normal, their means are both μ (the mean of the population), and their standard deviations are both $\sigma_{\bar{x}} = \sigma / \sqrt{n}$. Explain why this is so (a picture might help).

QUIZ 2: An application to the sociology of sports

The athletic departments of the Big Ten universities (of which there are actually 11) plus Notre Dame—or a total of 12 schools in all—have decided to hold a volleyball tournament. Table 2 contains a listing of the 12 schools and additional information about them. Use this information to answer questions 1–4.

1. In selecting a college at random, (a) what is the probability that it is in Indiana? (b) What is the probability that it is *not* in Indiana?
2. Using the information in question 1, (a) what is the probability that a college chosen at random will be either from Michigan or Ohio? (b) What is the probability that the school will be from any state other than Michigan or Ohio?
3. Use the information in question 1. In deciding the two teams to play in the first game, a college was selected at random, replaced back in the pool of 12, and a college was selected again. (a) What is the probability that a public school and a nonpublic school were selected in that order? (b) Under these circumstances, what is the probability that Michigan would play Michigan State? (*Hint:* In how many ways can this happen?)

TABLE 2   Twelve universities, states, and types

College	State	Public (P) or nonpublic (N)
U. of Illinois	Illinois	P
Indiana U.	Indiana	P
U. of Iowa	Iowa	P
U. of Michigan	Michigan	P
Michigan State U.	Michigan	P
U. of Minnesota	Minnesota	P
Northwestern U.	Illinois	N
U. of Notre Dame	Indiana	N
Ohio State U.	Ohio	P
Penn State U.	Pennsylvania	P
Purdue U.	Indiana	P
U. of Wisconsin	Wisconsin	P

4. For this question, group all of the schools in Indiana, Ohio, and Michigan together into group A and group the others into B. Create the probability distribution for selecting schools in A or B in two successive draws (with replacement).

5. Each member of a population of several thousand students was asked to indicate the amount of time it takes them to reach school from home. The distribution was approximately normal with a mean $\mu = 20$ minutes and a standard deviation $\sigma = 4$ minutes. Express a travel time of 26 minutes as (a) a deviation and (b) a z score.

6. Using the information in question 5, (a) what travel time would a student have if her deviation were –2 minutes? (b) What travel time would a student have if his z score were +0.75?

7. Using the information in question 5, (a) what is the probability that a student travels for 24 minutes or more? (b) What is the probability that a student travels between 18 and 22 minutes?

8. From the population described in question 5, above, a sample of $n = 100$ was selected. Its $\bar{x} = 18$ minutes and its $s = 2$ minutes. (a) Calculate the difference between the sample mean and the population mean. (b) Calculate the standard error of the mean, $\sigma_{\bar{x}}$, with σ known to be 4 minutes. (c) Convert the sample mean to a standard score.

9. (a) Construct the 95% and 99% confidence intervals around the sample mean in question 8. (b) Does the population mean fall inside of either or both of these confidence intervals? Which one(s)?

10. In the situation given in question 8, assume that *you do not know σ*. Under this new condition, (a) construct the 95% and 99% confidence intervals around the sample mean. (b) Does the population mean fall inside of either or both of these confidence intervals? Which one(s)?

Extra credit (up to 5 points): If the population mean falls within the 95% confidence interval around a sample mean, will it always fall within the 99% confidence interval around the sample mean? Why or why not?

QUIZ 3

1. In a class of 10 students, 4 are from Detroit, 3 are from the suburbs of Detroit, 2 are from other parts of Michigan, and 1 is from Ohio. (a) In selecting a student at random, what is the probability that he or she is from the suburbs? (b) What is the probability that the student is not from the suburbs?

2. Using the information in question 1, (a) what is the probability that a student chosen at random will be either from Detroit or the suburbs? (b) What is the probability that the student will be from any place in Michigan?

3. Using the information in question 1, if we select a student at random, replace that student back in the pool of 10, and select a student again, (a) what is

the probability that in both selections the student will be from other parts of Michigan? (b) Under these circumstances, what is the probability that one student will be from Michigan and the other will be from Ohio? (*Hint:* In how many ways can this happen?)

4. The hypothetical situation in question 1 was actually tested in two experiments. In the first experiment, each of 100 researchers selected a student at random. It turned out that 32 of the 100 students selected were from Detroit. In the second experiment, each of 1,000 researchers selected a student at random. Which of the following is the most likely result of the second experiment: (a) fewer than 320 of the 1,000 selections were from Detroit; (b) exactly 320 were from Detroit; or (c) more than 320 were from Detroit? Explain your answer.

5. A recent entrance exam, with a maximum score of 100 points, was given to several thousand students. It turned out that the distribution was approximately normal with a $\mu = 75$ points and a $\sigma = 5$ points. (a) Express a raw score of 80 as (a) a deviation and (b) a standard, or z, score.

6. Using the information in question 5, express a raw score of 62.5 as (a) a deviation and (b) a z score.

7. Using the information in question 5, what is the probability that someone gets a raw score of 85 or above? What is the probability that someone gets a raw score between 62.5 and 75?

8. A sample of $n = 16$ was selected from the thousands of students who took the exam described in question 5. Its $\bar{x} = 72.5$ and its $s = 3.0$. (a) Calculate the difference between the sample mean and the population mean. (b) Calculate the standard error of the mean, with σ known to be 5 points. (c). Convert the sample mean to a standard score.

9. Construct the 95% and 99% confidence intervals around the sample mean in question 8.

10. In the situation given in question 5, assume that you now *do not* know σ. Under this new condition, construct the 95% and 99% confidence intervals around the sample mean in question 8.

Extra credit: Does the population mean fall within any of the confidence intervals you constructed in questions 9 and 10? Which one(s)?

Bivariate Applications

Using Induction and Association in Sociological Research

The five chapters in this section (10 through 14) apply the principles of hypothesis testing introduced in Chapter 9 to the types of problems typically encountered in sociological research. All of these are bivariate; that is, they involve two variables: an independent (I) and a dependent (D). In some of these applications, one or both variables are nominal; in others, one or both are ordinal; and in others, one or both are numerical (see table IV.1). In each case, our purpose is to understand in a precise way *the relationship between I and D*: How and to what degree do they vary *together*, that is, "co-vary"?

The procedure includes the two basic steps of description and induction. In the first step, techniques are used to describe the relationship between two (or more) variables. These techniques are referred to as measures of *association,* because we use them to understand the extent to which the variables are associated with one another. These range from a simple comparison between the means of two groups (as in Chapter 10) to the calculation of statistics based upon means, sample size, and standard deviations, such as the correlation coefficient r (as in Chapter 13).

The second basic step uses inductive logic to test hypotheses about the association between I and D. Our purpose is to establish whether or not the observed relationship is statistically significant (as opposed to being merely a chance association).

Chapter 10 focuses on the two sample t-test. This applies to problems in which the independent variable is non-numerical and has two attributes (male/female, employed/unemployed, wealthy/poor, etc). The dependent variable is numerical (income in dollars, GPA, number of hours of TV watched each week, etc.). Chapter 11, on analysis of variance (ANOVA), continues along these lines with applications to situations in which the independent variable has three or more attributes (rural/urban/suburban, high-school graduate/community-college graduate/college graduate/advanced degree, etc.). Chapter 12 introduces several techniques for measuring association and testing hypotheses about the relationship between two variables, neither of which is numerical. For reasons to be discussed in the chapter, these are referred to *non-parametric* applications.

TABLE IV.1   Road map for Part IV

| Chapter | Level of measurement | |
	Independent	Dependent
10	Non-numerical, 2 attributes	Numerical
11	Non-numerical 3 or more attributes	Numerical
12	Non-numerical	Non-numerical
13	Numerical	Numerical
14	Numerical	Numerical

Chapters 13 and 14 focus on bivariate correlation and regression, respectively. These techniques are used for situations in which both variables are numerical. Each chapter includes measures of association and procedures for hypothesis testing that are among the most widely used in sociological and related social science research. The techniques of bivariate correlation and regression summarize and conclude a first course in applied statistics, and they represent the logical bridge to more advanced applications.

10

Two-Sample *t*-Tests and an Application to the Study of Altruism

This and the following chapter extend the principles of hypothesis testing introduced in Chapter 9 to bivariate applications in which one of the variables is numerical and the other is nominal or ordinal. Our general introduction to hypothesis testing presented a set of steps that apply to a wide range of situations, provided that certain conditions can be assumed. Among these is the assumption of random sampling. You will recall that the reason why random selection of samples is important is that the researcher can then make use of a sampling distribution to locate a sample mean, in relation to likely parameters. The techniques and illustrations presented in this chapter take advantage of this connection and therefore also assume random sampling and employ sampling distributions.

The hypotheses considered here and in Chapter 11 refer to the difference(s) between or among the means of two or more groups into which a population has been divided. Thus, the sampling distributions that are used to establish confidence intervals and critical regions refer not to a range of potential sample means but to a range of potential sample *differences* of means. This situation makes it necessary to introduce additional tables that list the values of statistics to beat, as well as alternative measures of calculated statistics and degrees of freedom. Beyond these specific matters, however, the general procedure for testing hypotheses should now be somewhat familiar and will, in any case, become increasingly so. That is:

1. The null and research hypotheses are stated in words and symbols.
2. A statistic is *calculated* based on sample information: n, $\bar{x}$, $(x_i - \bar{x})$, and s^2.
3. A corresponding statistic is taken from a *table* of values from the appropriate sampling distribution.
4. The calculated and table statistics are compared, and a decision is made based on the following rule: *If the calculated statistic is greater (in absolute value) than the table statistic, we reject the null hypothesis. Otherwise, we fail to reject the null.*

These steps are applied to two of the major types of difference-of-means significance tests. The first, covered in this chapter, is the two-means *t*-test, which uses a version of the *t* statistic introduced earlier. Within this category are several refinements, the most important of which are featured here. The second type of test, covered in Chapter 11, is one-way analysis of variance (ANOVA), which uses the *F* statistic to test hypotheses concerning differences among three or more means.

One additional version of the *t*-test, not covered in this chapter, is employed with a non-numerical variable (in the univariate case) or variables (in bivariate applications). In these situations, we do not compare means or calculate variances, because non-numerical variables do not have means or variances. In the place of means, we use *proportions*. This type of *t*-test is featured in the online Chapter 15.

The *t*-Test of the Difference Between Two Means

As noted, the research problems featured in this chapter are all bivariate. In this first application, the independent variable is a *dichotomy*—that is, a nominal- or ordinal-level variable with two and only two attributes. The dependent variable is numerical, for which the attributes are numbers such as dollars, points, or trips taken. The research focuses on a population that consists of two groups (numbered 1 and 2) defined in terms of the attributes of the independent variable—for example, gender (e.g., 1 = male and 2 = female), type of student (1 = new, 2 = returning), class in school (1 = upper, 2 = lower), and so on. In addition, information exists about the distribution in each group of values of the numerical dependent variable—for example, income in dollars, exam scores in points, etc.

Under these conditions, a probability sample of size *n* is drawn from the population.[1] Means, sample sizes, variances, and standard deviations are then calculated for each of the two groups: $\bar{x}_1$ and $\bar{x}_2$, n_1 and n_2, s_1^2 and s_2^2, and s_1 and s_2. Hypotheses are established; then a "cooked" score ($t_{calculated}$) is derived from the difference between sample means ($\bar{x}_1 - \bar{x}_2$), sample sizes, and variances; and the test is conducted.

The nature of the hypotheses and, to an extent, the testing procedures will differ according to whether the test is of the two-tailed or one-tailed type. Therefore, we first briefly examine these two types of tests based on the definitions of *t* the end of Chapter 9 and then describe and illustrate each procedure under various conditions.

Calculated t *as a Measure of Association*

The main reason for deriving a $t_{calculated}$ value is to compare it to a t_{table} value in testing hypotheses. But in the two-sample applications featured in this chapter, $t_{calculated}$ also stands on its own as a descriptive measure of the degree of *association* between the two variables: the dichotomous independent variable and the numerical dependent variable. With this and other measures of association, we are creating a number or numbers that indicate the extent to which the two variables vary together (or co-vary).

The size of $t_{calculated}$ indicates how closely the two variables in a particular sample are associated. And because it is a "cooked" score, it can be directly compared to the $t_{calculated}$ values of other samples, and even of other pairs of variables—provided that one is a dichotomy and the other is numerical.

The value of $t_{calculated}$ can be 0, or it can be positive or negative. If $t_{calculated} = 0$, we can say that there is no association, or that the variables do not co-vary at all. This indicates that there is no overall difference in the sample values for the dependent variable between the units with one or the other value on the independent variable. For example, we might observe the number of trips home (the dependent variable) taken by students (the "units") in two groups, "new" and "old" (the independent). In calculating t we find that it equals 0. In practice, this occurs when $\bar{x}_1 - \bar{x}_2 = 0$ (the means are equal); in this example, it occurs because each group might average five trips.

The larger the $t_{calculated}$ in absolute value, the greater is the degree of association between the two variables. This occurs when the absolute value of $\bar{x}_1 - \bar{x}_2 > 0$. A very high absolute value indicates that the two are strongly associated, and that it makes a real difference in terms of the value of the dependent variable which group a specific student (or other unit) is in. A positive $t_{calculated}$ indicates that $\bar{x}_1 > \bar{x}_2$, and a negative $t_{calculated}$ indicates that $\bar{x}_1 < \bar{x}_2$. The sign of $t_{calculated}$ is not of interest in two-tailed tests, but it is important in one-tailed tests, as we shall see.

Two-Tailed Versus One-Tailed Tests

Two-Tailed

We have already performed a two-tailed test in the univariate situation discussed earlier. You will recall that the term "two-tailed" refers to the location of the critical region, the area under the curve of the sampling distribution that includes values of the $t_{calculated}$ that would lead to rejection of the null hypothesis, H_0. When we set our level of significance $\alpha = .05$ or $.01$ in two-tailed tests, we divide the proportion into two equal parts: one (.025 or .005) for the left tail and the other (.025 or .005) for the right tail. The null hypothesis associated with this division of α always specifies "is equal" or "is the same," or "no, there is no difference," whereas the research hypothesis (H_r) specifies "is not equal," "is not the same," or "yes, there is a difference." Thus, if the absolute value of the calculated statistic (that is, ignoring its sign) lies within the confidence interval and not in the critical region, because it is smaller than t_{table}, the null hypothesis is not rejected. If the absolute value of the calculated statistic falls outside of the confidence interval, however, because it is larger than t_{table}, then the null hypothesis is rejected. For example, if t_{table} is 2.00, values of $t_{calculated} = +1.5$ and -1.5 both indicate failure to reject the null, whereas values of $t_{calculated} = +2.5$ and -2.5 both indicate rejection of H_0.

By the rules of probability, if $\alpha = .05$, the probability of rejecting H_0 if $t_{calculated}$ is positive is .025 and the probability of rejecting H_0 if $t_{calculated}$ is negative is .025. Thus, the probability of rejecting H_0 one way or another is .025 + .025 = .05. Similarly, if $\alpha = .01$, the probability of rejecting H_0 if $t_{calculated}$ is positive is .005 and the probability of rejecting H_0 if $t_{calculated}$ is negative is .005. Thus, the probability of rejecting H_0 one way or another is .005 + .005 = .01.

One-Tailed

In contrast to the two-tailed test, a one-tailed test locates the critical region only in the left (negative) or the right (positive) tail. For this reason, the sign of $t_{calculated}$ *is* relevant. The null hypothesis associated with this situation does *not* specify equality, sameness, no difference, and the like. Rather, it specifies the negation of a stated direction of difference. That is, "not greater than (not +)" or "not less than (not –)." Accordingly, the research hypothesis does not specify merely "no difference." Rather, in keeping with the associated null hypothesis, the research hypothesis specifies "greater than (+)" or "less than (–)."

Thus, if $t_{calculated}$ lies within the confidence interval and not in the critical region, it is because its value—including the sign—is *not greater than* the table value in one case or *not less than* the table value in the other. These are the conditions under which the null hypothesis is not rejected. But if the null specifies "not greater" and the calculated statistic (sign included) *is* greater than the table statistic, then the null is rejected. Likewise, if the null specifies "not less" and the calculated statistic (sign included) *is* less than the table statistic, then the null is also rejected. To reiterate, the one-tailed test makes the sign of the calculated statistic an essential piece of information, whereas it is irrelevant in the two-tailed case.

If $\alpha = .05$ (or .01) and the null hypothesis specifies "not greater," the probability of rejecting H_0 if the calculated statistic is positive is .05 (or .01), and the probability of rejecting H_0 if the calculated statistic is negative is 0. This is because any value that is not greater indicates acceptance. If $\alpha = .05$ (or .01) and the null hypothesis specifies "not less," the probability of rejecting H_0 if the calculated statistic is negative is .05 (or .01), and the probability of rejecting H_0 if the calculated statistic is positive is 0. This is because any value that is not less indicates acceptance. An alternative header row (labeled "1-tail") in table A.2 is used to find the column that contains the table t value. This row locates the entire critical region of .05 or .01 in one or the other tail, rather than splitting it between the two tails.

Two-Tailed Tests with Independent Subsamples

The *t*-tests we are considering in this section are designed to test the significance of the difference between the means of two groups, or *subsamples*, within a randomly selected sample. The purpose is to help in making decisions concerning the difference between the two groups within the population from which the sample is drawn.

Before continuing, however, it needs to be stressed that two-sample *t*-tests are also used when the means being compared are *not* from two separate—that is, independent—subsamples. Testing with independent subsamples is certainly one possibility, and the one to be covered first. But researchers are often interested in the difference between a sample mean observed at one point in time and the mean of the *same* variable for the *same* sample observed at another point—in brief, "before and after." This type of comparison is based on a procedure described as *paired samples* or *the same sample measured twice*. In these terms, the independent-groups test can be viewed as *two different samples measured once*.

We return to the before-and-after situation below, but here we assume that a randomly selected sample has been divided into two mutually exclusive groups along the lines of the attributes of a dichotomous independent variable. Further, the values of the subsample means, variances, and standard deviations have been (or can easily be) calculated. These are used to derive a sample statistic, $t_{calculated}$, that reflects the difference between the two group means. Under these assumptions, the generic two-tailed test involves the following two hypotheses, in symbols and words:

$H_0: \mu_1 = \mu_2$. The mean of the first group in the population is *equal* to the mean of the second group in the population. An equivalent statement is $H_0: \mu_1 - \mu_2 = 0$. There is *no difference* between the two group means in the population.

$H_r: \mu_1 \neq \mu_2$. The mean of the first group in the population is *not equal* to the mean of the second group in the population. An equivalent statement is $H_r: \mu_1 - \mu_2 \neq 0$. There *is a difference* between the two group means in the population.

As in the case of the univariate test, the calculated statistic is *t*. And, for the two tailed test, the table value, t_{table}, is once more found in the column located by the "2-tail" header of table A.2. Here the raw score is the difference between the sample means $(\overline{x}_1 - \overline{x}_2)$, and the calculated *t* value is a standardized or "twice-cooked" score: a deviation divided by a standard deviation.

$$t_{calculated} = \frac{x_1 - x_2}{s_{\overline{x}_1 - \overline{x}_2}}.$$

Here, the deviation of interest is simply the difference between the two sample means, that is, $(\overline{x}_1 - \overline{x}_2)$. The standard deviation by which the difference between sample means is divided is, as in the univariate case, an estimated standard error. Here, however, it is the *estimated standard error of the differences*, symbolized as $s_{\bar{x}_1 - \bar{x}_2}$.

In Chapter 7 we defined a sampling distribution as a theoretical probability distribution that includes the set of all possible statistics of a certain type (all means, standard deviations, and so on) for sample of size n. There and in Chapter 8 the statistic of interest was the mean, and the sampling distribution of means was used. Here we are using a sampling distribution that is similar to the sampling distribution of the means. But it consists not of all possible sample means, $\bar{x}$. Rather, it is the set of all *differences* between the group means ($\bar{x}_1 - \bar{x}_2$) of all possible samples of sizes n_1 and n_2 drawn from the population, as shown in figure 10.1. One of these differences, of course, is that in the

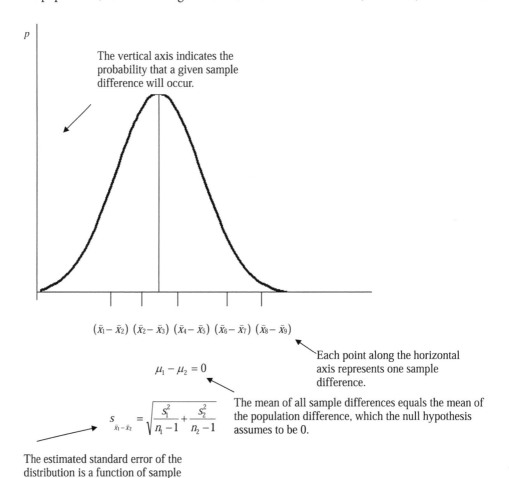

$$(\bar{X}_1 - \bar{X}_2) \ (\bar{X}_2 - \bar{X}_3) \ (\bar{X}_4 - \bar{X}_5) \ (\bar{X}_6 - \bar{X}_7) \ (\bar{X}_8 - \bar{X}_9)$$

Each point along the horizontal axis represents one sample difference.

$$\mu_1 - \mu_2 = 0$$

The mean of all sample differences equals the mean of the population difference, which the null hypothesis assumes to be 0.

$$s_{\bar{x}_1 - \bar{x}_2} = \sqrt{\frac{s_1^2}{n_1 - 1} + \frac{s_2^2}{n_2 - 1}}$$

The estimated standard error of the distribution is a function of sample sizes and variances.

FIGURE 10.1   The sampling distribution of differences between two means, from samples of sizes n_1 and n_2.

observed sample. The others are derived from the numerous samples not observed. As figure 10.1 indicates, the mean of this sampling distribution is equal to $\bar{x}_1 - \bar{x}_2$, which the null hypothesis always assumes to be 0.

Because it is an estimate, the sampling distribution of differences, $s_{\bar{x}_1 - \bar{x}_2}$, is derived from sample statistics, in particular from the sizes of the two subsamples and their respective variances. Although the formula appears somewhat complicated, on inspection it becomes evident what is involved:

$$s_{\bar{x}_1 - \bar{x}_2} = \sqrt{\frac{s_1^2}{n_1 - 1} + \frac{s_2^2}{n_2 - 1}}.$$

The estimated standard error of the differences between sample group means ($s_{\bar{x}_1 - \bar{x}_2}$) measures the degree of dispersion of the sampling distribution of differences (how spread out it is). In effect, it is an average of the group standard deviations, weighted by the sample sizes minus 1. It is, thus, a function of the average distances *between* group values and their respective means *within* samples.

As in the univariate case, the clue as to the degrees of freedom is found in the denominator of the standard error measure. As can be seen, these are $n_1 - 1$ and $n_2 - 1$. Because $n_1 + n_2$ equals the total sample size, n_{total}, this is the same as saying

$$d.f. = n_{total} - 2.$$

Two comments need to be made about this estimated standard error. First, its adequacy depends on how close the two variances, s_1^2 and s_2^2, are to being equal. If they are nearly equal, then no further steps are required. But if their values are very different, both the calculated t value and the degrees of freedom must be adjusted. The problem here is determining what "nearly equal" and "very different" mean. Rather than take up the technical details here, let us recommend one of two possible alternatives: (1) Simply assume that the variances are equal enough, in the knowledge that additional error is occasionally to be expected. (2) Use the results provided by IBM SPSS Statistics Base or another statistical package. These include significance tests concerning the equality of the variances as well as sets of calculated t values and degrees of freedom for each situation, equal and unequal variances, from which the researcher can choose.

The second aspect of the estimated standard error of differences that deserves mention is its reference to *between*- and *within*-group dispersion, as measured by the variance. The principle employed here is that the statistical significance of a difference between group sample means, $\bar{x}_1$ and $\bar{x}_2$, depends on the size of the between-group variance compared to the size of the within-group variance. If the former is *small* relative to the latter, then there is little difference between the means and the null hypothesis is *not* likely to be rejected. If the former is *large* relative to the latter, then there is *substantial difference* between the means, and the null hypothesis *is* likely to be rejected. This principle applies in a very prominent way in the ANOVA *F* test, as we shall soon see.

An Illustration of a Two-Tailed Independent-Sample Test

To illustrate this procedure, let us return to our example of household incomes used in earlier chapters. As in Chapter 8, we have randomly selected a sample of 50 households and have recorded the income of each. In addition, we have divided the sample into two groups representing those households that have recently moved to the community (Group 1, "recent") and those that have resided in the community for several years (Group 2, "older"). The length of residence, with the attributes "recent" and "older," is the independent variable.

We can now state our hypotheses in symbols and in words.

$H_0: \mu_1 = \mu_2$. The mean income of the recent households in the population is *equal* to the mean income of the older households in the population. An equivalent statement is $H_0: \mu_1 - \mu_2 = 0$. There is *no difference* between the recent and older household mean incomes in the population.

$H_r: \mu_1 \neq \mu_2$. The mean income of the recent households in the population is *not equal* to the mean income of the older households in the population. An equivalent statement is $H_r: \mu_1 - \mu_2 \neq 0$. There *is a difference* between the recent and older household mean incomes in the population.

The basic statistics for the entire sample were calculated and were found to be $n = 50$, $\bar{x} = \$5,819.56$, and $s = \$3,887.35$. The frequency distribution for the independent variable is shown in table 10.1. Thus, $n_1 = 34$ and $n_2 = 16$. The group-specific statistics are

$$\bar{x}_1 = \$7,760.62$$
$$\bar{x}_2 = \$1,694.81$$

TABLE 10.1   Length of residence table

Length of residence	*n*	*%*
Recent	34	68
Older	16	32
Total	50	100

$$s_1 = \$3,179.35$$
$$s_2 = \$661.99$$

The difference between the group means is

$$\bar{x}_1 - \bar{x}_2 - = \$7,760.62 - \$1,694.81 = \$6,065.81.$$

Without going much further, some things are already clear. Most important, there appears to be a very large difference between the incomes of the two groups, with the recent incomes more than four times higher than the older. In addition, the variances seem to be quite unequal. The difference of approximately \$2,500 between their standard deviations is magnified many times by squaring each value (that is, $s_1^2 = \$60,227,222.78$, whereas $s_2^2 = \$438,230.66$). Although we will assume equality, we will also check to see whether the outcome would have been different if this assumption were not made.

We can now calculate our sample t statistic,

$$t_{calculated} = \frac{\bar{x}_1 - \bar{x}_2}{s_{\bar{x}_1 - \bar{x}_2}}.$$

First, we solve for the estimated standard error,

$$s_{\bar{x}_1 - \bar{x}_2} = \sqrt{\frac{s_1^2}{n_1 - 1} + \frac{s_2^2}{n_2 - 1}} = \sqrt{\frac{\$60,227,222.78}{33} + \frac{\$438,230.66}{15}}$$

$$= \sqrt{\$1,825,067.30 + \$29,215.38} = \sqrt{\$651,313.56}$$

$$s_{\bar{x}_1 - \bar{x}_2} = \$807.04.$$

Thus,

$$t_{calculated} = \frac{\$6,065.81}{\$807.04} = 7.52.$$

This value of $t_{calculated}$ can now be compared to the values found in table A.2 at $\alpha = .05$ and .01 and $d.f. = 48$. Because $d.f. = 48$ is not listed, we must round down to 40, where we find that at $\alpha = .05$ $t_{table} = 2.021$, and at $\alpha = .01$ $t_{table} = 2.704$.

Our calculated t value is greater than the table value, at both levels of significance: $t_{calculated} = 7.52$, whereas $t_{table} = 2.02$ and 2.70, at .05 and .01, respectively. Thus, we *reject the null hypothesis.* We are 95% and even 99% confident that there is a difference between recent and older mean incomes in the population.

Incidentally, if we had assumed unequal variances, $t_{calculated}$ would have been 10.645 and $d.f. = 39$, according to IBM SPSS Statistics Base. For $d.f. = 39$ (rounded to 30) at $\alpha = .05$ $t_{table} = 2.042$, and at $\alpha = .01$ $t_{table} = 2.750$. So, in this case, the null hypothesis would be rejected regardless of the assumption about equal or unequal variances.

One-Tailed Tests with Independent Samples

A one-tailed test is appropriate when the researcher has reason to believe—ideally because a theory so indicates—not only that two group means in the population are unequal but that a specific one is actually greater than the other. In this case, the null and research hypotheses are stated differently from those for a two-tailed test, and the decision to reject or fail to reject the null hypothesis includes an added step. As noted above, the column determined by the "1-tail" header of table A.2 in Appendix A, rather than that determined by the "2-tail" header, is used to determine the value of t_{table}.

In the process of formulating a one-tailed hypothesis, it is preferable for the sake of clarity to attend first to the research hypothesis. In this way, the group whose mean is expected to be the larger can first be identified. It is sometimes possible to designate arbitrarily this as "group 1" and the other "group 2," regardless of the way they may have been initially coded. If this can be done, then the research hypothesis will always be

$H_r: \mu_1 > \mu_2$. The population mean of the first group is *greater than* the population mean of the second group.

The statement of the null hypothesis in symbols and words is thus

$H_0: \mu_1 \leq \mu_2$. The population mean of the first group is *not greater than* the population mean of the second group.[2]

For the sake of the following discussion, we will call this the "first group greater" situation.

When it is not possible for the researcher to assign the designation "group 1" arbitrarily to the group expected to have the larger of the two population means, it may be necessary to hypothesize that group 1 has the smaller mean of the two. In this case, the research and null hypotheses will be

$H_r: \mu_1 < \mu_2$. The population mean of the first group is *less than* the population mean of the second group.

$H_0: \mu_1 \geq \mu_2$. The population mean of the first group is *not less than* the population mean of the second group.[3]

For the sake of the following discussion, we will call this the "first group less" situation.

The extra step in the procedure, referred to earlier, is necessary because in a one-tailed test the sign of $t_{calculated}$ is relevant. And it is this sign that must be determined prior to identifying t_{table} in the one-tailed column of table A.2. The numerator of the statistic $(\bar{x}_1 - \bar{x}_2)$ is decisive because the denominator, $s_{\bar{x}_1 - \bar{x}_2}$, will always be *positive*. Thus, if $\bar{x}_1 > \bar{x}_2$, then $\bar{x}_1 - \bar{x}_2$ will be positive and $t_{calculated}$ will be positive as well. If $\bar{x}_1 < \bar{x}_2$, Then $\bar{x}_1 - \bar{x}_2$ will be *negative*, as will $t_{calculated}$.

As a consequence, if the sign of $t_{calculated}$ agrees with the research hypothesis, it should then be compared with the appropriate t_{table} and the accept-or-reject decision made in the usual way. However, if the sign of $t_{calculated}$ does not agree with the research hypothesis, then *the null hypothesis must be retained with no reference to the table.*

In detail, for the "first group greater" situation, if $t_{calculated}$ is positive, the first group sample mean must therefore be greater. In this case, $t_{calculated}$ should be compared to t_{table} at the appropriate α and *d.f.* A determination is then made concerning whether the positive difference $\bar{x}_1 - \bar{x}_2$ is large enough to "beat" the table. However, if $t_{calculated}$ is negative, the first group sample mean must be less than the second. In this case, $t_{calculated}$ cannot possibly beat the table because it is negative and the reject region is in the positive tail. Therefore, the null hypothesis is not rejected.

For the "first group less" situation, if $t_{calculated}$ is negative, the first group sample mean must therefore be less than the second. In this case, $t_{calculated}$ should be compared to t_{table} at the appropriate α and *d.f.* A determination is then made concerning whether the negative difference $\bar{x}_1 - \bar{x}_2$ is large enough to beat the table. However, if $t_{calculated}$ is positive, the first group sample mean must therefore be greater than the second. In this case, $t_{calculated}$ cannot possibly "beat" the table because it is positive and the reject region is in the negative tail. Therefore, the null hypothesis is not rejected. Table 10.2 summarizes this decision rule.

An Illustration of a One-Tailed Independent-Sample Test

The earlier illustration, for which we used recent and older household incomes, can be quickly adapted to a one-tailed test. However, because the results are already known, there is not much suspense about the outcome. We can make things a bit more interesting by selecting another sample (also $n = 50$) and using it in a one-tailed test. We

TABLE 10.2   Decision rule for one-tailed *t*-test

Research hypothesis	Null hypothesis	Sizes of sample means	Sign of difference $\bar{x}_1 - \bar{x}_2$	Sign of $t_{calculated}$	Next step
$H_r: \mu_1 > \mu_2$	$H_0: \mu_1 \leq \mu_2$	$\bar{x}_1 > \bar{x}_2$	+	+	Find t_{table}, compare to $t_{calculated}$, and decide.
$H_r: \mu_1 > \mu_2$	$H_0: \mu_1 \leq \mu_2$	$\bar{x}_1 < \bar{x}_2$	–	–	STOP. Retain H_0.
$H_r: \mu_1 < \mu_2$	$H_0: \mu_1 \geq \mu_2$	$\bar{x}_1 < \bar{x}_2$	–	–	Find t_{table}, compare to $t_{calculated}$, and decide.
$H_r: \mu_1 < \mu_2$	$H_0: \mu_1 \geq \mu_2$	$\bar{x}_1 > \bar{x}_2$	+	+	STOP. Retain H_0.

obviously have good reason to believe that recent household incomes are greater than older household incomes. On this basis, with "1" representing the recent households and "2" older households, our research hypothesis is:

$H_r: \mu_1 > \mu_2$. The mean income of the recent households in the population is greater than the mean income of the older households in the population.

The statement of the null hypothesis in symbols and words is:

$H_0: \mu_1 \leq \mu_2$. The mean income of the recent households in the population is not greater than the mean income of the older households in the population.

The statistics for the (entire) new sample are $n = 50$, $\bar{x} = \$5,113.28$, and $s = \$3,753.99$. The frequency distribution for the independent variable is shown in table 10.3. The group-specific statistics are

$$d.f. = 50 - 2 = 48$$
$$\bar{x}_1 = \$7,597.10$$
$$\bar{x}_2 = \$1,683.24$$
$$s_1 = \$3,035.15$$
$$s_2 = \$574.77$$
$$\bar{x}_1 - \bar{x}_2 = \$5,913.87$$
$$s_{\bar{x}_1 - \bar{x}_2} = \$672.68.$$

Therefore,

$$t_{calculated} = \frac{\bar{x}_1 - \bar{x}_2}{s_{\bar{x}_1 - \bar{x}_2}} = \frac{\$5,913.87}{\$672.68} = 8.792.$$

Because this is a one-tailed test with the research hypothesis specifying that $\mu_1 > \mu_2$, we need to establish whether the sign of $t_{calculated}$ is positive. If it is, then we determine t_{table} from table A.2. But if $t_{calculated}$ is negative, then we automatically accept the null hypothesis. Clearly, $t_{calculated}$ is positive.

Next, we find t_{table} at $d.f. = 48$ (rounded to 40). At $\alpha = .05$ and .01, based on the columns indicated by the "1-tail" header, t_{table} is 1.684 and 2.423, respectively. Comparing these to

TABLE 10.3   Length of residence table

Residence	f	%
Recent	29	58
Older	21	42
Total	50	100

$t_{calculated} = 8.792$, we can reject the null hypothesis. As expected, we conclude that the recent households in the population most probably do have a higher average income than the older households.[4] Box 10.1 contains an additional illustration of a one-tailed test.

Before-and-After *t*-Test

One of the most common uses of the difference-of-means *t*-test is for research in which a single group is measured twice (also discussed in Box 10.1). The first measurement occurs before the passage of a certain amount of time or, in experimental studies, before a stimulus or "treatment" is applied. The second occurs after an interval of time elapses or following the treatment. If control groups are used in an experimental study, then the real treatment is withheld from them; often, in medical testing, they receive a placebo. The role of the *t*-test is to measure the group and establish its mean for a numerical dependent variable and then, treating the passage of time or the experimental stimulus as the independent variable, establish the mean afterward.

In this situation, μ_1 represents the unobserved population mean and $\bar{x}_1$ represents the observed sample mean at the time of the first measurement; μ_2 and $\bar{x}_2$ represent the population and sample means at the time of the second measurement. The difference in the population means $(\mu_1 - \mu_2)$ is stated in the null hypothesis, and the difference in the sample means, $\bar{x}_1 - \bar{x}_2$, is converted to a $t_{calculated}$ value. This value is then compared to a t_{table} to test one of the two types of null hypotheses discussed above:

1. The two-tailed, $H_0 : \mu_1 = \mu_2$, there is no change in the mean between time 1 (before) and time 2 (after).
2. The one-tailed, either:
   a. $H_0 : \mu_1 \leq \mu_2$, the mean did not decrease between time 1 and time 2; or
   b. $H_0 : \mu_1 \geq \mu_2$, the mean did not increase between time 1 and time 2.

The sample means of the before $(\bar{x}_1)$ and after $(\bar{x}_2)$ raw scores are calculated with these formulas:

$$\bar{x}_1 = \frac{\sum_{i=1}^{n} x_{i1}}{N}, \text{ and } \bar{x}_2 = \frac{\sum_{i=1}^{n} x_{i2}}{N}, \quad \text{where } x_{i1} \text{ is the "before" raw score of the } i\text{th unit and } x_{i2} \text{ is the "after" raw score of the } i\text{th unit.}$$

Substituting for Degrees of Freedom and $s_{\bar{x}_1 - \bar{x}_2}$

The basic procedure used in the case of independent samples is also followed with before-and-after tests. However, the fact that only one group (the entire sample) is being measured makes it necessary to alter some of the calculations. The most obvious change is that the degrees of freedom no longer equal $n - 2$, because we have not divided the population and sample into two groups. Instead, $d.f. = n - 1$, underscoring the fact that we are concerned with only one group (although it is measured twice).

The other major substitution in the before-and-after test is for the estimated standard error of the differences ($s_{\bar{x}_1 - \bar{x}_2}$). The estimated standard error of the differences is no longer a valid estimate of the standard deviation of the sampling distribution. This is because we are no longer dealing with the sampling distribution of the differences between group means. Instead, the correct sampling distribution is that of the averages of before-and-after differences. The appropriate term is thus called the (estimated) *standard error of the mean difference,* and it is symbolized as $s_{\bar{D}}$.

The method of calculating $s_{\bar{D}}$ involves several complicated steps, to be shown below. But, assuming that we have found the value of $s_{\bar{D}}$, for the before-and-after test,

$$t_{calculated} = \frac{x_1 - x_2}{s_{\bar{D}}}.$$

As usual, this $t_{calculated}$ is to be compared with a t_{table} at $d.f. = n - 1$ and $\alpha = .05$ or $.01$. The column of table A.2 specified by the "2-tail" header is used for two-tailed tests, and the column specified by the "1-tail" header is for one-tailed tests.

Calculating $s_{\bar{D}}$

The formula for the standard error of the mean difference is

$$s_{\bar{D}} = \frac{s_D}{\sqrt{n-1}}.$$

To find it, we first need to calculate s_D (note that there is no bar above the D in the subscript), which is referred to as *the standard deviation of the before-after differences.* This is derived from raw data using the procedure shown in table 10.4.

Following the formula, because

$$s_{\bar{D}} = \frac{s_D}{\sqrt{n-1}},$$

we can restate

$$t_{calculated} = \frac{\bar{x}_1 - \bar{x}_2}{s_D/(n-1)}.$$

An Illustration of the Before-and-After Test

To illustrate the procedure of before-and-after testing, we return to the study of dorm students and their travels home. In Chapter 4, data were presented on the number of trips each of 15 students took during a particular semester. In Chapter 9, we discussed a program that would provide a small travel allowance for a certain maximum number of trips. Here we extend the illustration further by supposing that this policy has been initiated.

TABLE 10.4   Worksheet for s_D

To find s_D

1. Subtract the "after" raw score from the "before" raw score for each unit in the sample, $x_{i1} - x_{i2}$, where x_{i1} is the "before" raw score of the ith unit and x_{i2} is the "after" raw score of the ith unit. Each of these is a "difference," symbolized as D_i, of which there is one for each of the n units in the sample.
2. Next, square each D_i to eliminate the possibility that positive differences will cancel negative ones. These are symbolized as D_i^2.
3. Sum these squared differences. This produces the sum of the squared differences term,

$$\sum_{i=1}^{n} D_i^2 = \sum_{i=1}^{n} \left(x_{i1} - x_{i2} \right)^2.$$

4. Divide this sum, $\sum_{i=1}^{n} D_i^2$, by n to obtain the average of the squared differences:

$$\frac{\sum_{i=1}^{n} D_i^2}{n}$$

5. Next, find the mean of the "before" raw scores and the mean of the "after" raw scores, which will be used in the denominator of $t_{calculated}$. The familiar formulas for these are

$$\overline{x}_1 = \frac{\sum_{i=1}^{n} x_{i1}}{n}$$

$$\overline{x}_2 = \frac{\sum_{i=1}^{n} x_{i2}}{n}$$

6. Find the difference between these, $(\overline{x}_1 - \overline{x}_1)$, which is the difference between the "before" and "after" means.
7. Next, subtract the difference in step 6 from the sum in step 4:

$$\frac{\sum_{i=1}^{n} D_i^2}{n} - (\overline{x}_1 - \overline{x}_1)^2$$

The square root of this difference is s_D. Thus,

$$s_D = \sqrt{\frac{\sum_{i=1}^{n} D_i^2}{n} - (\overline{x}_1 - \overline{x}_2)^2}.$$

BOX 10.1   **Statistics for Sociologists**

The Study of Altruism and an Application to the t-Test

Altruism is a type of social action whose purpose is to benefit others, without regard to the well-being of the self. It is as much a part of the human condition as is its opposite, *egoism*, which is defined as social action intended to benefit the self without regard to the well-being of others. Its importance in sociology is underscored by the fact that the term *altruism* (and *egoism,* as well) was coined by the founder of the discipline, Auguste Comte, in the mid-nineteenth century, although scholars and ordinary people alike had shown an interest in the phenomenon long before then (for a summary of this research, see Barber (2004) and Delega and Grzelac (1982)).

Recent research in sociology and several other fields has demonstrated that altruism has an important role to play in human relations.[*] Some of the most influential studies in this area were conducted by Pitirim A. Sorokin (1880–1968), the first Chair of the Department of Sociology at Harvard University and 1964 President of the American Sociological Association. Sorokin believed that if we could unlock the secrets of altruism, the knowledge gained would contribute to what he called "the ennoblement of human personality."

> The practice of kindness and love is one of the best therapies for many mental disorders; for the elimination of sorrow, loneliness and unhappiness; for the mitigation of hatred and other antisocial tendencies, and, above all, for the ennoblement of human personality, for release in man of his creative forces, and for the attainment of union with God and peace with oneself, others, and the universe (Sorokin 1948: 225).

Since Sorokin's death in 1968, several studies have supplemented his approach. Among the most important are those of Kristen Renwick Monroe, especially in relation to her discovery of the key cognitive orientation, *perception of a common humanity* (Monroe, 1996; 2001). According to Monroe, the more that people view humanity as an integral whole and see the differences between nations, genders, classes, and other in-group and out-group divisions as unimportant, the more likely they are to perform altruistic acts.

In contrast to these lofty ideals, it often seems as if we live in a society that is driven by fear of others rather than a desire to help them (see Glassner, 1999). As we reach adulthood, the media inundate us with atrocities, robberies, muggings, and rapes. Rarely, if ever, are we told that we live in a safe place, free from harm. What are the

---

[*] Simmons (1991) made this point emphatically in her Presidential Address to the Midwest Sociological Society; and the recent collection by Field (2001) traces the history of the concept in sociology and related disciplines.

effects of these constant messages? Do they alter our perceptions of the world and of humanity? Do they create anxiety and thus serve as a barrier to altruistic behavior?

Research on Altruism[**]

An exploratory research project intended to provide answers to these questions was undertaken during the 2003–2004 academic year. The basic design of the study was to compare two groups of people: one consisting of individuals who had experiences that caused serious fear and anxiety, the other a control group whose members did not have such experiences. It was hypothesized that the groups would differ with respect to their beliefs in a common humanity and would thus also differ in the extent to which they were altruistically inclined. Prior to the study, it was not clear whether the survivors of fearsome experiences would be less or more fearful. Certainly the experience would affect them. But would it make them more afraid, or would the fact that they did survive make them less anxious about what is, after all, inevitable? This dilemma led to the decision to perform two-tailed *t*-tests, as noted below.

The extensive scholarly literature on death and dying indicates that anticipation of one's own death or that of a close relative or friend is strongly associated with fear, especially in U.S. culture. Thus, in light of Monroe's work, the researchers sought to understand how these specific fears may affect or serve as a barrier to altruistic behavior by altering one's perception of a common humanity. This connection led to the decision to employ in the study (1) an experimental group of cancer survivors (either in remission or living with the active disease) and (2) a matched control group of cancer-free individuals.

Again in keeping with Monroe's approach, members of both groups were interviewed in depth about their experiences and attitudes. A total of $n = 32$ subjects consisted of 19 non–cancer survivors and 13 cancer survivors. Of these, 24 were female and 8 were male. The results, which are summarized by Weinstein and Corwin (2006), shed much light on the relationship of interest. They seemed to support the hypothesis concerning the relationship between fear, on one hand, and the perception of common humanity/altruism connection, on the other.

Following the interviews, the subjects completed a questionnaire that included scales intended to measure the key variables:

- The Collett-Lester Fear of Death Scale
- The Self-Report Altruism Scale
- Perceptions of a Common Humanity Scale

[**] The research reported here was conducted by Jennifer Haskin Corwin for her M.A. thesis at the Department of Sociology, Anthropology, and Criminology, Eastern Michigan University, 2005.

Sample Scale Items

1. Collett-Lester

Based on the following scale, how much do the following items disturb you or make you anxious:

	Not at all		Somewhat		Very
	1	2	3	4	5

The shortness of life	1	2	3	4	5
Missing out on so much after you die	1	2	3	4	5
Dying young	1	2	3	4	5
How it will feel to be dead	1	2	3	4	5

2. Self-Report Altruism Scale

Please indicate the number of times in the past 12 months you have performed the following actions using the following scale:

1 = Never
2 = Once
3 = More than Once
4 = Often
5 = Very Often

I have assisted someone experiencing car trouble	1	2	3	4	5
I have given someone directions	1	2	3	4	5
I have made change for someone	1	2	3	4	5
I have given money to someone who needed (or asked for) it	1	2	3	4	5
I have done volunteer work for a charity	1	2	3	4	5

3. Perceptions of a Common Humanity Scale

Please indicate the most accurate response for you, in terms of the following items. Please answer all questions to the best of your ability using the following scale:

Immediate Family Only = 1
(Spouse/Children/Parents)

Extended Family & All of the Above = 2
(Aunts, Uncles, etc.)

Friends & All of the Above = 3

FIGURE 10.2   Sample scale items for altruism study.

Neighbors & All of the Above = 4

Co-workers/In-Group Members/Club Affiliates & All of the Above = 5

Acquaintances & All of the Above = 6

Strangers & All of the Above = 7

Please indicate to whom you would *be willing* to lend money for a period of 1 month	1	2	3	4	5	6	7
Please indicate to whom you would give a ride in your car, if the need were to present itself	1	2	3	4	5	6	7
Please indicate to whom you would give assistance if they were stranded	1	2	3	4	5	6	7
Please indicate to whom you would give up your place in line	1	2	3	4	5	6	7

FIGURE 10.2   (continued)

Each is a Likert scale (see Chapter 3) with a minimum of 1 point and a maximum of 5 points. Sample items for each scale are shown in figure 10.2 (a fourth scale was used but is not included here).

   The scores on each of these scales were used as the dependent variable in a two-tailed *t*-test of independent means. The independent variable is group membership: whether or not an individual was a cancer survivor.

   The hypotheses tested were:

- $H_0: \mu_1 = \mu_2$. There is no difference in the population between the mean scale scores of survivors and non-survivors.
- $H_r: \mu_1 \neq \mu_2$. The population mean scale scores do differ between groups.

   As table 10.5 indicates, the means of the two sample groups did differ on each of the variables (with the control group scoring higher on each). In combination with the results of the in-depth interviews, these findings support the view that some degree of association exists among the variables; however, they are inconclusive regarding specifically *how* they are related.

   By the criteria of the *t*-test, the results do *not* suggest a statistically significant relationship between the independent variable and any of the dependent variables. As shown in table 10.6, the differences between the means are 0.53 (fear of death), 0.23 (altruism), and 0.33 (perception of common humanity). The largest of these differences

TABLE 10.5   Independent-sample *t*-test: no cancer/cancer

Dependent variable	Grouping variable	n	x̄	s
Total fear	No cancer	18	3.03	0.643
	Cancer	13	2.5	0.925
Perception of common humanity	No cancer	18	5.09	0.655
	Cancer	13	4.86	1.225
Altruism	No cancer	17	3.2	0.493
	Cancer	13	2.88	0.558

is on the fear of death scale. In terms of the question raised above, here is some evidence that the cancer survivors are *less* fearful than others. Yet none of these differences is large enough to justify rejecting the null hypothesis. According to the results in table 10.6, in every case $t_{calculated} < t_{table}$.

Beyond the demonstration of how the independent-sample *t*-test is applied, a lesson learned from this experiment is that the researcher must sometimes accept null hypotheses. As in this case, other aspects of the study were more promising. There are many possible reasons why the results did not turn out as hoped—including a problem with the validity of one or more of the scales. We do know that much additional work is needed on this problem. We can be assured that the results of this experiment, disappointing as they may have been, will prove valuable as we continue to explore altruism and the ways in which it is associated with other sociological phenomena.

TABLE 10.6   *t*-test for equality of means: no cancer/cancer

Scale	Variances	$\bar{x}_1 - \bar{x}_2$	$t_{calculated}$	d.f.	t_{table}	Decision
Total fear	Equal	0.53	1.868	29	2.045	Do not reject H_0
	Unequal		1.763	20.1	2.086	
Perception of common humanity	Equal	0.23	0.668	29	2.045	Do not reject H_0
	Unequal		0.609	17.0	2.110	
Altruism	Equal	0.33	1.697	28	2.048	Do not reject H_0
	Unequal		1.668	24.1	2.064	

Information was then collected on student travel during the first semester, following implementation of the plan, and it was compared to the patterns observed prior to the change. The researchers assumed that if any change in travel patterns occurred, it would be an increase. That is, the subsidies would make it possible to take one or more free trips in addition to the usual number.

In order to determine whether this was a correct assumption, the researchers performed a one-tailed before-and-after *t*-test, using the following null and research hypotheses:

$H_0: \mu_B \geq \mu_A$. The mean number of trips in the population did not increase after the policy was put into effect.

$H_r: \mu_B < \mu_A$. The mean number of trips in the population did increase after the policy was put into effect.

The raw data and calculations are shown in table 10.7. These findings indicate that the average number of trips did increase after the policy, from 2.53 to 3.07 per student. Several of the students, including Allison, Charles, and Janella, did take one or two additional trips, whereas Brenda, Frank, and others did not change their patterns. In contrast, Dawn actually took one less trip. Now, because the administration wishes to generalize these results to the entire dorm population, it tested the null hypothesis shown above.

TABLE 10.7   Data on travel patterns for 15 students, before and after the new policy

Student	Before: number of trips home	After: number of trips home	Difference, D	D^2
Allison	3	4	−1	1
Brenda	2	2	0	0
Charles	0	1	−1	1
Dawn	5	4	1	1
Eugene	3	4	−1	1
Frank	3	3	0	0
Glen	5	5	0	0
Harriet	2	3	−1	1
Ian	1	2	−1	1
Janella	1	3	−2	4
Kris	3	3	0	0
Leora	2	2	0	0
Mike	0	2	−2	4
Nancy	4	5	−1	1
Jaepil	4	3	−1	1
Totals	38	46	−10	16
Means	$\bar{x}_B = 38/15 = 2.53$	$\bar{x}_A = 46/15 = 3.07$	$\bar{D} = -10/15 = -0.67$	$\sum_{i=1}^{n} D_i^2 / n = 16/15 = 1.07$

The first step is to find $t_{calculated}$, for which we need to derive s_D and $s_{\bar{D}}$. The quantities to be substituted for the symbols in the equation

$$s_D = \sqrt{\frac{\sum\limits_{i=1}^{n} D_i^2}{n} - (\bar{x}_1 - \bar{x}_2)^2}$$

are found at the bottom of table 10.7. Thus,

$$s_D = \sqrt{1.07 - 0.54^2} = \sqrt{1.07 - 0.2916} = \sqrt{0.778} = 0.882$$

Now, $s_{\bar{D}} = s_D/(n-1) = 0.882/14 = 0.063$. Therefore

$$t_{calculated} = \frac{\bar{x}_1 - \bar{x}_2}{s_{\bar{D}}} = \frac{-0.54}{0.063} = -8.57$$

Because this is a one-tailed test, the next step is to compare the sign of t to the sign of the hypothesized difference between the means. We see that the research hypothesis indicates that $\mu_B < \mu_A$, and under this condition $\mu_B - \mu_A < 0$. Therefore the difference between the sample means as well as the calculated t should be negative, which they are. If they were not, then there would be a discrepancy between the research hypothesis and the outcome, which would signal acceptance of the null without reference to the table. However, because there is agreement in this case, we do go to table A.2, "1-tail" column at $d.f. = 14$ and $\alpha = .01$ and $.05$. We see that $t_{table} = 1.761$ and 2.624 at the respective levels of significance.

With $t_{calculated} = -8.57$, we reject the null hypothesis and accept the research hypothesis. It is likely that the policy does increase the travel patterns of dorm students.

Summary

In this chapter, we expanded or discussion of confidence intervals and the close relationship they have with hypothesis testing that began in Chapter 9. Here, we turned to situations in which the researcher is interested in generalizing about the difference (or lack of difference) between two sample means for the population from which the samples were drawn. In this context, the widely used t-test was introduced and illustrated. We saw that different variations of this procedure are employed, depending on whether samples are truly independent (as opposed to being the same sample measured twice) and whether our null hypothesis states "no difference" between population means or indicates that one is "less than" or "greater than" the other.

These basic concepts and procedures are relevant to some extent in all of the inductive applications that follow. They are especially relevant to analysis of variance (ANOVA), the subject of Chapter 11. ANOVA simply takes the techniques used in the two-means test (such as finding $t_{calculated}$) and extends them to cases in which we are comparing three or more means (where $t_{calculated}$ is replaced by $F_{calculated}$). The main reason we calculate a t value (or an F value in Chapter 11) is to use it in hypothesis testing—an inductive application. But it is worth emphasizing that these statistics can also be used descriptively as measures of the association between the variables involved. Although this is an incidental point here, it becomes increasingly important as we move to the later chapters. A discussion of testing the difference between proportions can be found in the online Chapter 15.

KEY TERMS

Before-and-after test: A test of the difference between two means, using the t statistic, that represent the observations on one group made at two different times. Also called a paired-samples test.

Critical region: The portion of a sampling distribution, found in one or both of its tails, that indicates that the null hypothesis should be rejected. The critical regions most commonly used in hypothesis testing contain 5% ($\alpha = .05$) or 1% ($\alpha = .01$) of all possible population parameters such as ($\mu_1 - \mu_2$).

Estimated standard error of the differences: A statistic used to evaluate the standard deviation of the sampling distribution of differences when the standard deviations of the population groups are not known.

Independent samples: The two groups of distinct individuals compared in the t-test of mean differences.

Two-tailed tests: Tests of hypotheses in which the null states "no difference" (e.g., between sample means).

WEB SITES TO BOOKMARK

1. www.physics.csbsju.edu/stats/t-test.html
   This site contains a clear introduction to the t-test and its proper use.

2. www.physics.csbsju.edu/stats/Paired_t-test _NROW_form.html
   Here the focus is specifically on two-sample tests.

3. http://nimitz.mcs.kent.edu/~blewis/stat/tTest .html
   This interactive site from Kent State University includes a note on why t is referred to as "Student's t" (see note 6 in Chapter 8).

4. www.graphpad.com/Calculators/ttest1.cfm
   Here is an easy-to-use t-test calculator.

5. www.animatedsoftware.com/statglos/sgttest.htm
   This is a glossary that includes definitions of "t-test" and related terms.

6. http://www.geometry.net/scientists/gosset _william.php
   This site is dedicated to the life and work of William Gosset ("Student"; see note 6 in Chapter 8).

SOLUTION-CENTERED APPLICATION

The manager of a large engineering company has decided to experiment with a telecommuting system, in which employees would work from home and communicate by e-mail, fax, and telephone. The experiment was designed to provide several pieces of information, including the impact of the new system on the employees' morale and on their productivity. The research team hired to evaluate the experiment formed two groups of randomly assigned employees, each consisting of 20 individuals. The first, the experimental group, was designated as group A. The other, the control group, was designated B. Group A would work at home for three weeks, while the members of group B would maintain their normal routines.

Prior to the study the members of each group were given two tests, each scored on a scale of 0 to 10 points. The first was the morale test, with 0 indicating very low morale and 10 indicating high morale. The second was the productivity test, with 0 indicating low productivity and 10 indicating high productivity. After the three-week period, the tests were administered again. Table 10.8

shows the means and the standard deviations for each group on each test.

Individual "before" and "after" scores were not provided to the researchers, so paired-sample tests were not possible. Nevertheless, they were able to use the data in the table to test several hypotheses, including the following (stated as null hypotheses):

A. H_0: The morale of the two groups did not differ before the three weeks.

B. H_0: After the three weeks, the morale of group A was lower than or equal to the morale of group B.

C. H_0: The productivity of the two groups did not differ before the three weeks.

D. H_0: After three weeks, the productivity of group A was higher than or equal to the productivity of group B.

Using the data above and the techniques introduced in the first part of this chapter, test these hypotheses. Based on your conclusions, what can you say about the effectiveness of the telecommuting experiment?

TABLE 10.8   "Before" and "after" measures of morale and productivity

	Group A	Group B
Morale before	$\bar{x} = 8.0, s = 0.8$	$\bar{x} = 8.1, s = 0.8$
Morale after	$\bar{x} = 6.0, s = 1.0$	$\bar{x} = 8.0, s = 0.8$
Productivity before	$\bar{x} = 7.5, s = 0.5$	$\bar{x} = 7.6, s = 0.6$
Productivity after	$\bar{x} = 9.0, s = 1.0$	$\bar{x} = 7.5, s = 0.7$

Comparing Three or More Samples in Small-Group Research

This chapter continues our introduction to inductive techniques for comparing differences of means that we began in Chapter 10. The procedures to be discussed here are in many ways similar to those used in two-sample t-tests. For example, we test a pair of hypotheses: (1) H_r, the research hypothesis, which states what we expect to be true; and (2) H_0, the null hypothesis, which states the opposite. The hypotheses refer to parameters—characteristics of a population, and in particular, a set of population means (μ).

As with the two-tailed t-test, the null hypotheses of interest in this chapter state that there is *no difference* between the means. The research hypotheses state that the means *do differ*. To test the hypotheses, we employ statistics—sample data, particularly sample means, deviations, variances, and sample sizes. These statistics are then used to calculate a "cooked" score, which, in the case of the t-test, we symbolized as $t_{calculated}$. Next, we find a value from a table of values along a frequency distribution(s), symbolized as t_{table} when the distribution is the t distribution (table A.2). To find the correct t_{table}, we had to specify a level of significance ($\alpha = .05$ or $.01$) and a number of degrees of freedom ($d.f.$) based on the sample size(s), n. Finally, we compare $t_{calculated}$ to t_{table} and make a decision to reject the null hypothesis or not, based on the decision rule.

The procedures featured in this chapter, known as *analysis of variance* (ANOVA), are designed to test hypotheses that refer to the differences among three or more means.

One-Way Analysis of Variance

The type of ANOVA to be discussed in this section, *one-way* ANOVA, is a bivariate application.[1] In place of $t_{calculated}$ and the t distribution, ANOVA uses the F statistic. As in the case of the t-test for the difference of two means, the dependent variable in ANOVA is numerical (tuition in dollars, age in years, etc.), and the independent variable is either nominal or ordinal.

However, rather than being a dichotomy, the independent variable must now have at least three attributes. For example, the variable might be "type of university," with the attributes "private," "religious," and "public"; "region of the country," with the attributes "North," South," "East," and "West"; or class, with the attributes "freshman," sophomore," junior," and "senior." These attributes divide the population and the samples drawn from it into three or more groups, each of which has its own size, mean, variance, and so on.

The hypotheses of interest are *always* two-tailed. The research hypothesis does not specify that one population mean is greater (or less) than another, only that the means *are* or *are not equal*. These are presented as follows.

$H_0: \mu_1 = \mu_2 = \mu_3 = \cdots = \mu_k$, where k is the number of groups. There is no difference among the population means for the variable of interest.

$H_r: \mu_i \neq \mu_j$, for at least one pair i, j. There is a difference between at least two of the population means for the variable of interest. With three groups, 1, 2, and 3, i and j might be 1 and 2, or 1 and 3, or 2 and 3, etc.

In applying the t-test to the difference between two means in Chapter 10, we noted that if the population variances, σ_1^2 and σ_2^2, cannot be assumed to be equal, the procedure needs to be altered (when deriving $t_{calculated}$ and when determining $d.f.$). The same applies to the ANOVA F test for three or more means, where the population variances for each group are $\sigma_1^2, \sigma_2^2, \ldots, \sigma_k^2$.

In the following discussion, we shall assume equal population variances, with the understanding that this assumption may not always be warranted. In lieu of an alternative method, we can use the fact that the differences between the subsample variances, $s_1^2, s_2^2, \ldots, s_k^2$, are known and that they reasonably reflect the differences between population variances. So we can observe the size of the sample variance differences to decide informally whether the assumption is valid. If the sample differences appear small, then nothing further needs to be done. If they seem to be large, then our decision to reject or fail to reject H_0 should be stated with a caution.

The F *Sampling Distribution*

The sampling distribution used with ANOVA is neither the normal (z) nor the t distribution, although it is related to these. Rather, it is the F distribution, shown in table A.3 in the Appendix. Like the t distribution, this is actually a set of theoretical probability distributions of all sample differences among means, with each distribution corresponding to the number of attributes of the independent variable, which is the number of groups into which the population is divided. The correct distribution for any given test is determined by subtracting 1 from the number of groups to determine the *between-groups d.f.* (abbreviated as $df_{between}$):

$$df_{between} = k - 1.$$

where k stands for the number of groups: For example, if $k = 3$, then $df_{between} = (3 - 1) = 2$; if $k = 4$, then $df_{between} = 3$, and so on. These are shown as the columns in table A.3.

Once the correct distribution is determined, then we use the total sample size n_{total} to locate the correct table value, F_{table}. In particular, from n_{total} we subtract k to get the *within-groups d.f.*, or df_{within}:

$$df_{within} = n_{total} - k$$

The "within" refers to within the groups. If our total sample size, $n_{total} = 35$ and $k = 3$, then $df_{within} = 35 - 3 = 32$, and so on.

The table for the F distribution is usually presented in two sections, one for $\alpha = .05$ and one for $\alpha = .01$. Table A.3 has this format, and to illustrate its use we will refer to both sections. Here we have assumed that $df_{between} = (k - 1) = 2$ and $df_{within} = n_{total} - k = 32$.

To find the appropriate F_{table} value, we first select α to put us in the correct section of the table. We begin with $\alpha = .05$. Next, we locate the *column* that corresponds to $df_{between}$; here it is the column with "2" at the top. Next, we find the *row* that corresponds to df_{within}, which is 32, rounded down to "30" (as we rounded down to the next smaller available *d.f.* when looking up t_{table} in table A.2).[2] The cell in the "2" column and the "30" row has the value 3.32. This is our F_{table} at $\alpha = .05$ for 2 and 30 degrees of freedom. At $\alpha = .01$, this procedure gives an F_{table} value of 5.39.

You can compare these table values to our original "cooked" scores, the z or standard scores. Recall that in the normal distribution, the table z at 95% (.05) = 1.96, and at 99% (.01) it is 2.58. In the table for the F distribution, as the *d.f.* values increase, moving to the right and down the table, the F_{table} values decrease until they reach 1.96 in the .05 section at *d.f.* = 24 and 25 and they reach 2.58 in the .01 section at *d.f.* = 24 and 26 *d.f.* In fact, the F_{table} values get even smaller than these at very large *d.f.* values. This indicates that the F distribution is not normal for small sample sizes or few groups, and more leeway is needed to reject the null hypothesis. But at a particular point, with large n_{total} and k, the distribution is normal. With very large *d.f.* values, *less* leeway is needed than with a normal distribution.

The Calculated F Ratio

As in the case of confidence intervals with σ not known (Chapter 9) and two-sample *t*-tests (Chapter 10), the researcher calculates a statistic or "cooked score." This score is based on sample information: n, $\bar{x}$, and s^2. In ANOVA this score is $F_{calculated}$. Because of the way it is calculated, F is never a negative number (which is a hint as to why there are no one-tailed tests with ANOVA).

We see that there is one sample size, one mean, one variance, and so on for each of the k groups or subsamples. These are designated as n_1, n_2, . . . , n_k (the subsample sizes do not need to be equal); $\bar{x}_1$, $\bar{x}_2$, . . . , $\bar{x}_k$; and s_1^2, s_2^2, . . . , s_k^2. We also have corresponding values for the entire set of the k groups: n_{total}, $\bar{x}_{total}$, and s_{total}^2, where $n_{total} = n_1 + n_2 + \cdots + n_k$.

Like the z and t statistics, $F_{calculated}$ is a *ratio*: one quantity divided by another quantity. However, in the case of F the word "ratio" is used explicitly to emphasize the fact that it is measuring the one quantity in direct relation to the other: the numerator of the ratio measures *between*-group characteristics, and the denominator measures the characteristics *within* the groups. Thus, as a ratio $F_{calculated}$ describes the *between/within* aspects of our sample and its k subsamples.

In testing hypotheses with ANOVA, we compare $F_{calculated}$ to the F_{table} value at the appropriate α (.05 or .01), $df_{between}$, and df_{within}. Following the decision rule, we then determine whether the null hypothesis should be rejected. We will return to this decision step following a closer look at $F_{calculated}$.

The F Ratio as a Measure of Association

In Chapter 10 it was pointed out that $t_{calculated}$ can be used as a measure of the degree of association between the independent and dependent variables. The same is true of $F_{calculated}$. In fact, in this case it is a very meaningful measure. Because F is the ratio of *between*-group and *within*-group characteristics, it indicates the extent to which the k groups are actually different with respect to the dependent variable.

A large $F_{calculated}$ tells us that the differences in the values of the dependent variable between the groups are large relative to the differences in the values within the respective groups. In other words, the degree of association is high: the independent and dependent co-vary substantially. Although it is a relative matter, $F_{calculated} = 10.0$ or above (i.e., the between-group differences are at least 10 times as large as the within-group differences) is usually considered to be very high.

Although $F_{calculated}$ is never negative, it can be quite small, with a lower limit of 0. A zero value, which in practice rarely occurs, indicates that there are *no* differences in the values of the dependent variable between the groups. That is, the independent and dependent variables are completely unassociated—they do not co-vary at all. Similarly, a small but nonzero $F_{calculated}$, such as 0.36, indicates that differences between groups are minimal compared to the within-group differences. These relationships are illustrated in figure 11.1.

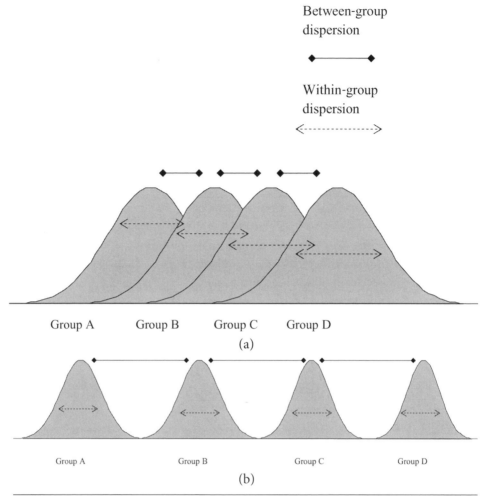

FIGURE 11.1   (a) Much within-group dispersion and little between-group dispersion (small $F_{calculated}$); (b) little within-group dispersion and much between-group dispersion (large $F_{calculated}$).

Decomposing the F Ratio

The value of $F_{calculated}$ is derived from sample data by combining (1) a set of squared deviations with (2) the *between* and *within* degrees of freedom. The final formula is symbolized as the ratio

$$F_{calculated} = \frac{MS_{between}}{MS_{within}},$$

where *MS* stands for "mean square" (for mean of the squared deviations).

The concept of the squared deviation was introduced in Chapter 7 in terms of the numerator of the important measure of dispersion, the sample variance:

$$s^2 = \frac{\sum_{i=1}^{n}\left(x_i - \bar{x}\right)^2}{n}.$$

Here $\left(x_i - \bar{x}\right)^2$ is one of n squared deviations. This concept is applied in ANOVA to determine whether the dispersion between the k groups is greater than the combined dispersion within the groups, and, if so, how much greater. The two sets of frequency polygons in figure 11.1 illustrate this *between/within* relationship that F is measuring.

Figure 11.1(a) depicts a situation in which the between-groups dispersion is relatively small and the within-groups dispersion is relatively large. We can see that the groups are not well defined and that there is considerable overlap between them. Thus, knowing which group a certain unit is part of does not necessarily indicate its value for the dependent variable of interest. Figure 11.1(b), in contrast, depicts a situation in which the between-groups dispersion is great and the within-groups dispersion is relatively small. In this case, the groups are separate and well defined, and there is little overlap. Here, knowing the group to which a unit belongs is a reliable indicator of its relation to the dependent variable, with group A consistently containing the lowest values and group D the highest. In both cases, dispersion is measured by s^2, sample variance—hence the name of the procedure, "analysis of variance."

Because in figure 11.1(a) the ratio of between to within variance is low, the distribution will produce a relatively small $MS_{between}$, a relatively large MS_{within}, and an $F_{calculated}$ with a low value. In hypothesis testing, this is likely to lead to failure to reject the null hypothesis. The distribution shown in figure 11.1(b), on the other hand, will produce a large $MS_{between}$, a small MS_{within}, and an $F_{calculated}$ with a high value. This is likely to lead to rejection of the null.

Calculating the F Ratio

Knowing that $F_{calculated} = MS_{between}/MS_{within}$, we can now consider how are the MS values in the numerator and denominator are derived. This derivation requires that we first find $df_{between}$, df_{within}, and the between and within sums of squares, symbolized as $SS_{between}$ and SS_{within}. The term "sum of squares" is a shortened version of "sum of deviations from the mean, squared," and is familiar as the numerator of the formula for sample variance: $\Sigma(x_i - \bar{x})^2$. In calculating the F ratio, $SS_{between}$ and SS_{within} are also sums of squared deviations from a mean; but here there is more than one mean to be considered. Each of the k groups has a mean, and there is a mean for all k groups combined. The formulas developed in this section take these differing means into account. Similarly, in addition to a degrees-of-freedom value and sum of squares for *between* (numerator) and *within* (denominator) values, there is also a total degrees of freedom, $df_{total} = df_{between} + df_{within}$, and a total sum of squares, $SS_{total} = SS_{between} + SS_{within}$. These do not appear in the formula, but they are used for intermediate calculations.

1. The numerator of $F_{calculated}$, $MS_{between}$, is the *average of the deviations between the k groups,* of which the typical term is $n_i(\bar{x}_i - \bar{x}_{total})^2$, where i is one of the groups. These are added together to create $SS_{between}$, the between-groups sum of squares:

$$SS_{between} = \sum_{i=1}^{k} n_i(\bar{x}_i - \bar{x}_{total})^2$$

This sum is then divided by $df_{between}$. The formula is, thus,

$$MS_{between} = \frac{SS_{between}}{df_{between}}.$$

2. Similarly, MS_{within}, in the denominator, is an average of the deviations *within* each of the k groups, of which the typical term is $(x_{ji} - \bar{x}_j)^2$, where x_{ji} is an individual score in group j and $\bar{x}_j$ is the mean for that group. These are added together to create SS_{within}, the within-groups sum of squares:

$$SS_{within} = \sum_{j=1}^{k} \sum_{i=1}^{n_j} (x_{ji} - \bar{x}_j)^2.$$

This sum is divided by df_{within}. The formula is, thus,

$$MS_{within} = \frac{SS_{within}}{df_{within}}.$$

The ratio of these two averages, $MS_{between}/MS_{within}$, gives us $F_{calculated}$. It is the size of the ratio that indicates the degree of association between the independent and dependent variables and, thus, the extent to which the groups are independent. When this ratio is compared to F_{table}, we can determine whether the null hypothesis, $H_0: \mu_1 = \mu_2 = \cdots = \mu_k$, should be accepted.

An Illustration of ANOVA

To illustrate one-way ANOVA, we return to our study of household incomes. In addition to collecting information on monthly incomes and length of residence, the researchers ranked the respective property values of the houses. The ranking has four values: 1 (low), 2 (average), 3 (high), and 4 (very high). These were determined on the basis of the assessment of the property at the time of purchase. Using these attributes, the population and the sample of households can be divided into the four corresponding groups.

From earlier illustrations, we have a fairly good idea about the central tendency and dispersion of the population and of several samples with $n = 50$ that were randomly drawn from it. We have also used the t-test to determine that it is quite likely that incomes vary between recent and older households. With the data on property values at hand, we can now carry this investigation further by using ANOVA to test whether average incomes vary among the four ranked groups. First, we should note that the dependent variable, income, is numerical, as is required in ANOVA. The independent variable, property value group, is ordinal with three or more attributes. (A nominal-level independent variable with three or more attributes would also be legitimate.) The appropriate null and research hypotheses are:

$H_0: \mu_1 = \mu_2 = \mu_3 = \mu_4$. The households whose property has low value in the population have the same mean income as those with average, high, and very high property values.

$H_r: \mu_i \neq \mu_j$, for at least one pair i, j. At least two of the ranked groups in the population have different mean incomes.

To test these hypotheses, a sample of $n = 50$ households was drawn from the population, shown in table 11.1 (49 households are listed because one of the households in the original sample did not report income and was counted as missing). Table 11.2 summarizes the sample statistics. We can see that for the 49 households as a whole, the mean income is just over $5,100, and the standard deviation is just over $3,600.

Each of the four rows below the "Entire sample" row in table 11.2 contains information about one of the ranked groups, from "low" to "very high." Clearly, the groups differ in size from $n_1 = 9$ to $n_2 = 18$, and in other respects. Of greatest importance in terms of ANOVA are the differences between the group means. These vary from $\bar{x}_1 = \$2,771.11$ to $\bar{x}_4 = \$9,610.00$. Moreover, the group means vary in direct relation to the ranking of the groups, with $\bar{x}_4 > \bar{x}_3 > \bar{x}_2 > \bar{x}_1$. From looking at the groups in the sample, it certainly appears that the means of the groups from which the sample was drawn are not equal. However, in order to be confident about such a generalization, we need to establish whether or not the differences among the observed means in the sample are *significant*. That is the purpose of the F test, performed through the following steps and summarized in table 11.3.

1. The first step is to derive $F_{calculated} = MS_{between}/MS_{within}$. Following the procedure outlined above, we begin by finding $SS_{between}$, the between sum of squares. This was done with SPSS and turned out to be quite a large number, 2.8×10^8 (with rounding), or about 280 million.
2. Next, we find $df_{between}$, which is equal to $k - 1$. With $k = 4$ groups, $df_{between} = 3$.

TABLE 11.1   Incomes and property values for ANOVA illustration

Monthly income	Property value[a]	Monthly income	Property value[a]
$ 500	2	$ 4,980	3
786	2	4,980	2
940	1	5,600	2
1,074	1	5,785	2
1,100	2	5,852	3
1,191	1	6,020	2
1,270	3	6,175	2
1,556	2	6,225	3
1,620	1	6,290	2
1,620	3	6,525	1
1,696	2	6,730	3
1,700	1	6,840	2
1,717	2	7,087	2
1,816	3	7,758	3
1,940	4	8,740	3
1,995	2	9,120	3
2,054	3	11,015	4
2,349	2	11,017	4
2,684	4	11,160	4
3,240	1	11,172	4
3,700	3	11,362	4
4,050	1	11,680	4
4,100	2	11,950	4
4,600	1	12,120	4
4,600	2		

[a]1 = low; 2 = average; 3 = high; 4 = very high.

TABLE 11.2   Descriptive statistics for data in table 11.1

Group	n	$\bar{x}$	s
Entire sample	49	$5,103.69	$3,617.55
Low prop. value	9	$2,771.11	$1,952.38
Average prop. value	18	$3,843.11	$2,332.80
High prop. value	12	$4,988.75	$2,854.52
Very high prop. value	10	$9,610.00	$3,869.03

TABLE 11.3   ANOVA worksheet for data in table 11.1

	SS^a	d.f.	MS	$F_{calculated}$	F_{table}	Decision
Between	2.8E+08	3	9.4E+07	12.126		
Within	3.5E+08	45	7.7E+06			
Total	6.3E+08	48				
$\alpha = .05$					2.84	Reject H_0
$\alpha = .01$					4.31	Reject H_0

^{a}These values are given in scientific notation, indicating that they have been rounded. As discussed in Appendix B, the decimal point should be moved to the right eight places. Thus, the (rounded) $SS_{between} = 280,000,000$, etc.

3. We can now replace the values in the formula, $MS_{between} = SS_{between}/df_{between} = 2.8 \times 10^8/3 = 9.4 \times 10^7$ (about 94 million).

4. From the SPSS printout, we found that SS_{within}, the within-groups sum of squares, is 3.5×10^8 (with rounding), about 350 million.

5. The within-groups sum of squares is to be divided by df_{within}, which is $n - k = 49 - 4 = 45$.

6. Now, we can replace the values in the formula $MS_{within} = SS_{within}/df_{within} = 3.5 \times 10^8/45 = 7.7 \times 10^6$ (about 8 million).

7. Thus,

$$F_{calculated} = \frac{MS_{between}}{MS_{within}} = \frac{93,599,405.2}{7,719,172.065} = 12.126.$$

This appears to be a large F value, indicating a strong association between income and property values for the sample. Next, it is to be compared with the appropriate F_{table}.

According to table A.3, at *d.f.* values of 3 and 45 (rounded to 40) with $\alpha = .05$ and .01, the F values are 2.84 and 4.31, respectively. We therefore reject the null hypothesis at both levels of significance. One or more pairs of groups in the population are highly likely to have unequal mean incomes; property values are likely to affect income. Although we have not proved it formally, it certainly appears that the households with the higher property values in the population have the higher incomes and those with the lower property values have the lower incomes.

Post-Hoc Tests: Determining the Pair(s) Contributing to a Significant *F* Ratio

The F test can help decide whether the group means in the population are all likely to be equal (as stated in the null hypothesis) or whether at least two of them are unequal. However, as just illustrated, when the null hypothesis is rejected, the F test cannot in itself indicate *which* pair or pairs may be unequal, nor can it determine which of the two means in any pair is the greater. For these purposes, several *post-hoc* (after the fact) procedures have been established and are widely used.[3] The most common among these are the LSD (not the psychedelic, but "*least significant difference*") and the Tukey HSD (*honestly significant difference*) tests. Many of these are similar to the difference-of-means *t*-test, and, in fact, the LSD procedure uses a series of *t*-tests. The main reason why these special procedures are used is that they can determine which pair(s) of groups contributed to the significant $F_{calculated}$ in one step. When the SPSS one-way ANOVA command is used, an option is provided to apply one or more post-hoc procedures. The Tukey HSD post-hoc test was run on the data of the preceding illustration, and the results indicated that the differences between the following pairs are significant, all at both $\alpha = .05$ and .01:

Low and Very High $(\bar{x}_1 - \bar{x}_4)$

Average and Very High $(\bar{x}_2 - \bar{x}_4)$

High and Very High $(\bar{x}_3 - \bar{x}_4)$

The question of when and how one employs these various tests is among the most puzzling issues in contemporary applied statistics. In fact, there is even a joke about it on the "Internet Gallery of Statistics Jokes."[4] In addition, their formulas are somewhat complicated. Our suggestion for the kinds of elementary applications discussed in this chapter is to do either of the following:

1. Make informal determinations concerning which of the pairs of means is most likely to be contributing to the significant *F* (and which of the means is the larger) simply by observation, as we have done, above.
2. Perform difference-of-means *t*-tests on the most likely pairs (or on all pairs if all seem to be candidates).

We illustrate the second option, *t*-tests, using the property value/income example in the preceding section.

With the four property value groups, there are six possible pairs of sample means whose differences might have contributed to the significant *F*. Table 11.4 lists these and all of the other information necessary to perform a one-tailed *t*-test on each pair. Because of our earlier observation that property values and incomes varied together, we will be testing in every instance the following null and research hypotheses:

$H_0: \mu_1 \geq \mu_2$. The mean income in the population of the lower-ranking group is *not less* than the mean income of the higher-ranking group.

TABLE 11.4   *t*-tests on pairs of means for a post-hoc ANOVA determination

Pair of group means	Difference in $	$s_{\bar{x}_1-\bar{x}_2}$[a]	$t_{calculated}$	d.f.	t_{table}, one-tailed $\alpha = .05$	$\alpha = .01$	Decision
$\bar{x}_1 - \bar{x}_2$	−1072.00	1134.25	−0.945	25	1.708	2.485	Fail to reject H_0
$\bar{x}_1 - \bar{x}_3$	−2217.64	225.13	−2.00	19	1.729	2.539	Reject at $\alpha = .05$, fail at $\alpha = .01$
$\bar{x}_1 - \bar{x}_4$	−6838.89	1276.56	−4.774	17	1.740	2.552	Reject
$\bar{x}_2 - \bar{x}_3$	−1145.64	1035.43	−1.025	28	1.701	2.467	Accept
$\bar{x}_2 - \bar{x}_4$	−5776.89	1095.79	−4.946	26	1.706	2.473	Reject
$\bar{x}_3 - \bar{x}_4$	−4621.25	1189.61	−3.222	20	1.725	2.528	Reject

[a] $s_{\bar{x}_1-\bar{x}_2} = \sqrt{s_1^2/(n_1-1) + s_2^2/(n_2-1)}$

$H_r: \mu_1 < \mu_2$. The mean income in the population of the lower-ranking group *is less* than the mean income of the higher-ranking group.

As table 11.4 indicates, all of the $t_{calculated}$ values are negative. Thus, in all cases, $\bar{x}_1 > \bar{x}_2$. Because the ordering is as predicted, the next step is to find the appropriate t_{table} values. Here we see that three of the six pairs produced *t* values with significant results at $\alpha = .05$ and .01, and two of the other three pairs produced *t* values that are not significant at either level. One of the pairs has a *t* value that is significant at $\alpha = .05$ but not at .01.

The pairs that contributed to the ANOVA decision to reject H_0 are (1) low and high property values, (2) average and high property values, (3) very high and high property values, and probably (4) low and very high property values. For these we rejected the *t*-test null hypotheses and concluded that the groups' mean incomes do indeed differ in the predicted direction: the households with the lower property values have the lower incomes. These results also agree with those of the Tukey HSD, although Tukey is more conservative—as it will always be—in not counting the low and very high pair as making a contribution.

Taken together, these results suggest that the households with the very highest property values clearly have the highest incomes. Moreover, they are the *only* group whose incomes are significantly higher than the others' at both $\alpha = .05$ and .01. Differences in the sample between the low and average, the average and very high, and so on, are not large enough to allow us to conclude that these means are unequal in the population.

Box 11.1 illustrates the application of ANOVA to a before-and-after testing problem.

| BOX 11.1 | **Statistics for Sociologists** |

Small-Group Research and the Difference Means

The study of small groups is the branch of microsociology that links interactions and dyadic (two-person) relationships to meso-level phenomena such as formal organizations. Because it typically deals with the dynamics of naturally occurring aggregates—families, work groups, athletic teams, etc.—many researchers see it as the approach that best demonstrates how sociological principles operate. It is also one of the most widely applied sociological specialties and has helped to shape policies and programs in education, industry, and clinical contexts. There are numerous books on the subject, and courses on small groups are offered at most colleges and universities. The field has its own scholarly journal, *Small Group Research*, which is published four times a year and is available to subscribers online at http://sgr.sagepub.com/.

Famous Experiments

A classic study of small-group dynamics, conducted in the 1920s and 1930s by George Elton Mayo, continues to influence the theories and vocabulary in sociology and related fields to the present. This is the Hawthorne Western Electric Study (Mayo, 1945; Roethlisberger and Dickson, 1939), a pioneering research project that examined working conditions at a plant that manufactured telephone equipment near Chicago, Illinois. Its findings led to the establishment of the field of "Human Relations in Industry," which emphasizes the importance of addressing the needs of workers beyond purely production-oriented concerns.

Among the concepts that this study made popular are "formal and informal norm" and "rate-busting." A formal norm is a behavioral standard that is considered official and is usually part of a written code of rules or laws (see also Chapter 6, Box 6.1). An informal norm is shared by members of a smaller group within a larger organization. It is a standard that is "understood" to apply to group members, but it is usually not written down. "Rate-busting" refers to the practice in which a member of a work group produces at a level that management stipulates by a formal norm, even when it is more than what the team's informal norm requires. It is considered deviant behavior by the team, even though it is conformity according to the official rules.

Another familiar concept that the study produced, and which in fact is named after the study, is the "Hawthorne effect." This came from the observation that work groups would perform differently, and more in keeping with the formal norms, when they knew they were being observed than when they believed that no one was watching.

This is one of the effects that researchers performing controlled experiments now routinely attempt to avoid.*

Since the days of the Hawthorne Study, small-group research has been conducted in a wide variety of settings and on an equally wide range of topics. Two of these studies, conducted by social psychologists, have received considerable attention because of ethical issues they raised concerning the appropriateness of experimenting with human subjects. One is the Milgram Study (see Miller, 1986), in which the research team led by Stanley Milgram induced student participants to believe that they were inflicting pain on other participants (although they were actually not causing *physical* harm). The other, the Zimbardo Study (after research director Philip Zimbardo), had a group of students play the roles of prisoners and inmates in a mock jail. Over the course of a few days, the students began to take their roles too seriously and the experiment had to be halted.**

A Small-Group Study of Prejudice

The principles of small-group research are illustrated in the following application of the before-and-after *t*-test. In our discussion of experimental design in Chapter 3, we referred to a study in which the level of prejudice of experimental subjects was measured before and after viewing a film. The object was to determine whether seeing the film (the independent variable) affected the level of prejudice (the dependent variable). This type of research has actually been conducted on many occasions, with a range of variations in the types of subjects, the specific experimental conditions, the kind of film that is shown, and so on.

In one version of the experiment, groups of 10 individuals were selected at random from all students enrolled in Introductory Sociology at a large university. These groups met with an instructor several times during the semester as small discussion sessions to go over the lecture material and reading assignments. Three of the groups (A, B, and C) were chosen—again, at random from the set of 10—for the purpose of the experiment. A fourth group (D) was designated as a control group.

Early in the semester, the students in each of the three experimental groups and the control group were administered a pre-test designed to measure their level of ethnic prejudice. This is a simple five-item scale, each item having a 0 or 1 answer. Total scores range from 0 to 5, with the higher scores indicating higher degrees of prejudice.

---

* An extensive body of literature has grown up around the study. Much of this work has been archived in the Hawthorne Studies Collection. See the online guide at www.library.hbs.edu/hc/wes/collections/.
** Zimbardo maintains a web site on this study that includes photographs and an interactive Q&A link. Go to http://www.prisonexp.org/.

TABLE 11.5   Conditions of small-group prejudice study

Group	Pre-test	Discussion before film	Watch film	Discussion after film	Post-test
A	Yes	Yes	Yes	Yes	Yes
B	Yes	Yes	Yes	No	Yes
C	Yes	No	Yes	No	Yes
D (control)	Yes	No	No	No	Yes

In the middle of the semester, the experimental groups—but not the control group—were shown a popular film about the Holocaust, *Europa Europa* (1991). At the end of the semester, all four groups were administered a post-test, very similar but not identical to the pre-test. In addition, two of the experimental groups (A and B) conducted a continuing discussion of prejudice prior to the showing of the film, and one of the groups (A) also had discussions of the film following its showing. These different conditions are summarized in table 11.5.

The researcher's expectation was that the level of prejudice would decline in the groups that saw the film. It was also believed that prejudice would decline more where there was prior discussion and decline the most where there was discussion before *and* after the showing.

Table 11.6 summarizes the results for each of the groups, listing the respective mean scores on the pre-test ($\bar{x}_1$) and the post-test ($\bar{x}_2$) and the differences between the pre-test and post-test means ($\bar{x}_2 - \bar{x}_1$). A 0 difference would indicate no improvement, because the pre- and post-tests results would be the same. A positive difference would indicate an *increase* in the level of prejudice, because the pre-test score would be greater than that of the post-test. A negative difference would indicate a *decrease* in the level of prejudice, because the post-test score would be greater than that of the pre-test. You can see that the signs of the differences are all negative, indicating that the post-tests all showed some improvement. The next-to-last column lists the standard error of the mean difference, ($s_{\bar{D}}$), calculated as shown in the text.

TABLE 11.6   Data and calculations for *t*-tests

Group	Pre-test mean	Post-test mean	Difference	Standard error	$t_{calculated}$
A	4.0	2.3	−1.7	0.43	−3.95
B	3.9	2.5	−1.2	0.41	−2.93
C	3.2	2.2	−1.0	0.53	−2.26
D	2.8	2.6	−0.2	0.36	−0.56

$t_{table} = 1.83$ at $d.f. = 9, a = .05$; $t_{table} = 2.82$ at $d.f. = 9, a = .01$.

Finally, with this information we derived the $t_{calculated}$ for each group, shown in the last column.

The Before-and-After t-Test

With the information shown in table 11.6, we can test the hypotheses about the likely effects of the film and related discussion in the entire population (of all possible study groups of introductory sociology students at the university) as a before-and-after *t*-test, as discussed in Chapter 10. Because the researchers anticipated not just a difference between the pre-test and post-test but actual improvement, this is a one-tailed test. The research hypothesis of interest, which applies to each of the four groups, is:

$H_r: \mu_1 < \mu_2$. The mean score on the pre-test for the population is less than the score on the post-test.

The associated null hypothesis is:

$H_0: \mu_1 \geq \mu_2$. The mean score on the pre-test for the population is *not* less than the score on the post-test.

Because each group has $n = 10$, and because the before-after *t*-test uses $d.f. = (n-1)$, $d.f.$ in each case is 9. Table A.2 shows a t_{table} value of 1.83 for one tail, $\alpha = .05$, at $d.f. = 9$ At $\alpha = .01$, the corresponding t_{table} value is 2.82.

With $t_{calculated} = -3.95$, we know from the minus sign that we are in the negative tail as required by the "<" symbol in the research hypothesis. We can then compare the values of $t_{calculated}$ and t_{table}, noting that the absolute value of $t_{calculated}$ is larger than t_{table} at both the .05 and .01 levels. We thus reject the null hypothesis and conclude that the film and discussion would probably have the desired effect on all study groups in the population.

By the same reasoning, we would conclude that the difference between pre- and post-test scores is significant, even when there was no discussion after the showing, as in group B (although the pre- and post-test difference was not as great as in group A). The $t_{calculated}$ for group C, which saw the film but had no discussion, is significant at .05 but not at .01, which suggests that discussion of some type does make a difference. Finally, we cannot reject the null hypothesis at either .01 or .05 in the control group. The difference between pre-test and post-test scores was negative, as anticipated, but it is too small to make a statistical difference.

The results of this study support the view that prejudice can be reduced in a group setting. Of perhaps greater importance, they support the view that the reduction is

TABLE 11.7 Data for ANOVA: individual differences between two scores

	Group A	Group B	Group C	Group D
	−1.3	−1.4	−1.0	−0.2
	−1.6	−2.3	−1.3	−0.4
	−1.0	0	−1.5	−0.2
	−1.5	−1.2	−1.0	−0.2
	−1.1	−1.1	−1.1	−0.5
	−2.3	−1.3	−0.9	0.0
	−1.9	−2.4	−0.5	−0.2
	−2.4	−0.6	−0.7	+0.2
	−1.8	−0.7	−1.0	+0.3
	−2.1	−1.2	−1.0	−0.3
Means	−1.70	−1.22	−1.00	0.15

most substantial (and statistically significant) when specific measures such as showing a film and having group discussion are used.

An Analysis of Variance

We can extend this investigation one step further with an application of one-way ANOVA, as discussed in this chapter. The improvement in test results for each of the 10 students in each group is shown in table 11.7. These are the values for the dependent variable. The independent variable is the type of experience that the students had, categorized into the four groups A, B, C, and D. In this experiment, we are seeking to establish whether or not the differences observed between the group means (the last row in table 11.7) can be generalized to the entire population of students.

The relevant hypotheses are:

$H_0: \mu_1 = \mu_2 = \mu_3 = \mu_4$. The improvement in test results in the population is the same regardless of the experience of group members.

$H_r: \mu_i \neq \mu_j$. for at least one pair i, j. At least two of the groups in the population have different levels of improvement..

Using the data in table 11.7, $F_{calculated}$ was derived according to the equation

$$F_{calculated} = \frac{MS_{between}}{MS_{within}}.$$

TABLE 11.8   ANOVA results

	Sum of squares	d.f.	Mean square	F
Between groups	12.597	3	4.199	18.568
Within groups	8.141	36	.226	
Total	20.738	39		
Post-hoc (Tukey) results				
Significantly different pairs	A and C	A and D	B and D	C and D
Mean difference	−0.700	−1.550	−1.070	−0.850

The values for solving the equation are as follows:

$$MS_{between} = \frac{SS_{between}}{df_{between}} = \frac{12.597}{3} = 4.199$$

$$MS_{within} = \frac{SS_{within}}{df_{within}} = \frac{8.141}{36} = 0.226$$

$$F_{calculated} = \frac{4.199}{0.226} = 18.568.$$

With 3 and 36 (rounded to 30) degrees of freedom, the F_{table} values are 2.92 and 4.51 at $\alpha = .05$ and .01, respectively. We can reject the null hypothesis. There is little doubt that the groups in the population would have different levels of improvement.

Now, as noted in the text, we can use a post-hoc test to determine *which* pairs of groups contributed to the significance of the F ratio. The results of the Tukey test are shown at the bottom of table 11.8. You can see that the improvement level of group D, the control group, differed significantly from that of each of the other three groups. In addition, the difference between A and C was also statistically significant.

The use of ANOVA verifies and expands upon the results of the two-sample *t*-tests. Showing the film and having related discussion has a clear impact on the student's degree of prejudice, at least as measured by the scale used in the experiment.

Summary

Like the various versions of the *t*-test, one-way ANOVA is designed to help the user explain observed differences between sample means on a numerical variable in comparing two (*t*-test) or more (ANOVA) groups. If such differences are found, then there are two possibilities. The first, which is stated in our null hypothesis, is that the differences are the result of chance, the random differences that always arise in random sampling; this is known as "sampling error." The other possibility is that the sample differences are a true reflection of actual differences between population means. This is stated in our research hypotheses.

The calculations used in deriving the t and F statistics discussed in this and the previous chapters convert the observed sample differences into "cooked" scores that can then be compared to standard tables. The conversion process removes the effect of such distracting features as the sample size and the units used to measure the numerical variable (pounds versus dollars, months versus years, etc.) With this accomplished, and with the help of the tables, we can ask, "Is the observed difference so small that it probably (95 or 99 percent of the time) is the result of chance, or is it large enough for us to say that it reflects a true population difference?"

In the following chapters, we extend this type of reasoning to applications involving other situations and levels of measurement. This begins with a discussion of non-numerical variables in Chapter 12.

KEY TERMS

ANOVA: Abbreviation for *analysis of variance*. A statistical technique used to test for the differences among three or more means.

Between- and within-group differences: individual score differences whose ratio determines the size of the F statistic.

F test: The statistical test used in ANOVA and related applications. It is based on the F ratio of mean squares between to mean squares within.

Mean square: In calculating the F ratio, this is the sum of squares (between or within) divided by the degrees of freedom (between or within).

Post-hoc test: Test performed to determine which pair(s) of groups caused a significant F in ANOVA.

One-tailed tests: Tests of hypotheses in which the research hypothesis indicates specifically which mean is expected to be larger than the other.

Sampling distribution of differences: The set of all differences between the means of pairs of samples drawn from the same population.

Sum of squares: Abbreviation for "sum of the squared deviations from the mean."

WEB SITES TO BOOKMARK

1. http://nimitz.mcs.kent.edu/~blewis/stat/anova.html
   This is an ANOVA interactive site.
2. http://trochim.human.cornell.edu/tutorial/rehberg/popper.htm
   Here is an introduction to ANOVA from Cornell University.

3. www.wolfram.com/solutions/statistics/functions/functions_anova.html
   This web site, maintained by the makers of *Mathematica* Statistical Solutions, contains an interactive ANOVA program with basic definitions of related terms.

TABLE 11.9   "Diversity" scores for employees

ID#	EA	AfA	LA	AsA
1	75	70	85	85
2	65	90	75	90
3	80	85	70	100
4	70	65	80	65
5	85	85	60	75
6	50	75	90	80
7	60	85	80	90
8	75	70	70	85
9	45	85	85	$n = 8$
10	90	$n = 9$	75	
11	70		$n = 10$	
12	75			
$n = 12$				

SOLUTION-CENTERED APPLICATION

A large corporation is interested in developing a cultural awareness program for its employees. A sociologist has suggested that a single program for all employees is not likely to be as effective as one that is tailored to specific ethnic groups. The reason given is that minorities tend to know more about the culture of the majority than members of the majority group know about minorities. Thus, different basic types of information and different teaching techniques are required for different groups.

Before initiating the program, the company decided to test the prospective student employees to judge whether the backgrounds of the groups were sufficiently different to justify separate types of training. Four groups (abbreviations in parentheses) were represented in the population of employees: non-Latino European Americans ("EA"), non-Hispanic African Americans ("AfA"), Latino Americans of any race ("LA"), and non-Hispanic Asian Americans ("AsA"). A small sample was taken from each group (total $n = 39$), and a test was administered to determine each individual's knowledge about the groups to which s/he did *not* belong. These were graded on a scale of 0 to 100, with the results shown in table 11.9.

With these data, create an SPSS file and determine whether there are significant group differences using the ANOVA command, as discussed in the latter parts of this chapter. If there are differences, indicate the pair(s) of groups whose scores are the main contributors to the overall difference.

Association and Induction in Qualitative Sociology

From Private Problems to Public Issues

In our introduction to hypothesis testing in Chapter 9, we explored several techniques for generalizing from samples to populations via the use of sampling distributions. These all share a very important feature: they all focus on sample and population *means*, *standard deviations*, and *variances*. In this chapter, we consider similar inductive applications with the kinds of variables for which no such measures of central tendency and dispersion exist. These, of course, are variables at the nominal or ordinal level of measurement, to which the concepts of a population (or sample) mean, standard deviation, and variance do not apply. Because the mean and similar measures are such important *parameters* in the applications considered to this point, those applications are known as "parametric" techniques. The approaches represented in this chapter are referred to as *nonparametric*.

Two techniques are discussed in separate sections in the following pages: chi-square and rank-order correlation. Here we revisit the widely employed technique of bivariate analysis: the *measurement of association*. You will recall that this is essentially a kind of description whose object is to characterize the extent to which the two variables in a sample co-vary or change together. As is the case in parametric applications, these measures of association are also used inductively as "calculated" values to test the significance of the relationships. This combination of description and induction is extended to parametric applications—correlation and regression—in Chapters 13 and 14.

Two-Way (Bivariate) Chi-Square

This section introduces *two-way chi-square*, the best-known and most widely used member of a family of nonparametric techniques used in the interpretation of crosstabs.[1] In these applications, a crosstab (such as table 12.1), which displays the relationship between two (or more) non-numeric variables (in this case, school "competitiveness

TABLE 12.1   Crosstab/contingency table

Competitiveness ranking	Affiliation		
	Private	*Public*	*Total*
Low	6 (18.8%)	3 (16.7%)	9 (18.0%)
Average	10 (31.3%)	10 (55.6%)	20 (40.0%)
High	6 (18.8%)	2 (11.1%)	8 (16.0%)
Very high	10 (31.3%)	3 16.7%)	13 (26.0%)
Total	32 (100.0%)	18 (100.0%)	50 (100.0%)

ranking" as low, average, high, and very high and "affiliation" as public or private), is treated as a *contingency* table. The term *contingency* applies to an event whose outcome follows from the occurrence of another event. The logical expression "if *a* then *b*" (*a* ⇒ *b*) is referred to as a relationship of contingency (between *a* and *b*). Another way to say this is "*b* is contingent on *a*."

As was stressed in Chapter 2, contingency is different from *cause and effect*. Although contingency is one of the conditions necessary to establish cause and effect, other conditions are also required. You will recall that these are (1) time ordering, such that the cause precedes the effect, and (2) the absence of an alternative cause or causes. The fact that chi-square and related techniques can shed light on the contingencies between variables is not meant to imply that in themselves they can go further and establish these other two conditions.

What chi-square *can* do is determine whether the observed contingencies in a crosstab could have occurred by chance alone, or whether they are more likely to reflect an authentic relationship between the variables of interest. This determination has both a descriptive and an inductive component. In the first case, descriptively, the chi-square techniques are used to calculate a statistic that measures the strength of the *association* between the variables: the degree to which they are actually related to one another. This measure is always positive, and it ranges from 0 on up. The closer it is to 0, the weaker the association; the higher the number, all things considered, the stronger the association.

The inductive component of chi-square involves the familiar procedure of comparing the calculated statistic to a corresponding value in a table that is based on a sampling distribution. These two values are then compared to test a null hypothesis, here stating "no relationship in the population" between the variables, following the rule that if the calculated statistic is less than the table statistic, the null is not rejected.

One of the reasons that chi-square is so popular is that it can be used with variables at any level of measurement. It is true that there are several techniques that are appropriate when one or both of two variables are numerical, and these are almost always preferable to contingency techniques. There are even some techniques specifically adapted to ordinal-level variables, one of which will be discussed in the next section. But chi-square and its relatives can be applied to any of these and to pairs of nominal-level variables as well. In addition to this, the calculation of chi-square and its interpretation are easy to understand, and they make especially clear the fundamental approach in inductive statistics of comparing observations to chance expectations.

Chi-Square as a Measure of Association

The chi-square statistic that is used to measure the strength of the association between two variables has the symbol χ^2, the Greek letter chi (χ) that is squared. Because this same statistic is also used for induction, in keeping with the notation used in other applications, we will distinguish between $\chi^2_{calculated}$ and χ^2_{table}. The formula for the calculated statistic is:

$$\chi^2_{calculated} = \Sigma \frac{(f_o - f_e)^2_{i,j}}{f_{ei,j}}.$$

Each of the symbols in the equation is defined in the subsequent paragraphs.

Whereas the calculation of z, t, and F statistics all begin with sample means, standard deviations, and variances, those quantities cannot be used with nonparametric statistics such as $\chi^2_{calculated}$ because the variables of interest are usually nominal or ordinal. Instead, we begin here with the crosstab/contingency table. For purposes of comparison, we reproduce the data in table 12.1 as table 12.2, with a few alterations that will assist in the calculations. As is always done with crosstabs, we have not only listed the frequencies in each cell but also included the *marginals*: the row totals, the column totals, and the grand total (n).

TABLE 12.2   Crosstab (contingency table) with raw data (observed frequencies)

Competitiveness ranking	Affiliation		
	Public	*Private*	*Total*
Low	$f_o = 6$	$f_o = 3$	9
Average	$f_o = 10$	$f_o = 10$	20
High	$f_o = 6$	$f_o = 2$	8
Very high	$f_o = 10$	$f_o = 3$	13
Total	32	18	50

Here we face a situation discussed in Chapter 4, where we are not especially concerned about which variable is independent and which is dependent. Yet it is still necessary to select the variable whose attributes form the columns, with the other's attributes forming the rows. The results of calculating chi-square and using it as a measure of association *are not in any way affected by which variable is on the columns and which is on the rows.* A choice needs to be made, however, one way or the other. Most often, the choice is made on the basis of which variable is considered to be the probable cause of the other. So, although not required mathematically, we do select an independent variable and a dependent variable for practical purposes. In this example, we are using the colleges data set and are treating type of administration (public versus private) as the independent and using the columns for its two attributes. Level of competitiveness is thus the dependent variable, and the rows are labeled with its attributes.

In each cell in table 12.2 we have not included the percentages, and we have labeled the frequency as f_o. This stands for *observed frequency*. As the name indicates, it is the number of units observed to have the pair of attributes associated with each cell: six schools are private and less competitive, three are public and less competitive, and so on.

In the formula for $\chi^2_{calculated}$, you will also note the symbol f_e. This stands for *expected frequency*; it is another frequency that is *not* observed. Instead, it is the frequency that *would be expected* in each cell by chance alone if the marginals—the row and column totals—remained as they are. Imagine that we had an object (a stone, coin, etc.) for each of the 50 schools in the sample, and we tossed all of them in the air in a random manner many, many times. The only limitations on the tossing are that that 32 would always have to be private, 9 would have to be less competitive, 20 would have to be average, and so forth. That is, the marginals would always have to remain as they were in the original crosstab. Under these conditions, in the long run the frequencies would display a certain *expected pattern*. These are the expected frequencies.[2]

To find this set of f_e values, we do the following:

1. Multiply each row total by each column total.
2. Divide the result by *n*.

For example, to calculate f_e for the expected frequency in the cell located in the first row, first column, we find the first row's total, which is 9. Next we find the first column's total, which is 32. Multiplying them, we get $9 \times 32 = 288$. Dividing by *n*, which is 50, for the cell in the first row, first column,

$$f_e = 288/50 = 5.76.$$

Likewise, the cell in the second column (which has a total of 18) of the first row (which has a total of 9) will have an expected frequency of

$$f_e = (9 \times 18)/50 = 162/50 = 3.24.$$

Note that sum of the expected frequencies for the first row is $5.76 + 3.24 = 9$. This is the row total. In fact, it will always be the case that the sum of the expected frequencies in any row or column will be the same as that row or column's marginal. This is because we established the condition that our chance expectations must allow the marginals to remain the same.

These results indicate that if chance alone were operating, under the stated conditions, the contingent outcome would be 5.76 public schools with a "less" ranking and 3.24 private schools with a "less" ranking. These can be compared to the observed frequencies of 6 and 3, respectively.

This procedure for finding expected frequencies is summarized by the following formula:

$$f_{ei,j} = \frac{(\text{row } i \text{ total})(\text{column } j \text{ total})}{n}.$$

In other words: the expected frequency of the cell in row i, column j is equal to the total in row i multiplied by the total in column j, divided by the sample size, n.

Using this formula, the set of expected frequencies for our crosstab are as follows:

$$f_{e1,1} = (9)(32)/50 = 5.76; \qquad f_{e1,2} = (9)(18)/50 = 3.24$$

$$f_{e2,1} = (20)(32)/50 = 12.8; \qquad f_{e2,2} = (20)(18)/50 = 7.2$$

$$f_{e3,1} = (8)(32)/50 = 5.12; \qquad f_{e3,2} = (8)(18)/50 = 2.88$$

$$f_{e4,1} = (13)(32)/50 = 8.32; \qquad f_{e4,2} = (13)(18)/50 = 4.68$$

These results have been inserted in each cell of the crosstab in table 12.3.

TABLE 12.3   Contingency table with observed and expected frequencies

Competitiveness ranking	Affiliation		
	Public	Private	Total
Low	$f_o = 6, f_e = 5.76$	$f_o = 3, f_e = 3.24$	9
Average	$f_o = 10, f_e = 12.8$	$f_o = 10, f_e = 7.2$	20
High	$f_o = 6, f_e = 5.12$	$f_o = 2, f_e = 2.88$	8
Very high	$f_o = 10, f_e = 8.32$	$f_o = 3, f_e = 4.68$	13
Total	32	18	50

Without going any further, it is obvious that the observed and the expected frequencies do not agree. Thus, we can conclude that, to some extent, the relationship between a school's affiliation and its competitiveness ranking is not merely the result of pure chance. However, it is possible to go further with this analysis and determine more precisely what "some extent" means.

The next step is to calculate the differences between the observed and expected frequencies to find the set of $(f_o - f_e)_{i,j}$ values. These are:

$$(f_o - f_e)_{1,1} = 6 - 5.76 = 0.24; \qquad (f_o - f_e)_{1,2} = 3 - 3.24 = -0.24$$
$$(f_o - f_e)_{2,1} = 10 - 12.80 = -2.80; \quad (f_o - f_e)_{2,2} = 10 - 7.20 = 2.80$$
$$(f_o - f_e)_{3,1} = 6 - 5.12 = 0.88; \qquad (f_o - f_e)_{3,2} = 2 - 2.88 = -0.88$$
$$(f_o - f_e)_{4,1} = 10 - 8.32 = 1.68; \qquad (f_o - f_e)_{4,2} = 3 - 4.68 = -1.68$$

These differences do provide a better idea of the extent of the discrepancies between the observed and the expected frequencies. They range between an absolute value of 0.24, in the case of the less competitive schools, to 2.80, for the average schools. The second greatest difference, in absolute value, is in the highly competitive category.

The figures also reveal that the sum of the differences for each row and each column is 0, with the negative differences canceling out the positive ones. Because there are two entries for each row, the entries are identical in absolute value and opposite in sign. This feature also follows from our stipulation that row and column totals must remain fixed. Thus, in a row with two entries, if the first difference between the observed and expected frequencies is d, then the second difference must equal $-d$. For the first row these are +0.24 and −0.24, for the second row they are −2.80 and +2.80, and so on.

The next step in our analysis of the differences between observed and expected frequencies involves combining all of them (all eight in this illustration), in part through addition, into one convenient measure. This measure is the $\chi^2_{calculated}$. As usual, the fact that positive and negative differences cancel each other when added together indicates that they should be squared (this is the source of the "square" in "chi-square"). So we need to derive the set of $(f_o - f_e)^2_{i,j}$ values, which are:

$$(f_o - f_e)^2_{1,1} = 0.24^2 = 0.058; \qquad (f_o - f_e)^2_{1,2} = (-0.24)^2 = 0.058$$
$$(f_o - f_e)^2_{2,1} = (-2.80)^2 = 7.84; \qquad (f_o - f_e)^2_{2,2} = (2.80)^2 = 7.84$$
$$(f_o - f_e)^2_{3,1} = (0.88)^2 = 0.774; \qquad (f_o - f_e)^2_{3,2} = (-0.88)^2 = 0.774$$
$$(f_o - f_e)^2_{4,1} = (1.68)^2 = 2.82; \qquad (f_o - f_e)^2_{4,2} = (-1.68)^2 = 2.82$$

The chi-square statistic does include the sum of the squared differences between observed and expected frequencies, but it includes more. In fact, it is a *weighted average* of these differences, in which each term is expressed as the ratio between the difference and its expected frequency. In doing this, we control for the distorting effect of rows or columns whose frequencies are very large but whose differences may be relatively small and of rows and columns whose frequencies are very small but whose differences may be relatively large. This is done by dividing the squared differences by the respective expected frequencies to obtain the set of $(f_o - f_e)^2_{i,j} / f_{ei,j}$ values. In our example, these are:

$$\frac{(f_o - f_e)^2_{1,1}}{f_{e1,1}} = \frac{0.058}{5.76} = 0.010$$

$$\frac{(f_o - f_e)^2_{1,2}}{f_{e1,2}} = \frac{0.058}{3.24} = 0.018$$

$$\frac{(f_o - f_e)^2_{2,1}}{f_{e2,1}} = \frac{7.84}{12.80} = 0.613$$

$$\frac{(f_o - f_e)^2_{2,2}}{f_{e2,2}} = \frac{7.84}{7.20} = 1.088$$

$$\frac{(f_o - f_e)^2_{3,1}}{f_{e3,1}} = \frac{0.774}{5.12} = 0.151$$

$$\frac{(f_o - f_e)^2_{3,2}}{f_{e3,2}} = \frac{0.774}{2.88} = 0.269$$

$$\frac{(f_o - f_e)^2_{4,1}}{f_{e4,1}} = \frac{2.82}{8.32} = 0.331$$

$$\frac{(f_o - f_e)^2_{4,2}}{f_{e4,2}} = \frac{2.82}{4.68} = 0.603$$

With these ratios between the differences and the expected frequencies derived, we have all that is needed to find $\chi^2_{calculated}$ by the formula

$$\chi^2_{calculated} = \sum_{i,j} \frac{(f_o - f_e)^2_{i,j}}{f_{ei,j}}.$$

In our example,

$$\chi^2_{calculated} = 0.010 + 0.018 + 0.613 + 1.088 + 0.151 + 0.269 + 0.331 + 0.603 = 3.083.$$

This number, 3.083, measures the degree to which the two variables, "competitiveness ranking" and "affiliation," are associated in our sample. It can be used to make comparisons with other samples drawn from the same population or with samples drawn from different populations but with the same (or equivalent) variables and attributes. It is not 0, which as we noted earlier indicates that there is an authentic (as opposed to pure chance) component to the association. Nevertheless, because $\chi^2_{calculated}$ does not have an upper limit, we cannot say how strong this association is in an *absolute* sense. It is greater than 2.0 and less than 4.0, but not much more can be said beyond this from a descriptive perspective.

Before moving on to consider this matter more closely, let us review the steps involved in deriving $\chi^2_{calculated}$. Once the crosstab/contingency table is created, with each cell containing an observed frequency, f_o:

1. Find an expected frequency, f_e, for each cell by the formula $f_{ei,j} = $ (row i total)(column j total)$/n$.
2. Find the set of $(f_o - f_e)_{i,j}$ values by subtracting each expected frequency from its corresponding observed frequency.
3. Find the set of $(f_o - f_e)^2_{i,j}$ values by squaring each difference.
4. Find the set of ratios of the squared differences to the expected frequencies, $(f_o - f_e)^2_{i,j} / f_{ei,j}$.
5. Sum these together to derive chi-square: $\chi^2_{calculated} = \Sigma_{ij} (f_o - f_e)^2_{i,j} / f_{ei,j}$.

Using Chi-Square for Inductive Applications

Researchers often employ chi-square to test hypotheses concerning the degree of association between two non-numerical variables in a population. As in other hypothesis-testing situations, this procedure uses a sampling distribution that displays the probability of occurrence of all possible sample statistics. Like the t and F distributions, the chi-square distribution is actually a set of distributions and associated curves, one of which corresponds to each possible *d.f.* However, because it is nonparametric, the chi-square distribution is unique in at least three relevant ways.

1. First, in contrast to the others, the chi-square is not a distribution of sample means or proportions. Rather, it is a distribution of all possible $\chi^2_{calculated}$ values. The practical consequence is that here we do not convert our sample statistic to a standardized or "cooked" score but rather use it directly in comparison to the table value, which is χ^2_{table}.
2. The second difference between chi-square and other significance tests is that, with chi-square, when *d.f.* is small, the sampling distribution is highly skewed. In particular, it is a positive skew in which, as you will recall, more than one-half of the cases (here chi-square values) are below the average of the distribution. Because this is a two-tailed test, with a small *d.f.*, the high degree of skew increases the range of

$\chi^2_{calculated}$ values that indicate rejecting the null hypotheses. As *d.f.* increases, the distribution comes closer to being normal.

3. The third somewhat unique feature of the chi-square distribution is that its number of degrees of freedom does not depend directly on the sample size, *n*. Rather, its *d.f.* is derived from the number of attributes of each of the two variables, which translates into the number of rows and the number of columns in the contingency table.

Degrees of Freedom with Chi-Square

The sampling distributions of parametric measures are derived from sets of equations involving *n*, $\bar{x}$, and *s* or s^2. But because means and the like do not apply to nonparametric measures, a different approach is required with chi-square.

Here, *d.f.* is determined by subtracting 1 from the number of rows and 1 from the number of columns and then multiplying the results. The formula is:

$$d.f. = (r - 1) \times (c - 1).$$

Thus, as in our example, if there are 4 rows and 2 columns,

$$d.f. = (4 - 1) \times (2 - 1) = 3 \times 1 = 3.$$

The smallest possible *d.f.* is 1, which occurs in the simplest crosstab with only 2 rows and 2 columns. In that case, $d.f. = (2 - 1) \times (2 - 1) = 1 \times 1 = 1$.

The manner in which degrees of freedom is calculated with chi-square makes it especially clear why this concept is so important in inductive statistics. In general, it tells the researcher (and the reader of research reports) the *degree* to which the results of a significance test reflect the actual data as opposed to being merely the outcome of the way the data are manipulated. That component of the results derived from the data is quantified as the degrees of *freedom*. In parametric applications, this is tied to the number of unknowns in a given set of equations. Once the degrees of freedom (1, 2, 3, ...) or number of unknowns is used, the rest of the results are determined by the rules of mathematics.

Let us consider the simple case of a 2 × 2 contingency table with the observed frequencies for a sample with *n* = 70 shown in table 12.4. As noted above, with a 2 × 2 table, *d.f.* = 1. We see that the frequencies are 10, 15, 20, and 25. The row marginals are

TABLE 12.4   A 2 × 2 contingency table

Dependent variable	*Independent variable*		
	Attribute c	*Attribute d*	*Totals*
Attribute *a*	10	15	25
Attribute *b*	20	25	45
Totals	30	40	70

TABLE 12.5   The 2 × 2 contingency table with only the marginals

	Independent variable		
Dependent variable	*Attribute c*	*Attribute d*	*Totals*
Attribute *a*			25
Attribute *b*			45
Totals	30	40	70

25 and 45, and the column marginals are 30 and 40. Next, by way of experiment, table 12.5 shows the same table with the frequencies deleted but the marginals unchanged. Now, in table 12.6, we have exercised our one degree of freedom by inserting any number (as long as it is not larger than the smallest marginal) in any of the four cells. For no special reason, we chose to place a 12 in the lower left cell. As table 12.7 indicates, once this choice is made, the other three cell entries are determined: Because 12 and the entry in the lower right cell must add to 45, that entry must be $(45 - 12) = 33$. Because 33 and the entry in the upper right must equal 40, the entry must be 7 $(40 - 7) = 33$, and so on.

You might want to try this yourself with another cell and another number, or see how the principle works with 2, 3, or more degrees of freedom. What this demonstrates is that although the configuration of observed frequencies of a crosstab might seem unique, only in one, or two, or another limited number of cells are the entries *free* to vary. Once these have been determined, the contents of the other cells are fixed. For

TABLE 12.6   The 2 × 2 contingency table with one degree
of freedom exercised

	Independent variable		
Dependent variable	*Attribute c*	*Attribute d*	*Totals*
Attribute *a*			25
Attribute *b*	12		45
Totals	30	40	70

TABLE 12.7   The 2 × 2 contingency table with all other cells
determined once one degree of freedom is exercised

	Independent variable		
Dependent variable	*Attribute c*	*Attribute d*	*Totals*
Attribute *a*	18	7	25
Attribute *b*	12	33	45
Totals	30	40	70

example, in table 12.4, once we established that there were 10 observations with attributes *a* and *c*, then the number of observation with the other pairs of attributes could no longer vary; they had to be 15, 20, and 25.

Testing Hypotheses with Chi-Square

Table A.4 in Appendix A contains χ^2_{table} values at selected degrees of freedom. It is used to test hypotheses according to the same set of rules that apply to the other significance tests that we have considered. Unlike the values in other sampling distributions, however, the ones shown in table A.4 do not decrease as *d.f.* increases. Rather, they increase as well, reflecting that fact that the larger the number of rows and columns, the higher the value of the chi-square statistics can be. Remember that the calculated statistic is a raw score rather than a standardized value such as *z, t,* and *F*.

The null and research hypotheses do not really have a form "in symbols," as do those formulated for parametric tests, for we cannot use the usual symbols such as μ, =, >, <, 0, or − in nonparametric applications. However, there is a "generic" form of chi-square hypothesis that can remind us of the nature of the test being performed:

H_0: There is no association between the two variables in the population.

H_r: There is an association between the two variables in the population.

The hypotheses "in words" state the variables and the nature of the association specifically. For our example with the variables "competitiveness ranking" and "affiliation," these would be:

H_0: Private schools and public schools in the population do not differ in competitiveness ranking. Both categories have the same proportions of low, average, high, and very high schools.

H_r: Private schools and public schools in the population differ in competitiveness ranking. The categories do not have the same proportions of low, average, high, and very high schools.

To test this null hypothesis, we use the $\chi^2_{calculated}$ derived from table 12.3, which is 3.083. The $d.f. = (r-1) \times (c-1) = (4-1) \times (2-1) = 3 \times 1 = 3$. Locating the χ^2_{table} in Table A.4 at $d.f. = 3$ (the third row) and for $\alpha = .01$ and .05, we find 7.82 and 11.3, respectively. Either of these χ^2_{table} values is larger than $\chi^2_{calculated}$. Thus, we fail to reject the null hypothesis at both levels of significance. We have *not* shown that affiliation makes a difference in competitiveness ranking. The nonzero value of $\chi^2_{calculated}$ for our sample could be the result of sampling error.

This concludes our discussion of bivariate chi-square. For applications using three or more variables, see the online Chapter 15.

| **BOX 12.1** | **Statistics for Sociologists** |

From Private Problems to Public Issues

FIGURE 12.1   C. Wright Mills (1916–1962) left an endur-
ing legacy in sociology, in part through his definition of
the field as "the intersection of history and biography."
©Yaroslava Mills. Used with permission.

Because sociology focuses on aggregates rather than individuals, it affords us the
opportunity to view private problems as public issues. According to C. Wright Mills
(1959), who is widely cited for making this observation, contemporary society tends
to isolate people from one another so that they do not have a chance to see their own
lives as part of a larger, collective experience. As a result, when we are confronted by a
problem, such as being laid off from work, we tend to internalize and personalize our
plight, blaming ourselves. Thus, we view the situation as a private problem. Yet, more
often than not, what we perceive to be a private problem is widely shared and is, in
fact, a public issue. So, in the case of layoffs, the problem may well reside not in the
failings of individual workers but in the company's or industry's policies, or in the laws
that regulate businesses. Consider the following example.

With recent changes in education policy, students are now required to take standardized examinations to measure achievement and to determine whether they should be
promoted to the next grade or held back. As a result, parents are receiving frequent official
reports about their children's performance. As might be expected, some of these reports
indicate that children are performing below the minimum standards, suggesting serious
problems. At issue is *whose* problems these are: Is it the fault of the students and their
lack of preparation and/or support at home, or are the schools failing the children?

Many of the parents take these poor reports personally, concluding that there is
something wrong with their parenting or with the students' motivation, capacity to
learn, etc. For those who feel this way, theirs is a *private problem* that demands changes

at home and with the students' orientation toward school. But an alternative explanation is that these parents are not alone and that parents throughout the school or the entire school system feel the same way. If true, this indicates that a public issue has emerged that requires a change in policy rather than in parenting practices.

The statistical technique of chi-square can help to resolve such dilemmas. In particular, it can employ information that pertains to a small sample of parents who believe that they have a private problem. It then uses the sample information to estimate the extent to which the problem is shared in the larger population, which can indicate the extent to which the problem is actually a public issue.

In a certain school district, a random sample of 225 parents of school-age children was drawn from a population of about 75,000 such parents. Two simple questions are asked of the sample parents:

1. Is your child performing below standard on the exams?
2. Who do you feel is responsible for the performance of students?

Note that each of these two variables is nominal level.

The results are shown in table 12.8. The independent variable is perception of children's performance and the dependent is belief about who is responsible. The observed frequencies are shown in **bold**, the column percentages (the appropriate percentages for measuring the impact of the independent on the dependent variable) are in parentheses, and the expected frequencies are in *italics*. The expected frequencies were calculated by the formula $f_e = n_{row} \times n_{col}/n_{total}$.

Looking at the observed data, we can see that 47% of the parents whose children are having problems in school believe that it is the child's responsibility and an additional 41% blame themselves, for a total of 88%. In contrast, only 32% of the parents whose children are performing well attribute it to the students and an additional 34% credit themselves, for a total of 66% in these two categories. For the parents whose children are having problems, only 12% attribute it to the schools whereas 34% of

TABLE 12.8   Crosstab showing imputed responsibility for children's performance

| Who is most responsible for children's performance | Children performing below standard | | |
	Yes	*No*	*Total*
Child	**40** (47) *32.1*	**45** (32) *52.9*	85 (38)
Parents	**35** (41) *31.4*	**48** (34) *51.6*	83 (37)
School	**10** (12) *21.5*	**47** (34) *35.5*	57 (25)
Total	85 (100)	140 (100)	225

the parents whose children are doing well assign responsibility to the schools. Based on the assumption of random sampling, with about 75,000 parents in the entire population, just under 38%, or approximately 28,500, have children performing below standard. Of these, 88%, or approximately 25,000, blame their children or themselves.

Even if we were to reduce the estimate by one-half, to 12,500, it is obvious that the parents who blame their children or themselves for performing below standard in the sample are not alone. Although we can't say with absolute certainty, we can safely conclude that this is indeed a public issue that might well demand policy change in the schools.

To determine the extent to which the two sets of parents in the sample differ, a chi-square statistic was calculated as follows.

(1) $\dfrac{\left(f_o - f_e\right)^2}{f_e} = 1.44;$ (2) $\dfrac{\left(f_o - f_e\right)^2}{f_e} = 1.44;$ (3) $\dfrac{\left(f_o - f_e\right)^2}{f_e} = 0.41;$

(4) $\dfrac{\left(f_o - f_e\right)^2}{f_e} = 0.41;$ (5) $\dfrac{\left(f_o - f_e\right)^2}{f_e} = 6.20;$ (6) $\dfrac{\left(f_o - f_e\right)^2}{f_e} = 6.20$

$\chi^2_{calculated} = 16.1$

A chi-square value of this size indicates that there are indeed differences between the parents whose children are performing below standard and those whose children are doing well, and that this difference is greater than would be expected by chance alone. For the sample, at least, the first set of parents is clearly more likely to blame their children and themselves as opposed to the schools. Again, this suggests that they view this as their private problem.

Finally, the $\chi^2_{calculated}$ was used to test the following hypotheses:

H_0: The two sets of parents in the population do not differ with respect to who they believe is responsible for the performance of the children.

H_r: The two sets of parents in the population do differ with respect to who they believe is responsible for the performance of the children.

At *d.f.* = (rows − 1)(columns − 1) = (3 − 1)(2 − 1) = 2, the following table values were found: at $\alpha = .05$, $\chi^2_{table} = 5.99$; and at $\alpha = .01$, $\chi^2_{table} = 9.21$. Comparing these to $\chi^2_{calculated}$ = 16.1, we can reject the null hypotheses at both levels of significance. We can conclude that in the population, parents whose children are performing below standard tend strongly to believe that it is their or their children's fault. Yet there are many thousands of parents in this situation, suggesting that it is likely to be a structural problem best treated as a public issue.

Rank-Order Correlation

The other technique to be considered in this chapter is rank-order correlation. Like bivariate chi-square, it is a measure of association between two non-numerical variables that can also be used as a test of significance. With rank-order correlation, however, both variables must be ordinal-level. The following discussion not only provides the basic steps for calculating and applying a useful nonparametric technique; it also serves as an introduction to the general topic of correlation. In Chapter 13 we take up the topic again in the case of two *numerical* variables.

Rank-Order Correlation as a Measure of Association

In measuring the extent to which two ordinal-level variables are associated in a sample with size n, rank-order correlation employs a statistic known as Spearman's rank-order correlation coefficient (after statistician Charles Spearman). *Correlation* is a specific type of association that measures the extent to which the variables vary together, or *co-vary*. The symbol for this coefficient is r_s, and it is derived by comparing the rankings of the units on one of the variables with the rankings on the other, unit by unit. You will recall this procedure from the before-and-after t-test, in which the "after" score is subtracted from the "before" score for each unit.

In fact, this is the first step in deriving r_s. Suppose that our two ordinal-level variables are called v and w. For each unit, we subtract its rank on v from its rank on w. This difference is designated D. This produces a set of $D_i = (v_i - w_i)$, for all i from 1 to n. Next, these differences are squared (again to counteract the effect of positive values and negative values canceling each other out) to produce a set of D_i^2. Finally, r_s is calculated via the following formula, which is a weighted average of the squared differences:

$$r_s = 1 - \frac{6 \sum_{i=1}^{n} D^2}{n(n^2 - 1)}.$$

With this formula, the resulting r_s is a number that ranges from -1.0 to $+1.0$. The sign indicates the *direction* of the relationship between the variables: whether it is *direct* or *inverse*. A positive $(+)$ r_s (a direct relationship) tells us that as the first variable increases in rank, the second variable also increases. A negative $(-)$ r_s (an inverse relationship) means that as the first variable increases, the second decreases.

The absolute value of r_s—its size, ignoring its sign—is symbolized as $|r_s|$. It indicates the *strength* of the association between the variables. A 0 signifies no association whatever. An $|r_s| = 1.0$ signifies a perfect correlation—that is, the rankings match exactly, either directly or inversely according to the sign. When $|r_s|$ lies between 0 and 1 (which

TABLE 12.9   Rank ordering of 13 colleges on graduation rate and age

College	Grad rate rank	Age rank
Boise State University	2.5	2.0
Southern Oregon State College	2.5	3.0
University of New Orleans	4.0	1.0
Youngstown State University	1.0	7.5
Massachusetts Maritime Academy	8.0	9.0
University of the Ozarks	5.0	10.5
Rockhurst College	6.0	6.0
Biola University	10.0	7.5
Spring Hill College	11.0	12.0
Emmanuel College	7.0	4.0
Tulane University	9.0	10.5
Connecticut College	12.0	5.0
Yale University	13.0	13.0

is usually the case), then the strength of the association is measured by its value: with .3 stronger than .4, .7 weaker than .9, and so on.

To illustrate this procedure, we have randomly selected a sample of 13 colleges and universities from the population used in previous applications. These are shown in table 12.9 along with each school's ranking on two ordinal-level variables: graduation rate and age of the institution. The table shows that Youngstown State University has the lowest graduation rate and Yale the highest. The youngest institution is the University of New Orleans, and the oldest is Yale.

You will notice that Boise State and Southern Oregon State College both have a rank of 2.5 on the graduation rate. This indicates that they were tied for 2nd and 3rd place and that they were each assigned a rank that is the average of the two: $(3 + 2)/2 = 5/2 = 2.5$. This is procedure is similar to that used when finding the median of a sample whose n is an even number.

There are also two ties on the age ranking variable. Youngstown State and Biola are tied for 7th and 8th youngest, and the University of the Ozarks and Tulane University are tied for 10th and 11th place.

In table 12.10 two columns were added that contain the results of the calculations for deriving the Ds and D^2s. For example,

Boise State: $D = $ (Grade Rate Rank − Age Rank) $= (2.5 − 2.0) = +0.5$; $D^2 = 0.25$

Southern Oregon State College: $D = $ (Grade Rate Rank − Age Rank)
$= (2.5 − 3.0) = −0.5$; $D^2 = 0.25$

The sum of the D^2s, shown at the bottom of the last column, is:

$$\sum_{i=1}^{13} D^2 = +150.5.$$

The sum can now be inserted into the equation for Spearman's coefficient, using $n = 13$.

$$r_s = 1 - \frac{6\sum_{i=1}^{n} D^2}{n(n^2 - 1)} =$$

$$r_s = 1 - \frac{6(150.5)}{13(13^2 - 1)} = 1 - \frac{903}{13(168)} = 1 - \frac{903}{2184} = 1 - 0.413 = +0.587$$

With its (+) sign, an $r_s = +0.587$ indicates a direct association, and the absolute vale of 0.587 says that it is moderately strong. As the age of a school in our sample increases, so does its graduation rate. There are certainly exceptions, which can be seen in tables 12.9 and 12.10; this is far from a perfect correlation. However, it is also well above zero. We

TABLE 12.10   Calculations for rank-order correlation based on table 12.9

College	Grad rate rank	Age rank	D	D²
Boise State University	2.5	2.0	0.5	0.25
Southern Oregon State College	2.5	3.0	0.5	0.25
University of New Orleans	4.0	1.0	3.0	9.00
Youngstown State University	1.0	7.5	−6.5	42.25
Massachusetts Maritime Academy	8.0	9.0	−1.0	1.00
University of the Ozarks	5.0	10.5	−5.5	30.25
Rockhurst College	6.0	6.0	0.0	0.00
Biola University	10.0	7.5	2.5	6.25
Spring Hill College	11.0	12.0	−1.0	1.00
Emmanuel College	7.0	4.0	3.0	9.00
Tulane University	9.0	10.5	−1.5	2.25
Connecticut College	12.0	5.0	7.0	49.00
Yale University	13.0	13.0	0.0	0.00
Total for the 13 colleges, $\sum_{i=1}^{13} D^2$				150.50

would be safe to assume that, for this sample at least, the graduation rate of a school does depend to some extent on its age.

Significance Tests with Rank-Order Correlation

The last qualification, "for this sample at least," should by this point serve as a reminder that the application of rank-order correlation can be taken one step further. This is to answer the question "But is it significant?" As a measure of association between the variables within our sample, r_s turned out to have the moderate, positive value of +0.587. With this in mind, can we say that, in the *population* from which the sample was drawn, the rankings between age and graduation rate are correlated? As in the case of chi-square, the answer to this question comes from a test of significance of the (not "cooked") statistic itself.

This now familiar procedure begins with the statement in symbols and words of the null and research hypotheses. For rank-order correlation the hypotheses are two-tailed. The next step is to calculate the statistic; but, as we have done here, it has already been calculated in measuring the degree of association. For the sake of comparison we label it "$r_{s\ calculated}$." As with $\chi^2_{calculated}$, it is the absolute value of this measure that is compared to the table value rather than the standardized or "cooked" score required for the z, t, and F tests.

Thus, we can go directly to the appropriate table, which is table A.5. At $\alpha = .05$ or .01 and the correct degrees of freedom we can find $r_{s\ table}$. With Spearman's rank-order correlation, the degrees of freedom, $d.f. = n$ itself, which is the same as the number of pairs. (This is evident in the table, in which the rows are designated "number of pairs.") As usual, if the absolute value of $r_{s\ calculated}$ is less than $r_{s\ table}$, we do not reject the null hypothesis; otherwise we reject the null.

Because we want our hypotheses to refer to the rank-order correlation *in the population*, we need to introduce a new symbol. This is ρ_s, the Greek letter rho with the subscript s (for Spearman). The ρ is the Greek equivalent of the Roman r, and it is employed here in keeping with our practice of using Roman letters for the sample (x, $\bar{x}$, s, and s^2) and Greek letters for the population (μ, σ, and σ^2). Thus, the (two-tailed) hypotheses are:

H_0: $\rho_s = 0$. There is no correlation between the graduation rate ranking and the age ranking of the schools in the population. The two sets of rankings are independent.

H_r: $\rho_s \neq 0$. There is a (nonzero) correlation between graduation rate ranking and age ranking of the schools in the population.

Here, $d.f. = n = 13$; but we note that 13 does not appear in table A.5. According to the instructions beneath the table, we use the greatest lower value that does appear in the table, which is 12. Thus, at $\alpha = .05$, $r_{s\ table} = 0.591$ and at $\alpha = .01$, $r_{s\ table} = 0.777$. With $r_{s\ calculated} = 0.587$, we find that the rank-order correlation in the sample is strong enough to indicate rejecting the null at $\alpha = .05$, but it is not strong enough to indicate rejection at $\alpha = .01$. We can therefore conclude that we are 95% confident that there is a rank-order correlation in the population, but we are not 99% confident. If we were required to be in error no more than 1% of the time, we would have to say that the rank-order correlation in the sample of +0.587 could be the result of sampling error rather than reflecting a true correlation in the population.

Summary

It should now be clear that a fairly complete logic of association and induction for non-numerical variables has been developed to parallel that used with numerical data. Some of these tools and techniques are referred to as "nonparametric" statistics, because the parameters of greatest interest in numerical applications—the population mean (μ) and the population standard deviation (σ)—do not exist for nominal- or ordinal-level variables. Although it might be preferable to use only parametric measures, scientists—and especially social scientists—must at times work with phenomena that are not quantifiable. To meet this challenge, chi-square and rank-order correlation are often used and are considered to be essential parts of the toolkit of contemporary applied social statisticians.

KEY TERMS

Association: The relationship between two or more variables as observed in samples.

Chi-square: The statistic based on observed and expected frequencies, which describes the relationship between non-numeric values in a contingency table.

Contingency table: A cross tabulation between two (or more) variables used for calculating chi-square.

Correlation: A type of association that focuses on the degree to which variables vary in conjunction with one another.

Expected frequencies: The frequencies in each cell of a contingency table that would occur if chance alone were operating with a given set of marginals.

Measure of association: A descriptive statistic that measures the degree to which variables are related.

Nonparametric: Statistical techniques and principles that apply to non-numeric data. With such data, the key *parameters* of other applications, μ and σ, do not exist.

Observed frequencies: The frequencies that are actually observed for each cell in a contingency table.

Rank-order correlation: The degree of association between the ranks of a pair of variables.

Spearman's r: The most common measure of rank-order correlation.

WEB SITES TO BOOKMARK

1. http://www.statsoft.com/textbook/nonparametric-statistics/
   An overview of nonparametric statistics from Statsoft that includes references to chi-square and Spearman's *r*.

2. http://math.hws.edu/javamath/ryan/ChiSquare.html
   The mathematics department at Hobart and William Smith Colleges has provided This clear and well-illustrated discussion of chi-square.

3. http://www.stat.tamu.edu/~west/applets/chisq-demo.html

   An online calculator for finding table values of chi-square, posted by the Texas A&M University Department of Statistics

4. http://faculty.vassar.edu/lowry/ch3b.html

   Richard Lowry at Vassar College has posted this concise discussion of Spearman's rank order correlation

SOLUTION-CENTERED APPLICATIONS

1. One frequently reads or hears a claim that the educational level in the states of the United States varies by region. That is, the level in the West differs from that in the South, and so on. For this application, you are to assume that you have been asked to conduct some basic research on the subject by the Department of Education. You are to use the 50 states (plus Washington, DC) as your units of observation.

   • Based on the criterion of the percentage of the population with a ninth-grade education or less, create a variable with three ranked categories: (1) low-percentage states, (2) medium-percentage states, and (3) high-percentage states. The other variable will be region.

   • Using a contingency table and the chi-square statistic, describe in a few sentences the relationship between the two variables, decide whether regional variation in educational level does occur, and indicate whether or not your findings are statistically significant.

2. This application is similar to the preceding one, but here we will apply rank-order correlation. The states will still be the units of observation, but instead of region, the independent variable will now be income.

   • The first step is to rank the states (1) according to the percentage of the population with a ninth-grade education or less and (2) by median income. This can be done by hand, but it is much easier with SPSS.

   • Next, analyze the data using Spearman's rank-order correlation.

   • Write a brief report on your findings, discussing the relationship between the two variables and the extent to which your findings are statistically significant.

Correlation Description and Induction in Comparative Sociology

In the several bivariate applications featured in previous chapters we considered cases involving the combination of (1) non-numerical and non-numerical variables and (2) non-numerical and numerical variables. For example, the chi-square and its family of measures apply to two variables at the nominal and/or ordinal level of measurement. The difference of means *t*-test and ANOVA are used when the independent variable is either nominal or ordinal and the dependent is numerical. In contrast, this and the following chapter introduce bivariate applications in which *both* variables are numerical.

As in Chapter 12, the discussion here and in Chapter 14 includes both descriptive and inductive approaches. That is, we will learn how to observe and describe the ways in which our independent and dependent variables are *associated* with one another, and we will learn how to test the extent to which such associations are statistically significant.

We begin with the most basic step in correlation/regression: translating raw data into the form of a scatterplot. The remainder of the chapter is divided into two subsections that correspond to the first two parts (see table 13.1) of linear correlation and regression analysis: correlation description and correlation induction. Chapter 14 takes up the latter two parts: regression description and regression induction.

Data for Correlation and Regression: The Scatterplot

The techniques to be discussed here and in Chapter 14 assume that the researcher has a random sample of *n* units for which there are values on each of two interval- or ratio-level variables. Table 13.2 contains a data set that we will use to illustrate several of the principles and concepts of correlation and regression. The sample consists of 66 randomly selected nations of the world, listed in alphabetical order. For each nation the values on five variables are shown: the total population size in millions (POP), the infant mortality rate (IMR), the urbanization rate (percentage of the population

TABLE 13.1   The four parts of correlation and regression

	Description	*Induction*	*Chapter*
Correlation	1	2	13
Regression	3	4	14

living in cities, URB), per capita gross national product (GNP), and the average life expectancy in years (male and female combined, LEXP). These are the kinds of data used by the World Bank, the United Nations Development Program, and other nongovernmental and governmental international aid agencies in their social research (see Box 13.1). Major applications include policies that determine the recipients and the terms of development loans, types and amounts of agricultural assistance, and the need for family planning programs.

BOX 13.1 **Statistics for Sociologists**

The World Bank Statement on Comparative International Data

Statistics form the foundation upon which sound policy is built. The mission of the World Bank's Data Group is to provide high-quality national and international statistics to clients within and outside the Bank and to improve the capacity of member countries to produce and use statistical information. As part of the international statistical system, the Data Group works with other organizations on new statistical methods, data collection activities, and statistical capacity–building programs. This group also coordinates the analytical and statistical work related to monitoring progress toward the Millennium Development Goals.

As the demand for good-quality statistical data increases, timely and reliable statistics are key inputs to the broad development strategy. Improvements in the quality and quantity of data on all aspects of development are essential if we are to achieve the goal of a world without poverty. Good data are needed to set baselines, identify effective public and private actions, set goals and targets, monitor progress, and evaluate impacts. They are also an essential tool of good government, providing a means for people to assess what governments do and helping them to participate directly in the development process.

This statement and data seta are available at http://web.worldbank.org/WBSITE/EXTERNAL/DATASTATISTICS/0,,contentMDK:21725423~pagePK:64133150~piPK:64133175~theSitePK:239419,00.html

TABLE 13.2 Population size and related variables, 1996–1998

Country	POP[a]	IMR[b]	URB[c]	GNP[d]	LEXP[e]
Albania	3.3	20.4	37	820	72
Antigua and Barbuda	0.1	18	36	7,330	74
Australia	18.7	5.3	85	20,090	78
Bahamas	0.3	19	86	—	72
Barbados	0.3	14.2	38	—	75
Belize	0.2	34	51	2,700	72
Bolivia	8	75	58	830	60
Brazil	162.1	43	76	4,400	67
Burkina Faso	11.3	94	15	230	47
Cameroon	14.3	65	44	610	55
Central African Rep.	3.4	97	39	310	46
China	1242.5	31	30	750	71
Comoros	0.5	77	29	450	59
Costa Rica	3.5	11.8	44	2,640	76
Cuba	11.1	7.2	74	—	75
Denmark	5.3	5.8	85	32,100	75
Dominican Republic	8.3	47	62	1,600	70
El Salvador	5.8	41	50	1,700	69
Estonia	1.4	10	70	3,080	68
Fiji	0.8	17	46	2,470	63
French Guyana	0.2	14	—	—	74
Gambia	1.2	90	37	—	45
Ghana	18.9	66	35	360	56
Guadeloupe	0.4	7.9	99	—	77
Guinea	7.5	153	29	560	45
Haiti	7.5	74	33	310	51
Iceland	0.3	5.5	92	26,580	78
Iran	64.1	35	61	—	67
Israel	6	6.7	90	15,870	78
Japan	126.4	3.8	78	40,940	80
Kenya	28.3	62	27	320	49
Kuwait	1.9	10	100	—	72
Latvia	2.4	16	69	2,300	70
Liberia	2.8	108	45	—	59
Lithuania	3.7	10	68	2280	71
Macedonia	2	16.4	60	990	71
Malaysia	22.2	10	57	4,370	72

Continued

TABLE 13.2   Population size and related variables, 1996–1998 (*Continued*)

Country	*POP[a]*	*IMR[b]*	*URB[c]*	*GNP[d]*	*LEXP[e]*
Malta	0.4	10.7	89	—	77
Mauritius	1.2	21	43	3,710	70
Moldova	4.2	20	46	590	66
Mozambique	18.6	134	28	80	44
Nepal	23.7	79	10	210	55
New Caledonia	0.2	8	71	—	72
Niger	10.1	123	15	200	47
Oman	2.5	27	72	—	70
Panama	2.8	22	55	3,080	74
Peru	26.1	43	71	2,420	69
Portugal	10	6.9	48	10,160	75
Reunion	0.7	9	73	—	74
Rwanda	8	114	5	190	43
St. Vincent/Grenadines	0.1	19	25	2,370	73
Saudi Arabia	20.2	29	80	—	70
Sierra Leone	4.6	195	36	200	34
Slovenia	2	4.7	50	9,240	75
South Africa	38.9	52	57	3,520	58
Sudan	28.5	70	27	—	51
Sweden	8.9	3.9	83	25,710	79
Taiwan	21.7	6.7	75	—	75
Thailand	61.1	25	31	2,960	69
Tunisia	9.5	35	61	1,930	68
Uganda	21	81	14	300	40
United Kingdom	59.1	6.1	90	19,600	77
Uzbekistan	24.1	26	38	1,010	70
Vietnam	78.5	38	20	290	67
Yemen	15.8	77	25	380	58
Zimbabwe	11	53	31	610	40

Source: Population Reference Bureau.

Note: (—) indicates missing data.

[a]POP, population in millions.

[b]IMR, infant mortality rate (number of deaths before age 1 per 1,000 births in a given year).

[c]URB, urbanization (percentage of the population living in cities).

[d]GNP, gross national product per capita (US$).

[e]LEXP, life expectancy (combined male and female).

Previous analysis has shown that population size, which ranges between 0.1 and 1,242.5 million with a mean of 35.0 million, is not associated in any "interesting" ways with the other variables. So we will set it aside for the sake of this analysis and work only with the last four variables.

Table 13.3 shows the descriptive statistics for these four variables: number of countries reporting values on each variable (valid n), ranges, minimum and maximum values, means, and standard deviations. There are six possible pairings for this set of four variables: IMR and URB, IMR and GNP, etc. As we discuss the various aspects of correlation and regression, we shall look closely at one specific pair—IMR and URB—and list the findings for the other five.

Once we have selected a pair of appropriate variables, we must decide which of the two should be treated as the independent. According to current theory in this area of study, it is likely that neither actually is the probable cause of the other but that both are the result of level of socioeconomic development. For purposes of measuring association, it does not make a difference, because the results will be the same regardless of which variable is selected as the independent or dependent. However, because we are forced to make the choice for the sake of creating tables and graphs, it seems more reasonable to assume that urbanization affects infant mortality rather than the other way around.

To distinguish between the two, we refer to values of URB as x, its mean as $\bar{x}$, and its standard deviation as s_x. The values of IMR will then be designated as y, its mean will be $\bar{y}$, and its standard deviation s_y.[1] Next, we note the respective means and standard deviations. These are: for IMR, $\bar{x} = 41.8$ and $s_x = 41.2$; for URB, $\bar{y} = 52.4$ and $s_y = 24.4$. We can see that the variability in IMR, as a proportion of the value of its mean (0.99), is the greater of the two (for URB this proportion is 0.47).

TABLE 13.3   Descriptive statistics for population size and the four other variables for the sample in table 13.2

Variable[a]	n[b]	Min	Max	Mean	Std. Dev.
POP	66	0.1	1,242.5	35.0	209.2
IMR	66	3.8	195	41.8	51.4
URB	65	5	100	52.4	26.9
GNP	50	80	40,940	5,315	877.6
LEXP	66	34	80	67.5	11.9

[a]See table 13.2 and the text for variables.

[b]n refers to the total number of countries for which data were available for each variable.

Creating the Scatterplot

With the decision made that URB is the independent and IMR the dependent variable, we move to the next step of creating a special graph known as a *scatterplot* (sometimes called a *scattergram*). For this we use the familiar technique of graphing on a rectangular coordinate system.

You will recall that this system has two axes, as shown in figure 13.1: the horizontal or *x*-axis and the vertical or *y*-axis. The *x*-axis will stand for the independent (*x*) variable and the *y*-axis will stand for the dependent (*y*). The point at which the two axes meet, the (0,0) point, is the origin. The axes divide the page into four parts, or quadrants, which are numbered counterclockwise from the upper right: I, II, III, and IV. All values to right of the *y*-axis are positive, and all values to the left are negative. All values above the *x*-axis are positive, and all values below it are negative. Thus, everything in quadrant I has a positive *x* and a positive *y* (+,+). In quadrant II, *x* is negative and *y* is positive (−,+); in quadrant III, both are negative (−,−); and in quadrant IV, *x* is positive and *y* is negative (+,−). In creating our scatterplots in this chapter we will use variables that have only values equal to zero or above—no negative values. This is very helpful, because we then only need to work in the first quadrant, as shown in the inset to figure 13.1.

As you probably recall from a course in algebra, to create a plot we mark off, for each unit, the value of the *x* variable on the *x*-axis and the value of the *y* variable on the *y*-axis. Then, we draw a vertical reference line from the *x* value and a horizontal reference line from the *y* value. Where the two reference lines intersect, we designate a point that is identified by the *coordinates* (*x,y*). The process is repeated until the coordinates are plotted for all units.

Using the data set in table 13.2 and the variables URB and IMR, we see that our first nation is Albania, with a value of 37 (percent) on the independent variable and 20.4 on the dependent. Figure 13.2 shows how these coordinates are plotted. Figures 13.3 and 13.4 show the coordinates for the next two countries: Antigua and Barbuda, and Australia, respectively. Finally, figure 13.5 contains the plot for all nations for which data are available. At this point, the plotting procedure is complete.

The Best-Fitting Line: Slope

The next step takes us closer to the realm of correlation description. It is easy to see that the scatterplot creates a pattern representing the relationship between the independent and dependent variables. The purpose of correlation description is to examine that relationship so that we might judge how, if at all, the variables vary together, or are "co-related." In our example, we can ask: Are highly urbanized nations likely to have high IMRs? Or is it the other way around, such that high rates of urbanization go with low levels of infant mortality? Is the relationship consistent, so that every nation with

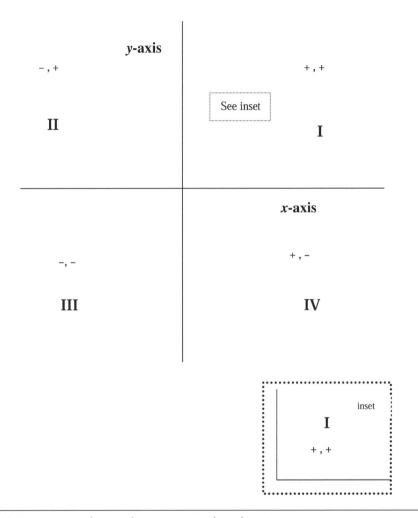

FIGURE 13.1   Rectangular coordinate system and quadrant I.

a specific level of urbanization has about the same infant mortality rate? Or is it the case that two nations with similar urbanization rates can have substantially different IMRs?

Correlation description answers such questions by determining two features of the scatterplot: slope and shape.

1. First is its *slope* or orientation. Does it tend to slope upward like this ↗? Or does it slope downward like this ↘?
2. Second is its *shape*. Is it closely clustered, as shown in figure 13.6? Or is it highly dispersed, as in figure 13.7?

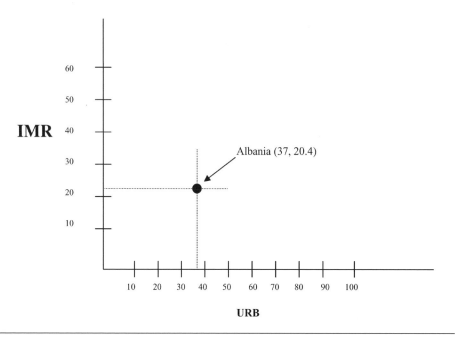

FIGURE 13.2   URB and IMR: the coordinates for Albania.

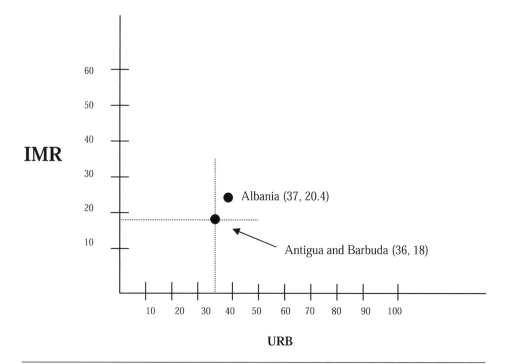

FIGURE 13.3   URB and IMR: the coordinates for Albania and for Antigua and Barbuda.

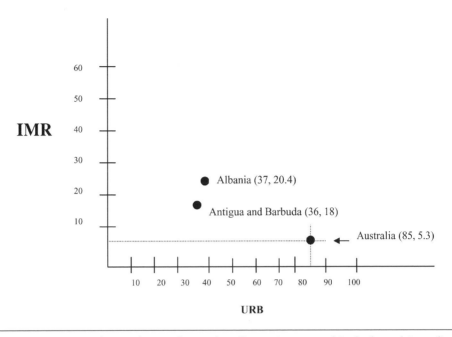

FIGURE 13.4   URB and IMR: the coordinates for Albania, Antigua and Barbuda, and Australia.

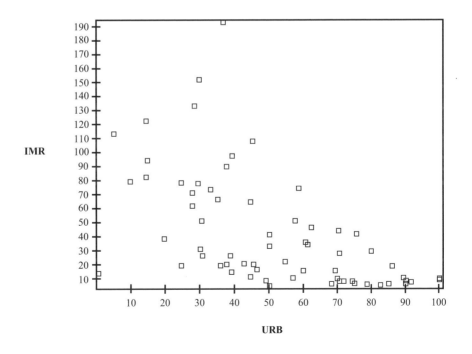

FIGURE 13.5   URB and IMR, the complete scatterplot: the coordinates for all countries.

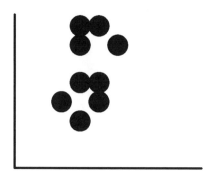

FIGURE 13.6   Scatterplot illustration.

It should be emphasized that correlation, in contrast to regression, is directly concerned with the scatterplot itself. This is because we are seeking to determine the degree of association between variables in the sample, and the scatterplot represents the actual observations of sample data.

Yet the easiest and most common method of informally determining the slope and shape of the plot is to sketch in—actually or mentally—a line that appears to fit the plot better than any other line. By "fit" we mean that it covers or come close to covering the maximum number of points. This *best-fitting* line, which is what it is usually called, is not actually part of the plot. But because it is based on the plot, we can describe the slope and shape in relation to it.

The best-fitting line can be drawn more precisely than by merely sketching it in. In fact, there is a familiar formula that is used to determine the line exactly, which is discussed later in this chapter. This exact line has two names, one of which—the *least squares line*—indicates how it is derived. The other name, the *regression line*, is featured in regression description and induction.[2] For this reason, correlation and regression

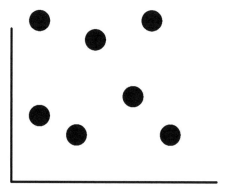

FIGURE 13.7   Scatterplot illustration 2.

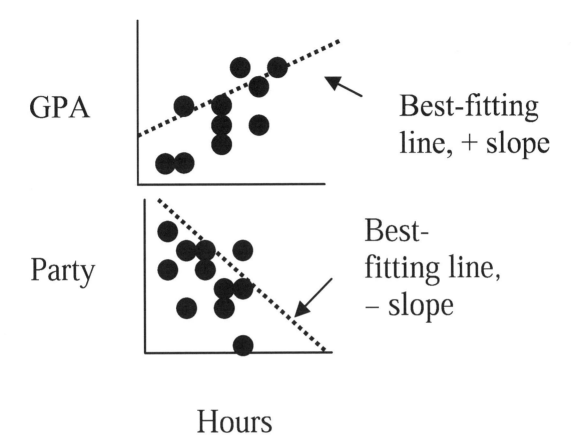

FIGURE 13.8   (a) Scatterplot with best-fitting line, positive correlation; (b) scatterplot with best-fitting line, negative correlation.

are actually two complementary parts of a single set of techniques. In particular, regression focuses on the exact best-fitting line derived from a correlation scatterplot.

Using the best-fitting line to judge the scatterplot's slope, we determine what happens to the *y*-coordinate (IMR in our example) when the line's *x*-coordinate (urbanization rate) increases. If the *y*-coordinate also increases, we have an increasing or *positive* (+) *slope*. If the *y*-coordinate decreases when *x* increases, we have a decreasing or *negative* (−) *slope*. In the case of a positive slope, the relationship between the two variables is termed *direct*, or a *direct correlation*. With a negative slope we call the relationship *inverse*, or an *inverse correlation*. These terms were introduced in Chapter 12 in connection with Spearman's rank-order correlation.

Figures 13.8(a) and (b) illustrate these two possibilities with a different, smaller sample. Figure 13.8(a) plots information for a sample of 10 recent college graduates. Here the independent variable is number of hours per week the graduate spent studying while enrolled

(Hours), and the dependent variable is grade point average at graduation (GPA). As we might expect, the slope of the best-fitting line is positive and the correlation between the two variables is direct: The more one studies, the higher the GPA. Figure 13.8(b) includes the same independent variable, but it introduces another dependent variable that applies to the 10 students: the number of weeknight parties the graduate attended while a student (Party). Here we see that the best-fitting line has a negative slope, indicating an inverse correlation: The more a student studies, the less he or she goes out on weeknights.

Determining the Slope

Before continuing on to the second aspect of correlation description, the shape of the scatterplot, let us use the reference line method to determine whether the scatterplot shown in figure 13.5 indicates a direct or inverse correlation between urbanization and IMR. With the use of the best-fitting line shown in figure 13.9, the answer is clear. It is an inverse correlation: As the urbanization rate increases, infant mortality decreases.

Thus far we have drawn the best-fitting line by informal estimation. But it does have a property that can help us to draw it a little more accurately and bring us closer to

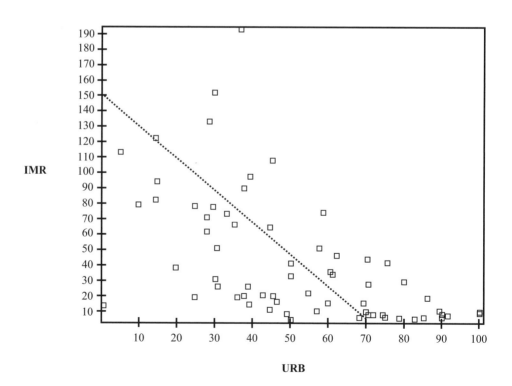

FIGURE 13.9   The complete scatterplot: the coordinates for all countries with best-fitting line.

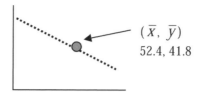

FIGURE 13.10   The sample means fall on the best-fitting line.

determining the actual regression line. That is, the coordinates made up of *the two means*, $(\bar{x}, \bar{y})$, will *always fall on the line*. Thus, we can better estimate the line in figure 13.9 by noting that it not only has a negative slope but also passes through the point (52.4, 41.8). This is shown in figure 13.10. We discuss this property further in relation to regression.

As noted, we seek to describe the shape of the scatterplot in terms of how closely packed or clustered its *n* points are. With the use of the best-fitting line, we can be more exact in how we state this feature, because we can indicate the extent to which the points literally "line up"—that is, how well they fit the best-fitting line.

Nonlinear Correlation

Before continuing, let us recall that the type of correlation and regression we are focusing upon here is the *linear* type. The reason is that we describe the plot's shape in relation to a *straight line*. Other approaches seek to fit the data to other shapes, such as parabolas or exponential curves, as shown in figures 13.11 and 13.12. It is often the case that nonlinear correlation conveys a more accurate picture of the relationships under investigation.

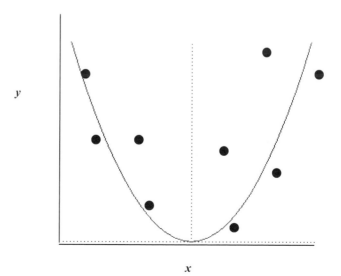

FIGURE 13.11   A parabola, a curve used in nonlinear correlation.

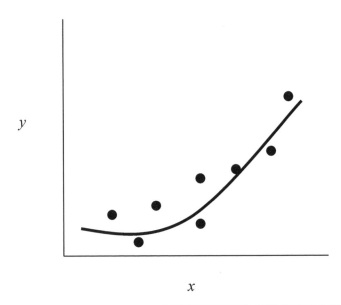

FIGURE 13.12   An exponential curve, also used in nonlinear correlation.

For example, the correlation between TV-watching hours and age is probably closer to being parabolic, with the young and old watching more than the middle-aged. As another example, population growth over time is generally exponential.

Nevertheless, we start with the line because it is the simplest shape in one important respect: Its slope does not vary regardless of the value of the independent variable—the slope, or rate of change (discussed below), is *constant*. If, for example, the slope of a line is positive between $x = 0$ and $x = 10$, then it will also be positive between $x = 10$ and $x = 100$ and between $x = 100$ and $x = 1,000$, etc. In contrast, note that the parabola in figure 13.11 has a negative slope up to its lowest ("turning") point, and then the slope becomes positive.

The Best-Fitting Line: Shape

Looking back on figures 13.6 and 13.7, it is clear that between the two, not only does the former indicate a more compact scatterplot, but its points lie closer to the best-fitting line. In this case, we would conclude that the correlation illustrated in figure 13.6 is "stronger" or "higher," and that in figure 13.7 is "weaker" or "lower." Now, depending on the degree to which the plot does fit the best-fitting line, a correlation (whether negative or positive) can range between perfect and none at all.

A *perfect correlation*—the strongest or highest possible kind—is one in which all of the points of the plot fall exactly on the line. In contrast, a situation of *no correlation*

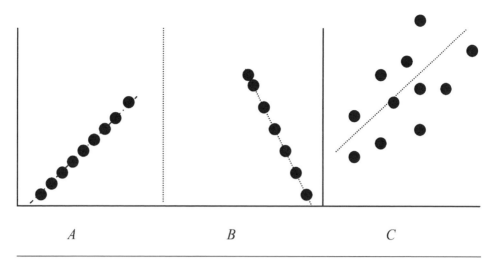

A   *B*   *C*

FIGURE 13.13   Perfect correlations (*A*, direct; *B*, inverse) and a correlation that is neither perfect nor 0 (*C*).

between the independent and dependent variables is one in which the scatterplot is so dispersed that there is no best-fitting line: every possible line fits as poorly as any other. These two extremes are pictured in figures 13.13 and 13.14, respectively. Panel *A* of figure 13.13 shows a perfect direct correlation, and panel *B* shows a perfect inverse correlation. Slope really doesn't apply to the case of no correlation, because there is no best-fitting line to guide us. There are infinite intermediate possibilities between a perfect correlation and no correlation, one of which is depicted in panel *C* of figure 13.13. In seeking to measure correlations of this type, a number is assigned whose absolute

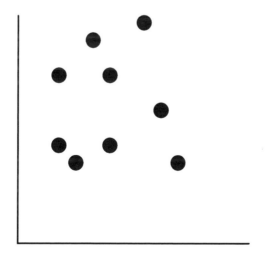

FIGURE 13.14   No correlation.

value lies between 0 and 1, and whose sign indicates a positive (+) or negative (−) slope.

The shape of the scatterplot is measured by this number, with higher absolute values indicating a stronger correlation and lower absolute values indicating a weaker correlation. We now turn to correlation description.

Correlation Description

Early in the twentieth century, the influential agronomist and statistician Karl Pearson devised a way to measure the slope and strength of a bivariate linear correlation that continues to be used today as the principal descriptive tool in the field. In his honor, the measure is often referred to as the "Pearsonian coefficient of correlation" or more simply by its symbol: "Pearson's r." This lowercase r is also called the "correlation coefficient" or, more exactly, the "linear correlation coefficient." Whatever we call it, it is an ingenious and easy way to understand the statistic. To mention that it is a statistic is a reminder that it is a characteristic of a sample and that it is calculated using sample data.

Measuring Correlation with Pearson's r

Following the method of measuring the slope and shape of the scatterplot, Pearson's r can have a + sign, or it can have a − sign, or it can equal zero. A positive r indicates that the scatterplot has a positive slope and that the correlation between the independent and dependent variables is direct. A negative sign indicates an inverse correlation. And a zero indicates no slope (a horizontal line than tends neither upward nor downward). The absolute value of r measures the shape of the scatterplot; and it ranges between 0, indicating no correlation, and 1, which stands for a perfect correlation. So, combining the sign and size together,

$$+1.0 \geq r \geq -1.0.$$

This can also be shown as a scale that represents the possible range of values of r, as in figure 13.15.

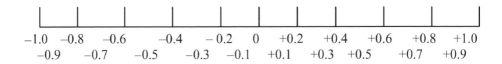

FIGURE 13.15   Scale of possible r values.

Beginning at the 0 point in the middle of the scale, as one moves outward in either direction, the correlation becomes stronger: inversely to the left and directly to the right. With this measure, then, we can clearly judge the slope and shape of a plot, and we can easily compare one plot with another.

Suppose that in the illustration of the correlation between hours studied and GPA, one sample of 10 graduates produced an *r* of +0.75. We would be justified in saying that as study time increased, so did GPA, and we would also be right in believing that it is a pretty strong or close correlation. Now, suppose that in another test of the same relationship with a different set of graduates, the *r* turned out to be +0.60. In comparing the two sets of results, we could conclude that our second survey agreed with the first in showing a direct relationship between the variables. However, we would also be led to believe that in the second test the correlation, although still fairly strong, was not as strong as in the first. Perhaps the discrepancy was the result of differences in the composition of the samples, the personalities of the graduates, or another reason.

Similarly, we might compare the results of the first survey, with *r* = +0.75, to the results of the survey in which the independent variable was number of parties attended. Suppose that the *r* produced in the "parties" survey was −0.75. In this case we could say that the two sets of results varied in that the correlation in the case of parties was *inverse*. Increases in the value of the independent variable were associated with *lowering* the value of the dependent (GPA). However, we would also want to point out that the strength of the correlations was equal—and quite substantial.

In our examination of the relationship between level of urbanization and infant mortality rate for the sample of 66 nations, calculations made using SPSS showed that the *r* for this relationship is −0.626. First, we see by the negative sign that this result verifies the impression that there is an inverse correlation between the variables. The more highly urbanized a country is, the lower its infant mortality rate. Moreover, it is a fairly strong relationship: not 1.0, of course, but quite a distance from 0.

Calculating r

As is true of most of the statistics introduced in this text, Pearson's *r* is a ratio; it measures one quantity divided by another quantity. We made explicit mention of this property in the case of the *F* ratio used in analysis of variance; we will return to *F* in Chapter 14. Unlike *F* and most of the other ratios considered earlier—but like Spearman's rank-order correlation coefficient—*r* cannot exceed 1.0 in absolute value. Unlike *F* and chi-square, which are always positive, *r* can be either positive or negative.

As a ratio, the numerator of *r* measures the degree to which the independent and dependent variables vary together (co-vary) in a clear pattern—that is, the degree to which the points of the scatterplot actually line up on the best-fitting line. The denominator measures all of the variability that occurs in each of the two variables, whether or not the variation occurs in a clear pattern that links the two. In other words, it measures the locations of all the points on the scatterplot, whether or not they fall on the best-fitting line. The numerator can be positive or negative, depending on whether the coordinates of the points fall above or below the means of the respective variables. The denominator is always positive, because, like the standard deviation and some other statistics, it involves squaring and then taking the positive square root. Thus, a positive numerator indicates a positive slope to the best-fitting line and a direct relationship. A negative numerator indicates a negative slope and an inverse relationship.

The numerator consists of n terms, one for each unit of the sample. Each term combines by multiplication the degree to which the x and y values differ from their respective means. For x this is $(x - \bar{x})$, and for y this is $(y - \bar{y})$. Each of the n terms is the product of these deviations:

$$(x_i - \bar{x})(y_i - \bar{y}).$$

The numerator of r contains the sum of each of these n products. For what may be obvious reasons, this is called the "sum of products," or SP.

$$SP = \sum_{i=1}^{n} [(x_i - \bar{x})(y_i - \bar{y})].$$

The entire numerator is derived by dividing this sum by n. The result is the average of the products of the deviations:

$$\frac{\sum_{i=1}^{n} [(x_i - \bar{x})(y_i - \bar{y})]}{n}.$$

The denominator of r measures separately (a) the degree to which each x value differs from its mean, which is simply the standard deviation of x,

$$s_x = \sqrt{\frac{\sum_{i=1}^{n} (x_i - \bar{x})^2}{n}},$$

and (b) the degree to which each y value differs from its mean—the standard deviation of y:

$$s_y = \sqrt{\frac{\sum_{i=1}^{n} (y_i - \bar{y})^2}{n}}.$$

To derive the complete denominator, we then multiply s_x by s_y:

$$\sqrt{\frac{\sum\limits_{i=1}^{n}(x_i-\overline{x})^2}{n}}\times\sqrt{\frac{\sum\limits_{i=1}^{n}(y_i-\overline{y})^2}{n}}.$$

Finally, bringing the numerator and denominator together, we get r:

$$r=\frac{\dfrac{\sum\limits_{i=1}^{n}[(x_i-\overline{x})(y_i-\overline{y})]}{n}}{\sqrt{\dfrac{\sum\limits_{i=1}^{n}(x_i-\overline{x})^2}{n}}\sqrt{\dfrac{\sum\limits_{i=1}^{n}(y_i-\overline{y})^2}{n}}}.$$

This can be simplified somewhat because the n in the numerator and the two $\sqrt{n}$'s in the denominator cancel each other out and both sums in the denominator can then be placed under the same square root sign:

$$r=\frac{\sum\limits_{i=1}^{n}[(x_i-\overline{x})(y_i-\overline{y})]}{\sqrt{\left(\sum\limits_{i=1}^{n}(x_i-\overline{x})^2\right)\left(\sum\limits_{i=1}^{n}(y_i-\overline{y})^2\right)}}.$$

The two factors in the denominator—the standard deviations *without* the division by n—are each referred to as the *sum of squares*. As in ANOVA, discussed in Chapter 11, this is short for *the sum of deviations squared*. The first is the sum of squares in x, abbreviated as SS_x, and the other is the sum of squares in y, abbreviated as SS_y.

Recall that the numerator of r is called the sum of the products (SP), which measures the extent to which the independent and dependent variables vary together.

$$SP=\sum\limits_{i=1}^{n}[(x_i-\overline{x})(y_i-\overline{y})]$$

As the independent increases a given amount, the value of the SP indicates whether the dependent increases (decreases) a constant or proportional amount. For example, suppose that x increases from 1 to 2 and y increases 2 to 4. Then, if x increases from 2 to 3, does y increase from 4 to 6? And if x increases from 3 to 5, does y increase from 6 to 10, and so forth? If the answer to these questions is "yes," then we know that the rate of change of y is constant, and their scatterplot forms a line.

The denominator, which is the square root of the product of the sum of squares, is symbolized as $\sqrt{SS_x SS_y}$. It measures the total of all the variations for both variables—the cases in which they vary together and those in which they do not. Thus, the formula for *r* in its most simplified version is

$$r = \frac{SP}{\sqrt{SS_x SS_y}}.$$

The numerator can be positive or negative (or zero) according to whether the dependent variable increases (+), decreases (−), or does not change at all (0) when the independent increases. The denominator is always positive because we are taking a positive square root.

A large *r* (in absolute value) means that the ratio is close to 1.0, which occurs as $\sqrt{SS_x SS_y}$ approaches the absolute value of *SP*. When they are exactly equal—that is, *r* = 1.0—we know that *all* of the variation observed in the dependent variable occurs in exact proportion to the variation in the dependent: they vary together perfectly. As we saw, the scatterplot of such a relationship would line up perfectly along the best-fitting line, because the slope, or rate of change, is constant. An *r* of zero means that *none* of the variation in the dependent variable occurs in a constant or exact proportion to the change in the independent. In such a case, there really is no "best"-fitting line, as the scatterplot is much dispersed.

Absolute values of *r* ranging between 0 and 1 reflect the value of the ratio of *SP* to $\sqrt{SS_x SS_y}$. For example, an *r* = +0.5 indicates that *SP* is one-half the size of $\sqrt{SS_x SS_y}$ and that *x* and *y* vary directly. An *r* = −0.25 indicates that they vary inversely and that *SP* is one-fourth of $\sqrt{SS_x SS_y}$, and so forth.

An Illustration

To illustrate how *r* is calculated, we return in table 13.4 to the example of the study habits and GPAs of our 10 college graduates. In column 1 we find the actual number of study hours reported by each student. These range from 2 for student *j* to 20 for student *a*. The mean, shown at the bottom of the table, is 9.0 hours. Column 2 shows the GPAs for each of the 10 students. These range from 2.0 (out of 4.0) for student *e*, who reported studying 6 hours per week, to 3.9 for student *f*, who reported studying 14 hours per week.

The mean for this variable, shown at the bottom of the table, is 3.04. With this information, along with the scatterplot shown in figure 13.16, we can make a fairly safe guess that the variables are *directly* related to one another and that the relationship is moderately strong. Certainly it is not a perfect 1.0 because, for example, the student with the lowest GPA did not report studying the least; nor does the student who studied the most have the highest GPA. But there is enough of a relationship to produce an *r* that will be well above 0.

TABLE 13.4   Raw data and calculations for finding the correlation coefficient between hours spent studying and GPA, $n = 10$

	1	2	3	4	5	6	7
Student ID	*Study hours (x)*	*GPA (y)*	$(x - \bar{x})$	$(y - \bar{y})$	$(x - \bar{x})^2$	$(y - \bar{y})^2$	$(x - \bar{x})(y - \bar{y})$
a	20	3.8	11	0.76	121	0.58	8.4
b	7	2.3	−2	−0.74	4	0.55	1.5
c	10	3.5	1	+0.46	1	0.21	0.5
d	10	3.4	1	+0.36	1	0.13	0.4
e	6	2.0	−3	−1.04	9	1.08	3.1
f	14	3.9	+5	+0.86	25	0.74	4.3
g	12	3.6	+3	+0.56	9	0.31	1.7
h	4	2.7	−5	−0.34	25	0.11	1.7
i	5	2.7	−4	−0.34	16	0.11	1.4
j	2	2.5	−7	−0.54	49	0.29	3.8
Totals	90	30.4			$SS_x = 260$	$SS_y = 4.14$	$SP = 26.6$
Means	$\bar{x} = 9.0$	$\bar{y} = 3.04$					

To determine the value of r, we find each graduate's deviation from the mean of x and from the mean of y, as shown in columns 3 and 4 in table 13.4. By multiplying the two sets of deviations together, we get the 10 terms shown in column 7. And when we add these terms, we get the sum of 26.6 at the bottom of column 7. This, of course, is SP, the numerator of the r statistic. Because it is a positive number, we now know for certain that the correlation between x and y is direct: the more one studies, the higher the GPA. To find the denominator of r, which is $\sqrt{SS_x SS_y}$, we first need to square the deviations in x and in y. These are found in columns 5 and 6, respectively. At the bottom of these columns, are the two sums. We see that $SS_x = 260$ and $SS_y = 4.14$.

The next step is to find the square root of the product $SS_x \times SS_y$. We find the product, which is 1072.2, and then take the square root to find the denominator of r, which is 32.7 (recall that the denominator will always be a positive number). The last step is to divide the numerator by the denominator: 26.6/32.8. Thus $r = +0.81$. As suspected, the correlation is neither perfect nor entirely absent. An r of +0.81 indicates a fairly strong direct correlation: these graduates' GPAs were definitely related to the amount of time that they spent studying, but not consistently so.

The Coefficients of Determination and Alienation

Having discussed the key features of the scatterplot, its slope and shape, from several perspectives, we have almost completed our exploration of correlation description. We

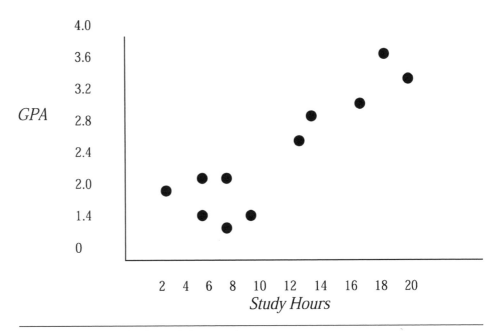

FIGURE 13.16   Scatterplot for study hours and GPA

have noted that the correlation coefficient, *r*, is a ratio that measures the degree to which (1) the independent and dependent variables co-vary (*SP*) compared to (2) all of the variation in both variables combined ($\sqrt{SS_x SS_y}$). When they are the same, $r = \pm 1.0$, which is to say that all variation is co-variation. If *SP* equals exactly one-half of $\sqrt{SS_x SS_y}$, then $r = \pm 0.50$, and so on. Now we can take this analysis of *r* one step further by changing the ratio into a proportion. The procedure is simply to square *r*, multiply it by itself, to produce the *coefficient of determination = r^2*.

The coefficient of determination is always positive (because it is a square), and it indicates *the proportion of variation in y that is accounted for by variation in x*. Like *r*, it ranges between 0 and 1.0. But, unlike *r*, it directly accounts for how consistently *y* changes as *x* changes. In this way, it allows us to judge directly the value of the independent variable as an explainer of the dependent on an easily understood scale. If r^2 = 1.0, then we give it a score of 100%; it explains the entire dependent. If r^2 = 0.50, then we give it a score of 50%; it explains one-half, and so on. In terms of the scatterplot, the coefficient of determination indicates as a proportion or percentage how closely the points are to the best-fitting line. In our illustration of the urbanization–IMR relationship, where $r = -0.626$, then $r^2 = 0.382$, indicating that nearly 40% of the variation in IMR is explained by level of urbanization, or about 0.4 of the points fall on or near the line. This relationship is illustrated in figure 13.16.

The complement of the coefficient of determination is called the *coefficient of alienation* (or *non-determination*). It measures the proportion of the variation in y that x does *not* explain; or the proportion of points that do *not* fall on the line. Its formula is simply

$$Coefficient\ of\ alienation = 1 - r^2.$$

So if $r^2 = 1.0$, the coefficient of alienation equals $(1 - 1.0) = 0$. That is, there is nothing left to explain after the independent variable does its job. If r^2 is equal to 0.5, so is the coefficient of alienation $(1 - 0.5) = 0.5$: one-half the job of explaining still remains. If $r^2 = 0.27$, then the coefficient of alienation equals 0.73, that is, 73% of the variation is *un*explained, and so on.

Because the absolute value of r is always 1.0 or below, the coefficient of determination is always less than r, except if $r = 1.0$ or 0. This is because any number less than 1.0 decreases when it is squared. This means that r itself does *not* directly indicate the degree to which the independent variable is an effective explainer of the dependent. For instance, if a correlation study produced an $r = 0.5$, we might be tempted to say that it is a "halfway decent" correlation. Strictly speaking, this is not true. Of course, 0.5 lies halfway between 0 and 1.0, but this is only a ratio of the co-variation to all variation. It is not meant to be understood as a true proportion. Instead, in order to judge whether a correlation is "halfway decent," we need to square r, thereby producing a smaller number. Thus, an r of 0.5 is only "a quarter of the way decent," because $r^2 = 0.25$. A "halfway decent" r would equal 0.707, because r^2 then produces a proportion of 0.5, or 50%. Table 13.5 compares r values with their corresponding coefficients of determination.

The respective r and r^2 values for the relationships between the variables in table 13.3 are shown in table 13.6. Clearly, these are all moderately strong to strong correlations, with r^2 values ranging from 0.220 for GNP and IMR to 0.803 for IMR and LEXP. In fact, the latter coefficient of determination is misleadingly high because of the phenomenon of *autocorrelation*, the correlation between a variable and itself. One of the main

TABLE 13.5 r and r^2

r	r^2	r	r^2
0	0	0.6	0.36
0.1	0.01	0.7	0.49
0.2	0.04	0.8	0.64
0.3	0.09	0.9	0.81
0.4	0.16	1.0	1.0
0.5	0.25		

TABLE 13.6   Bivariate correlation table

Independent variable	Dependent variable	r	r²
GNP	URB	0.666	0.444
GNP	IMR	−0.469	0.220
URB	LEXP	0.693	0.480
GNP	LEXP	0.543	0.295
IMR	LEXP	−0.896	0.803

components used to measure average life expectancy is the infant mortality rate. So the strong correlation between the two variables is not very informative.

The correlations between GNP and URB, URB and LEXP, and GNP and LEXP are all direct: wealthy countries tend to be highly urban and to have high average life expectancies. The correlations between GNP and IMR and between IMR and LEXP are inverse: wealthy countries have low infant mortality rates, and countries with high infant mortality rates have low average life expectancies.

Summary of Correlation Description

We have now completed our discussion of correlation description, which is summarized in table 13.7. This application focuses on the scatterplot, a graphic presentation of the relationship between two numerical variables. To create the scatterplot, the value of the independent and dependent variables for each of *n* units is plotted on an *x, y* coordinate system. We then find (a) the slope and (b) the shape of the plot. This is aided by using a reference line called the "best-fitting line"—which is determined by a formula in regression analysis and is also called the "regression line."

The next step is to calculate the Pearsonian correlation coefficient, *r*, and note its sign and size. A positive sign indicates a direct relationship, one in which an increase in the independent variable is accompanied by an increase in the dependent. A negative sign indicates an inverse relationship, in which an increase in *x* leads to a decrease in *y*. The shape of the scatterplot (in relation to the best-fitting line) is indicated by the absolute value of *r*, which varies between 0 and 1.0. The larger size of *r*, the more closely

TABLE 13.7   The four parts of correlation and regression II

	Description	Induction
Correlation	Plot, sign, and size of r; r^2, $(1 - r^2)$	2
Regression	3	4

the plot fits the line. Finally, by squaring r, we find r^2, the coefficient of determination, and the coefficient of alienation $1 - r^2$. These coefficients are proportions ranging between 0 and 1.0 that indicate the efficiency or lack of efficiency of x in explaining the variation in y.

Correlation Induction

If, as in the case of the 66-nations illustration, we can assume we have a random sample, we can then take our correlation analysis one step further. That is, we can ask how far the correlation results can be generalized to characterize the population from which the sample was drawn. The purpose of *correlation induction* is to make this determination.

When we follow the steps of correlation description, summarized above, we still do not know whether the correlation observed in the sample accurately reflects the correlation in the population. That is, if we could plot *all* coordinates in the population (of more than 200 nations), not just the n in our sample, would we find any correlation at all? This is another way to ask the question: Given the sign and size of r and the size of r^2, is it *statistically significant*?

As in other inductive applications, when we seek to determine the significance of a result based on sample information, we are about to test a hypothesis about the population—a null hypothesis, in particular. As always, our decision to accept or reject is based on whether the statistic summarizing the sample information is large enough to exceed a standard value found in the appropriate table. With the exception of the difference of means discussed in Chapter 10, all the tests used in this book, including that associated with correlation, are two-tailed. Thus, the sign of the statistic is irrelevant; its absolute value is what we compare to the table.

In the case of correlation, there are alternative approaches to the hypothesis-testing procedure, one of which is based on the two-tailed t-test. Here we omit the t-test approach to introduce a method that is widely used and is intuitively the clearest.[3] The statistic it uses is r^2 itself, which for this purpose is symbolized as $r^2_{calculated}$. This means that no special calculations are performed for the inductive part of correlation. All we need, in addition to an appropriate table value, r^2_{table}, are r^2 and n, both of which we have already employed in the descriptive part.

What we ask in correlation induction is, "Based on the size (absolute value) of $r^2_{calculated}$ from my sample, is there a correlation in the population?" We follow the practice of using Roman letters for statistics and Greek letters for parameters. With the statistic r^2, the population parameter counterpart is the Greek equivalent of r, which is ρ (pronounced *rho* and introduced in connection with Spearman's rank-order correlation in Chapter 12). Thus, the null hypothesis, "there is no correlation in the population" translates to

$$H_0: \rho = 0.$$

And the research hypothesis is

$$H_r: \rho \neq 0.$$

As in other hypothesis-testing situations, use of the table (here table A.6) requires that we know the degrees of freedom (*d.f.*) and α, level of significance. In the latter case, we continue to let $\alpha = .05$ and/or $\alpha = .01$. To find degrees of freedom in correlation induction we subtract 2 from *n* (1 for the independent variable and 1 for the dependent):

$$d.f. = n - 2.$$

In table A.6, as in most other tables (with the exception of chi-square), we see that as the number of degrees of freedom increases, the value of r^2_{table} decreases. That is, the larger the sample, the easier it is to reject the null hypothesis. Looking at the data in table 13.3, with such large $r^2_{calculated}$ values and with sample sizes ranging between 50 and 66, one would suspect that the relationships between URB and GNP and the others are significant, even before finding r^2_{table}.

Just to be sure, however, let us test the six null hypotheses that there is no correlation in the population between the respective variables. The appropriate values from table A.6 are shown in columns 5 and 6 in table 13.8.

As we had anticipated, all of the correlations in the sample are significant at both levels of significance. It is true that the calculated value of *r* for the pair GNP and IMR is not much larger than the table value at $\alpha = .01$ (in part because of the small *n*). Nevertheless, it is larger. Thus we can safely say, with 99 percent confidence, that each pair of variables is correlated to some extent in the population (that is, in the set of all the world's nations).

TABLE 13.8   Six null hypotheses

1	2	3	4	5	6	7
Variables	$r_{calculated}$	$r^2_{calculated}$	*d.f.*	r^2_{table}	r^2_{table}	*Decision*
				$\alpha = .05$	$\alpha = .01$	
URB and IMR	−0.626	0.392	63	0.063	0.106	Reject
GNP and URB	0.681	0.464	48	0.092	0.154	Reject
GNP and IMR	−0.471	0.222	48	0.092	0.154	Reject
URB and LEXP	0.693	0.480	63	0.063	0.106	Reject
GNP and LEXP	0.546	0.298	48	0.092	0.154	Reject
IMR and LEXP	−0.896	0.803	64	0.063	0.106	Reject

TABLE 13.9   The four parts of correlation and regression III

	Description	*Induction*
Correlation	Plot, sign, and size of r; r^2, $1 - r^2$	H_0: $\alpha = 0$. Use r^2 from descriptive part; table A.6: $\alpha = .05$ and/or .01, $d.f. = n - 2$
Regression	3	4

This illustration completes our overview of bivariate correlation induction. With the method used here, it is not necessary to calculate additional statistics. Table A.6 is arranged so that we simply compare our already-derived $r^2_{calculated}$ with the table value at $n - 2$ degrees of freedom and $\alpha = .05$ and/or .01. The null hypothesis we are testing is that there is no correlation in the population: H_0: $\rho = 0$.

The correlation row in the table of the four parts of correlation and induction, table 13.9, has now been completed. Next, we will move on to Chapter 14 and regression description.

Summary

Bivariate linear correlation is a technique for establishing the degree of association between two sample numerical variables (descriptive) and testing hypotheses about the corresponding degree of association in the population (inductive). The procedure begins with a scatterplot, which is a graphic representation of the relationship between the two variables. Using sample information, principally the means and standard deviations, the r, r^2, and $1 - r^2$ statistics are calculated and interpreted. Correlation induction uses $r^2_{calculated}$ in comparison to an r^2_{table} value to determine whether there is likely to be a nonzero correlation in the population.

These techniques can be extended to situations in which three or more variables are involved, which takes us to multivariate correlation. For more on this, see the online Chapter 15. Bivariate approaches are revisited in Chapter 14, which covers the closely related topic of linear regression.

KEY TERMS

Autocorrelation: The tendency for two variables to be highly correlated because they are essentially measuring the same thing.

Best-fitting line: A line drawn informally on the scatterplot that seems best to represent the linear trend of the plotted points.

Coordinates: the pair of values for each case on the x and y variables.

Direct correlation: A correlation for which the variables increase (or decrease) in value together.

Inverse correlation: A correlation for which an increase in the value of one variable is associated with a decrease in the value of the other.

Least squares line: The formal version of the best-fitting line based on minimizing the squared distances between it and the points of the scatterplot.

Negative slope: The type of slope for which an increase in the horizontal (x) produces a decrease in the vertical (y).

Pearson's r: The measure of bivariate linear correlation, named after pioneer statistician Karl Pearson.

Positive slope: The type of slope for which an increase in the horizontal (x) produces an increase in the vertical (y).

ρ (rho): The symbol for the correlation coefficient in a population, for which Pearson's r is an estimate.

Scatterplot: A graph that shows the relationship between the independent (x) and the dependent (y) variables with points representing the x and y values for each case as coordinates.

Slope: The number of units of vertical (y) change for every unit of horizontal (x) change.

WEB SITES TO BOOKMARK (FOR CHAPTERS 13 AND 14)

1. www.stat.uiuc.edu/~stat100/java/guess/PPApplet
   .html
   This fun site from the University of Illinois allows the user to create any scatterplot. Based on this, the program will calculate the appropriate correlation and regression coefficients.

2. spike.me.psu.edu/~ME082/Learning/Stat_2/
   stat_2.html
   Here you will find definitions of basic terms, formulas, and a clear illustration of the concepts in this and the following chapter.

3. www.uvm.edu/~dhowell/StatPages/More_Stuff/
   CorrReg.html

   This site has clear definitions and several illustrations of correlation, regression, and related concepts.

4. www.acad.sunytccc.edu/instruct/sbrown/ti83/
   regress.htm
   Here is another interactive site that creates scatterplots and then calculates correlation and regression coefficients.

5. acad.cgu.edu/wise/applets/Correl/correl.html
   This is a highly interactive site that uses a scatterplot as the starting point for a tutorial on correlation and regression. Claremont (CA) Graduate College maintains this site.

Solution-Centered and SPSS Applications on both correlation and regression follow Chapter 14.

Regression Description and Induction in the Sociological Study of Globalization

Our introduction to bivariate correlation in Chapter 13 focused on the scatterplot, produced by graphing the x- and y-coordinates of each unit in our sample. We have seen how useful it is to create, or at least to imagine, a reference line that best fits the scatterplot. For with such a line we are reminded that the kind of correlations we seek are *linear*; and it is easier to envision the two main aspects of the scatterplot of interest in linear correlation: the *slope* and the *shape* of the plot.

Linear *regression* techniques set the scatterplot aside to focus specifically on this best-fitting line. Once we have established, via correlation analysis, (1) the direction (the sign of r) and the extent to which the points of the plot fit the line (the sizes of r and r^2) and (2) whether or not r is significant, we remove the points and concentrate only on the line. It is as if we were saying, "I know that the points fit the line in a certain way—with a negative slope, or a positive slope, or very well, or very poorly, etc.—but now let us *assume that they all line up perfectly.*"

Regression Description

Based on this procedure, we reexamine the relationship between the independent and the dependent variables, now assuming that it is represented by the line itself. These steps are illustrated in figure 14.1. Under these conditions, the best-fitting line is given its proper name: *the regression line.*

The goal of regression description is, thus, to *describe the regression line*. As in correlation, the first feature to be considered is slope. In contrast to correlation, however, shape is not relevant. By assuming the plot itself away, we have forced the shape to be perfectly linear. Instead, the second aspect of description is the *position* of the line. We discuss position in a moment, after taking another look at the concept of slope.

You will recall from algebra that the slope of a line measures the *impact* of the independent (x) variable on the dependent (y). If the slope is small in absolute value, then

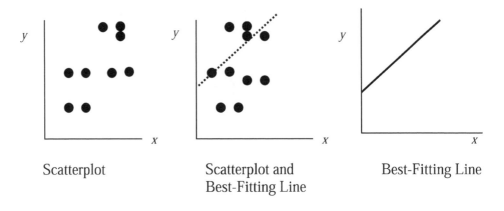

FIGURE 14.1   Regression diagram 1.

x has little effect on *y*; if the slope is large, then *x* has a considerable effect on *y*. If the slope is 0, then there is no effect. Of course, when *x* and *y* are sociological variables, the slope of their regression line is very important, for it indicates how strong an impact a phenomenon such as gross national product has on infant mortality rate, and so on.

Not only does the magnitude of the slope vary in absolute value, from 0 on up (there is no upper limit); its sign also varies. As we saw in the case of correlation, an upward slope, in which an increase in *x* leads to an increase in *y*, is designated as positive (+). A downward slope, in which an increase in *x* leads to a decrease in *y*, is designated as negative (–). From this it follows that *the sign of r and the sign of the slope of the associated regression line are always the same.* This is because the best-fitting line, which becomes the regression line in regression analysis, and *r* are both based on the same scatterplot.

The Slope and y-Intercept

Slope

In correlation analysis, we are interested in the slope of the scatterplot—as reflected in the slope of the best-fitting line—only insofar as it is positive (upward) or negative (downward). In regression analysis, we want to be more exact. This is accomplished not only by determining the sign of the slope but also by assigning it a quantitative value. This leads to the formal definition of the slope of a regression line, which is universally symbolized by a lowercase *b*.

b = slope: the number of units that *y* changes when *x* increases by one unit

As mentioned in the preceding section, a key property of a straight line is that there is only one slope, regardless of the value of *x*. If *x* increases from, say, $1.00 of GNP to

$2.00, the amount of change in y is the same when x goes from $101 to $102 as when x goes from $553 to $554. If the slope is 2% when $x = $101, it is always 2%.

The larger the slope (in absolute value), the steeper the line is inclined. Figure 14.2 illustrates this concept with several different slopes. In the upper row we have a set of positive slopes, increasing in steepness from +0.5 to +3.0. The bottom row shows increasingly steeper negative slopes. In the center is an illustration of no slope—that is, a horizontal line. Can you see how, as the slope of the line increases in absolute value, the impact of the x variable on the y variable increases? That is, there is increasingly more change per unit (more change in IMR per dollar of GNP, etc.).

Intercept

Now, in addition to the slope, the other feature that characterizes a line is what we have called its "position." By this we mean the point at which it intersects the y-axis. You will notice that this point, called the *y-intercept*, is where the regression line's x value equals zero; this is because every point along the y-axis has the coordinates $(0,y)$, just as every point along the x-axis has the coordinates $(x,0)$. The y-intercept is a number, designated by the lowercase letter a, that indicates at what value y is to be set as we begin to trace the slope of the line, and thus where we begin to measure the impact x has upon y.

a: the y-intercept; the value of y at which the regression line's x value equals zero

If there were 0 units of x (e.g., GNP)—even if this could never happen in reality—there would be a units of y (e.g., URB).

The y-intercept is not as important an indicator as the slope, because it is just a number that establishes the value of y compared to the scale by which x is measured. If, for example, we are examining a regression line that represents the relationship between GNP and URB, the y-intercept tells us what quantity needs to be added to (or subtracted from) GNP to convert dollars to percentage points.[1] The value of the y-intercept can be a negative number, even though we stipulated that we would remain in the first quadrant of the coordinate system. This occurs when the plot of all points creates a best-fitting line that is confined to the first quadrant, and does not cross the y-axis. (Only when we extend it does it cross, but then it ends up between quadrants IV and III, which have negative y values.)

Figure 14.3(a) shows some typical regression lines that have the same y-intercept but different slopes. For the sake of comparison, figures 14.3(b) and (c) show a set of regression lines that have (b) the same slope and different intercepts, and (c) different slopes and different intercepts. Notice in the first set of lines the feature to which we referred. That is, the y-intercept indicates the value of the dependent variable at which we start counting with $n = 0$—the change-of-scale property.

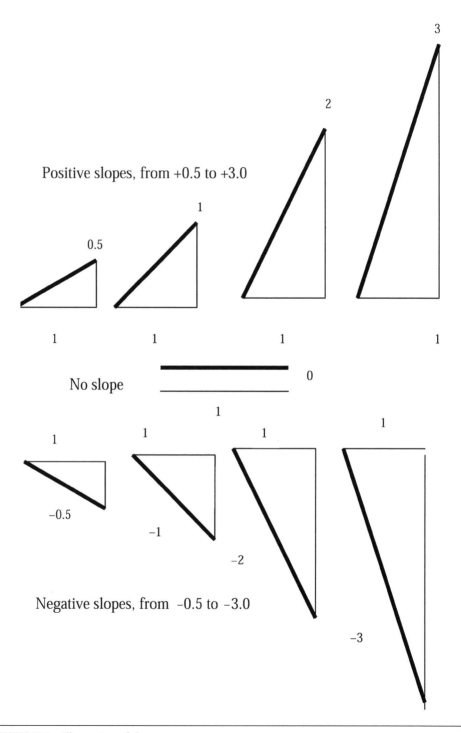

FIGURE 14.2   Illustration of slopes.

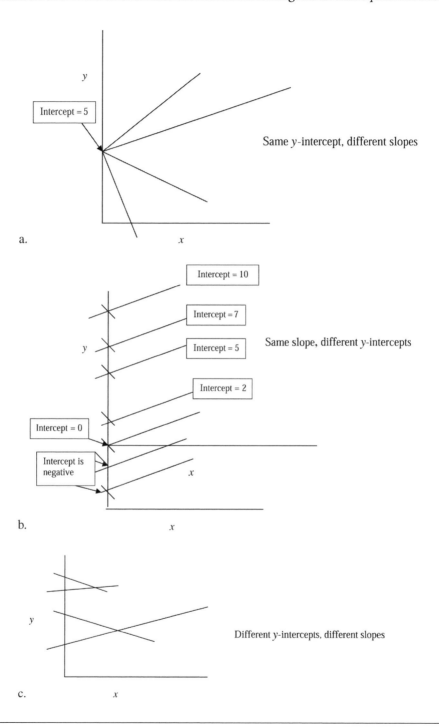

FIGURE 14.3   (a) Same *y*-intercept, different slopes; (b) same slope, different *y*-intercepts; (c) different *y*-intercepts, different slopes.

As you can see from figure 14.3(a), there are many (in fact, infinitely many) lines that share a given intercept. There are also many lines with the same slope but different intercepts; these are parallel lines. But there is one and only one line with a given intercept and a given slope. Just as two points determine a line, one point—the intercept (0,y)—and a slope also determine a line. In fact, the two statements represent the same principle. If you know that the intercept of a line is the point (0,5) and you know that for every unit change in x there is a change of 3 units in y, then you also know another point: 0 + 1 = 1 and 5 + 3 = 8. So, you can draw a line between (0,5) and (1,8); and it is the only line that can be drawn between these points. This is why we say that to describe a regression line fully, you need only to describe its slope and y-intercept. This process is illustrated in figure 14.4.

Measuring the Slope and the y-Intercept

Because the regression line is based on the scatterplot, we must return to the scatterplot and to the original set of *n* coordinates that make it up to measure the line's slope and y-intercept. You probably have realized that we have just defined the general equation in basic algebra that describes a line in slope/y-intercept form. This equation is the key to regression description. As it is usually written, the equation is a formula (a "recipe") for determining a unit's value on the dependent variable, y, given its value on the independent, x, variable. For example, it can be used for determining a student's GPA knowing the number of hours he or she studies, determining the urbanization rate

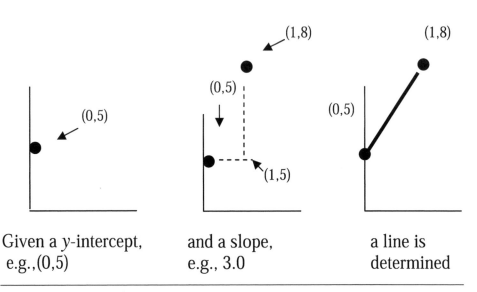

Given a y-intercept,   and a slope,   a line is
e.g.,(0,5)   e.g., 3.0   determined

FIGURE 14.4   Regression diagram 2.

of a country knowing its per-capita GNP, and so on. The general form of the equation is the familiar

$$\hat{y} = a + bx,$$

where $\hat{y}$ is the value of the dependent, x is the value of the independent, a is the y-intercept, and b is the slope. The "$\wedge$" sign over the y, called a circumflex, a caret, or simply a hat, is used to remind us that the y values derived are those that would be *predicted* if the scatterplot fit the line perfectly. Unless the correlation is perfect, many if not most predicted $\hat{y}$ values will be different from the actual observed y values (with no hat), that is, the ones that are part of the scatterplot. As an alternative to the hat, the predicted value of the dependent variable can be designated with a subscript p (for "predicted"), as with IMR_p in the following discussion.

Before we see how the necessary values for a and b are derived, let us illustrate how the equation works using the 66-nation data set. For the relationship between URB and IMR, SPSS analysis shows that $a = 97.9$ and $b = -1.06$. The b value means that for every unit change in URB (one percentage point), the IMR will *decrease* by 1.06 units (deaths per 1,000 infants). The a value means that if a country were to have 0% urbanization, its IMR would be 97.9 per 1,000. In equation form, this is:

$$IMR_p = 97.9 - 1.06 \times URB.$$

Notice that the slope, b, is negative. You will recall that r was also negative, so this is to be expected: it is an inverse relationship, where high URB goes with low IMR.

Now suppose that we have measured the urbanization rate of an imaginary country we'll call Freedonia and found it to be 65%. We can then solve for its (predicted) infant mortality rate as follows.

1. Multiply 65 by −1.06. This equals −68.9.
2. Subtract 68.9 from 97.9. This equals 29.
3. Therefore, Freedonia's (predicted) infant mortality rate is 29 per 1,000 (assuming, of course, that all points on the scatterplot fall perfectly on the regression line).

By way of comparison, suppose that we have found that another imaginary country, Gallardia, has an urbanization rate of only 30%. Would we expect its IMR to be higher or lower than that of Freedonia? Will the difference be great or small? According to the regression equation, Gallardia's IMR_p equals $97.9 - 1.06 \times 30 = 97.9 - 31.8 = 66.1$ per 1,000 (assuming that all points fall on the line). As the equation tells us, Gallardia's IMR_p is not only higher, it is more than twice as high, because its urbanization rate is less than half as high as Freedonia's.

Calculating Slope and Intercept

Like r, the slope of the regression equation, b, is calculated as a ratio. In this case, its numerator is also SP, $\sum_{i=1}^{n}[(x_i - \overline{x})(y_i - \overline{y})]$, and its denominator is a sum of squares:

$$b = \frac{\sum_{i=1}^{n}(x_i - \overline{x})(y_i - \overline{y})}{\sum_{i=1}^{n}(x_i - \overline{x})^2} = \frac{SP}{SS_x}.$$

This measures the degree to which the independent and dependent variables co-vary. However, the denominator is no longer $\sqrt{(SS_x SS_y)}$, which measures the total variation in both variables. Instead, the denominator is just SS_x:

$$SS_x = \sum_{i=1}^{n}(x_i - \overline{x})^2.$$

This measures the total variation in x alone. Thus, the formula for the slope is the ratio

$$b = SP/SS_x.$$

This indicates *the amount of variation in y as x varies*. Compare this to the definition of the slope of the regression line given above:

As a square, the denominator, SS_x, is always positive.

- If the numerator, SP, is positive, then b is positive, and y increases as x increases.
- If $SP = 0$, then y doesn't vary at all regardless of the value of x. In this case, $b = 0$ and there is *no slope*: the regression line is horizontal.
- If SP is negative, then y becomes smaller as x increases, and the slope is negative.
- If the absolute value of $SP = SS_x$, then $|b| = 1$, and the regression line increases or decreases, depending on the sign, at a 45° angle.

As noted, unlike the correlation coefficient, b can have an absolute value greater than 1.0. That is, the larger the value of absolute value of b, the more y varies in relation to x, with no maximum, and the steeper the slope.

The y-intercept, symbolized as a, is a number added to or subtracted from the slope so that y_p will be at the proper scale. Because the point whose coordinates are equal to the means of the two variables, $(\overline{x}, \overline{y})$, always falls on the regression line, we can substitute $\overline{x}$ for the x and $\overline{y}$ for the y in the equation. This ensures that the scale is adjusted correctly.

Thus, "on the average," we get this version of the regression equation:

$$\bar{y} = a + b\bar{x}.$$

To solve for a, we simply subtract $b\bar{x}$ from both sides of this equation. Thus:

$$a = \bar{y} - b\bar{x}.$$

Notice that if either $b = 0$ or $\bar{x} = 0$, then $a = \bar{y}$. If $\bar{y} = b\bar{x}$, then a is zero and the intercept is at the origin (the units of measurement can be treated as equivalent).

To summarize: In determining the formula for a regression line, we use the slope/y-intercept format:

$$\hat{y} = a + bx \quad \text{or} \quad y_p = a + bx,$$

where $\hat{y}$ or y_p is the predicted value of the dependent variable. The slope, which measures the impact of change in the independent variable on the dependent variable, is

$$b = \frac{\sum\limits_{i=1}^{n}(x_i - \bar{x})(y_i - \bar{y})}{\sum\limits_{i=1}^{n}(x_i - \bar{x})^2} = \frac{SP}{SS_x}.$$

And the intercept, the point at which the line crosses the the y-axis, is

$$a = \bar{y} - b\bar{x}.$$

Illustrating the Use of the Regression Line

We can apply these formulas to the example of study hours and GPA, presented in Chapter 13, table 13.4. We noted that $\bar{x} = 9.0$, $\bar{y} = 3.04$, $SS_x = 260$, $SS_y = 4.14$, and $SP = 26.6$ for our sample. The correlation coefficient for this relationship was $+0.81$, yielding a coefficient of determination of 0.66. These values reflect a strong direct correlation, with nearly two-thirds of the variation in GPA accounted for by the number of hours spent studying. At this point, we can solve for the regression line. The slope, b, equals SP/SS_x:

$$b = 26.6/260 = 0.102.$$

With $\bar{x} = 9.0$ and $\bar{y} = 3.04$,

$$a = 3.04 - (0.102)(9) = 2.12$$

So, our regression equation is:

$$GPA_p = 2.12 + (0.102) \times \text{study hours}.$$

In words: To find a student's predicted GPA, multiply 0.102 times the hours spent studying and add 2.12. The corresponding regression line is shown in figure 14.5.

The relationship between urbanization and infant mortality from the 66-nation sample has an r and r^2 of -0.626 and 0.392, respectively. The regression equation turned out to be be $IMR_p = 97.90 - 1.063URB$. The slopes, y-intercepts, and regression equations for this and the other bivariate relationships are shown in table 14.1.

Here are a few more illustrations with these equations. Suppose, for example, that our imaginary country of Freedonia has a GNP value of $10,000. Then, according to the equation in the second row of table 14.1, its urbanization rate would be

$$URB_p = 38.5 + (0.00171) \times (10,000) = 38.5 + 17.1 = 55.6\%.$$

According to the equation in the third row, its predicted infant mortality rate would be:

$$IMR_p = 57.7 - (0.00222) \times (10,000) = 57.7 - 22.2 = 35.5 \text{ per } 1,000.$$

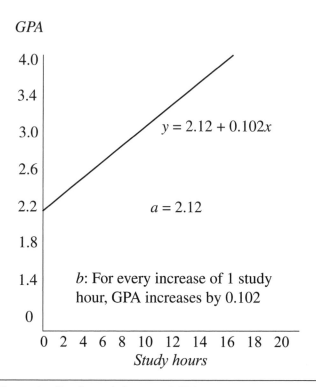

FIGURE 14.5   Regression line for study hours and GPA.

TABLE 14.1   Regression table for 66-nation sample

Variables	SS_x	SP	b	$\bar{x}$	$\bar{y}$	a	Equation
URB and IMR	3.797E+04	4.037E+04	−1.063	52.4	42.2	97.9	$IMR_p = 97.90 - (1.063)URB$
GNP and URB	4.094E+09	6.998E+06	+0.00171	5315	47.5	38.5	$URB_p = 38.5 + (0.00171)GNP$
GNP and IMR	4.094E+09	−9.131E+06	−0.00222	5315	45.9	57.7	$IMR_p = 57.7 - (0.00222)GNP$
URB and LEXP	3.797E+04	1.288E+04	+0.339	52.4	65.0	47.24	$LEXP_p = 47.24 + (0.339)URB$
GNP and LEXP	4.094E+09	3.032E+06	+0.00074	5315	63.9	59.94	$LEXP_p = 59.94 + (0.00074)GNP$
IMR and LEXP	1.104E+05	−2.852E+04	−0.258	41.8	65.1	75.94	$LEXP_p = 75.94 - (0.258)IMR$

And according to the equation in the fifth row, its predicted average life expectancy would be:

$$LEXP_p = 59.9 + (0.00074) \times (10{,}000) = 59.9 + 7.4 = 67.3 \text{ years.}$$

Least Squares and Regression Error

The regression line is the best-fitting line, for which the fit is rarely perfect. That is why we stipulate that the values of the dependent variable derived from the equations are estimates. The formulas for the slope and y-intercept are themselves estimates based on a specific set of conditions, in addition to the observed sample values. The conditions that are most often used in linear regression, and the ones that underlie the above equations, are expressed in the concept of the "least squares."[2]

The concept of least squares ensures that the line that is produced, as defined by its slope and y-intercept, is the one *from which the squared distances between it and each of the observed points are the absolute possible minimum.* That is:

- For every observed point (x,y) in the scatterplot, there exists a point on the regression line $(x,\hat{y})$, although they might coincide.
- The distance between them is represented as $(y - \hat{y})$. This difference is known as the *residual*; it is symbolized as *e* (because it is also a measure of error), where

$$e = (y - \hat{y}).$$

- The squared distance (residual squared) is e^2.

- The line created by the regression equation is the one that, on the average, equalizes the positive and negative distances. These are the distances between the points on the line and the observed points whose *y*-coordinates lie above it (positive distances) and the points whose *y*-coordinates lie below it (negative distances). The sum of the residuals, like the sum of the deviations from a mean, will be 0. Thus, the *a* and *b* of the line are calculated so that:

$$\sum e^2 \text{ is minimized and } \sum e = 0.$$

This approach to estimation is illustrated in figure 14.6, again using our study hours–GPA example from table 13.4. The vertical lines indicate the distance between the plotted point with a specific *x* value (hours studied) and the point on the regression line with that same *x* value. For example, Student *e*, with 6 hours of study time, has an observed GPA of 2.0. But the predicted GPA for *x* = 6 is 2.73, which results in a difference of –0.73. Moreover, student *a* has a predicted GPA of 4.17, which is an impossibility. Obviously, as we saw in our correlation analysis, hours studied do have some impact on GPA, but there is something else involved as well.

We can see from the table accompanying figure 4.6 that the sum of the differences (distances) is zero. This is the result of the way in which the slope and *y*-intercept of the line were calculated, that is, the least squares method: there is as much distance above the line as below it. The squared distances, which are of course all positive, are shown in column 5, and their sum is at the bottom of the column. This turns out to equal

$$\sum e^2 = 1.39.$$

As mentioned, another way to interpret the residual terms, *e*, is as the *error* that would be made if we were to use the regression equation to predict the *y* values instead of depending on the observed data. The distance between the point and the line on the graph in fact measures such *regression error*. There is, thus, one regression error term for each of the *n* units in the sample (although one or more might equal zero if the corresponding points of the scatterplot happened to fall exactly on the line). The sum of the error terms squared, $\sum e^2$, is thus also called the "error sum of squares," abbreviated as SS_{error}. It is a useful measure of the accuracy of the regression line as a predictor of the *y* values. In particular, the smaller the SS_{error}, the more accurate is the line and the closer is the fit between it and the original scatterplot.

A commonly used statistic that is based on SS_{error} serves the same function. However, it adjusts the quantity of error, or lack of fit, for the size of the sample. This allows us to compare regression lines and equations based on different sample sizes (because *n* does affect the magnitude of SS_{error}). This statistic is called the *standard error of the estimate*. Like the standard deviation, it is calculated by taking the square root of a specific sum of squares. This makes it more understandable as an average. In this case, it is an

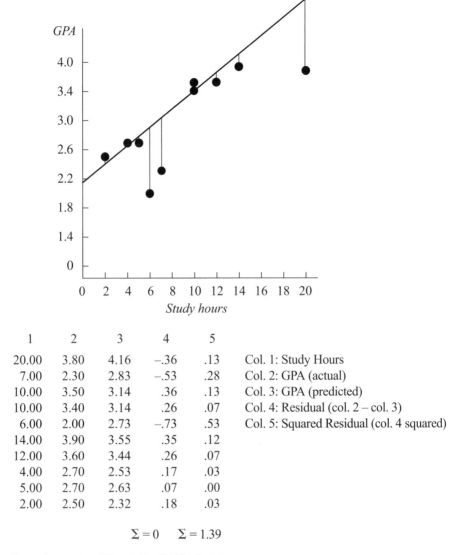

1	2	3	4	5	
20.00	3.80	4.16	−.36	.13	Col. 1: Study Hours
7.00	2.30	2.83	−.53	.28	Col. 2: GPA (actual)
10.00	3.50	3.14	.36	.13	Col. 3: GPA (predicted)
10.00	3.40	3.14	.26	.07	Col. 4: Residual (col. 2 – col. 3)
6.00	2.00	2.73	−.73	.53	Col. 5: Squared Residual (col. 4 squared)
14.00	3.90	3.55	.35	.12	
12.00	3.60	3.44	.26	.07	
4.00	2.70	2.53	.17	.03	
5.00	2.70	2.63	.07	.00	
2.00	2.50	2.32	.18	.03	

$$\Sigma = 0 \qquad \Sigma = 1.39$$

Regression equation: $\text{GPA}_p = 2.12 + (0.102) \cdot$ Study hours.

FIGURE 14.6 Regression line, equation, and residuals for study hours and GPA.

adjusted average of each of the n distances between the points in the plot and those on the line. The symbol for the standard error of estimate is $s_{y.x}$, and its formula is:

$$s_{y.x} = \sqrt{\frac{\sum_{i=1}^{n} e_i^2}{n-2}}$$

Illustrating with the data from our study hours–GPA example, we find that:

$$s_{y,x} = \sqrt{\frac{1.39}{8}} = \sqrt{0.175} = 0.419$$

That is, on the "average," there is a 0.419 difference between the students' actual grade point averages and those predicted by the regression equation.

The standard errors of the estimates for the regression equations using the 66-nation sample are shown in table 14.2. For this set of relationships, the IMR and LEXP pair has the lowest standard error of the estimate. Recall that they are also most highly correlated because they are close to measuring the same thing. At the other extreme, the greatest error is produced with GNP and IMR—in part because, as we observed earlier, they have the smallest n.

You have noticed that the denominator of the standard error of the estimate is $(n - 2)$, which indicates that it represents degrees of freedom—the same as used in correlation induction. Here, one degree is subtracted for the slope (b) of the regression equation and one is subtracted for the y-intercept (a). In reintroducing the idea of degrees of freedom, we are suggesting that our regression results—and $s_{y,x}$ in particular—will be used to make inferences about the population from which our sample is drawn. That is, we have come to the last of our main topics in correlation and regression: regression induction.

Before continuing, let us review the elements of regression description. The approach begins with the best-fitting line, which we now call the regression line. Our main focus is on its slope or b: its sign and size, and its y-intercept or a. These, in effect, describe the line in a unique way. The sign of b indicates whether the dependent variable increases (+) or decreases (–) as the independent increases, and it always agrees with the sign of the correlation coefficient. The size of b measures the impact of the independent variable on the dependent; the higher the absolute value of b, the more a change in x affects y. The y-intercept tells us the value of y when x is zero. It is a starting point, so to speak, that

TABLE 14.2   Regression equations and standard errors of estimates for 66 nations

Variables	Equation	$s_{y,x}$
URB and IMR	$IMR_p = 97.9 - (1.063)URB$	32.54
GNP and URB	$URB_p = 38.45 + (0.00171)GNP$	16.96
GNP and IMR	$IMR_p = 57.74 - (0.00223)GNP$	38.58
URB and LEXP	$LEXP_p = 47.24 + (0.339)URB$	8.66
GNP and LEXP	$LEXP_p = 59.94 + (0.00074)GNP$	10.49
IMR and LEXP	$LEXP_p = 75.94 - (0.258)IMR$	5.31

ensures that the scale remains the same as we go from dollars to percent, from hours to grade points, and so on.

Finally, because the regression line rarely is a perfect fit to the scatterplot, we must be able to characterize just exactly how far off the line is from the points (and vice versa). This is accomplished by measuring each of the n instances of regression error and summarizing them in measures such as the residuals $(y - \hat{y})$, the error sum of squares (SS_{error}), and the standard error of the estimate $(s_{y,x})$. These constitute the third of the four parts of correlation and regression, as shown in table 14.3.

Now, knowing what our regression line looks like and the extent to which it accurately portrays the observed relationship between x and y, we can ask one further question: Is it significant? To answer this, we turn to regression induction.

Regression Induction

Once we appreciate the importance of the residuals or regression error, $e = (y - \hat{y})$, there are several additional measures and techniques that are relevant to understanding and employing the concept more effectively. One of the most common of these uses ANOVA, introduced in Chapter 11, to measure and assess the amount of error observed in a specific relationship. This approach is used in SPSS and other applications and is discussed in this section. Another strategy, usually introduced in a second course in statistics, is to bring additional independent variables into the regression equation in the hope of reducing error. That is, we seek to explain y more successfully by identifying new variables (x_2, x_3, etc.) that, along with x, may have an impact. This process is described and illustrated in the online Chapter 15.

A third technique, discussed in this section, is parallel to that featured in connection with correlation induction. You will recall that in that context, we posed the question: "Knowing r and r^2 in my sample—the coefficients of correlation and determination— what can be said about the coefficient of correlation in the population?" In particular, we tested the null hypothesis that the population's correlation coefficient, symbolized as ρ, is zero: no correlation. This was phrased as the null hypothesis:

$$H_0: \rho = 0.$$

TABLE 14.3   The four parts of correlation and regression IV

	Description	*Induction*
Correlation	Plot, sign, and size of r; r^2, $1 - r^2$	$H_0: \rho = 0$. Use r^2 from descriptive part; table A.6: $\alpha = .05$ and/ or .01, $d.f. = n - 2$
Regression	Regression line: b, sign and size of its slope; a, its y-intercept; SS_{error}, $s_{y,x}$	4

In the case of regression, we also seek to generalize to the population, and in particular about the slope of the population regression line (for more on this inductive technique, see Hamburg, 1979: 279–281).

Testing the Significance of b

Once a and b, the intercept and slope, have been determined for a regression equation of the form $\hat{y} = a + bx$, we can get a fairly good idea from the scatterplot about how effective the equation is in predicting the y values from our sample x values. This is even clearer when we calculate the residuals, which measure the difference between the values of y predicted by the equation and the actual y values in the sample. This difference is the *error*, which we would of course like to be as small as possible.

Knowing as much as is possible about the regression equation, it is still of interest to establish the degree to which the equation can be generalized to the population from which our sample was drawn. Recall that the slope, b, is a measure of the amount of change that occurs in y for every unit change in x. The higher the absolute value of b, the greater the impact of x. Conversely, if the value of b is very low, then y is not affected very much by a change in x. And if $b = 0$, we know that there is no impact of x on y. Of course, only very rarely is b equal to exactly zero. But it is always possible that b is so small (in absolute value) that we cannot discount the likelihood that the regression line in the population from which the sample was drawn has no slope at all. In fact, that is the null hypothesis we test.

Recall that the Greek equivalent of r, which is ρ, is used to symbolize the correlation coefficient in the population. We would like to be consistent regarding regression and apply the rule that Greek letters stand for (population) parameters and Roman letters stand for (sample) statistics. However, the Greek equivalent of b, which is lowercase β, is universally used to stand for a statistic, the *standardized b* (see below). Thus, it cannot symbolize the slope in the population because it is being used for another purpose.

Instead, to indicate the slope of the regression line for the population, we use the uppercase Roman B (or the uppercase Greek *beta*, which is the same symbol). Thus, the null hypothesis we test in regression induction is written this way:

$H_0: B = 0$.

This indicates that the regression line that characterizes the relationship between x and y in the population has no slope. And the research hypothesis is:

$H_r = B \neq 0$.

That is, the regression line in the population does have a nonzero slope.

Recall that one thing that made our approach to correlation induction simple is that we did not need to calculate a separate statistic: we just used r^2. One reason for this is that

r^2 varies only between 0 and +1.0 and its size does not depend on the units of measure used for the variables. It does not matter whether we are correlating dollars and percents, hours and grade points, or rates and years. In its computation, correlation standardizes all values, and it is the standard (z) scores—which do not depend on units of measurement—whose relationship is measured. The slopes of regression equations, however, do depend on whether we are going from dollars to percents, hours to grade points, and so forth.

Therefore, a large b might reflect the scale of the measure (say, study hours to GPA) rather than a large change in y for a unit change in x. For example, when discussing study hours, one-half hour may not mean very much, whereas a small b that measures hours to GPA may reflect quite an impact. Doesn't a change of even 0.5 in one's GPA seem substantial?

For this reason, before we can test the above null hypothesis, we need to rescale b by performing a standardization, creating a "cooked" slope out of a "raw" one, as with other statistics. Here is where we use the symbol β properly. Based on the preceding discussion, to find β one must remove the effect of the units of measure of the x and y variables on the value of b. This is accomplished by dividing it by another error-based statistic, the *estimated standard error of b*, which is a kind of standard deviation. In particular, it is the ratio of $s_{y.x}$, the standard error of the estimate, to the square root of SS_x, the sum of squares of the independent variable. The symbol for the estimated standard error of b is s_b, and its formula is:

$$\text{Standard error of } b: s_b = \frac{s_{y.x}}{\sqrt{SS_x}} = \frac{s_{y.x}}{\sqrt{\sum_{i=1}^{n}(x_i - \bar{x})^2}},$$

where

$$s_{y.x} = \sqrt{\frac{\sum_{i=1}^{n} e_i^2}{n-2}}.$$

We next divide b by s_b to determine β, which is the standardized b. This division cancels out the effect of the units of measurement.

$$\beta = \frac{b}{s_b}.$$

To summarize to this point:

1. We seek to test the null hypothesis, H_0: $B = 0$ (there is no slope in the population).
2. This is done by first dividing the observed slope b by the estimated standard error of the slope to create a standardized b, whose formula is given above. That is,

$$\beta = \frac{b}{s_b}.$$

3. As in all other cases of hypothesis testing, the next step is to compare our calculated statistic to the corresponding table value. But which table?

Fortunately, the table to use in testing H_0: $B = 0$ is the familiar table of two-tailed t values (table A.2). This is appropriate because the standard error of the slope is a standard error term of a sampling distribution, which is not normal but approaches normal as n increases. The appropriate degrees of freedom are the same as those used in correlation induction, i.e., $(n - 2)$.

The study hours–GPA example, with $n = 10$ and $d.f. = (10 - 2) = 8$, can be used to illustrate this procedure. Earlier, we found that the regression equation for this pair of variables is

$$GPA_p = 2.12 + (0.102) \times \text{study hours}.$$

From figure 14.6 we found that

$$\sum_{i=1}^{n} e_i^2 = 1.39;$$

therefore

$$s_{y,x} = \sqrt{\frac{\sum_{i=1}^{n} e_i^2}{n-2}} = \sqrt{\frac{1.39}{8}} = .416.$$

Using the formula,

$$s_b = \frac{s_{y,x}}{SS_x},$$

with SS_x known to be 260 from Chapter 13 (table 13.4),

$$s_b = \frac{.416}{\sqrt{260}} = .416/16.1 = .0260.$$

We then find β by dividing b by s_b:

$$\beta = b/s_b = 0.102/0.0260 = 3.939.$$

This is our calculated statistic.

We compare this with the t_{table} value in table A.2 at $\alpha = .05$ and .01 and 8 degrees of freedom. These values turn out to be:

$$t_{table} = 2.306 \text{ at .05 and } 3.355 \text{ at .01.}$$

Because both table values are less than our calculated β of 3.939, we decide *to reject* the null hypothesis. A raw score slope of $b = 0.102$ is large enough to allow us to conclude that there is a nonzero slope in the population. We can say that study hours would prove to affect GPA if we had the appropriate data for all students in the population.

Analysis of Variance in Regression

Adapting ANOVA to regression induction is straightforward. The changes that need to be made are all related to the goal of our analysis. Recall that when ANOVA is employed to measure the association between two variables based on the difference between their means, as in Chapter 11, an $F_{calculated}$ is derived using data from three or more (k) independent subsamples. The F is a ratio of variation from the means *between* the samples to variation *within* the samples. A mean squared (MS) is calculated for each, so that $F_{calculated} = MS_{between}/MS_{within}$.

The inductive application for the difference between means tests the null hypothesis, $H_0: \mu_1 = \mu_2 = \cdots = \mu_k$, and the associated research hypothesis, $H_r: \mu_i \neq \mu_j$ for at least one pair i, j. An F_{table} value is found at $\alpha = .05$ and/or $.01$ and at two types of degrees of freedom: $df_{between} = (k - 1)$ and $df_{within} = (n - k)$. Then $F_{calculated}$ is compared to F_{table}, and a decision to reject or not reject the null is made according to the decision rule.

When applying ANOVA to regression analysis, we are no longer focusing exclusively on the difference between the means. Rather, we are interested in the differences between the observed values and the values predicted by the *regression* equation, for each of the n cases in the sample. These differences are the residuals or *error* terms, $e = (y - \hat{y})$.

Therefore, instead of thinking in terms of "between" and "within," we are concerned with the connection between *regression* (correct predictions) and *error* (incorrect predictions). In particular, a large value for F is evidence that the regression equation is relatively effective in predicting the actual values. A small value indicates that there is a relatively large amount of error.

Accordingly, the F ratio in regression is defined as:

$$F_{calculated} = \frac{MS_{regression}}{MS_{error}}.$$

As with the difference-of-means F ratio,

$$MS_{regression} = \frac{SS_{regression}}{df_{regression}} \text{ and } MS_{error} = \frac{SS_{error}}{df_{error}}.$$

For the degrees of freedom, instead of k groups, we have *two variables*, so $df_{regression} = 1$ and

$$df_{error} = n - 2.$$

This is the sample size minus the number of variables.

The sum of squares terms are

$$SS_{regression} = \sum_{i=1}^{n}(\hat{y}_i - \bar{y})^2.$$

TABLE 14.4   Summary of regression between GNP
and IMR

Variables (n = 50)	Correlation	Regression
GNP (ind.)	$r = -0.471$	$a = 57.74$
IMR (dep.)	$r^2 = 0.222$	$b = -0.00223$

This is the squared sum of the deviations of the predicted y values from the mean of y:

$$SS_{error} = \sum_{i=1}^{n} e_i^2.$$

And this is the squared sum of the residuals.

Combining these, we see that

$$F_{calculated} = \frac{MS_{regression}}{MS_{error}} = \frac{\sum_{i=1}^{n} (\hat{y}_i - \bar{y})^2}{\sum_{i=1}^{n} e_i^2 \Big/ (n-2)}$$

To illustrate, table 14.4 contains information on a regression analysis for the variables GNP and IMR from the international data set introduced in Chapter 13. We saw there that the variables have a moderate inverse relationship, as measured by an $r = -0.471$ and an $r^2 = 0.222$. Solving for a and b, the regression equation is:

$$IMR_p = 57.74 - (0.00223)GNP.$$

Table 14.5 shows the intermediate calculations for F as follows:

$$SS_{regression} = 20368.07; \; df_{regression} = 1; \; MS_{regression} = 20368.07$$

$$SS_{error} = 71442.47; \; df_{error} = 48; \; MS_{error} = 1488.39$$

$$F_{calculated} = \frac{MS_{regression}}{MS_{error}} = \frac{20368.07}{1488.39} = 13.68$$

Considering the sample size of $n = 50$, an F value this large suggests that the regression equation is successful in predicting GNP.

TABLE 14.5   Analysis of variance for regression of GNP and IMR

	Sum of squares	d.f.	Mean squares	$F_{calculated}$	F_{table}	
					$\alpha = .05$	$\alpha = .01$
Regression	20368.07	1	20368.07	13.68	4.085	7.314
Error	71442.47	48	1488.39			

These results can now be used for regression induction. As always with induction, we are interested in generalizing to the population (in this illustration, all nations in the world). As in the test of the significance of β, we want to know whether the regression equation in the population can predict the values of the dependent variable. Because $F_{calculated}$ does measure the effectiveness of the regression equation in the sample, it can be used to test the null hypothesis:

H_0: $B = 0$ (the regression line is horizontal—zero slope).

The associated research hypothesis is:

$H_r = B \neq 0$ (the regression line has a nonzero slope)

In the language of ANOVA, a zero slope indicates that there are *no* accurate predictions and that *error* is very large. This would translate to an F ratio for the (unknown) population regression equation with $MS_{regression} = 0$ and a very large MS_{error}.

The last two columns of the ANOVA table 14.5 lists the F_{table} values for $d.f. = 1$ and 48 (rounded to 40). From table A.3, at $\alpha = .05$, F_{table} is 4.085, and at $\alpha = .01$, F_{table} is 7.314. With an $F_{calculated} = 13.69$, we can *reject* the null at both levels of significance. Using ANOVA with regression, we can conclude that the regression equation in the population does have some predictive power beyond chance alone.

An Illustration of Regression Induction

We conclude this section with another look at the sample of 66 nations, for which n is considerably larger than in the study hours–GPA illustration. The relevant information is shown in table 14.6. This includes the slope, the standard error of estimate, the sum of squares for the independent variable, the estimated error of the slope, the calculated standardized β, and the table t values. The results indicate that the slopes of the relationships between URB and IMR (an inverse relationship) and between URB and LEXP (a direct relationship) are significant at both the .05 and .01 levels. This suggests that

TABLE 14.6   Significance tests of regression for 66 nations

Variables	*a*	*b*	$s_{y,x}$	SS_x	s_b	β	*t*	
							$\alpha = .05$	$\alpha = .01$
URB and *IMR*	97.9	−1.063	32.54	3.797E+04	0.167	−6.37	2.000	2.660
GNP and *URB*	38.45	0.00171	16.96	4.094E+09	0.000265	6.45	2.021	2.704
GNP and *IMR*	57.74	−0.00223	38.58	4.094E+09	0.000603	−3.70	2.021	2.704
URB and *LEXP*	47.24	0.339	8.66	3.797E+04	0.044	7.63	2.000	2.660
GNP and *LEXP*	59.94	0.00074	10.49	4.094E+09	0.000164	4.52	2.021	2.704
IMR and *LEXP*	75.94	−0.258	5.31	1.104E+05	0.0160	−16.16	2.000	2.660

TABLE 14.7   The four parts of correlation and regression, complete

	Description	*Induction*
Correlation	Plot, sign, and size of r; r^2, $1 - r^2$	H_0: $\rho = 0$. Use r^2 from descriptive part; table A.6: $\alpha = .05$ and/or $.01$, $d.f. = n - 2$
Regression	Regression line; b, sign and size of its slope; a, its y-intercept; SS_{error}, $s_{y, x}$	H_0: $B = 0$. Use ANOVA, table A.3, $\alpha = .05$ or $.01$., $d.f. = 1$, $n - 2$; or direct test of β, table A.2.

level of urbanization does impact these two, closely related, variables in the population. The fact that the number of degrees of freedom is so large (63, rounded to 60) helps considerably in establishing that the slope in the sample is not likely to be the result of chance alone.

As shown in table 14.7, we have now completed our four-part examination of correlation and regression. The box at the lower right summarizes the procedure of regression induction. In brief, here we test the extent to which the slope of the regression line formed by our sample data allows us to conclude that there is a nonzero slope, and thus an impact of x on y, in the population. To achieve this, we convert the slope in the sample, b, to a standardized score, β, that can be compared to table values of t (two-tailed). As always, we then compare our calculated and table values and base the decision to reject or not reject the null hypothesis on whether the calculated value is less than or equal to (do not reject) or greater than (reject) that in the table.

Summary

This and the preceding chapters have focused on the analysis of relationships between two or more numerical variables. The approach introduced here is the well-known and widely used linear correlation and regression. We observed that correlation and regression are not two separate sets of techniques but are instead closely connected to one another. We also stressed that each has a descriptive and an inductive aspect. Thus we divided the discussion into the four segments illustrated in table 14.7. The key to each of these subparts is the fact that we begin with a database that has, for each unit in a sample (e.g., a nation), values on the independent variables, x_1, x_2, etc., and the dependent, y, variable (e.g., urbanization and average life expectancy). This allows us to create a scatterplot on a coordinate system. Each point in this plot represents one unit, and its position along each axis stands for its value on the respective variable. We then determine the slope and shape of this plot, as measured by the correlation coefficient, r, with the help of a best-fitting line. This turns out to be the regression line, which acts to guide our description and generalization in correlation, and is the main object of study in regression.

| BOX 14.1 | **Statistics for Sociologists** |

The Sociology of Globalization

The phenomenon referred to as *globalization* is one of the most intensively studied, as well as one of the most controversial, topics in contemporary social science. It has captured the interest of specialists and nonspecialists alike. In fact, it is difficult to surf the Internet, watch TV, or read a newspaper without encountering discussion and debate about it. For many people, concern about globalization has been stimulated by one or more popular books on the subject, including the best-selling *The World Is Flat* by the *New York Times* journalist Thomas Friedman (2005).[*] Among the many scholarly works on the subject, *Sociology of Globalization* (Sassen, 2007), by one of the acknowledged leading experts in the field, Saskia Sassen, covers the topic especially well.[**]

As a sociological concept, *globalization* is a process that involves the evolution of humanity toward a single social, cultural, and political system, worldwide in expanse and transcending national borders. The editors of an early publication on the subject by the International Sociological Association made a special effort to emphasize this *process* aspect:

> If we already lived in a single world society then all the talk about globalization would be in the past tense. Instead, globalization is the present process of becoming global: globality itself lies in the future, but the very near future. Each major aspect of social reality (the structure, culture, and personality of traditional terminology) is simultaneously undergoing globalization, as witnessed by the emergence of the world economy, a cosmopolitan culture, and international social movements. (Albrow and King, 1990:1)

In this sense, globalization has been occurring ever since the beginnings of recorded history, if not before. During certain periods, such as the Crusades, the colonial era, and the Industrial Revolution, it has accelerated rapidly. It is definitely not a continuous and cumulative type of evolution, as it has always been characterized by reversals and contradictions. Nor has it ever been an entirely peaceful process; today, as in the past, globalization has been a major contributing factor to intergroup and international conflict.

The late twentieth and early twenty-first centuries have seen some of the most dramatic changes ever in the direction of globalization, most of which are technology-driven. Movies, cell phones, cable and satellite TV, and especially the Internet have taken us a long way toward what the communication theorist Marshall McLuhan first

---

[*] You can see Friedman discuss the book in an online video at http://mitworld.mit.edu/video/266/.
[**] For a brief overview of the sociology of globalization, see Weinstein (2005: Ch. 15).

labeled *the Global Village*. An equally influential force is the growth in the size and geographical reach of multinational corporations. Gigantic companies like Wal-Mart and the major automobile and energy corporations have brought about a previously unimagined uniformity and leveling ("flatness" in Friedman's terms) in the way people everywhere consume, work, think, and even dream. One company, McDonald's, has had such a profound effect that some sociologists, led by George Ritzer (2000), have equated *globalization* with *McDonaldization*.

As mentioned, the study of globalization is not without controversy. The most basic and largely unanswered question in this regard involves whether or not the process is benefiting the people of the world. Obviously, it is making some people, including the owners and managers of Wal-Mart, Exxon, and other multinationals, very rich and powerful. But what about ordinary people in the United States, Europe, and especially the poorer countries of Asia and Africa? Are they reaping rewards from globalization? Are they largely unaffected by it? Or is it making things worse for them, as the wealthy and powerful profit at their expense?

Of course, these are complex and difficult questions to answer. But quantitative research can provide some clues. In this context, the following illustration applies regression analysis to some interesting data on globalization and its impacts. Although linear regression cannot settle questions about whether globalization will bring progress, it can shed some light on how the process works.

Measuring Globalization

The data for this illustration includes a set of measures that are part of the general "KOF Index of Globalization."[***] As shown in table 14.8, three of these measures are *Economic Globalization*, *Information Globalization*, and *Cultural Globalization*. Each consists of a set of specific variables that indicate the degree to which a country's economy, information system, and culture, respectively, are connected with the global environment. The economic measure includes items such as trade and investment, the information measure includes Internet and cable TV use, and one of the items in the cultural measure is the number of McDonald's restaurants per capita. Data on these and many other variables were collected for 122 countries and for all years between 1995 and 2005, a selection of which are shown in table 14.9.

For the purposes of this analysis, nine variables were created from these indices, as listed in the upper part of table 14.8: one for each index for the year 2000 and for the year 2005, and one for each index that measures the change between the two years.

[***] KOF is an economic research center in Zurich, Switzerland. The Index and related information can be found online at: http://globalization.kof.ethz.ch/.

TABLE 14.8 Globalization indices

Economic	Information	Cultural	Other
Econ 2000	Info 2000	Cult 2000	Development Index (DI)
Econ 2005	Info 2005	Cult 2005	
Econ Change	Info Change	Cult Change	

A. *Economic Globalization*
   Trade (percent of GDP)
   Foreign direct investment, flows (percent of GDP)
   Foreign direct investment, stocks (percent of GDP)
   Portfolio investment (percent of GDP)
   Income payments to foreign nationals (percent of GDP)
B. *Information Globalization*
   Internet users (per 1000 people)
   Cable television (per 1000 people)
   Trade in newspapers (percent of GDP)
   Radios (per 1000 people)
C. *Cultural Globalization*
   Number of McDonald's restaurants (per capita)
   Number of Ikea stores (per capita)
   Trade in books (percent of GDP)

Source: Dreher, Axel, 2006. "Does Globalization Affect Growth? Empirical Evidence from a New Index." *Applied Economics* 38, 10: 1091–1110.

One additional variables, not part of the KOF index, was included: a development index that combines GNP, URB, IMR, and LEXP sub. This development measure assigns a number to each country, from 0 to 100, indicating its level of economic development (e.g., Uganda scored 16 and Japan scored 100 out of the 24 countries).

The results of the regression analysis are shown in table 14.10. For each pair of variables, it lists the intercept, slope, regression equation, r^2, the calculated F, degrees of freedom (from which you can determine the sample size by adding the two numbers together plus 1), and whether the F is significant at $\alpha = .05$ or .01.

Each of the first three equations regresses one of the globalization variables on DI, the development index. They are meant to help determine whether a country's level of socioeconomic development affects its level of globalization. The results indicate that it does indeed: the higher the level of development, the more globalized a country is. All of the F values are significant at $\alpha = .01$. The r^2 values tell us that development explains between approximately 33% and 56% of the variation in globalization.

The second set of three equations refers to the impact of level of globalization on economic growth. The results here indicate that there is little or no effect. All of the

TABLE 14.9   Globalization and development variables for selected countries

Country	Dev't Index	Global 2000	Global 2005	Global Change
Albania	52	46.53	48.51	1.99
Australia	86	77.74	71.02	−6.72
Bolivia	43	46.44	49.92	3.48
Brazil	60	46.85	45.25	−1.60
China	48	40.12	43.00	2.88
Costa Rica	60	67.48	66.91	−0.56
Denmark	92	87.97	88.00	0.03
Dominica	55	58.89	56.65	−2.24
Estonia	63	85.16	89.52	4.36
Fiji	51	60.20	56.59	−3.61
United Kingdom	87	80.62	80.83	0.21
Iceland	93	74.73	83.99	9.26
Israel	85	78.32	78.09	−0.23
Japan	100	44.72	47.45	2.73
Lithuania	64	67.02	73.31	6.29
Latvia	63	74.46	80.99	6.52
Malaysia	63	68.15	66.77	−1.37
Panama	60	71.12	69.93	−1.19
Peru	58	43.92	48.37	4.45
El Salvador	52	51.44	58.77	7.33
Slovenia	66	70.65	77.59	6.94
Sweden	90	86.54	87.49	0.95
Thailand	50	52.07	55.41	3.34
Tunisia	56	51.89	52.03	0.14
Uganda	16	36.12	39.92	3.79
Zimbabwe	26	52.78	56.70	3.92

Source: Dreher, Axel, 2006. "Does Globalization Affect Growth? Empirical Evidence from a New Index." *Applied Economics* 38, 10: 1091–1110.

Dev't. Index: Level of socioeconomic development, max. 100.

Global 2000: Combined economic, information, and cultural index for the year 2000.

Global 2005: Combined economic, information, and cultural index for the year 2005.

Global Change: (*Global 2005 − Global 2000*).

slopes are negative—high levels of globalization are associated with slow economic growth—but they are very small. Only one of the three the calculated *F's* is significant at $\alpha = .05$: the one with level of cultural globalization as the independent variable. The r^2 values are also very small, with none of the globalization variable explaining more than 4.5% of the economic growth. By this criterion, level globalization does not seem to have economic benefits for a country as a whole (which does *not* mean that it

TABLE 14.10   Bivariate regression equations for globalization variables

| Variables | | | | | | | |
Dep. (y)	Ind. (x)	a	b	Regression equation	r^2	F	α^a
Info 2005	DI	16.8	0.570	$\hat{y} = 16.8 + 0.570x$	0.413	20.4	.01
Econ 2005	DI	35.7	0.511	$\hat{y} = 35.7 + 0.511x$	0.336	17.7	.01
Cult 2005	DI	30.9	0.624	$\hat{y} = 30.9 + 0.624x$	0.564	37.5	.01
GDP Change	Info 2000	5.2	0.026	$\hat{y} = 5.2 - 0.026x$	0.041	3.5	
GDP Change	Econ 2000	3.9	−0.003	$\hat{y} = 3.9 - 0.003x$	0.001	0.05	
GDP Change	Cult 2000	5.2	0.024	$\hat{y} = 5.2 - 0.024x$	0.045	4.2	.05
Info Change	DI	−0.05	−0.003	$\hat{y} = -0.05 - 0.003x$	0.001	0.02	
Econ Change	DI	33.9	0.354	$\hat{y} = 33.9 + 0.345x$	0.011	0.4	
Cult Change	DI	−0.001	0.038	$\hat{y} = -0.001 + 0.038x$	0.141	3.6	

[a] α indicates the level of significance for F.

does not benefit some individuals or organizations within countries). The one possible exception, in the case of *Cult 2000*, suggests that having many McDonald's and Ikea stores leads to a relatively low rate of economic growth.

The last three equations examine the impact of level of development on *change* in level of globalization: that is, on globalization as a process. The results can be summarized in four words: "not much if any." The r^2 and the calculated F values are very small, and none of the F's is significant at $\alpha = .05$. The more and less developed nations appear to be globalizing at the same rate.

When viewed through the lens of linear regression with these specific variables, globalization appears to be at best a mixed blessing. Based on these—we should stress, limited—results, the more developed countries tend to be the most globalized. But globalization has not in itself brought dramatic economic growth anywhere.

In both cases, but especially with regard to regression, we observed how important it is to measure and understand error. In this case, error refers to the difference between the scatterplot—our observed data—and the slope and the intercept of the best-fitting/ regression line—our idealized relationship.

In the course of this discussion, we mentioned that one further step that can be taken in dealing with regression error is to seek to reduce it by introducing one or more additional variables into the regression equation. In fact, with this procedure, known as multiple regression, the major techniques in advanced statistics begin. For an introduction to multiple regression, see the online Chapter 15.

KEY TERMS

β *(beta)*: A standardized regression slope used in regression induction.

Error sum of squares: A measure of the overall accuracy of a regression line as a predictor of values of the independent variable. It is the sum of the squared residuals.

Regression line: The best-fitting line when used alone without direct reference to the scatterplot on which it is based; the line indicating the "ideal" relationship between x and y as if $r = 0$.

Residual: The difference between observed and predicted values of the dependent variable. It is a measure of error.

Standard error of the estimate: A measure of the average amount of error between observed and predicted values of y. It is computed by dividing the error sum of squares by $n - 2$ and taking the square root.

Sum of products: The sum of a set of terms, each of which is the product of a deviation from the mean of x and a deviation from the mean of y.

Sum of squares: Abbreviation for "sum of the squared deviations from the mean" (see Chapter 11).

SOLUTION-CENTERED APPLICATIONS

This final set of applications uses the regional census data set you created (in Chapter 3), along with the results of the related applications from earlier chapters. First, the data are used to illustrate the principles and techniques of correlation and regression. Then you will prepare a brief report of your findings on some of the regional characteristics of the U.S. population.

1. The correlation–regression application begins with selecting the three numerical variables from your data set. For the sake of convenience, we can label them x (this will be total population size), and y and z (the other two). Using the commands in the following SPSS application, you are to produce five sets of correlations and regressions: one for all 50 states and one for each of the four main regions. Each set of correlations and regression will include the three pairs of variables that can be created with x, y, and z. These are (1) x and y, (2) x and z, and (3) y and z. For each pair, select the independent and the dependent variable. For numbers (1) and (2), x will probably be the independent; but the choice will not be so clear with number (3).

   Start with the three SPSS runs for the nation as a whole. Then perform a separate run on each region. This will require you to create a subset of states for each of the regions with the "select cases" command.* Once you have completed each set of runs, do the necessary additional calculations and consult the appropriate tables. Finally, write a summary covering each of the following points (for the nation and for each region):

   • Describe the relationship between the two variables based on the scatterplot, r, and r^2.
   • Indicate whether the correlation is significant (include your H_0 and H_r here).
   • Describe the regression line.
   • Indicate whether the slope of the line is significant.
   • Summarize the relationships among the variables for the nation and all regions.

2. *A Research Report*: Collect the output and write-ups from the applications of the census data set from this and earlier chapters (Chapters 2–6 and Chapter 11). Using this material prepare a brief (approximately five-page) report that is intended to be read by a congressional committee considering legislation that will affect the regional distribution of federal funds. The report should:

---

*The steps are: click data, → select cases → click select if condition is satisfied → click unselected cases are deleted → click if bar → on this screen, click variable *region* from the list at the left into the equation box to the right → type in: = "northeast" → continue → OK.

- Indicate the role that region does (and does not) play in determining the characteristics you have measured.
- Discuss the relationships among the key variables, at the national and regional levels.
- Discuss the potential special needs of particular regions (e.g., high concentrations of elderly or disabled persons, high levels of poverty, etc.). Where possible, this discussion can also apply to specific states within regions.

- Summarize you findings with:
  a. Some suggestions about legislation and distribution of funds that have a regional component or impact
  b. Suggestion about additional data and further analyses that are needed to improve our understanding of the regional issues considered here

Testing Your Skills

Practice Quizzes for Chapters 10–14

The following two practice quizzes test your skills with topics covered in Chapters 10–14. They focus on difference of means tests (t and ANOVA), non-numerical variables, and correlation and regression.

Quiz 1

1. In a recent article in *The Academy* magazine, the authors claimed that they were 95% confident that football players at the major universities have an average GPA of 2.0. In support of this claim, data were shown for a sample of $n = 26$ schools. The mean for this sample was 2.1 grade points, and the standard deviation (s) was 0.2 point. Do you agree with the authors? Why or why not?

2. The same article referred to in question 1 also discussed the grade point averages of football players at schools in the Midwest, selecting a sample of $n = 11$ of these, and the East Coast, selecting $n = 8$ of these. The Midwest GPA was 2.30, and the East Coast GPA was 2.50. Further calculations showed that the estimated standard error of the difference, $s_{\bar{x}_1 - \bar{x}_2}$, was equal to 0.1 grade point. Select your own α and indicate whether you think that this study shows that there is a difference between the two sets of schools with regard to football players' GPAs. Why or why not?

3. A study of average commuting time, by class, of EMU undergraduate students who commute took a sample of 10 freshmen, 12 sophomores, 8 juniors, and 8 seniors. The average for the freshmen was 18 minutes, for the sophomores it was 15 minutes, for the juniors it was 20 minutes, and for the seniors it was 25 minutes. Using these means, the scores for each individual year, and the sample and subsample sizes, it was determined that the mean square *between* groups was equal to 11.2 and the mean square *within* groups was 3.5. Can you conclude that commuting time differs from class to class? Use $\alpha = .01$.

TABLE 1 Minority membership and attitude toward new plant

Glad about plant?	Minority	Non-minority	Totals
Yes	10	20	30
No	10	12	22
Totals	20	32	52

4. Table 1 shows the results of a study of a sample of 52 households chosen at random from the population of a small midwestern city. Each head of the household was asked two simple questions. One referred to whether or not they were members of a minority ethnic group, with a yes or no answer. The other referred to whether or not they were glad that a new auto parts plant had opened at the Interstate exit. Using these data, and an α of your choice, decide whether you think that minorities differ from non-minorities with regard to attitude toward the new plant.

5. Table 2 shows information for eight colleges on two variables. One is annual tuition and the other is percentage of minority students. Using these data, do the following:

   a. Create the scatterplot and estimate the best-fitting line.
   b. Describe the relationship between the two variables using r and r^2.
   c. Decide whether there is likely to be a nonzero correlation in the population.
   d. Determine the slope (b) and the intercept (a) for the regression equation.
   e. Describe the relationship between the two variables based on a and b.

TABLE 2 College tuitions and minority enrollment

College	Tuition, x	Minorities, y	$(x - \bar{x})$	$(y - \bar{y})$	$(x - \bar{x})^2$	$(y - \bar{y})^2$	$(x - \bar{x})(y - \bar{y})$
	($1,000)	(%)			SS_x	SS_y	SP
Idaho A&M	6	25	−2.3	4.6	5.3	21.2	−10.6
Milan State	18	10	9.7	−10.4	94.1	108.2	−100.9
Alaska Southern	10	18	1.7	−2.4	2.9	5.76	−4.1
Monroe Academy	2	30	−6.3	9.6	39.7	92.2	−60.5
Ohio Military	5	20	−3.3	−0.4	10.9	0.16	1.3
Wayne Tech	7	25	−1.3	4.6	1.7	21.2	−6.0
Ontario State	10	15	1.7	−5.4	2.9	29.2	−9.2
Eastern Nevada	8	20	−0.3	−0.4	0.09	0.16	0.12
Totals	66	163			156.	278.1	−189.9
Means	8.3	20.4					

Quiz 2

1. In a recent study of hurricane victims in Louisiana, it was determined that a sample of 100 households taken at random had been homeless for an average ($\bar{x}$) of 35 days and a sample standard deviation (s) of 5.0 days. The government agency asked the sociologists whether they could claim that they were 95% confident that the hundreds of thousands of households affected by the storm would average 37 days. What should the sociologists tell the agency? Why?

2. The government agency believed all the Louisiana households would have a different average number of homeless days from all Florida households. They knew from the study mentioned in question 1 that the Louisiana sample mean was 35 days. They did a similar survey with a sample of 100 Florida households and found its sample mean was 31 days. Further calculations showed that the estimated standard error of the mean difference was equal to 1.5 days. Select your own α and indicate whether you agree with the government. Why or why not?

3. A study of average grades in three social statistics exams, over a period of $n = 10$ years, showed that the average for the first exam was 78.5; for the second exam, 71.5; and 79.3 for the third exam. Using these means, the scores for each individual year, and the sample and subsample sizes, it was determined that the sum of squares *between* exams was equal to 225 and the sum of squares *within* exams was 211.4. Can the instructor conclude that student performance differs from exam to exam? Use $\alpha = .01$.

4. Table 3 shows the results of a study of a sample of 50 college faculty members. Each faculty member was asked two simple questions. One referred to whether the member was junior or senior faculty. The other referred to whether or not the member agreed with certain recent administrative changes at the university. Using these data, and an α of your choice, decide whether you think that junior faculty differ from senior faculty with regard to the administrative changes.

TABLE 3   Faculty attitudes toward administrative changes

Changes?	Faculty status		
	Junior	Senior	Totals
Agree	10	15	25
Disagree	20	5	25
Totals	30	20	50

TABLE 4   Raw data and calculations for finding the correlation coefficient between minutes spent by students commuting to class (x) and number of times students were late to their first class per semester (y), $n = 12$

ID #	x, minutes	y, late	$x - \bar{x}$	$y - \bar{y}$	$(x - \bar{x})^2$	$(y - \bar{y})^2$	$(x - \bar{x})(y - \bar{y})$
1	10	0	−13.33	−8.33	177.69	69.39	111.04
2	12	1	−11.33	−7.33	128.37	53.73	83.05
3	25	4	1.67	−4.33	2.79	18.75	−7.23
4	20	3	−3.33	−5.33	11.09	28.41	17.75
5	35	6	11.67	−2.33	136.19	5.43	−27.19
6	15	2	−8.33	−6.33	69.39	40.07	52.73
7	20	4	−3.33	−4.33	11.09	18.75	14.42
8	40	10	16.67	1.67	277.89	2.79	27.84
9	18	2	−5.33	−6.33	28.41	40.07	33.74
10	30	6	6.67	−2.33	44.49	5.43	−15.54
11	45	8	21.67	−0.33	469.59	0.11	−7.15
12	10	0	−13.33	−8.33	177.69	69.39	111.4
Totals	280	46			$SS_x = 1534.68$	$SS_y = 352.32$	$SP = 394.86$

$\bar{x} = 280/12 = 23.33$; $\bar{y} = 46/12 = 8.33$

5.   Table 4 shows information for 12 students on two variables. One is time spent commuting to class, and the other is number of times the student was late to the first class, per semester.

    a.   Create the scatterplot and estimate the best-fitting line. Describe the relationship using this scatterplot and reference line.

    b.   Describe the relationship between the two variables using r and r^2.

    c.   Decide whether there is likely to be a nonzero correlation in the population.

    d.   Determine the slope (b) and the intercept (a) for the regression equation.

    e.   Describe the relationship between the two variables based on a and b.

Extra credit: State in words and in symbols the hypothesis that is tested in the decision-making part of regression.

Appendix A

Tables

Table A.1 lists the areas under the normal curve (the z distribution) between 0 and a given z as shown in figure A.1.

TABLE A.1 Normal distribution

	\multicolumn{10}{c}{*Area between 0 and z*}
	0.00	*0.01*	*0.02*	*0.03*	*0.04*	*0.05*	*0.06*	*0.07*	*0.08*	*0.09*
0.0	0.0000	0.0040	0.0080	0.0120	0.0160	0.0199	0.0239	0.0279	0.0319	0.0359
0.1	0.0398	0.0438	0.0478	0.0517	0.0557	0.0596	0.0636	0.0675	0.0714	0.0753
0.2	0.0793	0.0832	0.0871	0.0910	0.0948	0.0987	0.1026	0.1064	0.1103	0.1141
0.3	0.1179	0.1217	0.1255	0.1293	0.1331	0.1368	0.1406	0.1443	0.1480	0.1517
0.4	0.1554	0.1591	0.1628	0.1664	0.1700	0.1736	0.1772	0.1808	0.1844	0.1879
0.5	0.1915	0.1950	0.1985	0.2019	0.2054	0.2088	0.2123	0.2157	0.2190	0.2224
0.6	0.2257	0.2291	0.2324	0.2357	0.2389	0.2422	0.2454	0.2486	0.2517	0.2549
0.7	0.2580	0.2611	0.2642	0.2673	0.2704	0.2734	0.2764	0.2794	0.2823	0.2852
0.8	0.2881	0.2910	0.2939	0.2967	0.2995	0.3023	0.3051	0.3078	0.3106	0.3133
0.9	0.3159	0.3186	0.3212	0.3238	0.3264	0.3289	0.3315	0.3340	0.3365	0.3389
1.0	0.3413	0.3438	0.3461	0.3485	0.3508	0.3531	0.3554	0.3577	0.3599	0.3621
1.1	0.3643	0.3665	0.3686	0.3708	0.3729	0.3749	0.3770	0.3790	0.3810	0.3830
1.2	0.3849	0.3869	0.3888	0.3907	0.3925	0.3944	0.3962	0.3980	0.3997	0.4015
1.3	0.4032	0.4049	0.4066	0.4082	0.4099	0.4115	0.4131	0.4147	0.4162	0.4177
1.4	0.4192	0.4207	0.4222	0.4236	0.4251	0.4265	0.4279	0.4292	0.4306	0.4319
1.5	0.4332	0.4345	0.4357	0.4370	0.4382	0.4394	0.4406	0.4418	0.4429	0.4441
1.6	0.4452	0.4463	0.4474	0.4484	0.4495	0.4505	0.4515	0.4525	0.4535	0.4545
1.7	0.4554	0.4564	0.4573	0.4582	0.4591	0.4599	0.4608	0.4616	0.4625	0.4633
1.8	0.4641	0.4649	0.4656	0.4664	0.4671	0.4678	0.4686	0.4693	0.4699	0.4706
1.9	0.4713	0.4719	0.4726	0.4732	0.4738	0.4744	0.4750	0.4756	0.4761	0.4767
2.0	0.4772	0.4778	0.4783	0.4788	0.4793	0.4798	0.4803	0.4808	0.4812	0.4817
2.1	0.4821	0.4826	0.4830	0.4834	0.4838	0.4842	0.4846	0.4850	0.4854	0.4857
2.2	0.4861	0.4864	0.4868	0.4871	0.4875	0.4878	0.4881	0.4884	0.4887	0.4890
2.3	0.4893	0.4896	0.4898	0.4901	0.4904	0.4906	0.4909	0.4911	0.4913	0.4916
2.4	0.4918	0.4920	0.4922	0.4925	0.4927	0.4929	0.4931	0.4932	0.4934	0.4936
2.5	0.4938	0.4940	0.4941	0.4943	0.4945	0.4946	0.4948	0.4949	0.4951	0.4952

(Continued)

TABLE A.1   Normal distribution (*Continued*)

	0.00	0.01	0.02	0.03	0.04	0.05	0.06	0.07	0.08	0.09
	Area between 0 and z									
2.6	0.4953	0.4955	0.4956	0.4957	0.4959	0.4960	0.4961	0.4962	0.4963	0.4964
2.7	0.4965	0.4966	0.4967	0.4968	0.4969	0.4970	0.4971	0.4972	0.4973	0.4974
2.8	0.4974	0.4975	0.4976	0.4977	0.4977	0.4978	0.4979	0.4979	0.4980	0.4981
2.9	0.4981	0.4982	0.4982	0.4983	0.4984	0.4984	0.4985	0.4985	0.4986	0.4986
3.0	0.4987	0.4987	0.4987	0.4988	0.4988	0.4989	0.4989	0.4989	0.4990	0.4990

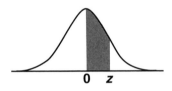

FIGURE A.1   The normal (*z*) distribution.

Table A.2 lists the critical values for Student's t distribution, at which the probability of $t_{calculated}$ falling in the tail (shaded in figure A.2) is equal to the values shown in the column heads.

TABLE A.2   Critical values of Student's t distribution

	Probability of exceeding the critical value					
df 2-tail	*0.20*	*0.10*	*0.05*	*0.02*	*0.01*	*0.005*
df 1-tail	*0.10*	*0.05*	*0.025*	*0.01*	*0.005*	*0.001*
1	3.078	6.314	12.706	31.821	63.657	318.313
2	1.886	2.920	4.303	6.965	9.925	22.327
3	1.638	2.353	3.182	4.541	5.841	10.215
4	1.533	2.132	2.776	3.747	4.604	7.173
5	1.476	2.015	2.571	3.365	4.032	5.893
6	1.440	1.943	2.447	3.143	3.707	5.208
7	1.415	1.895	2.365	2.998	3.499	4.782
8	1.397	1.860	2.306	2.896	3.355	4.499
9	1.383	1.833	2.262	2.821	3.250	4.296
10	1.372	1.812	2.228	2.764	3.169	4.143
11	1.363	1.796	2.201	2.718	3.106	4.024
12	1.356	1.782	2.179	2.681	3.055	3.929
13	1.350	1.771	2.160	2.650	3.012	3.852
14	1.345	1.761	2.145	2.624	2.977	3.787
15	1.341	1.753	2.131	2.602	2.947	3.733
16	1.337	1.746	2.120	2.583	2.921	3.686
17	1.333	1.740	2.110	2.567	2.898	3.646
18	1.330	1.734	2.101	2.552	2.878	3.610
19	1.328	1.729	2.093	2.539	2.861	3.579
20	1.325	1.725	2.086	2.528	2.845	3.552
21	1.323	1.721	2.080	2.518	2.831	3.527
22	1.321	1.717	2.074	2.508	2.819	3.505
23	1.319	1.714	2.069	2.500	2.807	3.485
24	1.318	1.711	2.064	2.492	2.797	3.467
25	1.316	1.708	2.060	2.485	2.787	3.450
26	1.315	1.706	2.056	2.479	2.779	3.435
27	1.314	1.703	2.052	2.473	2.771	3.421
28	1.313	1.701	2.048	2.467	2.763	3.408
29	1.311	1.699	2.045	2.462	2.756	3.396
30	1.310	1.697	2.042	2.457	2.750	3.385

(Continued)

TABLE A.2   Critical values of Student's *t* distribution (*Continued*)

	Probability of exceeding the critical value					
df 2-tail	*0.20*	*0.10*	*0.05*	*0.02*	*0.01*	*0.005*
df 1-tail	*0.10*	*0.05*	*0.025*	*0.01*	*0.005*	*0.001*
40	1.303	1.684	2.021	2.423	2.704	3.307
50	1.299	1.676	2.009	2.403	2.678	3.261
60	1.296	1.671	2.000	2.390	2.660	3.232
100	1.290	1.660	1.984	2.364	2.626	3.174
∞	1.282	1.645	1.960	2.326	2.576	3.090

This table is in the public domain. It was produced using APL programs written by William Knight, University of New Brunswick, Canada.

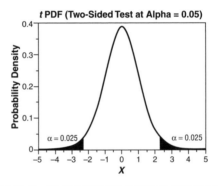

FIGURE A.2   Student's *t* distribution.

Table A.3 is actually two tables, one for the 5% significance level and one for the 1% significance level. They give the values for the F distribution, introduced in Chapter 11, at which the probability of $F_{calculated}$ falling within the shaded tail in figure A.3 is equal to the specified significance at the specified numbers of degrees of freedom within and between groups.

TABLE A.3 *F* distribution

df_{within}	$df_{between}$, 5% significance level									
	1	*2*	*3*	*4*	*5*	*6*	*7*	*8*	*9*	*10*
1	161.448	199.50	215.71	224.60	230.16	33.99	236.77	238.90	240.54	241.88
2	18.513	19.000	19.164	19.247	19.296	19.330	19.353	19.371	19.385	19.396
3	10.128	9.552	9.277	9.117	9.013	8.941	8.887	8.845	8.812	8.786
4	7.709	6.944	6.591	6.388	6.256	6.163	6.094	6.041	5.999	5.964
5	6.608	5.786	5.409	5.192	5.050	4.950	4.876	4.818	4.772	4.735
6	5.987	5.143	4.757	4.534	4.387	4.284	4.207	4.147	4.099	4.060
7	5.591	4.737	4.347	4.120	3.972	3.866	3.787	3.726	3.677	3.637
8	5.318	4.459	4.066	3.838	3.687	3.581	3.500	3.438	3.388	3.347
9	5.117	4.256	3.863	3.633	3.482	3.374	3.293	3.230	3.179	3.137
10	4.965	4.103	3.708	3.478	3.326	3.217	3.135	3.072	3.020	2.978
11	4.844	3.982	3.587	3.357	3.204	3.095	3.012	2.948	2.896	2.854
12	4.747	3.885	3.490	3.259	3.106	2.996	2.913	2.849	2.796	2.753
13	4.667	3.806	3.411	3.179	3.025	2.915	2.832	2.767	2.714	2.671
14	4.600	3.739	3.344	3.112	2.958	2.848	2.764	2.699	2.646	2.602
15	4.543	3.682	3.287	3.056	2.901	2.790	2.707	2.641	2.588	2.544
16	4.494	3.634	3.239	3.007	2.852	2.741	2.657	2.591	2.538	2.494
17	4.451	3.592	3.197	2.965	2.810	2.699	2.614	2.548	2.494	2.450
18	4.414	3.555	3.160	2.928	2.773	2.661	2.577	2.510	2.456	2.412
19	4.381	3.522	3.127	2.895	2.740	2.628	2.544	2.477	2.423	2.378
20	4.351	3.493	3.098	2.866	2.711	2.599	2.514	2.447	2.393	2.348
21	4.325	3.467	3.072	2.840	2.685	2.573	2.488	2.420	2.366	2.321
22	4.301	3.443	3.049	2.817	2.661	2.549	2.464	2.397	2.342	2.297
23	4.279	3.422	3.028	2.796	2.640	2.528	2.442	2.375	2.320	2.275
24	4.260	3.403	3.009	2.776	2.621	2.508	2.423	2.355	2.300	2.255
25	4.242	3.385	2.991	2.759	2.603	2.490	2.405	2.337	2.282	2.236
26	4.225	3.369	2.975	2.743	2.587	2.474	2.388	2.321	2.265	2.220
27	4.210	3.354	2.960	2.728	2.572	2.459	2.373	2.305	2.250	2.204
28	4.196	3.340	2.947	2.714	2.558	2.445	2.359	2.291	2.236	2.190
29	4.183	3.328	2.934	2.701	2.545	2.432	2.346	2.278	2.223	2.177

(Continued)

TABLE A.3   *F* distribution (*Continued*)

df_{within}	$df_{between}$, 5% significance level									
	1	*2*	*3*	*4*	*5*	*6*	*7*	*8*	*9*	*10*
30	4.171	3.316	2.922	2.690	2.534	2.421	2.334	2.266	2.211	2.165
40	4.085	3.232	2.839	2.606	2.449	2.336	2.249	2.180	2.124	2.077
41	4.079	3.226	2.833	2.600	2.443	2.330	2.243	2.174	2.118	2.071
50	4.034	3.183	2.790	2.557	2.400	2.286	2.199	2.130	2.073	2.026
60	4.001	3.150	2.758	2.525	2.368	2.254	2.167	2.097	2.040	1.993
70	3.978	3.128	2.736	2.503	2.346	2.231	2.143	2.074	2.017	1.969
80	3.960	3.111	2.719	2.486	2.329	2.214	2.126	2.056	1.999	1.951
81	3.959	3.109	2.717	2.484	2.327	2.213	2.125	2.055	1.998	1.950
100	3.936	3.087	2.696	2.463	2.305	2.191	2.103	2.032	1.975	1.927

df_{within}	$df_{between}$, 1% significance level									
	1	*2*	*3*	*4*	*5*	*6*	*7*	*8*	*9*	*10*
1	4052.19	4999.52	5403.34	5624.62	5763.65	5858.97	5928.33	5981.10	6022.50	6055.85
2	98.502	99.000	99.166	99.249	99.300	99.333	99.356	99.374	99.388	99.399
3	34.116	30.816	29.457	28.710	28.237	27.911	27.672	27.489	27.345	27.229
4	21.198	18.000	16.694	15.977	15.522	15.207	14.976	14.799	14.659	14.546
5	16.258	13.274	12.060	11.392	10.967	10.672	10.456	10.289	10.158	10.051
6	13.745	10.925	9.780	9.148	8.746	8.466	8.260	8.102	7.976	7.874
7	12.246	9.547	8.451	7.847	7.460	7.191	6.993	6.840	6.719	6.620
8	11.259	8.649	7.591	7.006	6.632	6.371	6.178	6.029	5.911	5.814
9	10.561	8.022	6.992	6.422	6.057	5.802	5.613	5.467	5.351	5.257
10	10.044	7.559	6.552	5.994	5.636	5.386	5.200	5.057	4.942	4.849
11	9.646	7.206	6.217	5.668	5.316	5.069	4.886	4.744	4.632	4.539
12	9.330	6.927	5.953	5.412	5.064	4.821	4.640	4.499	4.388	4.296
13	9.074	6.701	5.739	5.205	4.862	4.620	4.441	4.302	4.191	4.100
14	8.862	6.515	5.564	5.035	4.695	4.456	4.278	4.140	4.030	3.939
15	8.683	6.359	5.417	4.893	4.556	4.318	4.142	4.004	3.895	3.805
16	8.531	6.226	5.292	4.773	4.437	4.202	4.026	3.890	3.780	3.691
17	8.400	6.112	5.185	4.669	4.336	4.102	3.927	3.791	3.682	3.593
18	8.285	6.013	5.092	4.579	4.248	4.015	3.841	3.705	3.597	3.508
19	8.185	5.926	5.010	4.500	4.171	3.939	3.765	3.631	3.523	3.434
20	8.096	5.849	4.938	4.431	4.103	3.871	3.699	3.564	3.457	3.368
21	8.017	5.780	4.874	4.369	4.042	3.812	3.640	3.506	3.398	3.310
22	7.945	5.719	4.817	4.313	3.988	3.758	3.587	3.453	3.346	3.258
23	7.881	5.664	4.765	4.264	3.939	3.710	3.539	3.406	3.299	3.211

TABLE A.3 (*Continued*)

df_{within}	$df_{between}$, 1% significance level									
	1	**2**	**3**	**4**	**5**	**6**	**7**	**8**	**9**	**10**
24	7.823	5.614	4.718	4.218	3.895	3.667	3.496	3.363	3.256	3.168
25	7.770	5.568	4.675	4.177	3.855	3.627	3.457	3.324	3.217	3.129
26	7.721	5.526	4.637	4.140	3.818	3.591	3.421	3.288	3.182	3.094
27	7.677	5.488	4.601	4.106	3.785	3.558	3.388	3.256	3.149	3.062
28	7.636	5.453	4.568	4.074	3.754	3.528	3.358	3.226	3.120	3.032
29	7.598	5.420	4.538	4.045	3.725	3.499	3.330	3.198	3.092	3.005
30	7.562	5.390	4.510	4.018	3.699	3.473	3.305	3.173	3.067	2.979
40	7.314	5.179	4.313	3.828	3.514	3.291	3.124	2.993	2.888	2.801
50	7.171	5.057	4.199	3.720	3.408	3.186	3.020	2.890	2.785	2.698
60	7.077	4.977	4.126	3.649	3.339	3.119	2.953	2.823	2.718	2.632
70	7.011	4.922	4.074	3.600	3.291	3.071	2.906	2.777	2.672	2.585
80	6.963	4.881	4.036	3.563	3.255	3.036	2.871	2.742	2.637	2.551
100	6.895	4.824	3.984	3.513	3.206	2.988	2.823	2.694	2.590	2.503

This table is in the public domain. It was produced using APL programs written by William Knight, University of New Brunswick, Canada.

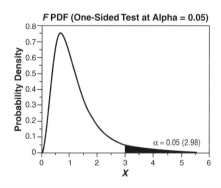

FIGURE A.3 *F* distribution.

Table A.4 gives the values for the chi-square distribution, introduced in Chapter 12, at which the probability that $\chi^2_{calculated}$ falls in the shaded area in figure A.4 equals the value given in the upper column head (or, perhaps more usefully, at which the probability that $\chi^2_{calculated}$ falls in the unshaded tail area equals the α value given in the lower column head) at the specified degrees of freedom.

TABLE A.4   Critical points of the chi-square distribution

d.f.	Cumulative probability												
	0.005	0.010	0.025	0.05	0.10	0.25	0.50	0.75	0.90	0.95	0.975	0.99	0.995
							$\alpha =$	.25	.10	.05	.025	.01	.005
1	0.39E-4	0.00016	0.00098	0.0039	0.0158	0.102	0.455	1.32	2.71	3.84	5.02	6.63	7.88
2	0.0100	0.0201	0.0506	0.103	0.211	0.575	1.39	2.77	4.61	5.99	7.38	9.21	10.6
3	0.0717	0.115	0.216	0.352	0.584	1.21	2.37	4.11	6.25	7.81	9.35	11.3	12.8
4	0.207	0.297	0.484	0.711	1.06	1.92	3.36	5.39	7.78	9.49	11.1	13.3	14.9
5	0.412	0.554	0.831	1.15	1.61	2.67	4.35	6.63	9.24	11.1	12.8	15.1	16.7
6	0.676	0.872	1.24	1.64	2.20	3.45	5.35	7.84	10.6	12.6	14.4	16.8	18.5
7	0.989	1.24	1.69	2.17	2.83	4.25	6.35	9.04	12.0	14.1	16.0	18.5	20.3
8	1.34	1.65	2.18	2.73	3.49	5.07	7.34	10.2	13.4	15.5	17.5	20.1	22.0
9	1.73	2.09	2.70	3.33	4.17	5.9	8.34	11.4	14.7	16.9	19.0	21.7	23.6
10	2.16	2.56	3.25	3.94	4.87	6.74	9.34	12.5	16.0	18.3	20.5	23.2	25.2
11	2.60	3.05	3.82	4.57	5.58	7.58	10.3	13.7	17.3	19.7	21.9	24.7	26.8
12	3.07	3.57	4.40	5.23	6.30	8.44	11.3	14.8	18.5	21.0	23.3	26.2	28.3
13	3.57	4.11	5.01	5.89	7.04	9.3	12.3	16.0	19.8	22.4	24.7	27.7	29.8
14	4.07	4.66	5.63	6.57	7.79	10.2	13.3	17.1	21.1	23.7	26.1	29.1	31.3
15	4.60	5.23	6.26	7.26	8.55	11.0	14.3	18.2	22.3	25.0	27.5	30.6	32.8
16	5.14	5.81	6.91	7.96	9.31	11.9	15.3	19.4	23.5	26.3	28.8	32.0	34.3
17	5.70	6.41	7.56	8.67	10.1	12.8	16.3	20.5	24.8	27.6	30.2	33.4	35.7
18	6.26	7.01	8.23	9.39	10.9	13.7	17.3	21.6	26.0	28.9	31.5	34.8	37.2
19	6.84	7.63	8.91	10.1	11.7	14.6	18.3	22.7	27.2	30.1	32.9	36.2	38.6
20	7.43	8.26	9.59	10.9	12.4	15.5	19.3	23.8	28.4	31.4	34.2	37.6	40.0
21	8.03	8.90	10.3	11.6	13.2	16.3	20.3	24.9	29.6	32.7	35.5	38.9	41.4
22	8.64	9.54	11.0	12.3	14.0	17.2	21.3	26.0	30.8	33.9	36.8	40.3	42.8
23	9.26	10.2	11.7	13.1	14.8	18.1	22.3	27.1	32.0	35.2	38.1	41.6	44.2
24	9.89	10.9	12.4	13.8	15.7	19.0	23.3	28.2	33.2	36.4	39.4	43.0	45.6
25	10.5	11.5	13.1	14.6	16.5	19.9	24.3	29.3	34.4	37.7	40.6	44.3	46.9
26	11.2	12.2	13.8	15.4	17.3	20.8	25.3	30.4	35.6	38.9	41.9	45.6	48.3
27	11.8	12.9	14.6	16.2	18.1	21.7	26.3	31.5	36.7	40.1	43.2	47.0	49.6

TABLE A.4   (*Continued*)

d.f.						Cumulative probability							
	0.005	0.010	0.025	0.05	0.10	0.25	0.50	0.75	0.90	0.95	0.975	0.99	0.995
							α =	.25	.10	.05	.025	.01	.005
28	12.5	13.6	15.3	16.9	18.9	22.7	27.3	32.6	37.9	41.3	44.5	48.3	51.0
29	13.1	14.3	16.0	17.7	19.8	23.6	28.3	33.7	39.1	42.6	45.7	49.6	52.3
30	13.8	15.0	16.8	18.5	20.6	24.5	29.3	34.8	40.3	43.8	47.0	50.9	53.7

This table is in the public domain. It was produced using APL programs written by William Knight, University of New Brunswick, Canada.

FIGURE A.4   Chi-square distribution.

Table A.5 gives the values for the distribution of Spearman's *r* (introduced in Chapter 12) for the given significance levels for the given numbers of pairs.

TABLE A.5 Distribution of Spearman's *r*

n	*0.05*	*0.01*
5	1	1
6	0.886	1
7	0.786	0.929
8	0.738	0.881
9	0.683	0.833
10	0.648	0.794
12	0.591	0.777
14	0.544	0.715
16	0.506	0.665
18	0.475	0.625
20	0.450	0.591
22	0.428	0.562
24	0.409	0.537
26	0.392	0.515
28	0.377	0.496
30	0.364	0.478

To use this table, compare your calculated value of ρ to the value of the appropriate α (0.05 or 0.01), taking into account how many pairs of scores you have. For example, a calculated ρ of 0.75, with 18 pairs of scores, is larger than the critical value of ρ at the 0.01 level of significance (0.625). You would conclude that your calculated value of ρ is likely to occur by chance less than one time in a hundred (i.e., it is highly significant). If your *n* is not in the table, use the greatest lower value (e.g., for an *n* of 17, use the table values for 16 [*n* is the number of *pairs* of scores]).

Used with permission of Dr. Graham Hole, University of Sussex.

Table A.6 gives the values for the distribution of Pearson's r^2 for the specified significance levels at the specified number of degrees of freedom.

TABLE A.6   Significance of r^2

	Distribution of r^2	
d.f. (n − 2)	*α = .05*	*α = .01*
1	0.994009	0.9998
2	0.9025	0.9801
3	0.770884	0.919681
4	0.657721	0.840889
5	0.570025	0.765625
6	0.499849	0.695556
7	0.443556	0.636804
8	0.399424	0.585225
9	0.362404	0.540225
10	0.331776	0.501264
11	0.305809	0.467856
12	0.283024	0.436921
13	0.264196	0.410881
14	0.247009	0.388129
15	0.232324	0.367236
16	0.219024	0.3481
17	0.207936	0.330625
18	0.197136	0.314721
19	0.187489	0.301401
20	0.178929	0.288369
21	0.170569	0.276676
22	0.163216	0.265225
23	0.156816	0.255025
24	0.150544	0.246016
25	0.145161	0.237169
26	0.139876	0.229441
27	0.134689	0.221841
28	0.130321	0.214369
29	0.126025	0.207936

(Continued)

TABLE A.6   Significance of r^2 (*Continued*)

d.f. (n – 2)	$\alpha = .05$	$\alpha = .01$
	Distribution of r^2	
30	0.121801	0.201601
40	0.092416	0.154449
60	0.0625	0.105625
120	0.031684	0.053824

Note: This table was calculated from the table of t values at the appropriate *d.f.*

Appendix B

Subscripts, Summation, and Scientific Notation

SUBSCRIPTS

Statisticians routinely use formulas to indicate how various measures, such as the mean or the standard deviation, are calculated. Many of these involve repeated operations with *series* of numbers. For example, the formula for the sample mean of a variable requires that we add the value of that variable for the first unit (individual, school, and so on), to the value of the second, to the value of the third, up to and including the value of the last, or *n*th, unit. For this and similar types of calculations, a technique known as *subscript notation* can make long and tedious calculations clearer and easier to understand.

The basis of this procedure is to assign each unit an *index* number from 1 to *n*. Ordinarily it does not matter which unit is assigned a given index number, so long as each has one index number that is distinct from all others (for example, there cannot be two number 5s). For the sake of convenience, when raw data come in the form of a list of units and associated values on variables—as in an SPSS data set—the index numbers are assigned in the same order as the list. In this way, it is no longer necessary to refer to a unit by its proper name such as "Susan" or "Eastern Michigan University" or "Australia." Instead, we can refer to them as unit 1, unit 2, unit 3, . . . , unit *n*. Note that the three dots (. . .), called an *ellipsis*, indicate missing items in a continuous list.

Once the index numbers are assigned, they are used to help distinguish between the values attained by different units on a given variable. For example, in the following table we have listed five units (students) with their names, the numbers assigned to them, and their values on the variable "GPA." Following the convention of using lowercase x's and y's to stand for values on numerical variables, we write the index number as a *subscript*, below the line that the x or y is on. So, we write x_1 to stand for "Susan's GPA" and y_1 to stand for "Susan's study hours." Thus, we can list all of the values as follows: $x_1 = 3.2$, $y_1 = 12$; $x_2 = 2.8$, $y_2 = 8$; $x_3 = 3.5$, $y_3 = 10$; $x_4 = 2.6$, $y_4 = 4$; and $x_5 = 3.8$, $y_5 = 9$.

Student name	Unit number	GPA (x)	Study hours (y)
Susan	1	3.2	12
Dave	2	2.8	8
Joan	3	3.5	10
Karen	4	2.6	4
Robert	5	3.8	9

Another key advantage of this system is that it allows us to refer to any given value (GPA, study hours, etc.) in a sample—as opposed to a specific one—by replacing the specific number with a letter. This is usually a lowercase i or j. Thus, x_i (or x_j) would refer to any observed GPA, also called as the "ith," and y_i (or y_j) would refer to any number of observed study hours. In this illustration, because $n = 5$, we could refer to all GPAs as:

$$\{x_i\colon i = 1 \text{ to } n, n = 5\}.$$

This is spoken as "the set of x sub i for all i from 1 to n, where n equals 5."

SUMMATION

The most common use of subscript notation in elementary statistics is with the summation sign, an uppercase Greek sigma: $\sum$. One way in which we can represent the sum of $\{x_i\colon i = 1 \text{ to } n, n = 5\}$ would be simply to show the addition, term by term:

$$x_1 + x_2 + x_3 + x_4 + x_5 = 3.2 + 2.8 + 3.5 + 2.6 + 3.8 = 15.9.$$

However, it is much more economical, especially when n is very large, is to use the summation sign. In its basic form, we want to indicate:

$$\sum x, \text{ which says "sum the } x\text{'s."}$$

From this, we can move to:

$$\sum_i x_i, \text{ that is, "sum the } x_i\text{'s."}$$

And finally, and most specifically:

$$\sum_{i=1}^{n} x_i.$$

This says: "Sum all x_i's beginning at the first and ending at the nth." Thus,

$$\sum_{i=1}^{n} x_i = x_1 + x_2 + x_3 + x_4 + x_5 = 3.2 + 2.8 + 3.5 + 2.6 + 3.8 = 15.9.$$

Of course, it isn't necessary to begin at 1 and end at n. If we wanted to add only the first three GPAs, we would write:

$$\sum_{i=1}^{3} x_i = x_1 + x_2 + x_3 = 3.2 + 2.8 + 3.5 = 9.5.$$

Notice that a 3 has replaced the *n* at the top of the summation sign. And if we wanted only the last two, we would write:

$$\sum_{i=4}^{n} x_i = x_4 + x_5 = 2.6 + 3.8 = 6.4.$$

Notice that a "4" replaced the "1" at the bottom of the summation sign.

We conclude by illustrating subscript notation with the summation sign for the other variable shown in the table above, y_i or study hours.

$$\sum_{i=4}^{n} y_i = 12 + 8 + 10 + 4 + 9 = 43.$$

Finding the mean of the two variables with this notation, we see that:

$$\bar{x} = \frac{1}{n}\sum_{i=1}^{n} x_i = \frac{15.9}{5} = 3.2; \quad \bar{y} = \frac{1}{n}\sum_{i=1}^{n} y_i = \frac{43}{5} = 8.6.$$

SCIENTIFIC NOTATION

When dealing with very large or very small numbers, statisticians often employ a system of rounding known as *scientific notation*. Although this book included this type of notation only in one or two cases, some books and articles and, especially, SPSS use it routinely.

Scientific notation reports values in this format:

$$\pm b\text{E}\pm exp \quad \text{or} \quad \pm b \times 10^{\pm exp},$$

where *b* is the "base," the uppercase E indicates that this is scientific notation, and *exp* stands for "exponent."

Here are two examples:

(1) 5.27E4; where *b* is +5.27 and *exp* is +4

(2) 1.718E−6; where *b* is +1.718 and *exp* is −6.

The *exp* is understood to be the power to which 10 is raised, after which the product is multiplied by *b*, so that E1 means $\times 10^1 = \times 10$, E2 means $\times 10^2 = 100$, E3 means $\times 10^3 = \times 1{,}000$, and so on. If the *exp* is negative, then it is understood to be a negative power of 10 and to follow the general rule that for any number, *A*,

$$A^{-exp} = \frac{1}{A^{exp}}.$$

Thus, if *exp* = −2, then E−2 = $1/10^2 = 1/100 = 0.01$. To covert scientific notation to common notation, we

multiply *b* by 10^{exp} (or, if *exp* is negative, by $1/10^{|exp|}$).

In the two examples, above, this would give us:

(1) $5.27E4 = 5.27 \times 10^4 = 5.27 \times 10{,}000 = 52{,}700.$

(2) $1.718E{-6} = 1.718 \times 10^{-6} = 1.718 \, \dfrac{1}{10^6} = 1.718 \times 0.000001 = 0.000001718.$

There is an easy shortcut for converting from scientific to common notation. Recall that to multiply or divide by any power of 10 you need only to move the decimal point *exp* number of places to the right if *exp* is positive and to the left if *exp* is negative, and fill in with zeros. Thus, in the first example, 5.27E4 tells us to move the decimal point four places to the right and fill in with zeros: one place gives us 52.7; two places gives us 527.0; three places gives us 5270.0; and four places gives us 52,700.0. In the second example, 1.718E–6 says to move the decimal point six places to the left and fill in with zeros: one place gives us 0.1718; two places, 0.01718; three places, 0.001718; four places, 0.0001718; five places, 0.00001718; and six places gives us 0.000001718.

Here are some additional examples:

(3) $940.0E2 = 94{,}000$

(4) $-3.76E8 = -376{,}000{,}000$

(5) $15.92E{-5} = 0.0001592$

(6) $-435.674E{-3} = -0.435674.$

In most cases the base will be "normalized"; that is, the exponent will be adjusted so that the base is greater than or equal to 1 but less than 10. So 940.0E2 will more likely be written 9.400E4; 15.92E–5 will be written 1.592E–4; and 435.674E–3 will be written 4.35674E–1.

The original practice was to write "$b \times 10^{exp}$." The notation using "E" was devised for use with computers that could not handle superscripts or the multiplication sign.

Appendix C

Answers to Selected Practice Quizzes

Chapters 3–6 (pages 138–143)

Quiz 3

1. Health is ordinal; Visits is interval; Residence is nominal and it is a **dichotomy**.

2.

Health	f	%	cf
Good	4	30.8	13
Fair	6	46.1	9
Poor	3	23.1	3
	N = 13	100.0	

Health	f	%	cf
Urban	7	54	13
Rural	6	46	6
	13	100	

(*cf* to be used in #4)

3.
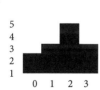

4. Modes: Health—Fair; Visits—2; Residence—Urban

5. Medians: Health—Fair; Visits—2

6. Mean: $\bar{x} = (\Sigma\, xf_x)/n = [(2 \times 0) + (3 \times 1) + (2 \times 5) + (3 \times 3)]/13 = 22/13 = 1.7$

7. Negative skew because mdn $x > \bar{x}$.

8.

	Residence (ind)		
Health (dep)	Urban	Rural	Totals
Good	0 (0%)	4 (67%)	4
Fair	4 (57%)	2 (33%)	6
Poor	3 (43%)	0 (0%)	3
Totals	7 (100%)	6 (100%)	13

Yes, there is a relationship between the independent, Residence, and the dependent, Health. Rural patients are healthier.

9.

Visits	f
2	2
3	2
	$n = 4$

10. $\bar{x} = [(2 \times 2) + (2 \times 3)]/4 = 10/4 = 2.5$ visits. Range $= 3 - 2 = 1$. $s^2 = [\Sigma(x - \bar{x})^2]/n$

x	$(x - \bar{x})$	$(x - \bar{x})^2$
2	0.5	0.25
2	0.5	0.25
3	−0.5	0.25
3	−0.5	0.25
		$\Sigma(x - \bar{x})^2 = 1.00$

$s^2 = [\Sigma(x - \bar{x})^2]/n = 1.00/4 = 0.25$. $s = \sqrt{0.25} = 0.5$.

Chapters 7–9 (pages 226–230)

Quiz 3

1. (a) $3/10 = .3$. (b) $1.0 - .3 = .7$, or $(4 + 2 + 1)/10 = 7/10 = .7$
2. (a) $4/10 + 3/10 = 7/10 = .7$. (b) $4/10 + 3/10 + 2/10 = 9/10 = .9$
3. (a) $(2/10) \times (2/10) = 4/100 = .04$. (b) Either the first is from Michigan and the second is from Ohio *or* the first is from Ohio and the second is from Michigan. That is: $(9/10) \times (1/10)$ or $(1/10) \times (9/10) = (9/100) + (9/100) = 18/100 = .18$.
4. (c) More than 320 were from Detroit. As the number of trials increases, the actual frequency gets closer to the theoretical frequency. Here the theoretical frequency is .40 or 400 out of 1,000. So, as the number of trials increases, the frequency should increase from 32/100 (.32) to something closer to 400/1,000 (.40).

5. (a) Deviation $= (x - \mu) = 80 - 75 = +5$. (b) $z =$ deviation/standard deviation $= 5/\sigma = 5/5 = 1.0$.

6. (a) Deviation $= (x - \mu) = 62.5 - 75 = -12.5$. (b) $z = -12.5/\sigma = -12.5/5 = -2.5$.

7. *Probability of raw score of 85 and above:* First, convert 85 to a z score $= (85 - 75)/5 = 10/5 = +2.0$. Then go to table A.1 and find the row that has 2.0 in the left-hand column of z values. Next look for the column that has the part of the z score that follows 2.0, which is 0.00. At the intersection of that row and column you will find .4772. This number is the portion of the area of the bell curve between the centerline $(z = 0)$ and $z = 2.0$; that is, it is the probability of a z score *between* 0 and 2.00. To get the portion of the area within the tail of the bell curve, the number in the table must be subtracted from 0.5. The difference, representing the probability of having a z score 2.0 or above, is $.5000 - .4772 = .0228$. *Probability of raw score between 62.5 and 75:* In question 6, we found the z value of a raw score of 62.5 to be -2.5. So we go to table A.1 and find 2.5 in the left-hand column of z values. Next, look at that row in the column under 0.00 to find the value .4938. This is the probability of a z score between -2.5 and 0, which is exactly the probability we need because $\mu = 75$.

8. (a) Difference $(\bar{x} - \mu) = 72.5 - 75 = -2.5$. (b) Standard error of the mean $\sigma_{\bar{x}} = \sigma / \sqrt{n}$. Assuming $\sigma = 5$, then $\sigma_{\bar{x}} = 5 / \sqrt{16} = 5/4 = 1.25$. (c) $z = (\bar{x} - \mu)/ \sigma_{\bar{x}} = -2.5/1.25 = -2.00$.

9. **95% CI** $= x \pm 1.96\sigma_{\bar{x}} = 72.5 \pm (1.96)(1.2) = 72.5 \pm 2.35 = $ **70.15 to 74.85**

$-1.96\sigma_{\bar{x}}$	$\bar{x} =$	$+1.96\sigma_{\bar{x}}$
$72.5 - 2.35 =$		$72.5 + 2.35$
70.15		**= 74.85**

99% CI $= x \pm 2.58\sigma_{\bar{x}} = 72.5 \pm (2.58)(1.2) = 72.5 \pm 3.10 = $ **69.40 to 75.60**

$-2.58\sigma_{\bar{x}}$	$\bar{x} =$	$+2.58\sigma_{\bar{x}}$
$72.5 - 3.10 =$		$72.5 + 3.10$
69.40		**= 75.60**

10. With σ not known, we must estimate the standard error of the mean with the formula.

$$s_{\bar{x}} = \frac{s}{\sqrt{n-1}}.$$

So $s_{\bar{x}} = \dfrac{3}{\sqrt{16-1}} = \dfrac{3}{\sqrt{15}} = \dfrac{3}{\sqrt{3.87}} = 0.76$.

95% CI $= \bar{x} \pm ts_{\bar{x}}$. At $d.f. = 16 - 1 = 15$ and $\alpha = .05$, $t = 2.131$. Therefore, 95% CI $= 72.5 \pm (2.131)(0.76) = 72.5 \pm 1.65 = 70.85$ to 74.15.

99% CI $= \bar{x} \pm ts_{\bar{x}}$. At $d.f. = 16 - 1 = 15$ and $\alpha = .01$, $t = 2.947$. Therefore, 99% CI $= 72.5 \pm (2.947)(0.76) = 72.5 \pm 2.24 = 70.26$ to 74.74.

Extra credit: The population mean, $\mu = 75.0$. It falls within the 99% CI with σ known. It is larger than the upper limit of the other three CIs.

Chapters 10–14 (pages 354–357)

Quiz 1

1. Create the 95% CI around the sample mean and see whether the supposed population mean falls inside or outside. If inside, agree; if outside disagree. Since σ is not known, the 95% CI $= \bar{x} = \pm t(s/\sqrt{n-1})$. The t value at $\alpha = .05$ and $d.f. = (26 - 1) = 25$ is 2.06. Therefore the 95% CI $= 2.1 \pm 2.06(0.2/5) = 2.1 \pm 2.06(0.04) = 2.1 \pm 0.082 = 2.018$ to 2.182. The supposed population mean of 2.0 or below lies entirely outside of the range. Do **not** agree.

2A. This is a two-tailed difference-of-means test. Calculated $t = (\bar{x}_1 - \bar{x}_2) / s_{\bar{x}_1 - \bar{x}_2} = (2.3 - 2.5)/-0.1 = -0.2/0.1 = -2.0$. At $\alpha = .05$, the table (A.2) t value for $d.f. = (11 + 8 - 2) = 17 = 2.110$. Because the calculated t is less than the table t, do not reject the null: there is no difference shown. The same decision occurs at $\alpha = .01$ because the table t value is 2.898.

2B. This is a one-tailed test. Because the hypothesis says that Eastern schools have a higher GPA, $(\bar{x}_1 - \bar{x}_2)$ and t must be negative, or else you accept the null with no further work. As calculated above, they are negative. So, we go to table A.2 at $d.f. = 17$. At $\alpha = .05$, the table value is 1.740, and at $\alpha = .01$, the table value is 2.567. You **can** reject the null at .05 but **you cannot** at .01.

3. The null hypothesis is H_0: $\mu_1 = \mu_2 = \mu_3 = \mu_4$. $N_{total} = 38$. Calculated $F = MS_{between}/MS_{within} = 11.2/3.5 = 3.2$. At $\alpha = .01$, the table (A.3) value of F at 3 and 34 (30) degrees of freedom is 4.51. Accept the null. There is not enough difference in the sample to conclude that there is a difference in the population.

4. This is a chi-square problem. The first step is to calculate the expected frequencies, where $f_e = $ (row marginal $\times$ column marginal)$/n$. (1) $(30 \times 20)/52 = $ **11.5.** (2) $(30 \times 32)/52 = $ **18.5.** (3) $(22 \times 20)/52 = $ **8.5.** And (4) $(22 \times 32)/52 = $ **13.5.** Next, calculate chi-square by the formula $\chi^2 = \Sigma[(f_o - f_e)^2/f_e] = [(10 - 11.5)^2/11.5] + [(20 - 18.5)^2/18.5] + [(10 - 8.5)^2/8.5] + [(12 - 13.5)^2/13.5] = 0.195 + 0.122 + 0.264 + 0.167 = 0.748$. The table chi-square at $d.f. = (2 - 1) \times (2 - 1)$ at $\alpha = .05$ is 3.84, and at $\alpha = .01$ it is 6.64. In both cases, do not reject the null hypothesis. You can't conclude that minorities differ from non-minorities.

5. (1) $r = \sum (x - \bar{x})(y - \bar{y}) / \sqrt{\sum (x - \bar{x})^2 \sum (y - \bar{y})^2} = 189.9/208.62 = \mathbf{0.91}$; $r^2 = \mathbf{0.83}$.
This is a very strong, inverse correlation: the higher the tuition, the fewer the minority students. The scatterplot also shows this.

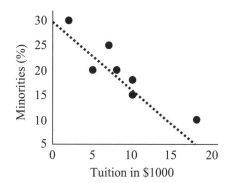

(2) Test the null hypothesis: $\rho = 0$ (there is no correlation in the population). The calculated r of .91 "beats the table" at $8 - 2 = 6$ *d.f.* at $\alpha = .05$ and .01. Reject the null. There is likely to be a correlation in the population.

(3) Slope $b = \Sigma(x - \bar{x})(y - \bar{y})/\Sigma(x - \bar{x})^2 = 189.9/-156.5 = -1.21$.
Intercept, $a = \bar{y} - b\bar{x} = 20.4 + (1.21 \times 8.3) = 20.4 + 10.04 = 30.44$.

(4) The regression equation is: $y = 30.44 - 1.21x$. To find a school's predicted percentage of minorities, multiply its tuition by -1.21 and add 30.44.

(5) Test the null hypothesis $B = 0$. This requires the F test at 1 and $(8 - 2) = 6$ *d.f.* The calculated F is MS_{reg}/MS_{error}. $MS_{reg} = (r^2)SS_y/1$; $MS_{error} = (1 - r^2)SS_y/6$. $MS_{reg} = 230.8$. $MS_{error} = 7.88$. $F = 230.8/7.88 = 29.3$. Table A.3 at .05 = 5.99 and at .01 = 13.79. In both cases reject the null. You can conclude that there is a slope in the population.

Appendix D

Formulas Used in This Book

Proportion (or probability):

$$p = \frac{f}{n}$$

Percentage:

$$pct\ (\%) = (100) \times p$$

Cumulative frequency:

$$cf_i = \sum_{i=1}^{k} f_i,\ \text{for } k \text{ attributes}$$

Cumulative percentage:

$$c\% = \left(\frac{cf}{n}\right) \times 100$$

Sample mean:

$$\overline{x} = \frac{\sum_{i=1}^{n} x_i}{n}$$

Deviation from sample mean:

$$dev_i = x_i - \overline{x}$$

Range:

$$R = x_{hi} - x_{lo}$$

Sample variance:

$$s^2 = \frac{\sum_{i=1}^{n} dev_i^2}{n}$$

Sample standard deviation:

$$s = +\sqrt{s^2}$$

Standard error of the mean:

$$\sigma_{\bar{x}} = \frac{\sigma}{\sqrt{n}}$$

Estimated standard error of the mean:

$$s_{\bar{x}} = \frac{s}{\sqrt{n-1}}$$

Standard scores:

For a sample:
$$z_i = \frac{dev_i}{s}$$

For a population:
$$z_i = \frac{z_i - \mu}{\sigma}$$

For a sampling distribution of means:
$$z_i = \frac{\bar{x}_i - \mu}{\sigma_{\bar{x}}}$$

Sampling error:

$$\text{Error} = \bar{x} - \mu$$

Margin of error, σ known:

For 95%: $\text{ME} = 1.96\sigma_{\bar{x}}$

For 99%: $\text{ME} = 2.58\sigma_{\bar{x}}$

Margin of error, σ not known or small sample:

$$\text{ME} = ts_{\bar{x}}$$

Confidence interval:

$$\text{CI} = \bar{x} \pm \text{ME}$$

t score (calculated):

$$t_{calculated} = \left(\frac{\bar{x} - \mu}{s_{\bar{x}}}\right)$$

Degrees of freedom:

For one-sample t-test: $d.f. = n - 1$

For two-sample t-test: $d.f. = n - 2$

For F test: $df_{between} = k - 1, df_{within} = n - k,$

where k *is* the number of groups, subsamples, or (for regression) variables

For chi-square: $(\text{rows} - 1) \times (\text{columns} - 1)$

For bivariate correlation: $n - 2$

Estimated standard error of the differences between means:

$$s_{\bar{x}_1 - \bar{x}_2} = \sqrt{\frac{s_1^2}{n_1 - 1} + \frac{s_2^2}{n_2 - 1}}$$

Estimated standard error of the mean differences (for the before-and-after t-test):

$$s_{\bar{D}} = \frac{s_D}{\sqrt{n-1}},$$

where s_D is the standard deviation of the before/after differences:

$$s_D = \sqrt{\frac{\sum_{i=1}^{n} D_i^2}{n} - (\bar{x}_1 - \bar{x}_2)^2}$$

Mean square:

Between:
$$MS_{between} = \frac{SS_{between}}{df_{between}}$$

Within:
$$MS_{within} = \frac{SS_{within}}{df_{within}}$$

F ratio (calculated):

$$F_{calculated} = \frac{MS_{between}}{MS_{within}}$$

Standard error of proportions:

$$s_p = \sqrt{\frac{pq}{n}} = \sqrt{\frac{p(1-p)}{n}}$$

Margin of error for proportions:

For 95%: $ME = 1.96 s_p$

For 99%: $ME = 2.58 s_p$

Confidence interval for proportions:

$$CI = p \pm ME$$

Combined sample proportion:

$$p* = \frac{n_1 p_1}{n_{total}} + \frac{n_2 p_2}{n_{total}}$$

$$q* = (1 - p*)$$

(Estimated) standard error of the difference of proportions:

$$s_{p_1-p_2} = \sqrt{\frac{p^* q^*}{n_1} + \frac{p^* q^*}{n_2}}$$

Chi-square:

$$\chi^2_{calculated} = \sum \frac{(f_o - f_e)^2_{i,j}}{f_{ei,j}}$$

Expected frequency:

$$f_{ei,j} = \frac{(\text{row } i \text{ total}) (\text{column } j \text{ total})}{n}$$

Spearman's rank-order correlation coefficient:

$$r_s = 1 - \frac{6 \sum\limits_{i=1}^{n} D^2}{n(n^2 - 1)} \quad \text{(if there are no tied ranks)}$$

Pearsonian correlation coefficient:

$$r = \frac{\sum\limits_{i=1}^{n} \left[(x_i - \bar{x})(y_i - \bar{y}) \right]}{\sqrt{\left(\sum\limits_{i=1}^{n} (x_i - \bar{x})^2 \right) \left(\sum\limits_{i=1}^{n} (y_i - \bar{y})^2 \right)}}$$

or

$$r = \frac{SP}{\sqrt{(SS_x SS_y)}}$$

Sum of the products in correlation and regression:

$$SP = \sum\limits_{i=1}^{n} \left[(x_i - \bar{x})(y_i - \bar{y}) \right]$$

Sum of the squares in x in correlation and regression:

$$SS_x = \sum\limits_{i=1}^{n} (x_i - \bar{x})^2$$

Sum of the squares in y in correlation and regression:

$$SS_y = \sum\limits_{i=1}^{n} (y_i - \bar{y})^2$$

Partial correlation coefficient:

$$r_{x_1y.x_2} = \frac{r_{x_1y} - r_{x_2y}r_{x_1x_2}}{\sqrt{(1 - r_{x_1x_2}^2)(1 - r_{x_2y}^2)}}$$

Multiple correlation coefficient:

$$R_{x_1,x_2,y} = \sqrt{\frac{r_{x_1y}^2 + r_{x_1y}^2 - 2r_{x_1y}r_{x_2y}r_{x_1x_2}}{1 - r_{x_1x_2}^2}}$$

or

$$R_{x_1,x_2,y} = \sqrt{r_{x_1y}r_{x_1y.x_2}^2(1 - r_{x_1y}^2) + r_{x_2y}r_{x_2y.x_1}^2(1 - r_{x_1y}^2)}$$

Bivariate linear regression equation:

$$\hat{y} = a + bx$$

Slope of bivariate regression line:

$$b = \frac{\sum_{i=1}^{n}(x_i - \overline{x})(y_i - \overline{y})}{\sum_{i=1}^{n}(x_i - \overline{x})^2} = \frac{SP}{SS_x}$$

y-intercept of a regression equation:

$$a = \overline{y} - b\overline{x}$$

Residual (regression error):

$$e = (y - \hat{y})$$

Sum of squares error:

$$SS_{error} = \sum e^2$$

Standard error of the estimate:

$$s_{y.x} = \sqrt{\frac{\sum_{i=1}^{n}e_i^2}{n-2}}$$

Estimated standard error of *b*:

$$s_b = \frac{s_{y.x}}{\sqrt{SS_x}} = \frac{s_{y.x}}{\sqrt{\sum_{i=1}^{n}(x_i - \overline{x})^2}}$$

Standardized b:

$$\beta = \frac{b}{s_b}$$

F ratio for regression:

$$F_{calculated} = \frac{MS_{regression}}{MS_{error}}$$

Mean square for regression:

$$MS_{regression} = \frac{SS_{regression}}{df_{regression}}$$

$$MS_{error} = \frac{SS_{error}}{df_{error}}$$

Sum of squares for regression:

$$SS_{regression} = \sum_{i=1}^{n}(\hat{y}_i - \bar{y})^2$$

$$SS_{error} = \sum_{i=1}^{n}e_i^2$$

Multiple regression equation:

$$\hat{y} = a + b_1 x_1 + b_2 x_2 + \cdots + b_k x_k, \text{ for } k \text{ variables}$$

Slope of multiple regression equation (two independent variables):

$$b_1 = \left(\frac{s_y}{s_1}\right)\left(\frac{r_{yx_1} - r_{yx_2}r_{x_1 x_2}}{1 - r_{x_1 x_2}^2}\right)$$

$$b_2 = \left(\frac{s_y}{s_2}\right)\left(\frac{r_{yx_2} - r_{yx_2}r_{x_1 x_2}}{1 - r_{x_1 x_2}^2}\right)$$

Intercept of multiple regression equation (two independent variables):

$$a = \bar{y} - b_1 \bar{x}_1 - b_2 \bar{x}_2$$

Chapter Notes

Chapter 1

1. This and most of the following chapters include a boxed section, entitled "Statistics for Sociologists." These are designed to illustrate the many ways in which sociology and applied statistics work together to help us understand and reconstruct the social worlds in which we live.

2. We will soon learn to refer to the number of units as *sample size* or, even more briefly, with a lowercase *n* (for "number").

3. Continually updated versions of FORTRAN are available for PC/Windows configurations and in digital format. These and a catalog of support products can be found at http://www.Fortran.com.

4. The AACS web site is at www.aacsnet.org, and the SP-ASA site is at www.techsociety .com/asa.

5. Members of AACS were asked to name the most useful book on applied research methods (most of which included some discussion of applied social statistics). The authors and titles of the four books receiving the most votes are identified with an asterisk in the References section at the end of this book.

Chapter 2

1. As you probably know, the word *data* is the plural form of the Latin singular, *datum*, meaning "something given." Thus, we say "data are," etc.

2. Some writers say *an hypothesis*, treating the initial "h" as a silent letter. In this book we follow the more common convention of saying *a hypothesis*, with the first "h" sounded.

3. These are basic operators in the sense that stringing them together can indicate more complex logical relations. For example, one might want to refer to the other sense of "or" that does not include "and." In that case, the sentence "I will take a course in sociology or anthropology" would be untrue if you took both. In logical terms you would say "I will take sociology or I will take anthropology but I will not take both." A symbol does exist to express this "exclusive or," and it is convenient. It is not necessary, however, because the same sense can be conveyed with a combination of some of the five basic operators.

4. Units are also referred to as "cases," "subjects," or "respondents," depending on the context of the research. Often the unit of analysis *is* the unit of observation, but in many important instances there is a difference between the two. The unit of analysis is the person or object that is assumed to have the characteristic(s) identified in the predicate of the hypothesis. The unit of observation is the person from whom the data are collected. If I were to ask a set of 10 students their ages and then compute their average age, the students would be the units of both analysis and observation. But if I were to ask the teacher to list for me the ages of 10 students in the class, again to calculate the average age, the students would still be units of analysis, but the teacher would be the unit of observation. The U.S. Census uses this convention when it determines characteristics of members of a household (the units of analysis) from one adult member of that household (the unit of observation).

Chapter 3

1. The Christian calendar was devised before Europeans learned to use zero as a number, so it does not refer to the year designated as that of the birth of Christ as 0, but rather as 1. The year before 1 C.E. is not 0 C.E. but 1 B.C.E. (Before the Common Era). This fact raised considerable controversy when the year 2000 was celebrated as the beginning of a millennium. Mathematically speaking, at midnight, January 1, 2000, only 1,999 years of the Common Era had elapsed. Thus, many people argued, the millennium "should" have been celebrated in 2001. This is a good lesson in what it means to have a mathematically arbitrary zero—or lack thereof.

2. Because a score of 200 is the lowest that can be achieved on the Scholastic Aptitude Test (SAT), one could argue that SAT score is an interval-level variable. That is, if 200 is the actual zero point, then a score of 800 is not really twice as high as a score of 400.

3. This use of the word "unit" is unrelated to the unit of observation/analysis discussed earlier. Rather, this is related to how variables and their attributes are measured: income in the unit dollars, education level in the unit years, etc.

4. This discussion of data collection techniques is meant only to answer the question "Where do social scientific data come from?" More detailed discussion and comparisons among these approaches are ordinarily reserved for courses in research methods. See, for example, Babbie (2005: Chapters 8–12).

5. Over the years, researchers have developed numerous techniques that simulate the experimental model under less-than-ideal conditions. By far, the most widely used text on this subject is the classic by Campbell and Stanley (1963).

6. SPSS and SPSS Student Version include sample data from NORC and several other sources.

Chapter 4

1. Note the lowercase "*x*" in parentheses next to the variable name in this and related tables. This is in keeping with the common practice of referring to numerical variables with the "*x*" symbol (and with "*x*" and "*y*" in bivariate applications).

2. The conditions to which we refer are those in which we can assume that the probability that any single attribute will be selected is the same as the probability that any other attribute will be selected. This is the principle of *equiprobability*, to be discussed in Chapter 6. If this cannot be assumed, then the frequencies must be weighted accordingly, and probability will reflect adjusted proportions.

3. The polygons (meaning "objects with many sides") with which we are most familiar, such as the rectangle, pentagon, hexagon, etc., are all *closed*. That is, each side is joined to another side on each end so that they fully enclose an "inside." However, a many-sided object need not be closed to qualify as a polygon. In addition, the number of sides can be *very* many (and *very* small) as they approach the limit of having an infinite number of sides, each of which is an infinitesimally small point. It is on this basis that we call open, smooth curves *polygons*.

4. It also applies to the process of urban growth, such that rapid growth in an earlier period eventually slows as the 100% saturation point is approached. Most of the highly industrialized countries such as the United States, Japan, and those in Western Europe are at or near the saturation point, whereas the less developed countries of Africa and much of Asia are in a rapid growth phase.

Chapter 5

1. Statisticians speak of the "moments" of a distribution. In this context, "moment" means importance, as in the word "momentous." The first moment—the most important feature—is central tendency. Other moments will be discussed in later chapters: the second moment is *dispersion*; the third moment is *skewness*; and the fourth moment is *kurtosis*—which is illustrated in Chapter 8. For brief definitions, formulas, and illustrations of the concept of moment, see http://geography.uoregon .edu/GeogR/topics/moments.htm.

2. To be exact, this is the *arithmetic* mean. Other types exist and are useful for various scientific purposes. These include the *geometric* and *harmonic* means.

3. This definition highlights the relationship between the mean and the median in any type of frequency distribution. It is related to the measure called skew*ness*, which is applied to the normal distribution or bell curve, to be discussed in Chapter 6. Skewness is the third "moment" or third most important measure (after the mean

and the variance; see note 3) of a distribution, and its formula involves the sum of deviations taken to the third power.

4. This type of symmetry is known as *bilateral*, or "two-sided," because of the mirror-image effect. There are other types of symmetry, including *radial* symmetry, in which two sides, top and bottom, and other pairs of segments are the same. This is the symmetry of snowflakes, for example.

5. Here is the proof that the sum of the deviations from the mean always equals zero. We can express the sum as:

$$\sum_{i=1}^{n}(x_i \sum \overline{x}) = \sum_{i=1}^{n}\left(x_i - \sum \frac{\sum_{i=1}^{n}x_i}{n}\right)$$

$$= \sum_{i=1}^{n}x_i - \sum n\frac{\sum_{i=1}^{n}x_i}{n} = \sum_{i=1}^{n}x_i - \sum_{i=1}^{n}x_i$$

$$= 0$$

Chapter 6

1. Dispersion is also sometimes referred to as "variability."

2. This is based on the formula for the number of pairs that can be formed with n units: number of pairs $= 1 + 2 + 3 + \cdots + (n - 1)$.

3. The other mathematically legitimate way to eliminate cancellation between negative and positive values is to take the absolute values of the negative deviations, symbolized by putting them between a pair of parallel lines (||). The absolute value of any number, positive or negative, is "unsigned" and treated as positive. Thus, for any number a, $|+a| = a$ and $|-a| = a$. For example, $|+7| = 7$ and $|-7| = 7$. When applied to deviations, the use of absolute values produces the set $|x_i - \overline{x}|$, each of which is either positive or, if $x_i = \overline{x}$, zero, but never negative. The resulting measure of dispersion, $\sum_{i=1}^{n}|x_i - \overline{x}|/n$, is called *the mean deviation*. It is occasionally used. However, it tends to underestimate the impact of very high and very low values, so it is not considered to be an effective measure of dispersion as compared to the variance and standard deviation.

4. This follows from the definition of "square root of x" as a number that, when multiplied by itself, equals x. Because a negative number multiplied by itself is positive and a positive number multiplied by itself is also positive, a positive x always has two square roots: one positive and the other negative.

5. They are, perhaps, more easily understood than to say: the positive square roots of the averages of the squared deviations.

Chapter 7

1. Symbols for population parameters are also used for any aggregate that is not a sample and, thus, not observed or observable. This is the reason why the symbols μ and σ are used for theoretical probability distributions, as we shall see toward the end of the chapter.

2. The definitive work on the subject remains Leslie Kish's classic *Survey Sampling* (New York: Wiley, 1990).

3. One common method that is well adapted to multi-stage cluster sampling is known as *pps,* which stands for *probability proportionate to size.* With this approach, clusters and possibly secondary sampling units are weighted by the sizes of their census populations. In this way, more populous clusters have a higher probability of being included in the sample than those with smaller populations. This reduces the likelihood that the final sample will be biased against, say, households that are located in large cities.

4. We use μ for the mean and σ for the standard deviation here to indicate that these are not observed sample data.

5. This has been termed "the gambler's fallacy" and is defined by *The Skeptic's Dictionary* as follows: "The gambler's fallacy is the mistaken notion that the odds for something with a fixed probability increase or decrease depending upon recent occurrences." For an interesting illustration, go to http://skepdic.com/gamblers.html.

6. Because the other kinds of probability samples are partly random, the sampling distributions discussed here can be used with them, but only if adjustments are made. For instance, each stratum of a stratified sample must be referred separately to its appropriate sampling distribution.

7. The normal or "bell" curve is the graphic form of the Gaussian distribution, named after its discoverer, the German mathematician Carl Friedrich Gauss (1777–1855). The curve—at least the left half of it—is somewhat reminiscent of the graph of the ogive, the cumulative frequency polygon (see Chapter 3). This is not a coincidence, because both distributions are based on exponential functions. The formula for the Gaussian distribution and its normal curve is $y = (1 / \sqrt{2\pi})e^{\pi x^2/2}$, where y is the height of the curve at a distance x from the vertical axis and π and e are constants approximately equal to 3.142 . . . and 2.718 . . . , respectively. Thus, if we know the value of a given mean, $\bar{x}_i$, then the probability that $\bar{x}_i$ will occur can easily be determined from the y value.

Chapter 8

1. We put "average" in quotation marks because the standard error is the square root of the sum of the squared deviations all divided by n, not the sum of the deviations divided by n. You will recall that the latter formulation always yields zero.

2. Here is another, equivalent way to interpret this equivalence between 95% of all sample means and 95% of all population means. Any given sample mean, $\bar{x}$, in a sampling distribution could have been drawn from a population with a mean, μ, that is equal to it, in which case $(\bar{x} - \mu) = 0$ and there is no error. Otherwise, it was drawn from a population with a mean that is either less than or greater than it, in which case $(\bar{x} - \mu) \neq 0$ and there is some error. To determine the range of population means that would lead to 47.5% error or less *below* their value or to 47.5% error or less *above* their value (for a total of 95% maximum error), we add or subtract 1.96 standard error units $(\sigma_{\bar{x}})$ to the value of $\bar{x}$.

3. *Leeway* is an interesting metaphor to use in inductive statistics. It is a nautical term that means to allow extra distance between one's boat and other boats or a dock on the boat's "lee" side, the side away from the wind. When the wind blows, the boat heads "leeward," so allowance must be made for this possibility. A sailor gives leeway, and a statistician leaves a margin of error. When a statistician sails, there ought never to be a collision. Unfortunately, the probability of zero collisions is only theoretical—as the sailing author of this book can attest!

4. If n is large but σ is not known, it is permissible to use n rather than $n - 1$ under the square root sign. For most applications, however, this is a trivial matter. So it is easier to learn only one formula, which is pretty much equivalent. For example, if $n = 100$, $\sqrt{n} = \pm 10.00$ and $\sqrt{n-1} = \sqrt{99} = \pm 9.95$, or a difference of one-half of 1%.

5. If we allow the numerator of a fraction to remain the same but reduce the size of the denominator, the whole fraction becomes larger. For example, $8/8 = 1$, $8/4 = 2$, $8/2 = 4$, $8/1 = 8$. This is basically the effect of using $n - 1$ as opposed to n in the denominator of the estimated standard error of the mean.

6. Many statistics students feel flattered that an important probability distribution is named in their honor. Unfortunately, this is just a coincidence. W. S. Gosset, a statistician who began working for the Guinness Brewery in Dublin, Ireland, in 1899, developed the t distribution while testing samples of barley destined for the famous Guinness Stout. To prevent disclosure of trade secrets, Guinness did not allow its employees to publish research findings. So to get his article "The Probable Error of a Mean" published without losing his job, Gosset chose to submit it under the alias "Student."

7. The concept of "degrees of freedom" refers to the systems of equations that are used to create statistical tables such as those in Appendix A. If we are working with a set of k equations, each of which has v variables, the degrees of freedom equal $(k - v)$. For,

say, 5 equations with 4 variables, *d.f.* = 1. This means that one variable is not deter-mined and is free to vary regardless of what the equations stipulate. If $k = v$, that is, *d.f.* = 0, then all of the variables are determined. Although a demonstration of how *d.f.* is derived would take us beyond the level of mathematics assumed here, its use with the chi-square statistic (Chapter 12) provides an easy-to-understand illustration.

8. As mentioned in the notes to Chapter 5, kurtosis is the fourth most important char-acteristic of a frequency distribution—the fourth "moment," after central tendency, dispersion, and skewness.

Chapter 10

1. This is a problem for which either pure random or stratified sampling may be appro-priate. We assume pure random sampling here, but the techniques can be easily adapted to stratified sampling (which employs random sampling within strata) through the use of weighting.

2. The symbol for "not greater than" is ≤. Literally, this reads "less than or equal to," which of course are the two ways in which a quantity can be "not greater than" another.

3. The symbol for "not less than" is ≥. Literally, this reads "greater than or equal to," which of course are the two ways in which a quantity can be "not less than" another.

4. The assumption of unequal variances would have made no difference in the decision. The $t_{calculated}$ would have been 10.24, with *d.f.* = 30. The corresponding table values at $\alpha = .05$ and .01 are 1.697 and 2.457, respectively, placing $t_{calculated}$ well into the critical region.

Chapter 11

1. Two-way ANOVA is used with three variables, two independent and one dependent; three-way ANOVA takes three independents and one dependent; and so on.

2. A easy way to remember whether to go to a column or a row is that $df_{between}$ is always a small number compared to df_{within}. You can see that the numbers heading the columns are smaller than those at the beginning of the rows. So $df_{between}$ is in a column and df_{within} is in a row.

3. SPSS provides 18 *post hoc* tests, 14 with equal variances assumed and 4 with unequal variances assumed.

4. Yes, there is a statistics jokes Web site: www.ilstu.edu/~gcramsey/Gallery.html. The joke, which runs for pages and pages, concerns a statistician whose research

produced a significant F. He was then interested in determining which pair(s) of means was responsible, but could not decide which test to use among all of the many choices. So he sought advice from the leading experts in the field at all of the major research universities with statistics programs. After receiving a variety of different "correct" answers, he published his findings as follows: "The contributing pair of means is $\bar{x}_1$ and $\bar{x}_2$, except in Berkeley, California, and Princeton, New Jersey. In the latter case, it is $\bar{x}_1$ and $\bar{x}_2$, but it is also $\bar{x}_2$ and $\bar{x}_3$. This is partly correct in Cambridge, Massachusetts, where the contributing pair changes as one moves farther from the Charles River. In Chicago, none of the differences is significant."

Chapter 12

1. Other members of the family include the median test, the goodness-of-fit test, and the one-way chi-square. From this point on in the text we use "chi-square" as a synonym for two-way chi-square.

2. Many statisticians warn that if expected frequencies are less than 10.0, an adjustment should be made because the degree of association would otherwise be overstated. The most popular of these is *Yates's correction*, which subtracts 0.5 from the absolute value of the difference between the observed and expected frequencies before squaring it (see below). Similarly, it is held that any chi-square for which expected frequencies are less than 5.0 should be avoided altogether. Although these points are well taken, it is acceptable at this elementary level for the researcher to report low expected frequencies (their values and the cells in which they are found) along with the $\chi^2_{calculated}$. This allows the reader not to take the results at face value as if there were no low expected frequencies.

Chapter 13

1. This is common practice in applications requiring two numerical variables: that is, x stands for the independent and y for the dependent. When three or more variables are involved, each of the independent variables is symbolized by x with an appropriate subscript: $x_1, x_2, x_3, \ldots$.

2. The literal meaning of the word "regression" is "going back." Its application in statistics refers to the tendency of the values of the dependent variables to be influenced by, or go back to, the mean of the independent variable. It was first coined by the British statistician Francis Galton (1822–1911).

3. The direct test used here employs a table (table A.6) that was derived from the respective t values by the formula $r^2 = t^2/(t^2 + d.f.)$.

Chapter 14

1. The two-dimensional graph for (x,y) coordinates has four quadrants: I, x and y both positive; II, x negative and y positive; III, x and y both negative; and IV, x positive and y negative. By using only positive values for all variables, we have remained in quadrant I. The three-dimensional graph for (x,y,z) coordinates has eight sections (octants): $+++, ++-, +-+$, etc. Again, we remain in the first octant.

2. In fact, there are other types of least-squares estimates than the one used here. This is the most common and the most straightforward (although it is not always the best). To distinguish it from the others, this type is referred to as "ordinary least-squares" or "OLS" for short.

References

Albrow, Martin, and Elizabeth King, eds. 1990. *Globalization, Knowledge, and Society*. London: Sage.

Babbie, Earl R. 2005. *The Basics of Social Research*. Belmont, CA: Wadsworth.

Bacon, Francis. 2004 [1620]. "*Novum Organum*." In G. Rees and R. Wakely, eds., *The Instauratio Magna, Part II: The Novum Organum and Associated Texts*. Oxford: Clarendon.

Barber, Nigel. 2004. *Kindness in a Cruel World: The Evolution of Altruism*. Amherst, NY: Prometheus Books.

Burawoy, Michael. 2004. "Public Sociologies: A Symposium from Boston College." *Social Problems*, vol. 51, no. 1, pp. 103–130.

Campbell, Donald, and Julian Stanley. 1963. *Experimental and Quasi-Experimental Designs for Research*. Chicago: Rand McNally.

Delega, Valerian J., and Janusz Grzelac. 1982. *Cooperation and Helping Behavior: Theories and Research*. New York: Academic Press Inc.

Dentler, Robert A. 2002. *Practicing Sociology: Selected Fields*. Westport, CT: Praeger.*

Dubois, William, and R. Dean Wright. 2001. *Applying Sociology: Making a Better World*. Boston: Allyn & Bacon.*

Durkheim, Émile. 1982. *The Rules of Sociological Method*. New York: Free Press.

Field, Alexander. 2001. *Altruistically Inclined? The Behavioral Sciences, Evolutionary Theory, and the Origins of Reciprocity*. Ann Arbor: University of Michigan Press.

Friedman, Thomas. 2005. *The World Is Flat*. New York: Farrar, Straus and Giroux.

Glassner, Barry. 1999. *The Culture of Fear: Why Americans Are Afraid of the Wrong Things*. New York: Basic Books.

Gouldner, Alvin W. 1964. *Patterns of Industrial Bureaucracy*. New York: Free Press.

Hamburg, Morris. 1979. *Basic Statistics*. New York: Harcourt Brace Jovanovich, Inc.

Hoover, Kenneth, and Todd Donovan. 2004. *The Elements of Social Scientific Thinking*, 8th. ed. New York: St. Martin's Press.

Kim, Jae-On. 1971. "Predictive Measures of Ordinal Association." *American Journal of Sociology*, vol. 76, no. 5 (March), pp. 891–906.

Kim, Jae-On. 1975. "Multivariate Analysis of Ordinal Variables." *American Journal of Sociology*, vol. 81, no. 2 (September), pp. 261–298.

Klayman, Douglas. 2007. "Why Is Public Sociology on Shaky Ground?" *Journal of Applied Social Science*, vol. 1, no. 1, pp. 36–43.

Mayo, Elton. 1945. *Human Problems of an Industrial Civilization*. Boston: Harvard University Graduate School of Business Administration.

Merton, Robert K. 1968. *Social Theory and Social Structure*. New York: The Free Press.

Miller, Arthur G. 1986. *The Obedience Experiments: A Case Study of Controversy in Social Science*. New York: Praeger.

Mills, C. Wright. 1959. *The Sociological Imagination.* New York: Oxford University Press.

Monette, Duane, Thomas Sullivan, and Cornell Dejong. 2002. *Applied Social Research: Tool for the Human Services.* Belmont, CA: Wadsworth.*

Monroe, K. R. 1996. *The Heart of Altruism: Perceptions of a Common Humanity.* Princeton, NJ: Princeton University Press.

Monroe, K. R. 2001. "Morality and a Sense of Self: The Importance of Identity and Categorization for Moral Action." *American Journal of Political Science,* vol. 45, no. 3, pp. 491–507.

Myrdal, Gunnar. 1944. *An American Dilemma: The Negro Problem and Modern Democracy.* New York: Harper & Bros.

Popper, Sir Karl Raimund. 2002 [1959]. *The Logic of Scientific Discovery.* London, New York: Routledge.

Rawls, John. 1971. *A Theory of Justice.* Cambridge, MA: Belknap Press.

Ritzer, George. 2000. *The McDonaldization of Society.* Thousand Oaks, CA: Pine Forge Press.

Roethlisberger, Fritz J., and William J. Dickson. 1939. *Management and the Worker.* Cambridge, MA.: Harvard University Press.

Sassen, Saskia. 2007. *Sociology of Globalization.* New York: W. W. Norton.

Scheff, Thomas J. 1994. *Microsociology: Discourse, Emotion, and Social Structure.* Chicago: University of Chicago Press.

Shadish, William R., Thomas D. Cook, and Donald T. Campbell. 2002. *Experimental and Quasi-Experimental Designs for Generalized Causal Inference.* Boston: Houghton Mifflin.*

Simmons, Roberta G. 1991. "Presidential Address on Altruism and Sociology." *Sociological Quarterly,* vol. 32, no. 1, pp. 1–22.

Smith, Robert B. 1978. "Nonparametric Path Analysis: Comments on Kim's 'Multivariate Analysis of Ordinal Variables.'" *American Journal of Sociology,* vol. 84, no. 2 (September), pp. 437–448.

Sommer, Robert, and Barbara Sommer, eds. 2001. *A Practical Guide to Behavioral Research: Tools and Techniques.* New York: Oxford University Press.*

Sorokin, Pitirim A. 1948. *The Reconstruction of Humanity.* Boston: Beacon Press.

Sorokin, Pitirim A. 1956. *Fads and Foibles in Modern Sociology and Related Sciences.* Chicago: H. Regnery Co.

Steele, Stephen F., AnneMarie Scarisbrick-Hauser, and William Hauser. 1999. *Solution Centered Sociology: Addressing Problems through Applied Sociology.* Thousand Oaks, CA: Sage Publications.*

Stephens, Richard E. 2000. *Careers in Sociology.* Boston: Allyn and Bacon.

Straus, Roger A., ed. 2002. *Using Sociology: An Introduction from the Applied and Clinical Perspective,* 3rd ed. Lanham, MD: Rowman and Littlefield.*

Sullivan, Thomas. 2001. *Methods of Social Research.* Belmont, CA: Wadsworth.*

Turner, Jonathan H. 1993. *Classical Sociological Theory: A Positivist's Perspective.* Chicago: Nelson-Hall.

Turner, Stephen P., and Jonathan H. Turner. 1990. *The Impossible Science: An Institutional Analysis of American Sociology.* Newbury Park, CA: Sage Publications.

Weinstein, Jay. 2005. *Social and Cultural Change: Social Science for a Dynamic World.* Lanham, MD: Rowman and Littlefield.

---

* Leading nominee as "most useful text."

Weinstein, Jay, and Jennifer Haskin Corwin. 2006. "Fear of Death and Dying and Altruism: Toward a Theoretical Synthesis." In Elvira del Pozo, ed., *Integralism, Altruism and Reconstruction: Essays in Honor of Pitirim A. Sorokin*. Valencia: Universitat de València.

Wolff, Kurt. 1950. *The Sociology of Georg Simmel*. Glencoe, IL: Free Press.

Whyte, William Foote. 1955. *Street Corner Society: The Social Structure of an Italian Slum*. Chicago: University of Chicago Press.

Index

Note: All page numbers followed by an "f" refer to figures and all pages followed by a "t" refer to tables.

About the Author

Jay Weinstein is professor of sociology at Eastern Michigan University, where he also served as head of the Department of Sociology, Anthropology, and Criminology (1986–1990 and 2004–2006). His international experience includes two terms as Fulbright Professor in India and consulting work in Central and Eastern Europe with the Soros Foundation and the World Bank. He is the recipient of the Charles Horton Cooley and Alex Boros Awards for his contributions to applied sociology and the John F. Schnabel Award for Teaching Excellence. He has served as president of the Society for Applied Sociology and the North Central Sociological Association and as chair of the American Sociological Association Council on Sociological Practice. He is the author of numerous journal articles, book chapters, and books, including *Social and Cultural Change: Social Science for a Dynamic World, 2nd edition* (Rowman and Littlefield Publishers, 2005).